Akron at 200

\ SERIES ON OHIO HISTORY AND CULTURE

Series on Ohio History and Culture

Kevin Kern, Editor

Timothy H. H. Thoresen, *River, Reaper, Rail: Agriculture and Identity in Ohio's Mad River Valley, 1795–1885*

Mark Auburn, *In the President's Home: Memories of the Akron Auburns*

Brian G. Redmond, Bret J. Ruby, and Jarrod Burks, eds., *Encountering Hopewell in the Twenty-first Century, Ohio and Beyond. Volume 1: Monuments and Ceremony*

Brian G. Redmond, Bret J. Ruby, and Jarrod Burks, eds., *Encountering Hopewell in the Twenty-first Century, Ohio and Beyond. Volume 2: Settlements, Foodways, and Interaction*

Jen Hirt, *Hear Me Ohio*

S. Victor Fleischer, *The Goodyear Tire & Rubber Company: A Photographic History, 1898–1951*

Ray Greene, *Coach of a Different Color: One Man's Story of Breaking Barriers in Football*

John Tully, *Labor in Akron, 1825–1945*

Deb Van Tassel Warner and Stuart Warner, eds., *Akron's Daily Miracle: Reporting the News in the Rubber City*

Mary O'Connor, *Free Rose Light*

Joyce Dyer, *Pursuing John Brown: On the Trail of a Radical Abolitionist*

Walter K. Delbridge and Kate Tucker, editor, *Comeback Evolution: Selected Works of Walter K. Delbridge*

Gary S. Williams, *"No Man Knows This Country Better": The Frontier Life of John Gibson*

Jeffrey A. John, *Progressives and Prison Labor: Rebuilding Ohio's National Road During World War I*

John W. Kropf, *Color Capital of the World: Growing Up with the Legacy of a Crayon Company*

Steve McClain, *The Music of My Life: Finding My Way After My Mother's MS Diagnosis*

Jade Dellinger and David Giffels, *The Beginning Was the End: Devo in Ohio*

Peg Bobel and Linda G. Whitman, eds., *Native Americans of the Cuyahoga Valley: From Early Peoples to Contemporary Issues*

David Lieberth and Jon Miller, eds., *Akron at 200: A Bicentennial History*

For a complete listing of titles published in the series,
go to www.uakron.edu/uapress.

Akron at 200

A Bicentennial History

David Lieberth and Jon Miller, editors

 The University of Akron Press \ *Akron, Ohio*

All material copyright © 2025 by The University of Akron Press
All rights reserved • First Edition 2025 • Manufactured in the United States of America.
All inquiries and permission requests should be addressed to the Publisher,
The University of Akron Press, Akron, Ohio 44325-1703.

ISBN: 978-1-62922-310-0 (printed case)
ISBN: 978-1-62922-311-7 (ePDF)
ISBN: 978-1-62922-312-4 (ePub)

A catalog record for this title is available from the Library of Congress.

∞ The paper used in this publication meets the minimum requirements of ANSI/NISO z39.48–1992 (Permanence of Paper).

Cover photo: Reopening of Lock 3 in November 2024. Photo by Pritt Entertainment Group, courtesy of the City of Akron. Cover design by Amy Freels, based on typography design by Rebecca Schreiber

Akron at 200 was designed and typeset in Arno Pro with Museo titles by Rebecca Schreiber | Reflective Book Design.

Contents

Acknowledgements	vii
Introduction \ *David Lieberth and Jon Miller*	1
1 The Indigenous History of Akron \ *Eric Olson*	5
2 C. W. Howard and the Temperance Movement in Early Akron \ *Jon Miller*	13
3 Our Own John Brown \ *Donald R. Hicks*	39
4 Truth in Between: The Social and Political Environment of the 1851 Woman's Rights Convention in Akron, Ohio \ *Philathia Bolton*	53
5 An International City \ *Charlotte Gintert*	63
6 The Christian Churches of Akron: From the Gore to the Globe \ *Jane Gramlich*	85
7 Akron's Servants, 1900 to 1940 \ *Christi Blythin*	109
8 Akron—Home of Serial (and Cereal) Entrepreneurs \ *Christopher C. Esker*	122
9 Akron, Home of the World of Make-Believe \ *Sharon Moreland Myers*	137
10 Wendell Willkie: Akron's Favorite (Adopted) Son \ *Clair Dickinson*	153
11 The Wingfoots and Nonskids: Kings of Akron Baseball \ *Jeffrey Smith*	165

12	The Brightest Spot in the Underworld: Akron's Furnace Street Mission \ *Bill Hauser*	177
13	The Evangelists: From the Tenderloin to Television \ *Jody Miller Konstand*	201
14	Tees and Greens in the Rubber City \ *Jane Gramlich*	236
15	Some of Akron's Olympic Gold Medalists and Hall of Famers \ *Tim Carroll*	243
16	Fritz Pollard \ *Steve Love*	252
17	Akron in Broadcasting \ *Mark J. Price*	265
18	The Rise and Fall of Howard Street as a Black Business District \ *Rose Vance-Grom*	295
19	Julia Perry's Musical Legacy Shines a Light on Akron \ *Karla Tipton*	301
20	The Failure of the Akron Innerbelt \ *Seyma Bayram*	309
21	1968: A Year of Drama. A Year of Change \ *David Lieberth*	324
22	Black Intracity Migration to Maple Valley and the Copley Corridor in the 1960s \ *Shaneen Harris*	336
23	The Great Transition: Remembering the Akron Renaissance \ *Stephen H. Paschen*	347
24	The Akron Sound \ *David Giffels*	360
25	Akron's Queer History \ *Fran Wilson*	375
26	"You'll be Hearing from Us, Too": Citizen Volunteers and Environmentalism in Akron \ *Megan Shaeffer*	394
27	Neighborhood Development in the Twenty-First Century \ *Melanie Mohler*	407
	Index	421

Acknowledgements

The editors would like to acknowledge and thank the City of Akron and Mayors Dan Horrigan and Shammas Malik for their generous support of this project. Many people helped to bring this book together. The editors would also like to recognize and thank the members of the Akron Bicentennial Commission, listed below, as well as Chuck Ayers; Vic Fleischer, John Ball, Mark Bloom, Jennifer Davis, Hannah Kemp-Severence, and Rose Vance-Grom of Archives and Special Collections, The University of Akron; Stephanie Marsh of the City of Akron; Mary Plazo of Special Collections, Akron-Summit County Public Library; Cheryl Powell-Fuller, Executive Editor, *Akron Beacon Journal/BeaconJournal.com*, Regional Editor Northern Ohio—USA TODAY Network; Mark Price, General Assignment Reporter and History Writer, *Akron Beacon Journal*; Amy Freels, Julie Gammon, Brittany LaPointe, Thea Ledendecker, Gwen Bushen, and Isaiah Carter of The University of Akron Press; and Rebecca Schreiber of Reflective Book Design.

• • •

The Akron Bicentennial is a citizen-led initiative guided by a commission that has planned a series of events that speak to four bicentennial themes: Akron history, civic pride, innovation, and legacy. The goal is to showcase two hundred years of community contributions, achievements, and milestones so that citizens feel a sense of pride in the commemoration of Akron's rich history and the diversity of our city.

Members of the Commission

Honorary Commissioners

Ernest Pouttu	President and CEO, Harwick Standard Distribution
Hon. Elinore Stormer	Judge, Probate Court of Summit County
Dr. Cynthia Capers	Emeritus Dean and Professor, The University of Akron, College of Nursing
Marco Sommerville	Senior Advisor to the Mayor, Deputy Mayor for Intergovernmental Affairs

Commissioners ex officio

Dr. Paul Levy	Professor, The University of Akron
Kimberly Beckett	CEO, Downtown Akron Partnership
Gregg Mervis	CEO, Akron/Summit Convention and Visitor's Bureau
Leianne Neff Heppner	CEO, Summit County Historical Society
Pam Hickson Stevenson	Executive Director, Akron-Summit County Public Library
Megan Mannion	Learning Specialist, Akron Public Schools
Phil Montgomery	Director, Department of Finance and Budget County of Summit
Margo Sommerville	President, Akron City Council

Commissioners

Mark Greer	Executive Director, *Akron 200, Inc.*
Hon. Deborah Cook	Judge, United States Court of Appeals for the Sixth Circuit
Bronlynn Thurman	Program Officer, Cleveland Foundation
Andre Thornton	CEO, ASW Global
Sharon Connor	Council Representative, Akron City Council Ward 10
Joseph Tucker	Executive Director, South Street Mission
Mac Love	Co-Founder & Chief Catalyst, Art x Love
Kathryn Beck	Co-Artistic Director, Gum-Dip Theatre
Dr. Naresh Subba	Physics Dept., Kent State University, Bhutanese Community
Curtis Minter Jr.	Senior Fellow, Third Space Action Lab
James Weyrick	Ellet community historian and volunteer
Tina Boyes	Akron City Council Ward 9 representative
Demetrius Lambert-Falconer	Chief of Community Engagement for Summit Metro Parks
Dr. Harvey Sterns	Professor Emeritus, The University of Akron and Co-Chair, Age Friendly Akron

Staff

David Lieberth	Executive Secretary, President, the Akron History Center, Inc.
Gertrude Wilms	Chief of Staff to the Mayor of Akron, 2022–2023
Nannette Pitt	Chief of Strategy to the Mayor of Akron, 2024

Akron at 200

\ SERIES ON OHIO HISTORY AND CULTURE

Introduction

David Lieberth

•••

The only thing new in the world is the history you don't know.

—HARRY S. TRUMAN, 33RD PRESIDENT OF THE UNITED STATES

Planning for Akron's Bicentennial celebration in 2025 has its roots in the year 2000, when the Summit County Historical Society sponsored forty events to commemorate the Akron Centeseptequinary—the 175th anniversary of the city's founding.

The high point of the year 2000 was the opening of a time capsule installed in 1950 under the stone porch of the Simon Perkins Mansion. A new time capsule was created—filled with letters to the future by young people, to be opened in 2025 as part of the bicentennial.

Planning for the 200th anniversary began in earnest in April 2021, when I approached Mayor Dan Horrigan about appointing a mayoral advisory committee that would oversee the celebration that would begin in December 2024 and last through December 2025.

In January 2022, the mayor announced plans for the anniversary celebration and appointed four honorary chairs of a new Bicentennial Commission. In June, he named twenty-four men and women to the Commission, representing every ward in the city.

Early on, two activities were certain: the development of Akron's first enduring exhibit of the 200-year history of the city and the publication of a new history book.

The predicate for this new volume of history was established on the occasion of Akron's prior anniversaries—1925, 1950, and 1975.

Akron had been the subject of published histories before 1925, including *Historical Reminiscences* by Lucius V. Bierce (1854); Perrin's *History of Summit County* (1881); Howe's *History of Ohio* (1890); *Fifty Years and Over of Akron and Summit County* by former sheriff, mayor, and publisher Samuel Lane (1892); and Oscar Olin's *Akron and Environs* (1917).

Professor Olin took the lead in the publication of a Centennial history for the Summit County Historical Society, a 666-page anthology written by thirty-seven authors. Mayor of Akron D. C. Rybolt noted in an introduction that the hastily prepared book was written in a "popular" vein and was so rushed that "errors may have crept in."

Twenty-five years later, for the city's 125th anniversary, the Historical Society employed former *Akron Times* reporter-turned-author Karl Grismer to research and write what would be regarded as the most comprehensive history, beginning with his account of Native American nomads and advancing to the massive industrial successes that marked the first half of Akron in the twentieth century.

Grismer's 800-page book is superbly indexed and has remained a principal resource for anyone writing Akron history in the last seventy years. Notably, the volume enshrined a pantheon of Akron's founders in a 174-page biographical appendix. There are 421 (white) men and five women featured in the volume (two of the women won fame with nationally recognized singing careers). There was no account of women's contributions to Akron, and in a city that still had segregated cafeterias in 1950, there were no accounts of the Black leaders and communities that played such an important role in Akron's growth in the twentieth century.

In 1975, for Akron's sesquicentennial, the Historical Society commissioned Akron's premier historian Dr. George W. Knepper to create a coffee table book about the city, superbly illustrated with new and archival photographs assembled by Jack Gieck. *City at the Summit* reached the public in 1981. Gieck and Knepper produced a 1975 film with the same title.

The need for a new history is driven by the need to utilize the tools of science that we have today that were unavailable to previous authors: namely, the

Introduction

digitization of historical materials and the work in recent decades of archaeologists and anthropologists who have sharpened our understanding of populations of Native Americans that traveled through what is now the city of Akron.

Search engines and other innovations were unavailable to previous writers of history. (Of interest is that in the 1950s, when Goodyear Aircraft was assembling some of the nation's first guided missiles at its Akron plant, they met the need for greater computing power by inventing and making one of America's first analog computers that had "search" capability.)

Missing from earlier volumes of Akron history is an appreciation for the roles that women and African Americans played in the city. This new anthology also contains a written history of Akron's LGBTQIA+ community and attempts to correct much of the myth and legend that marked previous accounts of Indigenous people.

In March 2022, I invited twenty-two people who had written about Akron history to a meeting at the John S. Knight Center to discuss the feasibility of writing a new history of Akron. The goal of this project was to assemble new accounts of topics that may have been written about before, but without the advantages that we have today in researching historical people and events.

The anthology was produced under the guidance of Dr. Jon Miller, Director of The University of Akron Press. This new volume of history exists mainly because of his dedication and skill to make this happen.

The quote at the head of this introduction attributed to Harry Truman reads in full:

> There is not really anything new if you know what has gone before. What is new to people is what they do not know about their history or the history of the world.

The hope and expectation of this anthology is that the reader will learn something new about Akron's rich history. My personal mantra for the study of history comes from the author Jon Meacham in his book *American Gospel: God, the Founding Fathers, and the Making of a Nation:*

> To fail to consult the past consigns us to 'the tyranny of the present', the mistaken idea that the crises of our own time are unprecedented and that we have to solve them without experience to guide us. If we know how those who came before us found the ways and means to surmount the difficulties of their age, we stand a far better chance of acting in the moment with perspective and measured judgment.

David A. Lieberth
Executive Secretary, Akron Bicentennial Commission
President, The Akron History Center, Inc.
October 2024

Postscript

Akron at 200 brings forward and consolidates a great deal of new historical writing about the history of our city. The more we learn our history, however, the more we understand how much more there is to learn. This anthology treats a diverse range of subjects, and it was authored by a diverse group of Akronites. But *Akron at 200* does not pretend to be a comprehensive history. There is much more to learn.

As Director of The University of Akron Press, I hope that this book will inspire the writing of more books on Akron history, by even more authors, and I invite readers to contact The University of Akron Press for consultation, encouragement, and possible publication of new historical writing they would like to undertake to improve our shared future by advancing our understanding of our histories, ourselves, and our communities.

Jon Miller
Director, The University of Akron Press
Akron, Ohio
October 2024

\ **1**

The Indigenous History of Akron

Eric Olson

Exactly when people first settled in North America is debated—not in days, months, years, or even decades, but in thousand-year chunks. The current archaeological evidence indicates that humans have been in North America for over twenty thousand years. Exactly when people settled in North America does not change their status as first peoples. As Jay Custer succinctly put it, "Who cares if Indians came here from somewhere else and when, so long as they were here before Europeans." These first peoples are often referred to as pre-Clovis, which is a label that archaeologists use to categorize these first peoples, named for the culture associated with artifacts found in 1932 near the town of Clovis, New Mexico. There are no written records of what they called themselves. Paulette Steeves has suggested using the term Upper Paleolithic for this time period to be consistent with archaeological time periods from the eastern hemisphere.[1]

The landscape drastically changed as the Earth warmed and the ice melted. Rivers flowed in different directions than they do today, and the Great Lakes were in the process of forming. By the end of the Clovis period, roughly twelve thousand years ago, Lake Erie was roughly one-third of the size it is today. As the ice melted, new streams of melted ice water began to cut through natural sediment dams, causing much of the Great Lakes to form rapidly in flood events. Some archaeologists have suggested these rapid flooding events may be the impetus behind much of the flood creation stories common among Great Lakes Tribes.[2]

With the changing environment and climate came cultural shifts during what many archaeologists call the Archaic period. During this seven-thousand-year span, the climate continued to get warmer and wetter. The environment of Ohio was becoming more like the present. By the Middle Archaic Period (6,500 to 3,500 BCE), deciduous trees were growing across the state; these trees provided new foods, fuel, and building materials for people. By the Late Archaic (3500 BCE), the Lower Cuyahoga River, the portion that flows through modern-day Akron, connected to the rest of the rivers in Northeast Ohio. The Upper Cuyahoga River that formerly flowed south into the Tuscarawas was re-routed. Prior to the Late Archaic, the drainage divide between Lake Erie and the Ohio River would have been further north, perhaps as far north as Everett.[3]

The roughly two thousand years after the Archaic period is commonly referred to by archaeologists as the Woodland period, which is most well-known for the mound-building cultures that produced such earthworks as Fort Ancient, Hopewell Mound Group, Mound City, and Seip Earthworks in southwest Ohio. During this time, people farmed crops such as sunflowers, pumpkin, squash, beans, amaranth, goosefoot, and knotweed and continued hunting with atlatls, spears, traps, and nets.[4]

With the introduction of the bow and arrow and maize, around 800 CE, populations began to increase. Territory became more important to protect maize fields and hunting grounds crucial to vibrant village life. By 1000 CE, most people in Northeast Ohio were living in villages with palisades around them. The bow and arrow may have made hunting easier, but the higher rate of fire made possible with this new hunting technology made warfare easier, too.[5]

Within the Lake Erie basin, each major river generally had one large village within fifteen miles of the lake. Within the Cuyahoga River watershed, during the spring, summer, and fall, multiple families lived within the palisaded walls of the South Park Village near present-day Independence. Then, during the winter months, people spread out across the river valley in smaller camps. The South Park Village was not abandoned each winter, though its population did drastically decrease during the winter. This general pattern continued up until about 1650 CE. At its peak, the South Park village might have had a population of five hundred people.[6]

By the mid-1600s, the Ohio region had undergone a rapid change in economics. The European demand for furs (beaver in particular) led to an influx in hunting and warfare in the eastern Great Lakes. The relatively stable system of singular palisaded villages that dispersed to hunt every winter was broken up by this dramatic economic shift. Likewise, the introduction of foreign diseases by Europeans spread throughout the Americas and decimated many groups.[7]

The people living in the South Park village may have spoken either an Iroquoian language or an Algonquian language, but current archaeological and historical research has not put this debate to rest. What is clear, however, is that the neighboring Erie tribe's defeat by the Seneca Nation opened the "western door" leading to Northeast Ohio. Based on the accounts of French Jesuit missionaries, the Erie tribe lived along Lake Erie stretching from Erie, Pennsylvania, to just south of Buffalo, New York. The Seneca Nation, along with the other four nations of the Five Nations (Cayuga, Onondaga, Oneida, Mohawk), began to absorb or conquer neighboring tribes. Those Erie tribe members not killed in combat were adopted into the Seneca Nation. The people of the South Park Village, around the time the Erie were defeated, likely left their settlement and headed south or were adopted into the Seneca Nation. The Cuyahoga was now Seneca Territory.[8]

Contrary to local folklore, Fort Island in Fairlawn was not the "last stand" of the Erie. In 1988 and 1989, excavations by archaeologists at The University of Akron revealed a couple of post molds (remnants of a wooden post that was once placed in the ground) and an underwhelming number of artifacts. (It is possible the site once had a higher density of artifacts; collecting and looting by the public has removed an immeasurable amount of archaeological data from the site.) The lack of artifacts and features did not indicate to the archaeologists that the site represented a village site. The embankments that encapsulate the site (still visible today) may have served as earthen walls for a palisade. The radiocarbon dates from the post molds date to the 1300s CE. Given this information, even the most liberal interpretation of the site as a village from the 1300s puts Fort Island three hundred years too early to be the "last stand" of the Erie (leaving aside the lack of any evidence of Erie peoples west of Erie, Pennsylvania).[9]

As Seneca Territory, the Cuyahoga River became a frequent stopping point for hunting parties searching for furs to sell to Europeans. The village life that the people of South Park once knew was no more, though it is likely that the people still living and hunting in the Cuyahoga Valley were from Northeast Ohio and adoptees to the Seneca Nation. It was not a "no man's land" or "vacant." It was likely either during this period, or in subsequent times while the Seneca occupied and claimed the region, that the name *Cuyahoga* became the colloquial name for the river, attributed to the Mohawk word for *river*.[10]

This region was formally recognized by the British as Five Nations land in 1701 in the treaty of Nanfan, purported to transfer lands that were the Beaver Hunting Grounds from the Five Nations to the King of England. The treaty did not define clear boundaries on what the Five Nations claimed through right of conquest, but that was no concern of the British at the time. While the Five Nations interpreted the treaty as a right of use by the British, the British interpreted the treaty as a fee simple deed, granting them complete ownership. However, by the mid-1720s, the language of the Nanfan treaty came to a head as the French began building forts at Detroit, Niagara Falls, and Michilimackinac (located at the foot of Michigan's Mackinac bridge today).

In 1726, in Albany, the British had the Five Nations (now the Six Nations with the addition of the Tuscarora in 1722) sign an amendment to the treaty that set the Cuyahoga River as the formal western boundary. Around the same time, the Seneca in western New York were dealing with smallpox outbreaks. The construction of English and French forts on all sides of their territory led many Seneca to move from western New York to the Ohio Country. With the 1726 Albany Treaty, many Seneca now had a clearly defined western boundary marking how far they could migrate and still be within Seneca lands. By the 1740s, the Cuyahoga was very clearly the borderland between British merchants in Albany and Philadelphia, and French merchants in Detroit.[11]

As was common within the Seneca Nation and the other tribes of the Five Nations, representatives were appointed to govern the regions acquired during the seventeenth century. Within the Cuyahoga Valley, that representative was Conageresa, or Broken Kettle. Relatively few written accounts mention Conageresa, so there is not much to say about his personality or style of leadership. However, like most representatives of the time, he had a difficult job. In the 1740s the Cuyahoga Valley was split between French and British interests, with both attempting to set up trading posts along the Cuyahoga. In addition to these competing Europeans, Conageresa was the figurehead of a village of two thousand people, many of whom were not Seneca. The people living in Cuyahoga Town included members of the Ottawa, Ojibwe, Shawnee, Seneca, Cayuga, Mahican, and Lenape (Delaware).[12]

But where did Conageresa derive his authority? Many people in Ohio did not respect or recognize Seneca territorial claims, or the leaders they appointed. Some Seneca and Cayuga living in the Ohio country were commonly called the derogatory term *mingo*, a Delaware word meaning "treacherous one." However, the Five Nations were not the only Indigenous Nations claiming land in the Ohio country. The Wyandot (also known as Wendat or Huron) laid claim to the land west of the Cuyahoga and as far south as the Ohio River. The Miami claimed much of the western third of Ohio. The Delaware, forced from their homelands in the Hudson and Delaware River valleys, laid claim to east central Ohio. The Shawnee claimed the lands along the Scioto River.[13]

The Indigenous History of Akron

Many of these land claims were in competition with one another. In the case of both the Shawnee and the Delaware, their land claims were made through permissions from the Wyandot. By the end of the 1740s, these competing land claims struggled to coexist. Delegations sent to Philadelphia from Conageresa's village had failed to garner British support. Trader George Croghan's trading post had failed, as had French trader Saguin's. The British had better luck with the outpost at Pickawillaney, near modern Piqua, Ohio. However, this was too far into what the French considered *their* land, so in 1749 the French led an expedition down the Ohio River to place lead plates in the ground to formally claim the territory west of the Ohio River as French.[14]

This show of force by the French only heightened tensions in the Ohio country. The situation came to a boiling point in 1754. The Seven Years' War (also known as the French and Indian War) lasted until 1760 in the Ohio Country. The Cuyahoga Valley likely supplied soldiers and supplies to the war effort, though no battles occurred in Northeast Ohio. The French had withdrawn their forces from the Ohio country by 1760, and by 1763 they had ceded their territorial claims to the British.[15]

The next decade saw numerous conflicts, primarily at or near British forts, in response to poor British policy meant to curtail colonial settlers from migrating west into the Ohio Country. Seneca–Cayuga men played key roles in two of the most prominent conflicts, Guyasuta in Pontiac's Rebellion and Chief Logan in Lord Dunmore's War. Neither of these men had direct associations with the Cuyahoga Valley, though the wars they fought determined the fate of the valley.[16]

Despite the animosity towards the British during the 1760s, by the time of the American Revolution most of the Ohio Country supported the British. By the late 1770s, the Cuyahoga was mostly under the control of Delaware chiefs like Hopocan, Tegasah, and White Eyes. The attacks by belligerent settlers during the 1760s and the conclusion of Lord Dunmore's war made it clear to many Native Americans in Ohio that the British, while failing, were at least attempting to stem the flow of trespassers into the Ohio Country. American forces attempted to capture the Cuyahoga Valley only once during the revolution, in 1778. The British, the preceding winter, had built an ammunition magazine at the mouth of the Cuyahoga. In response, the Americans planned a campaign to attack the magazine from Fort Pitt via the Mahoning River. Before the army could reach the Cuyahoga, they turned back due to poor weather. The Americans then refocused their attentions to the south that same year near present-day Bolivar, where they constructed Fort Laurens.[17]

The fighting with Americans continued even after the British surrendered at Yorktown in 1781. None of the battles occurred in the Cuyahoga Valley, but by 1784, the Cuyahoga and the Portage Path were used to draw lines between "Indian Territory" and American Territory. The Treaty of Fort Stanwix of 1784 was signed by the Seneca Nation, but the following year the Americans sought the signatures of other tribes to release their claims to eastern Ohio lands in the treaty of Fort McIntosh. This western boundary, first formally established in 1726, would be recodified in 1795 with the signing of the Treaty of Greenville. However, these treaties, and the surveyors that came after them, did not lead to an immediate settlement by Americans. Native Americans, in particular Seneca–Cayuga and Shawnee, still continued to fight American forces and claim parts of Ohio.[18]

With the death of Tecumseh after the British abandoned him and his forces at the Thames in 1813, American settlers began migrating to the Cuyahoga in larger numbers. The populations remained small, but by the 1820s, the number of American settlers in the Cuyahoga Valley rivaled the population levels of the 1650s, when the South Park Village was at its peak. It would take another decade to approach the population of Conageresa's town in the 1740s. If the city of Cleveland can claim a population of fifteen in 1797, their founding year, then at no point in any year prior could anyone claim that the Cuyahoga Valley was not populated, vacant, a no man's land, or abandoned. Nor could anyone recognizing British Common Law and the concept of fee simple deeds claim that unoccupied land was not "owned" or under possession.[19]

During this brief dive into over twenty thousand years of history, information about the Portage Path was notably scant. While today the path is an important landmark and part of Akron's identity, it is mostly remembered in connection to boundary setting by colonists. Native Americans, accustomed to travel by foot or canoe and based in an economic system different from the marketplace of Europeans, did not envision the Portage Path as the land between Cleveland and New Orleans because nobody in Northeast Ohio was making trips between Cleveland and New Orleans (except, perhaps, Tecumseh). Those people interested in international commerce and commercialism recognized the shipping potential of the Portage Path, which was realized with the creation of the Ohio and Erie Canal in 1825. But before the canal were the Seneca, Cayuga, Delaware, Wyandot, Shawnee, Ottawa, and Ojibwe Nations who called (and many still call) this land home. These Nations still exist today, though their homes are far from Akron. However, "far" is a relative term based on the mode of transportation. Salamanca, New York, home of the Seneca Nation of Indians, is a sixty-two-hour walk from Akron. But it is only three hours by car.[20]

Notes

1. Jay Custer, "Faith, Science, and Native American Origins," *Pennsylvania Archaeologist* 79, no. 2 (2009): 64. For a thorough discussion of Upper Paleolithic archaeology in North America, see Paulette Steeves, *Indigenous Paleolithic of the Western Hemisphere* (University of Nebraska Press, 2021).

2. David Graeber and David Wengrow, in *The Dawn of Everything: A New History of Humanity* (Farrar, Straus, and Girroux, 2021), critique the term "archaic" as an insult to human history. They argue that it is often used to define the time before what archaeologists consider more interesting archaeology. Troy Holcombe et al., "Revised Lake Erie Postglacial Lake Level History Based on New Detailed Bathymetry," *Journal of Great Lakes Research* 29, no. 4 (2003): 681–704; Charles Herdendorf, "Research Overview: Holocene Development of Lake Erie," 112, no. 2 (2013): 24–36; Victoria Brehm, *Star Songs and Water Spirits* (Tustin: Ladyslipper Press, 2011).

3. J. P. Szabo et al, "Foundations from the Past: Clues to Understanding Late Quaternary Stratigraphy Beneath Cleveland, Ohio," *Journal of Great Lakes Research* 29 (2003): 566–80; Andrew Bauer et al., "Archaeological Site Distribution by Geomorphic Setting in the Southern Lower Cuyahoga River Valley, Northeastern Ohio: Initial Observations from a GIS Database," *Geoarchaeology* 26, no. 8 (2004): 711–29. For a thorough discussion of the Ohio Archaic, see Matthew Purtill, "The Ohio Archaic: A Review," in *Archaic Societies: Diversity and Complexity across the Midcontinent*, ed. Thomas Emerson, Dale McElrath, and Andrew Fortier (State University of New York Press, 2009), 565–600.

4. Bradley Lepper, *Ohio Archaeology: An Illustrated Chronicle of Ohio's Ancient American Indian Cultures* (Orange Frazer Press, 2005); William Dancey and Paul Pacheco, "A Community Model of Ohio Hopewell Settlement," in *Ohio Hopewell Community Organization*, ed. William Dancey and Paul Pacheco (Kent State University Press, 1997), 3–40.

5. Brian Redmond, "Reviewing the Late Prehistory in Ohio," in *Cultures Before Contact: The Late Prehistory of Ohio and Surrounding Regions*, ed. Robert Genheimer (Ohio Archaeological Council, 2000), 426–37; David Brose, *The South Park Village Site and the Late Prehistoric Whittlesey Tradition of Northeast Ohio* (Prehistoric Press, 1994); Lepper, *Ohio Archaeology*. See also Brian Redmond, "The First People: Ancient History of the Cuyahoga Valley and Northeast Ohio," in *Native Americans of the Cuyahoga Valley*, ed. Peg Bobel and Linda G. Whitman (University of Akron Press, 2024), 39–52.

6. Brose, *The South Park Village Site*; David Brose, "Late Prehistoric Societies of Northeastern Ohio and Adjacent Portions of the South Shore of Lake Erie: A Review," in *Cultures Before Contact: The Late Prehistory of Ohio and Surrounding Regions*, ed. Robert Genheimer (Ohio Archaeological Council, 2000), 96–120. See also Redmond, "The First People," 88–92.

7. Michael McConnell, *A Country Between: The Upper Ohio Valley and Its Peoples, 1724–1774* (University of Nebraska Press, 1992).

8. Brian Redmond and Katherine Ruhl, "Rethinking the 'Whittlesey Collapse': Late Prehistoric Pottery Migrations in Eastern Ohio." *Archaeology of Eastern North America* 30 (2002): 59–80; Redmond, "Reviewing the Late Prehistory." See also Colden Cadwallader, *The History of the Five Indian Nations, Depending on the Province of New-York in America* (1747; Cornell University Press, 1973).

9. There is extensive research demonstrating the Erie's furthest western extent was modern Erie, Pennsylvania. For examples, see E. S. Carpenter et al., "The 28th Street Site," *Pennsylvania Archaeologist* 19, no. 1–2 (1949): 3–16; David Bush and Charles Callander, "Anybody but the Erie," *Ohio Archaeologist* 34, no. 1 (1984): 31–35; Emerson Greenman, "Two Prehistoric Villages near Cleveland, Ohio," *The Ohio State Archaeological and Historical Quarterly* 43, no. 3 (1937): 325–63; Philip Shriver, "The Whittlesey People: Algonquian or Iroquoian?," *Ohio Archaeologist* 36, no. 4 (1986): 25; John Marwitt and Lisa Hartley, *A Management Summary of the 1989 Field School Excavation at Fort Island, 33 SU 9, Akron, Summit County, Ohio*, ed. Eric Olson, and Gavin DeMali (University of Akron Department of Anthropology).

10. Erminie Wheeler-Voegelin, "An Ethnohistorical Report," in *Indians of Northern Ohio and Southeastern Michigan*, ed. David Horr, vol. 1 (Garland Publishing, 1974); Henry Shetrone, "The Culture Problem in Ohio Archaeology," *American Anthropologist* 22, no. 2 (1920): 144–72; David Brose, "History as a Handmaiden to Archaeology?," *Ohio Archaeologist* 34, no. 1 (1984): 28–30; Philip Shriver, "A Large

Seventeenth Century Historic Contact Interment in the Cuyahoga Valley: An Iroquoian Piece in the Puzzle of What Happened to the Whittlesey Focus?," *Ohio Archaeologist* 35, no 4 (1985): 20–29. For specific references to Northeast Ohio as a "no-man's land," see George Knepper and Kevin Kern, "Along the Lower Cuyahoga: 1740–1805," in *Native Americans of the Cuyahoga Valley*, ed. Peg Bobel and Linda G. Whitman (University of Akron Press, 2024), 104.

11. Timothy Shannon, *Iroquois Diplomacy on the Early American Frontier* (Viking, 2008); George H. J. Abrams, *The Seneca People* (Indian Tribal Series, 1976), 20–23; Charles Whittlesey, *The Early History of Cleveland, Ohio* (Fairbanks, Benedict, and Company, 1867). There is still debate whether to call the document signed in 1701 and amended in 1726 a treaty or a deed. See Jim Windle and Paul Williams, "What about that 1701 Nanfan Treaty?," *Two Row Times* (December 28, 2016), https://tworowtimes.com/historical/1701-nanfan-treaty/.

12. McConnell, *A Country Between*, 69; Wheeler-Voegelin, "An Ethnohistoric Report"; Colin Calloway, *The Indian World of George Washington* (Oxford University Press, 2018), 51.

13. John Heckewelder, *History, Manners, and Customs of the Indian Nations* (The Historical Society of Pennsylvania, 1881); Wheeler–Voegelin, "An Ethnohistoric Report."

14. Shannon, *Iroquois Diplomacy*; Calloway, *Indian World*; Scott Weidensaul, *The First Frontier: The Forgotten History of Struggle, Savagery, & Endurance in Early America* (Houghton Mifflin Harcourt, 2012).

15. For a thorough narrative of the French and Indian War, see Calloway, *Indian World* and McConnell, *A Country Between*.

16. For information on Pontiac's Rebellion and Lord Dunmore's War, see chapter two of Colin Calloway's *The Shawnees and the War for America* (Penguin, 2007) and Calloway, *Indian World*. See also Anthony Wallace, *Death and Rebirth of the Seneca* (New York: Vintage, 1970). There are various sources on Chief Logan, but many were written over one hundred years ago. See "Logan: The Mingo Chief, 1710–1780," *Ohio State Archaeological and Historical Society Quarterly* 20, no. 2 (April, 1911): 137–75 and Franklin Sawvel, *Logan the Mingo Chief* (R. G. Badger, 1921). Chief Logan, contrary to what local folklore says, has no direct associations with Northeast Ohio. George Knepper and Kevin Kern (2024) also argue that there is no connection between Chief Logan and Northeast Ohio.

17. Helen Tanner, "The Location of Indian Tribes in Southeastern Michigan and Northern Ohio," in *Indians of Northern Ohio and Southeastern Michigan*, ed. David Horr, vol. 1 (Garland, 1974); Calloway, *Indian World*; Wheeler-Voegelin, "An Ethnohistoric Report." Fort Laurens was a short-lived fort, abandoned in 1779.

18. Wallace, *Death and Rebirth*; Calloway, *Shawnees*; Tanner, "The Location of Indian Tribes."

19. Calloway, *Shawnees*; Whittlesey, *Early History*, 357 and 456.

20. Canal Engineer James Geddes' 1823 *Canal Report* in so many words describes Akron as ideal for a canal because of the watershed divide that the Portage Path crosses. As a point of departure for boats between Cleveland and New Orleans, see Lucius V. Bierce, *Historical Reminiscences of Summit County* (Canfield, 1854) 21; Peter Cherry, *The Portage Path* (Western Reserve Company, 1911). For a more thorough discussion on the history of the Portage Path, see Peg Bobel and Linda G. Whitman's "Path Finding" (2024).

\ **2**

C. W. Howard and the Temperance Movement in Early Akron

Jon Miller

The story of the rise, fall, and recovery of Charles Wesley ("C. W.") Howard (1809–1898), one of Akron's pioneer entrepreneurs, illustrates many sides of the early history of Akron and the striving, human, and imperfect lives of its people. Howard's story spans the early formative period from the city's founding in 1825 into the early 1840s, when Akron was selected as the county seat of the newly formed Summit County.

The Year Without a Summer

C. W. Howard was the seventh of twelve children born to Harvey and Sarah Howard, who worked as farmers and tanners in Connecticut. The early nineteenth century was a hard time for children. There were high birth rates and high rates of infant and childhood mortality. Howard was the second baby his parents named Charles; their first Charles did not survive infancy. When he was eight, in 1817, Howard's parents decided to move their large family from Connecticut to Ohio.

The Howard family left Connecticut in a surge of migration westward. Moving to Ohio was a popular idea in New England in 1817, and one reason was the weather: in 1815 Mount Tambora erupted in Indonesia. The most powerful volcanic eruption in our known history put a continent-sized cloud of ash into the atmosphere. This cloud drifted eastward, dimming the sunlight and lowering temperatures. It traveled east around the globe, crossing the Pacific Ocean and causing agricultural catastrophes in North America and even in Western Europe. It also produced unprecedented variations in the weather. It made the strangest weather anyone could remember. Historians call 1816 "The Year without a Summer."[1] The *Connecticut Courant* wrote on June 11: "The weather has been extremely variable of late.... Winter garments were as common yesterday as in December."[2] Planting seasons were disrupted, harvests were thin, farms failed, and food prices soared. Reports and predictions of hardship caused by the freakish weather often appeared in the newspapers. Many New Englanders saw this as a good reason to move west and start over. Eastern newspapers carried good reports of the prospects for settlement in Ohio, and in 1816 this was sounding like a better and better idea.

Another reason for the surge of migration into the Western Reserve was the end of hostilities between Americans and Native Americans in this area. The War of 1812 had increased the violence between Americans and Native Americans throughout Ohio, and after about 1815 there was only a small population of Native Americans along the Cuyahoga River.[3]

The Howard family got halfway to Ohio before they stopped in the newly founded town of Preble, New York. They liked the area and settled there instead.

Middlebury

C. W.'s eldest brothers, Horatio (born in 1795) and Harvey (born in 1798), moved on to Ohio some years later, in their late teens or early twenties. They settled in Middlebury, now an Akron neighborhood. In the 1820s Middlebury was a thriving village nestled along the western bank of the Little Cuyahoga River, around the area of what is now the intersection of East Market Street and Case Avenue. In 1825 Middlebury had about five hundred residents, making it one of the most productive industrial and commercial centers in Northeast Ohio. For perspective, at this time Cleveland had about eight hundred residents. Karl Grismer describes Middlebury as a "lusty town" in the 1820s, a hard-working place with no churches and widespread, open, and heavy consumption of alcoholic beverages. Middlebury had six large general stores, a millinery store, a tailor, three boot and shoe makers, a hat maker, a physician, three attorneys, and an abundance of industry, much of it powered by the waters of the Little Cuyahoga River. There were two gristmills, two sawmills, a blast furnace, a forge, four blacksmith shops, a tannery, and a wool carding and cloth dressing mill. There were also factories for making nails, plows, chairs, soap, and candles.[4] The oldest Howard brothers joined this community and went into business. C. W. left the crowded Preble home and joined them in 1827, around the age of 17.

Disease

The early nineteenth century was also a time of deadly epidemics, especially in thriving population centers where there was no effective sanitation infrastructure. A very popular traveler's guide to Ohio told readers that the state's climate was "healthy," with the notable exception of areas near marshes and stagnated waters, where people were described as afflicted with frequent fevers and agues.[5] In the 1830s the alternation of shivering and fever was called an *ague*. Akron was one of these places near marshes and stagnated waters, and there were frequent fevers and agues in the years that it took to complete the construction of the canal.

The stretch of the Ohio and Erie Canal from Summit Lake to the Tuscarawas River south of Lake Nesmith was dug through swamp. Men labored waist-high in mud and water, through heavy rains and summer heat. These working conditions consistently made them sick. The work paid well, but the canal diggers were itinerant, impoverished workers, mostly from Ireland but also from Germany. They were poorly treated by the better-established white settlers. In 1879 Howard remembered downtown Akron, in the area of South Howard Street along the canal, as being temporarily dotted with "little Irish shanties" housing these laborers during the 1828 to 1831 years, which saw the completion of the canal.[6]

Today we might recognize their "fevers and agues" as diseases such as malaria, typhoid, and smallpox. These diseases, plus cholera, which spreads when sewage contaminates the source of the drinking water, killed many people in the area. Cholera was epidemic in 1832. In short, the area was unusually sickly in the late 1820s and early 1830s, and the value of Akron-area land fell for years after reaching early, speculative heights around 1828.[7]

Horatio Howard and Harvey Howard died of illness in 1828.[8]

Marriage to Calista Crosby

At this time one of Middlebury's most prominent citizens was Dr. Eliakim Crosby. Crosby is one of the most central figures in early Akron's history.[9] Crosby invented and led the project to divert the waters of the Little Cuyahoga River into downtown Akron, creating the Cascade Mill Race which delivered the waterpower responsible for the canal town's industrial boom in the 1830s.

In October 1830 Crosby's wife, Marcia Beemer Crosby, died while giving birth to their eighth child. At this time Eliakim was fifty-one years old; Marcia was thirty-six or thirty-seven. The child died in infancy.[10] Two months after the death of her mother, Crosby's eldest daughter, sixteen-year-old Marcia Calista Crosby (who went by the name Calista) married twenty-one-year-old C. W. Howard in Middlebury.[11] Crosby's prominence in Akron created significant opportunities for the young couple.

Youth

If we were to travel back in time to Akron in the middle of the nineteenth century, we might be stunned by the overall youth of the population. Compared to today, Akron was a village of children and younger adults, with only a sprinkling of old heads. A well-known photo of the Mustill Store from the 1860s includes twenty-five people. Fourteen appear to be children.

Here are some numbers to consider. The 2020 census showed that the median age of people in the United States was 38.8 years old, and 16.5 percent of Americans—about 1 in 6—were 17 years old or younger.[12] The 1840 census found that the median age of people in the United States was 17.8.[13] In Summit County, 56 percent of all people were 19 years old or younger, and 45 percent of all people were 14 or under. In other words, small children and teenagers outnumbered full-grown adults. And less than 7 percent of the population was 50 or older. In 2020, twice that percentage were older than 65. Summit County was a little younger than the nation as a whole in 1840, perhaps because the elderly did not migrate westward so much as the young.[14] Akron was a brand-new place for its earliest citizens—a new settlement of the United States—and it was stocked with young people hosting young travellers and welcoming young migrants.

This is a general truth about US history: the farther back we go, the younger the population was. And the farther back we go, the more all these children were stressed by the hardships of inadequate shelter, disease, nutritional deficiencies, physical abuse, and other adversities. This more hostile environment inhibited human growth. It reduced the overall stature of adults, and it delayed

A much-reprinted photo of twenty-five blurry people outside the Mustill Store near Lock 15. \ Special Collections, Akron-Summit County Public Library.

the onset of puberty. Children may have acquired some kinds of hard-earned wisdom as they survived such difficult circumstances, but their overall physical and mental development was slower than it is today, on average. For example, for nineteenth-century American girls the average age for the onset of menstruation was fifteen or sixteen; today the average age is twelve.[15] Fifteen- and sixteen-year-old males were regarded as "boys." Their age relative to the rest of the population did not change the perception of their immaturity. The people of Akron in the 1830s, like Americans everywhere in the 1830s, were smaller, younger, and less mature than Akronites of the same age today. Perhaps half of all Akronians in 1830s had not yet entered puberty.[16]

Still most teenagers worked, in or out of the home. School sessions were short and not universally attended. Schoolteachers were often teenagers themselves. It was a struggle to get to adulthood. Most children saw some hard times and were deprived of at least some of the essentials for healthy growth. Calista

Crosby was sixteen when she married C. W. Howard in late 1830. She had just experienced the death of her mother, and she was leaving her father's home to start her own family. She gave birth to a son in December of 1831. Like so many babies of the time, their boy did not survive the 1830s. His small grave is in Glendale Cemetery.

Waterpower and Crosby's Stone Mill

The Crosby and Howard families moved to Akron around 1831. In what might be the most significant story of early Akron, Calista's father, Dr. Eliakim Crosby, contrived with Simon Perkins and other major landowners to acquire a long, narrow, contiguous stretch of land from the Little Cuyahoga River to the canal at Akron. He then employed canal diggers to dig his famous "ditch" along this land, creating a man-made channel of water, called a *race*, or if it was used to power a mill, a *millrace*. In Akron it came to be known as the Cascade Mill Race. This ran along the Little Cuyahoga before turning south to run down the center of Main Street. It then plunged down Mill Street to the canal, where it flowed northward to power mills and other industries along the canal. This race would later become part of the "Cross-cut" or Pennsylvania and Ohio Canal, which opened in 1839 and connected Akron to Bolivar, Pennsylvania.[17]

Gravity created enough waterpower to power a series of mills and other manufactories. In this era before electrical infrastructure, the race was like a massive power line, once completed in 1833. The water ran in one building, powered it by turning a water wheel, and then ran out that building to enter another building, where it turned another water wheel. A long series of buildings were powered by the same race. In the 1830s, waterpower was the most significant need for industrial enterprise, and the Cascade Mill Race spurred rapid development in the area north of Market Street.

At the foot of Mill Street, Crosby built a massive structure that would be long known as the Stone Mill, a fixture of Akron throughout the nineteenth century. In 1833 a correspondent reporting about Akron for a Vermont newspaper noted how the "great dearth" of waterpower in "every part" of Ohio made Akron's "vast" waterpower "almost invaluable," and he described Crosby's "large stone Flouring Mill" as "built in a style not exceeded by any other in America." This same reporter also listed four furnaces, a gristmill, a distillery, a machine shop, three taverns, four stores, plenty of warehouses, three lawyers, two doctors, "mechanics of every description," and a total population of four or five hundred people.[18]

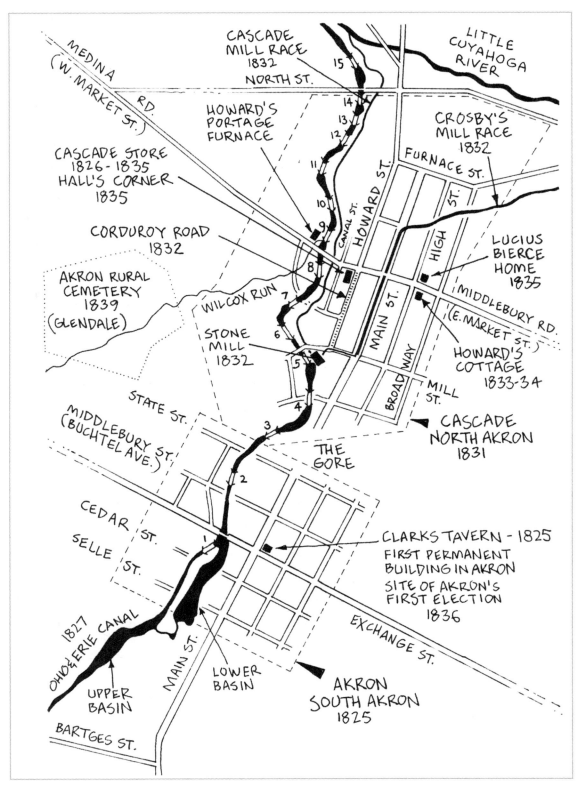
Maps of early Akron, featuring locations mentioned in this chapter. \ Maps by Chuck Ayers, 2024

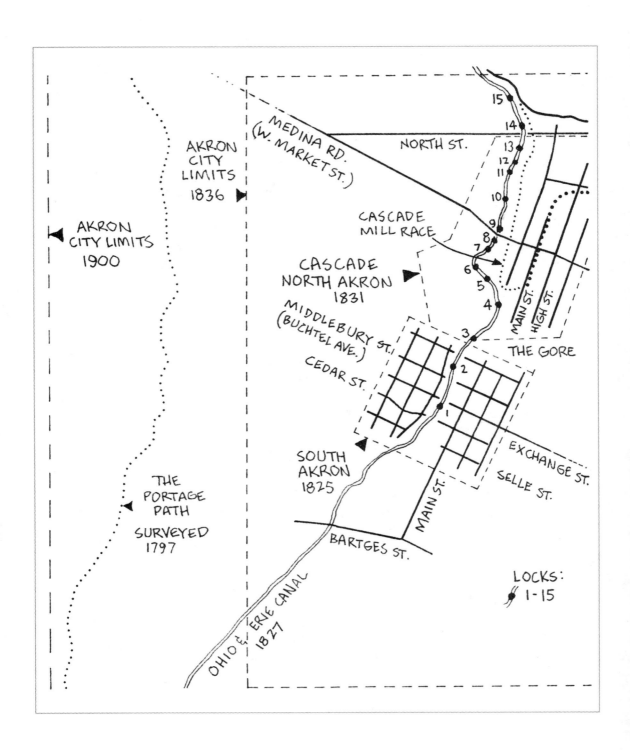

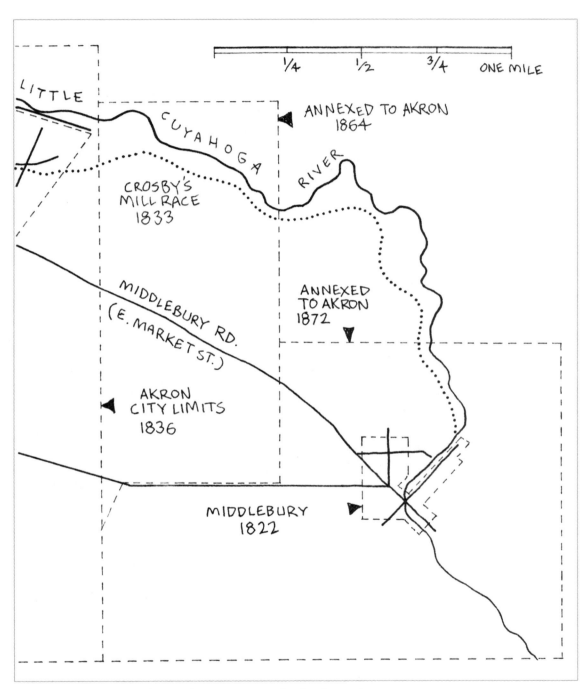

Maps of early Akron, featuring locations mentioned in this chapter. \ Maps by Chuck Ayers, 2024

Cascade, North Akron, and South Akron

By 1832, when the Stone Mill began operation and the canal was completed to the south, some of the sickness had abated, and property values began to pick up in the northern area of what is now downtown Akron. The decision of a court case involving the older Howard brothers over town lots in Akron describes the fluctuation and 1830s boom in property values. The elder Howard brothers agreed to buy town lots in 1828, shortly before dying from disease. Presumably they raised or borrowed this money through the success of their Middlebury business. They agreed to purchase the lots for five thousand dollars; a year later they were estimated to be worth not more than three thousand dollars. By 1840 these lots were estimated to be worth somewhere between thirty and forty thousand dollars.[19]

At the start of the boom in the early 1830s, Akron had two distinct halves. There was the original Akron as drawn up in 1825, in the area now around the Akron Children's Hospital and Exchange Street at Main. The first Akron post office was not far from the corner of Main and Exchange. This area came to be called "South Akron" because there was soon another booming commercial center to the north, in the millrace-powered industrial valley. This northern area developed two names, first "Cascade" and then "North Akron." The earliest store and hotel, built and opened before the completion of the millrace in anticipation of the development in the area, were called the Cascade Store and the Cascade House. When the area was officially platted, however, it was called "North Akron." The area went by both of these names for several years.[20]

South Akron and North Akron were separated by rough land called "the Gore." Today this is a colorful word, suggesting blood and violence. In the 1830s, a *gore* was a triangular piece of cloth sewn into the seam of a garment to make it bigger or better fitting. And so in the early 1830s the "Gore" was an undeveloped, heavily wooded, triangle-shaped area expanding from a point on the canal up the steep hill to the east. Today this is the downtown area north of University Avenue, including Lock 3 Park, the Civic Theater, the Peanut Shoppe, and the Akron Municipal Court. After residents petitioned for the change, North and South Akron were united by the State Legislature on March 12, 1836.[21] The area in the Gore became a kind of neutral ground, perfect for churches and government buildings serving both sides of town. The existence of such convenient and available property played a role in Akron's argument to become the seat of Summit County, which was created in 1840 out of pieces of what are now neighboring counties.

Crosby owned many valuable lots in North Akron, and he sold one that was just up the hill from the intersection of the canal and Market Street to his son-in-law for a low price. Seth Iredell, a Quaker living in the area, built a store for Howard on this lot. The Cascade Store was the first store—and when constructed, one of only three buildings—in North Akron.[22] With his partner Jonathan Fenn, Howard stocked the store, and when it opened in 1832, Iredell worked the counter, waiting on customers.[23]

Wilcox Run and Portage Furnace

A stream ran down from the hills west of Akron through what is now Glendale Cemetery. Known as the Wilcox Run, it appears on many early maps. Later it was called Willow Brook. The stream was quite pretty and added scenic charm to the cemetery. Population growth in the area led to deforestation and the digging of new wells, and the water level in the stream dropped. Willow Brook became more of a muddy bed. Eventually what remained of this waterway was moved underground into the sewer system.

In the 1830s Wilcox Run flowed out of Glendale, south of what is now Glendale Avenue, and down toward the canal. Howard and Fenn contrived to capture the flow of Wilcox Run in a race that they ran under Market Street and into their furnace, the Portage Furnace, which stood on what is now the site of the Diamond Grille.

Iron ore was hauled to this furnace from Zoar in Tuscarawas County on a canal boat named the *Dragon*. At Howard's blast furnace this iron ore was reduced into pig iron.[24] In the 1830s Akron had multiple foundries which cast pig iron into useful things such as ploughs, the gearing for mills, and wood-burning stoves.

Howard Street

By 1833 things were going well for C. W. Howard. He managed a store on the best corner in town for retail, and he owned a blast furnace producing large quantities of pig iron from the significant and newly discovered iron ore deposits south of the city, within easy reach of the canal. The land between his store and his father-in-law's mill at the foot of Mill Street was then a hollow, deeply gullied and difficult to walk through. C. W. Howard hired men to fill it in with logs and dirt to create a rough "corduroy" road from the Cascade Store to the Stone Mill. Not surprisingly, this road came to be known as Howard Street.[25] The original Howard Street—later called South Howard Street—lies today under Cascade Plaza.

As the fill dirt settled, the logs came to the surface and the street grew rougher. A letter to the editor of Samuel Lane's newspaper *The Buzzard* complained in

1837. The newly formed town council had collected a tax to improve the roads, but so far nothing had been done. "Market Street is in a miserable condition," the author wrote, "uneven, and badly gullied." Howard Street was "literally filled with lumber, timber, wood piles, &c." Market and Howard Streets were not paved until the 1860s, as numerous editorials in *The Summit Beacon* attest. "No other city in Ohio, of its size and business importance," they wrote, has "such shabby and slovenly streets." In this era of horse-drawn wagons, sewage cesspools, and no municipal trash collection, the streets came to be an "unfathomable depth" of the "filthiest kind of mud," comprised of "a thousand-and-one unwholesome substances, both animal and vegetable."[26] In November 1866, Howard Street was first paved with Nicholson pavement, a tiling of thick, square wood blocks. The editor of the *Beacon* described it as "the beginning of the 'good time coming' for our young and vigorous city."[27]

Hall's Corner

Akron had the best waterpower in the young State of Ohio, and the booming canal brought a great many people to town to witness its growth and potential. There was a good deal of speculation in town lots.

A sign of things to come, the Cascade Store failed in 1835. The economic environment was tumultuous for Akron and all American towns in the 1830s. There was a great deal of volatility in markets. The Akron area was flooded with counterfeit money, often brought into town from the Boston, Ohio, area, where it was made in difficult-to-access forested hideaways. (This Boston is now part of the Cuyahoga Valley National Park.)[28] Lending laws were loose, and financial literacy was limited. There was a great deal of usury, and there were few protections for the bankrupt.

In 1834, Howard's blast furnace failed. "Everybody went into iron making," he told the *Beacon Journal* in 1874. "And we all failed." Pig iron fell to $19 a ton from $30 a ton, and a glut of stoves brought their value from $60 a ton down to "nothing."

After the failure of his furnace, perhaps because he was overleveraged with debt, Howard sold the Cascade Store in 1835 to Philander D. Hall, who changed the name to Hall's Store and ran it until his death in 1892.[29] One of the most valuable commercial properties in Akron thus slipped from Howard's fingers. Throughout the nineteenth and well into the twentieth century, the corner of Howard and Market was known as "Hall's Corner."[30] The original wood-frame building burnt down in 1851 and was replaced by a three-story stone building or "stone block," as they called this style of commercial real estate. When the stone block was razed in the 1890s, it was considered perhaps the oldest landmark in the city.[31] Hall's Corner stood in the area that is now under the John F. Seiberling Federal Building and United States Courthouse.

Election of 1836

Akron held its first election in June 1836, as required by the charter uniting South Akron and North Akron in March 1836. Voting was restricted to white men who had lived in the town for at least six months. The election was held in a tavern on the northeast corner of Main and Market streets.

In what suggests some difference of opinion between Howard and his father-in-law, Howard ran as a Democrat, and Crosby ran as a Whig. These were the two main political parties of the 1830s. Crosby ran against Seth Iredell for mayor and lost. Looking back almost sixty years, Samuel Lane remembered Mayor Iredell as a "venerable Pennsylvania Quaker" who had been "thoroughly identified with the growth and prosperity" of South Akron, despite his more recent association with the Cascade Store. Howard ran for City Recorder and lost. In his well-known 1892 history of Akron and Summit County, Lane interpreted the result not as an expression of animosity toward the Howard family in particular, but rather as the result of sectional conflict between the original South Akron and the newer North Akron: according to him, Crosby was then regarded as "the very father" of North Akron.[32]

Drinking in Akron

Early city council meetings had another problem to address—the town was full of drunk people. The sober citizens wanted the town council to do something about it.

Akron was full of places to get a drink. Canal boats stalled at the locks for hours during the process of getting the boats over the hill from one side of town to the other. Canal travellers would head into town, looking for a place to rest and wait. Farmers and merchants who came to town to make deals might spend the night, with extra cash on hand.

In the 1830s water was not universally regarded as a beverage fit for people. Water was for horses and livestock. Farmers might enjoy drinking water from clear springs or unpolluted wells. But water in town could be downright nasty, if not full of sediment and other matter. Sources of drinking water in Akron would have been the river, the canal, cisterns filled by downspouts, and wells. Wooden cisterns might fill with mosquitos, another vector of disease, and then rot.

Wells were often polluted with sewage, which collected in cesspools—literal puddles—below outhouses. Americans did not begin to build infrastructure to deliver clean, drinkable water into town until the late 1840s. Akron's first "water works" delivered "an abundant supply of pure, cold, soft water" to the citizens on the west side of town in 1849.[33]

For a town of its size, Akron had a lot of public spaces selling alcoholic beverages by the glass. Hotels and taverns had dedicated barrooms. There were also a number of groceries—stores that sold provisions—that sold drinks by the glass.

In addition, private homes might host guests and serve alcohol one or two nights a week. Some private homes were at least rumored to be houses of gambling and/or prostitution, hosting private parties for men and boys. Professional gamblers, traders in counterfeit money, and idle men of means might congregate and drink there, as the numerous complaints about their behavior in Samuel Lane's late 1830s newspaper, *The Buzzard*, suggest.

People also drank in shops or offices, at places of work and business, where deals might be sealed with a glass of whiskey. And in the 1830s some laborers were still paid in part with daily rations of liquor, although more employers were trying to maintain a sober workplace. The town's factories ran dangerous or delicate equipment, and their owners did not want drunken men working on the premises, maiming themselves and damaging the machinery. The practice of drinking at work was abating, but it was still common.

Property owners, employers, and parents, however, worried about the influence of alcohol and drunkenness on the future of Akron and its people. They did not like to see Akron getting a bad reputation. And in the 1830s it very much was acquiring a bad reputation.

Sober citizens complained about the drunkenness and the "drunkards," as alcoholics were then called, in the Akron newspapers. In the *Buzzard* for November 4, 1837, a correspondent described a grocery by the canal frequented by men such as the "poor old hardened wretch ... so beastly drunk he could neither stand, sit, nor lie." This man was so drunk, all he could do was "tumble round upon the floor, more beastly than that the filthy swine" that could be found outside, wallowing in Akron's muddy streets.[34]

On June 24, 1836, the Akron Town Council passed an ordinance designed to curb drinking in the grocery stores. It said that if "any licensed grocer" permits, allows, or suffers any kind of intoxication on his premises, he could be fined anywhere between ten and one hundred dollars. As "Wilberforce" noted in *The Buzzard*, this ordinance was never enforced in 1836 or 1837.[35] In December 1837, the town council responded to growing public outrage about the failure to enforce this law. They explained that the June 1836 law empowered them to fine only *licensed* houses. And since they had not issued any licenses, they could not fine anyone.[36]

Like many towns in the 1830s, Akron had an extreme case of public drunkenness and related harms caused by problem drinking. The period from roughly 1810 to 1840 saw alcohol consumption and abuse rise to extremely high levels. Never before and never since have Americans consumed so much alcohol on a per capita basis. America was a hard-drinking nation in the 1830s, and Akron was a hard-drinking town.[37]

The Panic of 1837

A series of financial events, exacerbated by the Jackson administration's war with the Second Bank of the United States, contracted the unstable American economy in 1836. The value of crops failed, and a series of alarming financial events led to a panic, a run on the banks that triggered a severe depression lasting well into the 1840s.

Akron was affected severely. In the fall of 1837, an editorial in an Akron newspaper, *The American Balance*, noted the violent fluctuations in the prices of produce as a cause for capitalists and businessmen to cease trade. As a result, the paper noted, the "prevailing opinion is that in our large cities provisions will be very scarce and high during the coming winter" and consequently there will be "a great amount of suffering among the poor.... We look forward to a winter of horror such as has not been experienced since the early settlement of this country in a time of peace."[38] According to one account, only three of the fourteen stores in North Akron survived the downturn of 1837.[39]

C. W. Howard Imprisoned for Debt

In Akron the Howards lived in a pretty cottage on the southeast corner of Market and High streets, where the Akron Art Museum now stands, across Market Street from neighbor Lucius V. Bierce.[40] This was then the edge of town. The dirt road east to Middlebury passed through heavy forest.[41]

Howard had his house built in 1833 or 1834, and Bierce's house was built in 1835. For some time these two houses were regarded as the finest homes in Akron.[42] Just as Howard lost his prime retail location, so did he lose his fancy cottage. The house was known for decades as "The Bartges House" after its second owner, Dr. Samuel F. Bartges, and his wife, Catharine Ann Crump Bartges. Samuel Bartges was a physician who moved to Akron in 1842. Together the couple amassed a large portfolio of Akron-area real estate, including a good deal of valuable land that was platted and added to the southern part of the city, where Bartges Street now runs and where the Diamond Rubber and B. F. Goodrich factories were built east of the canal.[43]

Howard lost everything in the financial chaos of 1837. His father-in-law was unable or perhaps unwilling to bail him out. In 1830s Ohio a creditor could have his debtor imprisoned by paying a dollar or two a week to the jailor to cover the debtor's board. In the summer of 1837, Howard was imprisoned for debt by the lawyers of two corporate creditors.

One of these creditors was Tappan, Edwards, and Company, the Wall Street mercantile house of Arthur Tappan. During the May 1837 panic, news of his failure was one of the most reprinted stories of the financial collapse.[44] Arthur Tappan was a very wealthy philanthropist and abolitionist with a national reputation. Accounts of his financial embarrassment were often reprinted with highly emotional editorial content, reflecting the strong and contrasting opinions of his politics and abolitionist work.[45]

It's not clear why the son-in-law of Dr. Eliakim Crosby was left to languish in prison for so long. The Akron community responded to Howard's imprisonment with sympathy and anger. Imprisoned people were not able to labor and earn the money needed to support their families and repay their debts. Imprisonment for debt was widely regarded as an unfair and cruel practice, and the difficulties of 1837 further aroused public opinion against it. Joseph Vance, the Whig governor of Ohio from 1836 to 1838, described it as attracting "the attention of the benevolent and humane portion of society throughout every government advanced in the scale of civilization." He decried imprisonment for debt as "a relic of barbarism" and called for its immediate end. A bill abolishing the practice became law in March 1838.[46]

Samuel Lane's lively Akron paper, *The Buzzard*, often printed editorials against the treachery of usurious lenders in town and their cold-hearted readiness to imprison or, more often, appropriate all the property of the bankrupt.[47] At the end of January 1838, a letter to *The Buzzard* reported that C. W. Howard had been in prison "near a year." His property was all gone, and his wife and an infant son, "left dependent on charity," had "gone to Canada as a place more free from cold, unfeeling oppression than America." This editorial signed by "Rousseau" outed Arthur Tappan as the "unfeeling, unchristian creditor" who "severed the relation of husband and wife, parent and child, and sent misery, and woe, upon an amiable, and unoffending family."[48] In early March, Lane published another letter attacking "Rousseau" for dishonestly reporting on the extent of Arthur Tappan's involvement.[49]

C. W. Howard and the Temperance Movement in Early Akron   **29**

In March Howard wrote a letter to *The Buzzard* from Ravenna, where he had found some work near the county jail, doing writing for the clerk and sheriff. He expressed no ill will towards his creditors, but he did express his belief that they should pay him for the time he spent in jail. He urged the citizens of Akron to support the bill abolishing imprisonment for debt; Lane noted in his reply that this bill had passed. "Hereafter when running debt," Lane remarked, "I shall not have the 'horrors of a dungeon' staring me in the face."[50] In his 1892 history, Lane recalls that "it was said" that Rousseau's article was brought to the attention of Arthur Tappan, who then ordered Howard's immediate release. People in Akron may have wanted to believe this, but as Lane suggests, it's more likely that Howard was released because the legislature was in the process of abolishing the practice.[51]

Intemperance and Divorce

After release from debtor's prison, Howard "became intemperate." He took heavily to drink and became a "drunkard."[52] Habitual drunkenness was sufficient grounds for divorce in Ohio.[53] Calista divorced him.[54]

"No-fault" divorce was not established in Ohio until 1974, but in the 1830s and 1840s the state had a reputation for granting divorces easily. Courts were not interested in undertaking a thorough investigation, and they often made decisions after hearing only from witnesses friendly to one side of the case. "Perhaps there is no statute in Ohio more abused, than the statute concerning divorce and alimony," wrote one legal observer.[55] "Divorces are now the order of the day," wrote a Columbus correspondent to the *Summit County Beacon* who described himself as "heart sick" to see so many divorces granted "on the most trivial reasons."[56]

In 1852 Calista married Judge Leicester King, a devoted abolitionist who had been the Liberty party candidate for Ohio Governor in 1842 and 1844. Calista was thirty-nine and King was sixty-three. In the 1830s, King and General Simon Perkins owned "pretty much all the land" in North Akron.[57] A friend of the family, King had partnered with Simon Perkins and her father Dr. Crosby in the design of North Akron and the construction of the Cascade Mill Race.

Broadside advertising a Liberty Party convention in Akron in June 1844. A number of letters are upside down; this may have been a proof that survived because it never left the printing office. Calista Crosby's second husband, Leicester King, is featured as the Liberty Party candidate for Governor of Ohio. A third party, the Liberty Party, stood for the abolition of slavery during a time of intense loyalties to the larger parties, the Whigs and the Democrats. In the October 1844 gubernatorial election, King received just under 3 percent of the vote. \ Archives and Special Collections, University Libraries, The University of Akron.

Temperance

Throughout the nineteenth century, Americans expressed concern about the harm caused by the sale and consumption of alcoholic beverages. In the previous century, calls for a reduction in the consumption of alcoholic beverages had been issued mainly by religious organizations, especially from groups of Friends (Quakers) and from Protestant churches. They were joined by members of the medical community, led by Philadelphia's Dr. Benjamin Rush, a signer of the Declaration of Independence and the young country's leading medical authority. By the 1820s, as W. J. Rorabaugh shows in his book *The Alcoholic Republic*, there were very high levels of alcoholism, drinking problems, and real harm associated with such widespread and conspicuous drunkenness. Americans—especially white male Americans—consumed a staggering amount of alcoholic beverages.

As the nation's drinking problem intensified in the 1830s, a wide range of local, regional, and national organizations emerged to fight drunkenness. They did this by championing "temperance," the word they used to describe a durable, gritty sobriety. In the 1820s and early 1830s, temperance groups focused on dissuading respectable people, mainly young people of prosperous families, from consuming alcohol. They worked hard to associate upward social mobility and high social status with sobriety.

The 1830s also saw a rapid proliferation of printed reading material, as related technologies advanced with the ongoing industrial revolution. Newspapers started up all over. The cost of producing and shipping books fell. The appearance of cheap books fueled the public school movement, and there was widespread interest in reading and the development of literary traditions. American literature scholars have long regarded the antebellum decades as an "American Renaissance" for the literary arts.

Among the new, popular genres of reading material that were developed in the 1830s was the "temperance tale." These were short stories illustrating the advantages of sobriety to young men who wanted to get ahead. The main examples from this period were short stories by Massachusetts author Lucius Manlius Sargent. These were printed in pamphlet form and widely distributed. Sargent's tales were often copied into newspapers, which frequently published poetry and short stories in the 1830s, especially in periods between elections, when there were not so many political speeches to publish or partisan essays to print and reprint.

Toward the end of the 1830s temperance literature began to also focus on reforming the drunkard, which was then a new idea. In the November 9, 1837, number of Akron's Whig newspaper, *The American Balance*, Sargent's tale "Too Fast and Too Far; or, The Cooper and the Currier" ran on the front page. This story is prefaced with an editorial describing it as "truly American," describing a pair of young married brothers, a cask maker (a cooper), and a leather finisher (a currier). These brothers often get drunk and fight, for years, bringing harm and suffering to themselves, to their wives, and to their children. They are young, miserable drunkards.

At rock bottom, in a rare sober state of mind, one brother visits "a shrewd, honest, old Quaker" in the village, asking for advice about how to handle his debts. The Quaker replies that he needs time to think about it, but if the young man will not drink alcohol for one more day, he can come back and hear his advice. The young man does this. He returns, and the old Quaker says the situation is very difficult, and he needs a little more time. If the young man will not drink alcohol for a few more days, he can come back and hear his advice. He returns, and again the old Quaker asks for a little more time, saying he'll give good advice if he can stay sober a bit longer and come back in a few days. "One day at a time" thus becomes a week of sobriety. And soon the young man has been sober long enough to see positive changes in his health and in his family relationships. At this point the old Quaker persuades him to sign a temperance pledge, promising never to drink again, and afterwards, in sober enthusiasm, the young man visits his brother, their estrangement is ended, and the two young couples join a temperance society.

Early Akron had a Quaker community and Quaker leadership—the first mayor, Seth Iredell, was a Quaker—and this kind of story evidently resonated in the community. The appeal of these sobriety tales increased as people suffered through the long, cruel recession that began with the Panic of 1837.

Commanders of the Raging Canawl

The canal brought different types of people to Akron, and these people varied in social status and prosperity. Among the most admired and respected of these people was the canal boat captain. Canal boat captains styled themselves after the captains of boats on Lake Erie. To become the commander of a canal boat was to reach "a station of very great importance, indeed," Samuel Lane mused forty years later. "Very vividly" he remembered getting advice, after sharing his plan to move to Akron in 1835, to get a job in a downtown warehouse. This was recommended as the best way to start an Akron career that might carry him into the command of a canal boat.

Canal boat Captain Dan Hickox was "imperial in his imperious impudence" when at "the height of his maritime glory," surrounded by a "full galaxy of equally gallant and skillful navigators." Such men made things "lively," generally

C. W. Howard and the Temperance Movement in Early Akron

and particularly, on the busy canal.[58] Captain Roger H. Folger could be seen "daily promenading the hurricane deck of his noble craft, and, with stentorian yet melodious voice, transmitting orders to his subalterns—the helmsman, the bowser, the driver and the cook." Some captains went on to distinguished legal and political careers. Captain Folger went on to be the mayor of Massillon and a member of the Stark County Bar. Captain Noah M. Green, another "Commodore" of the "raging canawl" in the 1830s, was four times elected Justice of the Peace for Portage Township in the 1840s and 1850s.[59]

In Cleveland, another port town full of conspicuous public drunkenness, a lawyer, reformer, and politician named John A. Foote founded the Cleveland Temperance Society in 1839. Foote was also an officer in the antislavery societies of Cleveland and Cuyahoga County.[60] In 1880, he recalled Captain Reuben Turner, a boat captain that he met in the course of his legal practice. A weatherbeaten, dissipate man, Turner gave up drinking in the late 1830s for the sake of his good, loyal wife, who "loved him out of the ditch."[61]

The "reformed drunkard" was a novelty in the late 1830s. Temperance tales described hardened drinkers converting to sobriety, but in real life people did not see this happen very often. Impressed by Turner's sobriety, Foote invited him to tell the story of his reform at a temperance society meeting. Turner accepted the invitation and "astonished" everyone with his performance. In a series of speaking engagements, he "electrified the community" with the story of his recovery and "induced thousands to follow his example." A hardened and charismatic boat captain, Turner was just the type of man capable of appealing to a much broader audience than the usual temperance lecturer.

A wealthy gentleman from Rochester named Aristarchus Champion saw one of his appearances. He was so pleased by the performance and its effect on the audience, he offered Turner five hundred dollars to tour as a temperance lecturer for three months. Turner accepted.

Turner's first stop was Detroit, where he appeared with another plain-speaking man and recovered alcoholic, John H. Guptill. They presented themselves to the Michigan State Temperance Society's anniversary meeting on November 15, 1841, as "Delegates from the Cleveland Society of Reformed Drunkards." A reporter from the *Journal of the American Temperance Union* described the scene. A curious and "numerous audience" crowded every part of Detroit's largest church. The two men related their drinking experience and presented themselves as "men elevated to the position of moral instructors" from "the lowest degradation" through the "renovating power of temperance." Their powerful appeal to their "erring brethren" inspired twenty men to sign the pledge and form their own society for reformed drunkards.[62]

Turner and Guptill toured for two years, and their lectures inspired fifty thousand men to sign a pledge of total abstinence.[63]

The Washingtonian Movement

The recovery lecture tour of Captain Turner and John Guptill was part of a national movement characterized by large numbers of new people joining temperance societies. These people tended to be hard drinkers, laborers, mechanics, and their friends and family; they were not like the doctors, preachers, politicians, and capitalists who mainly supported earlier temperance societies. This moment in the progress of temperance organization came to be known as the Washingtonian Temperance Movement, as many of their societies were called Washington or Washingtonian Temperance Societies.

The origins of the Washingtonian movement are often traced to a group of hard-drinking Baltimore men who joined together and pledged mutual support and recovery in 1840. The difficult times of the ongoing recession, catalyzed by the proliferation of popular fiction describing the recovery of men who were addicted to alcohol, sparked explosive growth of Washingtonian temperance meetings and societies all over the country.[64]

Many features of Washingtonian temperance anticipate the development and success of Alcoholics Anonymous, which was founded in Akron almost one hundred years later in the Highland Square home of Dr. Robert "Bob" Smith. Unlike most of the previous temperance societies, Washingtonian meetings were not sponsored by a particular religious denomination or an august professional association. Washingtonian meetings were characterized by "experience" lectures, in which reformed drunkards described the depths of their alcoholism and their struggle to sobriety. Their leaders were not prosperous men who had enjoyed a lifetime of sobriety; they were reformed drunkards. Their focus was not on keeping young men sober, but on keeping the alcoholic sober. They promoted the idea of "every man brings a man," encouraging members to recruit and sponsor new members.

After Detroit, Captain Turner and John Guptill toured Northeast Ohio. They visited Medina, Akron, Cuyahoga Falls, Ravenna, Warren, Jefferson, Painesville, and Chardon before Christmas. A newspaper notice announcing the details of their tour called on "hard drinkers to come forward and look upon those who are reformed out of their ranks, and to learn how easy and how happy it would be for them to become sober men and useful citizens."[65]

At the end of November they came to Akron and stayed two nights. "Each night the house was crowded to overflowing with eager listeners," the *Summit*

County Beacon reported. One hundred and thirty Akron men signed a pledge of total abstinence, "including many who have been considered hopeless drunkards, as well as scores of moderate drinkers." On the morning of the third day, a number of Akron men organized a Washington Total Abstinence Society. Captain Turner remained in Akron long enough to swear in the officers, "two old grey-headed men and one young man in the prime of life." The scene "affected many to tears."[66]

The young man in the prime of life was C. W. Howard. Now the Secretary of Akron's Washingtonian Temperance Society, Howard gave notice in the *Summit County Beacon* of their intention to host a temperance celebration on Washington's birthday in February 1842, with the "old tar" Captain Turner returning to give an address.[67] On January 5, 1842, the *Beacon* noted that Akron's Washingtonian Society had between four and five hundred members, which is incredible considering that in 1840 the census counted only about sixteen hundred people living in Akron.

A procession of bands, military groups, dignitaries, clergymen, and Washingtonians wound its way through town on February 22, 1842, meeting up with "the Ladies" at the Stone Church for orations by Captain Turner and George Bliss, a prominent Akron lawyer, future mayor of Akron, and member of the United States House of Representatives from Ohio. The *Summit County Beacon* described the event as "a glorious day for Summit County," as the town "was filled to overflowing" with people who came to participate. They estimated the crowd at two thousand people and noted that not more than one-third could get close enough to the speakers to hear their orations. As part of the evening program, Howard gave an address.[68] In March at a temperance meeting in Medina, he also addressed "a large and respectable audience" who "listened with great interest to facts as they fell from the lips of a reformed drunkard."[69]

At this time Howard was attempting to make a living teaching penmanship and bookkeeping.[70] The Washingtonian Temperance Movement abated about as quickly as it formed, with many members moving into fraternal organizations with strong aspirations to respectability, such as the Sons of Temperance, which were often led not by reformed drunkards but by respectable citizens who had lived a long life of temperance. Like so many of the early citizens of Akron, Howard moved on. In the 1850s he was known to be living in Wilkes-Barre, Pennsylvania as an "upright, sober business man."[71]

Notes

1. Wolfgang Behringer, *Tambora and the Year Without a Summer: How a Volcano Plunged the World into Crisis*, trans. Pamela Selwyn (Medford: Polity, 2019). A full discussion of early migration and immigration patterns to Ohio can be found in Kevin F. Kern and Gregory S. Wilson, *Ohio: A History of the Buckeye State*, second ed. (Wiley-Blackwell, 2023), ch. 6.

2. Untitled weather report, *Hartford Connecticut Courant*, June 11, 1816, 3. Unless otherwise noted, newspapers are cited from digital versions through Newspapers.com.

3. See Olson, chapter 1.

4. Karl H. Grismer, *Akron and Summit County* (Summit County Historical Society, 1952), 70–71.

5. John Kilbourn, *The Ohio Gazetteer, or Topographical Dictionary*, tenth ed. (John Kilbourn, 1831), 49, Google Books.

6. "Akron's Pioneers," *Akron Summit County Beacon*, July 23, 1879, 4. To read more about the canal diggers, see John Tully, *Labor in Akron, 1825–1945* (University of Akron Press, 2020), 10–18; and Jack Gieck, *A Photo Album of Ohio's Canal Era, 1825–1913*, revised ed. (Kent State University Press, 1998), xvi.

7. "Howard et al. vs. Babcock et al.," *Condensed Reports of Decisions in the Supreme Court of Ohio*, ed. P. B. Wilcox (Isaac N. Whiting, 1840), 431, Google Books.

8. Kathie Wiegel, "Charles Wesley Howard (1809–1898)." *Find A Grave*, https://www.findagrave .com/memorial/141669069/charles-wesley-howard.

9. For more on Crosby's entrepreneurial and engineering achievements, see Jack Gieck, *Early Akron's Industrial Valley: A History of the Cascade Locks* (Kent State University Press, 2008). See also Lynn Metzger and Peg Bobel, eds., *Canal Fever: The Ohio & Erie Canal, from Waterway to Canalway* (Kent State University Press, 2009).

10. Kathie Wiegel, "Marcia Beemer Crosby (1793–1830)." *Find A Grave*, https://www.findagrave .com/memorial/116980391/marcia-crosby

11. *Akron Summit County Beacon*, "Akron's Pioneers," 4.

12. United States Census Bureau, "Census Bureau Releases New 2020 Census Data on Age, Sex, Race, Hispanic Origin, Households and Housing," May 25, 2023, https://www.census.gov/newsroom/press -releases/2023/2020-census-demographic-profile-and-dhc.html; United States Census Bureau, "Exploring Age Groups on the 2020 Census," May 25, 2023, https://www.census.gov/library/visualizations/ interactive/exploring-age-groups-in-the-2020-census.html.

13. "Table 7: Median Age of the Population: 1820 to 2000," Census 2000 PHC-T-9: Population by Age, Sex, Race, and Hispanic or Latino Origin for the United States: 2000, https://www2.census.gov/ programs-surveys/decennial/2000/phc/phc-t-09/tab07.pdf.

14. *Compendium of the Enumeration of the Inhabitants and Statistics of the United States* (Thomas Allen, 1841), 76–77, Census.gov.

15. Robert M. Malina, "Secular Changes in Size and Maturity: Causes and Effects," *Monographs of the Society for Research in Child Development* 44, No. 3–4 (1979): 59–102, JSTOR; Courtney E. Thompson, "Child-Mothers and Invisible Fathers: The Paradox of 'Precocious Maternity' and the Pervasiveness of Child Sexual Abuse in Nineteenth-Century America," *Journal of Women's History* 34, no. 4 (Winter 2022): 125–46, OhioLINK Electronic Journal Center; Gladys M. Martinez, "Trends and Patterns in Menarche in the United States: 1995 through 2013–2017," *National Health Statistics Reports* 146 (September 10, 2020), http://cdc.gov.

16. Examination of the archives of the *Akron Beacon Journal* shows that the citizens of Akron mainly called themselves "Akronians" in the nineteenth century, with the alternative "Akronites" gradually gaining in popularity and becoming the norm in the early twentieth century.

17. Gieck, *Early Akron's Industrial Valley*; also informative is "The Old Supplanted: The Plodding Mule of the Towpath Steps Aside," *Akron Beacon Journal*, August 25, 1900, 3.

18. M., "Hasty Sketches: Number 11," *Burlington (VT) Sentinel*, May 17, 1833, 1.

19. "Howard et al. vs. Babcock et al.," 431.

20. "Cascade Mills Were Landmark of Early Akron," *Akron Beacon Journal*, July 21, 1925, 3.

21. Grismer, *Akron and Summit County*, 92–99.

22. The others, according to the memory of eighty-five-year-old Mary Chambers, were Cobb's Tavern on Market Street by the canal and the Stone Mill (later part of the American Cereal Mill). "After Many Years Mrs. Chambers Returns to Scene of Early Life," *Akron Beacon Journal*, October 21, 1903, 9.

23. Lucius V. Bierce, *Historical Reminiscences of Summit County* (T. & H. G. Canfield, 1854), 27, Google Books; Samuel A. Lane, *Fifty Years and Over of Summit County* (Beacon Job Department, 1892), xl, 43; "Akron–Its Past," *Akron Summit County Beacon*, May 6, 1857, 3; *Akron Summit County Beacon*, "Akron's Pioneers."

24. *Akron Summit County Beacon*, "Akron's Pioneers"; *Akron Beacon Journal*, "After Many Years."

25. *Akron Summit County Beacon*, "Akron's Pioneers."

26. "Paving the Streets," *Akron Summit County Beacon*, January 25, 1866, 3.

27. "The New Pavement." *Akron Summit County Beacon*, November 15, 1866, 3.

28. Stephen Mihm, *A Nation of Counterfeiters: Capitalists, Con Men, and the Making of the United States* (Harvard University Press, 2007), ch. 4.

29. *Akron Summit County Beacon*, "Akron's Pioneers."

30. Herman Fetzer, "An Outline of Akron's History, Chapter 10: The Second Akron," *Akron Beacon Journal*, July 21, 1925, 6.

31. "An Old Landmark," *Akron Beacon and Republican*, January 28, 1892, 1.

32. Lane, *Fifty Years*, 49–50.

33. "The Cold Spring Company," *Akron Summit County Beacon*, June 20, 1849, 3.

34. Pollock, letter to the editor, *Akron Buzzard*, November 4, 1837, 1. Samuel Lane complains about the hogs running at large in town in *Akron Buzzard*, August 11, 1838, 2. I appreciate the Western Reserve Historical Society and the Archives and Special Collections at The University of Akron for making the *Buzzard* available to researchers.

35. Wilberforce, letter to the editor, *Akron Buzzard*, November 18, 1837, 1.

36. Untitled editorial, *Akron Buzzard*, December 16, 1837, 3.

37. The classic monograph on this epidemic of problem drinking is W. J. Rorabaugh, *The Alcoholic Republic* (Oxford University Press, 1979). See also Mark Edward Lender and James Kirby Martin, *Drinking in America: A History*, rev. and expanded ed. (The Free Press, 1987), 46–53.

38. Untitled editorial, *American Balance*, October 26, 1837, 3.

39. Charles Whittlesey Foote, "Chapter VIII: City of Akron," *History of Summit County with an Outline Sketch of Ohio*, ed. William Henry Perrin (Baskin & Battey, 1881), 331, Google Books.

40. Lane, *Fifty Years*, xl; *Akron Summit County Beacon*, "Akron's Pioneers."

41. "A Boy's Perseverance," *Akron Summit County Beacon*, August 1, 1888, 1.

42. Samuel Lane, "The Bierce House," *Akron Summit County Beacon*, September 5, 1883, 8.

43. Oscar Eugene Olin, *Akron and Environs: Historical, Biographical, Genealogical* (Lewis Publishing, 1917), 67, Google Books.

44. Daniel Walker Howe, *What Hath God Wrought: The Transformation of America, 1815–1848* (Oxford University Press, 2007), 502.

45. For example, see "Money Market," *Charleston (SC) Courier*, May 9, 1837, 2; "Arthur Tappan & Co.," *Brandon Vermont Telegraph*, May 10, 1837, 3; "Arthur Tappan," *Maumee City (OH) Express*, May 13, 1837, 2.

46. "The Governor's Message," *Maumee City (OH) Express–Extra* (December 23, 1837), 1; "Imprisonment for Debt," *Piqua (OH) Courier and Enquirer* (March 24, 1838), 3.

47. For example, see "Lay on Macduff," *Akron Buzzard*, December 2, 1837, 1.

48. Rousseau [pseud.], letter to the editor, *Akron Buzzard*, January 27, 1838, 4.

49. Young Cromwell [pseud.], letter to the editor, *Akron Buzzard*, March 10, 1838, 1.

50. C. W. Howard, letter to the editor, *Akron Buzzard*, March 24, 1838, 1.

51. Lane, *Fifty Years*, 69.

52. *Akron Summit County Beacon*, "Akron–Its Past."

53. Henry Folsom Page, *A View of the Law Relative to the Subject of Divorce, in Ohio, Indiana, and Michigan* (J. H. Riley, 1850), 172, Google Books.

54. "Pioneer: Charles W. Howard Was Among Akron's First Citizens," *Akron Beacon Journal*, May 26, 1898, 8.

55. Page, *A View of the Law*, vi–vii.

56. "Columbus Correspondence of the Summit Beacon," *Akron Summit Beacon*, January 24, 1844, 2.

57. Foote, "Chapter VIII: City of Akron," 331.

58. Samuel Lane, "Forty Years Ago: A Glimpse of Our City as It Then Appeared," *Akron Summit County Beacon*, June 16, 1875, 1.

59. Charles Whittlesey Foote, "Chapter VII," *History of Summit County, with an Outline Sketch of Ohio*, edited by William Henry Perrin (Baskin and Battey, 1881), 329, Google Books.

60. "John A. Foote," *Encyclopedia of Cleveland History*, ed. John J. Grabowski, Case Western Reserve University, https://case.edu/ech/articles/f/foote-john.

61. "Hon. John A. Foote's Remarks," *Annals of the Early Settlers Association of Cuyahoga County, Number 1* (Mount and Carroll, 1880), 58–60, Google Books.

62. "Michigan," *Journal of the American Temperance Union*, vol. 6, no. 2 (January 1842): 14, Google Books.

63. "Hon. John A. Foote's Remarks."

64. Lender and Martin, *Drinking in America*, 74–70; Jack S. Blocker, *American Temperance Movements: Cycles of Reform* (Twayne, 1989), 40–47.

65. "Washingtonian Notice," *Ohio Atlas and Elyria Advertiser*, November 10, 1841, 2.

66. "Temperance," *Akron Summit Beacon*, December 1, 1841, 2.

67. "Washington's Birth Day," *Akron Summit Beacon*, December 29, 1841, 3.

68. "Washingtonian Temperance Celebration," *Akron Summit Beacon*, February 16, 1842, 2; "Celebration of the Twenty Second," *Akron Summit Beacon*, February 23, 1842, 2.

69. "The Temperance Ball Rolling," *Akron Summit Beacon*, March 9, 1842, 2.

70. "New School," *Akron Summit Beacon*, January 19, 1842, 3.

71. *Akron Summit County Beacon*, "Akron–Its Past."

\ **3**

Our Own John Brown

Donald R. Hicks

John Brown's role in the harrowing events occurring in the 1850s at Osawatomie, Kansas, and Harpers Ferry, Virginia, along with the loss of innocent lives, may forever make him a subject of controversial interpretation.

Much of his life was spent in Akron, Hudson, Franklin Mills (now Kent), Richfield, and Tallmadge. It was here, during his formative years, that he came to abhor slavery. Later, people in these communities supported John Brown in his abolitionist endeavors.

He was born on May 9, 1800, into an abolitionist family in Torrington, Connecticut. In 1805, his parents Owen and Ruth (Mills) Brown moved their growing family to Hudson. Two years earlier, Ohio became the seventeenth state.

The journey from Hartford, Connecticut to the Ohio Western Reserve took forty-eight days. Owen and Ruth brought five children: Ruth (age 7), John (age 5), Salmon (age 3), Oliver (age 1), and Levi Blakeslee (age 11), an adopted son.

Owen and Ruth descended from pre-Revolutionary families who strongly adhered to Calvinist traditions. Their religion was the foundation of their values and established them as passionate abolitionists long before significant organized antislavery movements developed.

John Brown's mother died during childbirth in 1808. Brown's account of his childhood emphasized how much he would "pine after" her in subsequent years. Owen, left with five children to care for, married Sally Root in 1809. Although

Sally treated John Brown well, she and her stepson never established a close emotional bond. The marriage of Owen and Sally produced eight children. Altogether, Owen Brown fathered sixteen children from both marriages, with John Brown being his eldest living son.

Other Connecticut families like the Browns had forged similar paths to Ohio's Western Reserve, a large portion of land granted in 1662 to the Colony of Connecticut by King Charles II. As passable roads were constructed across Pennsylvania in the late eighteenth century, settlers from Connecticut and other eastern states came to the Ohio region, bringing with them established principles of their Calvinist faith and Puritan ideals which included antipathy to slavery. John Brown's Connecticut ancestors had opposed slavery for many generations.

Ohio Black Laws

Ohio's 1802 Constitution abolished slavery in the state. Nevertheless, provisions imposed austere restrictions on Black citizens, and sets of "Black Laws" were established to discourage the migration of fugitive slaves into the state. Black people could not vote, hold political office, testify in court against whites, attend public schools, serve in the military, or perform jury duty. Other related laws required Black people to post a $500 bond before establishing residency in Ohio. A Black resident who failed to secure a bond was required to be expelled from the jurisdiction. Black people were also compelled to register a document called "a certificate of freedom" at the county clerk of court before becoming employed. Without these papers, a free Black person would be at risk of being kidnapped, taken South, and sold into slavery.

In practice, the enforcement of Ohio's Black Laws was sporadic and arbitrary, but effective at discouraging and intimidating Black Americans. As abolitionist activism heated up in northeast Ohio during the 1830s, regional antislavery groups put pressure on legislators to repeal these laws. Such efforts had limited success as these laws were not fully repealed until 1886, more than twenty years after the end of the Civil War.

Owen Brown was instrumental in the founding of Western Reserve College. He labored with David Hudson, who was also a dedicated abolitionist, to set up multiple stations in Ohio for the Underground Railroad. As a boy, John Brown observed these two men and other like-minded folks make Hudson into a hotbed of abolitionist activity. During the War of 1812, when John Brown was twelve, his father dispatched him to deliver a herd of cattle to Detroit for General William Hull's army. While in the Michigan territory, John Brown observed an enslaved boy his own age get a severe beating with a shovel by his master. The memory of this event remained with John Brown throughout his entire life.

Augustus Washington, American (1820–1875). Portrait of John Brown, ca. 1846–1847. Daguerreotype, quarter plate: 3 ¼ × 4 ¼ inches (8.3 × 10.8 cm). The Nelson-Atkins Museum of Art, Kansas City, Missouri. Gift of the Hall Family Foundation in honor of the 75th anniversary of The Nelson-Atkins Museum of Art, 2008.6.4. \ Image courtesy of Nelson-Atkins Digital Production & Preservation.

As early as 1832, Owen Brown established the Western Reserve Anti-Slavery Society in Hudson and later the Free Congregational Church. The family had long been active in Hudson's First Congregational Church, and it was at this church that John Brown swore his famous 1837 oath: "Here before God, in the presence of these witnesses, I consecrate my life to the destruction of slavery."

In 1853, Frederick Douglass visited Hudson, spoke before the chapel at Western Reserve College, and stayed at Owen Brown's home.

Tallmadge was established in 1807 by David Bacon, a Congregationalist minister who left his ministerial assignment to a church in Hudson to found Tallmadge. Around 1812, he left Tallmadge and returned to Connecticut.

The Elizur Wright Sr. family came to Tallmadge from Connecticut in 1810 and started a preparatory academy in his home. In 1816, his son Elizur and John Brown both attended this academy. The Wrights were devoted abolitionists who may have been active supporters, if not agents, of the Underground Railroad. Tallmadge, because of its unique location as an intersection of eight different roads, served as an especially important hub for travel and, probably, for the Underground Railroad.

An 1810 house built by Elizur Wright Sr., now in the Goodyear Heights area of Akron, was formerly in Tallmadge before modern boundaries were established. The house may have served as a sanctuary for fugitive slaves. It was in this home that young John Brown attended school with Elizur Wright Jr.

On June 24, 1857, John Brown was in Tallmadge for the fiftieth anniversary of its founding. He may have been seeking funds and weapons for his future plans at Harpers Ferry.

In his own way, John Brown followed in his father's footsteps as an abolitionist, as a man of deep faith, and as an entrepreneur. Both men sired large families, with John Brown fathering twenty. In the realm of commerce, John Brown also raised cattle, operated tanneries, and speculated in real estate. However, he failed miserably in his many different business pursuits throughout his life.

In 1819, with the assistance of his father, John Brown started up his own tannery in Hudson. He prospered from his efforts and on June 21, 1820, he married Dianthe Lusk, "a neat, industrious, and an economical girl of excellent character." In 1825, he left Hudson, went east, and relocated Dianthe and their three children, John Jr., Jason, and Owen Jr., to wilderness land in New Richmond, Crawford County, Pennsylvania.

While living there, he and Dianthe brought forth four more children. Their four-year-old son Frederick died in New Richmond in 1831. A year later, an unnamed son died three days after birth. Dianthe died hours later.

John Brown's move to New Richmond in 1825 occurred in the same year as the founding of Akron. Distraught about the death of Dianthe, and a widower

Our Own John Brown

with five motherless children, he employed a housekeeper whose sixteen-year-old sister, Mary Day, occasionally came to his home.

On June 14, 1833, John Brown wed Mary Day in New Richmond. She took on the role of being a mother to five stepchildren. Ten months later, Mary gave birth to a daughter, Sarah, who would be the first of thirteen children born of her marriage to John Brown. Only six of these thirteen, however, would survive to adulthood.

In 1835 Brown and his family returned to Hudson, where a wealthy business-man invited Brown to join him in a tannery business. Brown and his fourteen-year-old son, John Jr., got to work at building the tannery in Franklin Mills (now Kent), six miles away.

The Panic of 1837, a financial crisis that started a national economic depression brought business failure once again to John Brown. He had speculated with bor-rowed money on the construction of the tannery and land purchases along the Cuyahoga River.

In 1837, while living in Franklin Mills, he joined the Franklin Congregational Church. At a worship service in 1838, Brown noticed that Black congregants were seated in the rear of the church. He announced to the assembly that such seating arrangements evidenced discrimination. He then brought the Black worshippers forward to the Brown family pew, and he moved himself and his kin to the back of the church.

By 1840, John Brown and his family left Franklin Mills and returned to Hud-son. He purchased a farm and once more attempted to attain some level of suc-cess. The financial turmoil which had begun as the Panic of 1837 continued to touch all levels of society. John Brown fell into arrears on his mortgage, and the lender initiated foreclosure. When the sheriff sought to evict John Brown and his family from the Hudson farm, he doggedly resisted. He was arrested for being disorderly and taken to jail.

No longer able to avoid his creditors, and still reeling from the effects of pri-or economic disruptions and imprudent speculation, he moved to Richfield in 1842. John Brown was adjudged bankrupt in federal court that same year. Now stripped of his home and most of his personal property, he rented housing for himself and his family from an old Hudson friend, Heman Oviatt. Pursuing the type of work he knew best, John Brown collaborated with Oviatt to raise sheep and operate a tannery.

The year before John Brown would move to Akron and go into the sheep busi-ness with Colonel Perkins, four of his children died from dysentery in a span of sixteen days. Charles, age five, died on September 11, 1843; Peter, age two, died on September 14; Sarah, age nine, died on September 22; and Austin, age 1, died on September 27.

Shouldering immeasurable grief, John Brown and his wife Mary buried their four young children in the Fairview Cemetery in Richfield. A single headstone holds the names of all four children, their ages, and dates of death. After more than 180 years, the limestone grave marker is weather-beaten and worn down by the wind but still stands tall.

Over the years he was in Richfield, he lived in three different homes. He worked hard at shepherding and leatherworking to honor his financial obligations and to get a fresh start. His knowledge of animal husbandry established him as a well-known expert in the sheep industry. His skills were so accomplished that he could tell the breed and quality of wool by feeling it in his hand while blindfolded.

Having heard of John Brown and learning more about his reputation, Colonel Perkins reached out to him in 1844. Situated on one hundred and fifty acres, the Perkins Mansion was surrounded by stony hills and sparse soil. After nearly ten years of raising cattle with limited success, Colonel Perkins considered a new idea. He wondered if his land might be better suited for a different agricultural purpose. He contemplated converting his land to the raising of sheep.

Upon meeting, the two men agreed to go into the wool business together and established the partnership of Perkins & Brown. Now forty-four years old, John Brown needed a way to move forward from the deaths of his children and the bankruptcy he had filed two years earlier.

The partnership between Perkins and Brown was forged and the terms allowed the Brown family to rent the clapboard residence that had served as a temporary home of Perkins and his wife, Grace, when they first moved to Akron in 1834, during the time that their mansion was being built.

John Brown was pleased to inhabit the well-built house. This new business arrangement would assure food, shelter, and income for his traumatized family, still struggling with grief over their recent losses. The partnership agreement between Perkins and Brown further called for them to share equally in the profits and losses and gave hope for added prosperity. The terms also allowed the Browns to have a garden, gather firewood, and undertake the butchering of meat for both families.

Perkins & Brown had early success and by 1846, John Brown was preparing to depart Akron to open a business office for the partnership in Springfield, Massachusetts, an important trade center for the burgeoning American wool industry. The business of Perkins & Brown was run as a farming cooperative where the two partners took on specific tasks and jointly shared profits and benefits.

Brown believed that having a mercantile office in Springfield would allow Ohio wool-producing clients to obtain greater profits for their superior product. In Akron, Jason and Owen watched over the flock which grew to thirteen

Our Own John Brown

hundred head. For his part, Colonel Perkins enlarged the Akron operations to include a three-story factory where different steps of sorting, cleaning, and grading of wool were performed before shipping it east to Springfield.

Brown's presence in Massachusetts provided him with an unforeseen opportunity when he formed the partnership with Perkins. In Springfield, he became well known among many of the leading abolitionists of the time. East Coast states were full of antislavery sentiment.

While Ohio had more passageways on the Underground Railroad than any other state, the tenor of its abolitionism was less passionate than in the East, where the most influential and ardent opponents of slavery lived. As Ohio bordered the slave states of Virginia (later, West Virginia) and Kentucky, it was a natural corridor to Northern free states and to Canada for those seeking freedom from Southern servitude. Travel through Ohio was often essential for people escaping slavery from the South. The active, outspoken antislavery campaigns going on in Ohio, while important, did not have the numbers or the intensity of the political efforts in the East. John Brown's move to Springfield, Massachusetts, brought him nearer to more fervent abolitionism.

As a result of the years he spent in Springfield and his travels within East Coast states, John Brown came to know Frederick Douglass, Sojourner Truth, William Lloyd Garrison, Harriet Tubman, Harriet Beecher Stowe, Gerrit Smith, and many other renowned antislavery proponents of the era. His relationships with these activists were founded on mutual contempt for the practice of slavery.

Throughout his life, he moved freely within different social circles where members were drawn from areas of business, religion, government, law, agriculture, or otherwise. People found him engaging and even charismatic. Frederick Douglass described his captivating blue eyes as "full of light and fire."

While in Springfield, John Brown immersed himself into a large established Black community, attended the Springfield Free Church, and openly employed emancipated and escaped slaves at the wool storage warehouse maintained by the firm of Perkins & Brown.

In 1849, Colonel Perkins and John Brown agreed to charter a ship to Liverpool, England filled with wool from the Perkins & Brown warehouse. Domestic wool prices were low, and John Brown believed he could make higher profits by selling directly to English wool merchants. The venture turned into a financial disaster that resulted in John Brown selling the wool in Europe for a price less than what he had been offered in Springfield. The failed excursion to Europe and other woolen business issues greatly diminished Colonel Perkins's wealth. Since his financial standing was greater than the beleaguered assets of Perkins & Brown, he shouldered primary responsibility for the settlement of the partnership debts.

Colonel Simon Perkins's relationship with John Brown was critical to providing the financial wherewithal to pursue his abolitionist activities while engaging in the wool business. Brown also made many trips to Canada, known as the "Promised Land" to enslaved people.

In Springfield, Brown observed Black people and white people who publicly advocated for militancy to bring an end to slavery. Although he had previously given thought to this approach, he had not yet encountered others who openly spoke about the necessity of such a course. It was in Springfield that John Brown came to embrace militant insurrection and accept the position that slavery could only be eradicated through armed rebellion. When he later returned to Akron, he sought support for his new plans.

The early years of the Perkins & Brown partnership were sufficiently successful to justify the establishment of a warehouse in Springfield. Perkins usually remained in Akron, watching over his farm operations and attending his other business responsibilities. Brown frequently returned to Akron as necessary to connect with his family and have discussions with Perkins. The extensive correspondence between the partners contains almost no information about John Brown's abolitionist activities in Springfield or anywhere.

While renting from Perkins in Akron, John Brown often secured fugitives about his home until they could be safely transported across Lake Erie to Canada. Grace Perkins was critical of the Browns and the way they conducted themselves. She said of John Brown, "He was always concerning himself with negros" and further described him as "often having several hidden at once about his place." Colonel Perkins did not openly embrace abolitionism, if at all. Despite the long partnership between the men, there is little information relating to Perkins's thoughts about slavery. When interviewed late in his life about John Brown's assault on the federal arsenal in Virginia, the Colonel stated that he thought the Harpers Ferry venture was "foolish."

Unquestionably, Perkins valued his relationship with John Brown, or it would not have lasted for more than ten years. Authors James S. and Margot Y. Jackson have said of Colonel Perkins: "Certainly his name has not been found listed among those raising money for or endorsing the ideals of John Brown's anti-slavery efforts." Although Perkins may not have charitably funded John Brown's abolitionism, their relationship allowed both to engage in other interests. The partnership was built on trust and honesty, and neither man is known to have questioned the integrity of the other. Brown had access to partnership funds, spending authority, and decision-making capacity, as did Colonel Perkins. It is clear that John Brown's place in the partnership benefited himself, his family, and provided stable income and housing throughout the times when they lived in Akron, Springfield, and North Elba.

On the issue of slavery, John Brown and his circle of supporters were a step ahead of many white Americans who believed the issue would resolve itself on its own over time. Many white citizens did not express themselves one way or another on the issue of slavery, at least in forms that we can access today as researchers.

The partners made a decision to wind down their operations in both Akron and Springfield. Changes in market conditions, significant financial losses, and overwhelming litigation brought the men to this conclusion. Neither John Brown nor Colonel Perkins demonstrated rancor toward each other. They had cooperated and communicated reasonably well over the years and generally had made decisions in the best interest of the company. With so many pending court cases and the length of time it would take to negotiate the lawsuits to conclusion, their continued cooperation and the application of their collective knowledge would be crucial. By the end of the partnership Perkins had started up other businesses which now occupied his attention and at least gave some assurance for future financial security.

Perkins's collaboration with John Brown lasted until 1856, when they resolved the final lawsuit relating to the financial problems of Perkins & Brown. The remaining business records of the partnership are insufficient to determine the profits and losses over the years of operation. However, in the end, responsibility for the monetary losses incurred by the partnership of Perkins & Brown fell upon Colonel Perkins. While the amounts were very substantial, they were not ruinous. Colonel Perkins, like his father General Perkins, exhibited qualities of being generous, calm, and industrious. Like his impact on Akron, Colonel Perkins's influence John Brown's life, while significant, cannot be measured. The circumstances of John Brown's many years of association with Perkins, in view of what Brown did and who he became, cannot be minimized.

In the spring of 1855, John Brown's five sons left Akron to seek farmland of their own in Kansas. The departure of his sons signaled the close of John Brown's involvement with Colonel Perkins as they had long worked on Perkins's farms in both Akron and Tallmadge.

Brown intended to settle down at the farm he had purchased from abolitionist Gerrit Smith in North Elba, New York. He moved his family to the farm in 1849. He relied greatly on his wife Mary and their children to maintain his 250-acre homestead in North Elba.

Although John Brown is buried at North Elba, he was rarely there.

In the mid-1850s, after concluding the lawsuits in Akron involving himself and Colonel Perkins, the bulk of John Brown's remaining years ended up being used to find financial support and supplies in the East and in Ohio, fighting border ruffians in Kansas, and making preparations for his assault on the arsenal at Harpers Ferry.

In June of 1855, Gerrit Smith assisted John Brown in raising money to be used against proslavery vigilantes in Kansas and Missouri. Later that summer John Brown returned to Ohio and made stops in Hudson and Akron, where he reached out to loyal sympathizers for money and weapons.

Within the Akron legal profession, many lawyers of the era opposed slavery and acted to bring about its demise. One important citizen was General Lucius V. Bierce, who exercised outsized influence in Akron. Bierce became a Republican in 1854 because of his loathing of slavery.

An outstanding lawyer, he assisted John Brown by supplying him with funds, army surplus broadswords, firearms, storage, and enlisting support from Akronites and many others within Summit County. Bierce himself was larger than life. The best-known lawyer in Akron, he served as mayor six times. Early in his career, he assumed leadership of his Ohio militia and appointed himself as brigadier general over his troops during the short-lived Patriot War in Canada from 1837 to 1839. He served as a judge in the 1850s and was elected as a state senator for a term in 1862. Bierce, like many others who settled in northern Ohio, was born in Connecticut but did not arrive in Akron until around 1836 when he was thirty-five. Bierce and John Brown's shared Connecticut roots gave them another common connection and likely shaped and cemented their mutual abolitionist sentiments. Whether raising money, providing weapons, or giving moral support to John Brown, Lucius Bierce was an outspoken supporter.

John Brown was no stranger to the legal system. His personal debts and other obligations relating to Perkins & Brown kept him involved in the Summit County courts over long periods. His many lawsuits within the Summit County courts may have been another way that he and General Bierce came to know each other.

Brown's five sons, who had moved to Kansas in 1855, wrote to their father about the antislavery violence of "border ruffians" which had followed the passage of the Kansas-Nebraska Act in 1854. After receiving this information, Brown soon left Ohio for Kansas with the weaponry supplied to him by General Bierce.

The triumphs that John Brown achieved at Osawatomie emboldened him and spread his fame through newspaper articles and by word of mouth. His elevated profile raised public consciousness about slavery and thereby lifted it up as the most politically significant issue of the time. There are no records to show that Bierce traveled to Kansas, but he nevertheless played an important part in John Brown's Osawatomie crusade. There are indications that the Old Stone School House built in the 1830s and still located today on Broadway Street in downtown Akron may have been the building where Bierce stored some of the arms and supplies which he provided to John Brown, although it is difficult to fully confirm.

Our Own John Brown

The donated arms included broadswords similar to, if not the same, as those used by Bierce's militia in the ill-fated 1837 Patriot War in Canada. Broadswords figured prominently in the 1856 Osawatomie conflict, known as the Pottawatomie Massacre, where John Brown and his men sought revenge for the sacking of Lawrence, Kansas. The use of the broadswords and the brutality of the killings has stained the reputation of John Brown ever since. Frederick Douglass, fellow abolitionist and friend of John Brown and Owen Brown, described the act as "a terrible remedy for a terrible malady."

It took John Brown many years to fully design a plan to wage his war against slavery. His key proposition called for establishing a base of operation in the Appalachian Mountains where many of the nation's four million slaves would join John Brown and take up arms to fight for their freedom. The base would be the starting point for a slave rebellion, which would attract freedom-seeking slaves from the South. He carefully drafted his military objectives and amassed money, weapons, and men.

On Sunday, October 16, 1859, at around eight o'clock in the evening, he and his army of eighteen men marched into Harpers Ferry. By ten they had seized the federal armory with its cache of one hundred thousand weapons. They then halted an incoming Baltimore & Ohio train, secured the two bridges leading in and out of town, and killed a free Black baggage porter. Brown and his men grabbed a small number of hostages and held them inside the armory.

Brown's soldiers skirmished with a local militia and townsfolk over the hours that followed. In the morning as employees of the armory arrived for work, they too were taken as hostages. Two small advance parties dispatched by John Brown into the countryside arrested two prominent Virginia slave owners and confiscated their slaves. These seemingly minor events ignited widespread fear of a mass slave uprising throughout the area. The psychological impact may have been John Brown's greatest victory.

On Monday, October 17, 1859, information about the seizure of the federal armory quickly reached high levels of government. President James Buchanan ordered that Marines be sent by train from Washington, DC, only fifty miles away. These troops arrived before midnight. Commanded by Colonel Robert E. Lee, the Marines waited until dawn on October 18, 1859, before charging the armory and putting down the insurrection. The Marines used only bayonets in their attack to avoid injuring hostages. The assault took only minutes and when it ended John Brown had been seriously wounded. Four of his men were killed or captured. Eleven hostages were released unharmed and two Marines were shot, one of whom died. Sixteen people were killed during the raid including ten of John Brown's men, two of whom were his sons. Charges of murder, conspiracy,

An 1856 daguerreotype of John Brown, taken after the fighting began in Kansas. \ Boston Athenaeum.

and treason were brought against John Brown and his six followers who were captured. Over the weeks ahead, all were taken to trial, convicted, and hanged by the state of Virginia.

John Brown was the first to be tried. On October 26, 1859, his trial began at the courthouse in Charles Town, Virginia, before Judge Richard Parker. Severely wounded, John Brown lay on a cot throughout most of the proceedings but listened and spoke up when necessary. On Monday, October 30, 1859, closing arguments were made. Forty-five minutes after commencing deliberations, the jurors returned verdicts of guilty on all charges. Sentencing took place on November 2, 1859, and Judge Parker ordered him to be hanged one month later on December 2, 1859. On the day of his execution, Virginia Governor Henry Wise, fearing that sympathizers might help John Brown escape, ordered that 1,500 soldiers be present. Once removed from the county jail, John Brown sat on top of his coffin as he was taken by horsedrawn wagon to the gallows.

Many in Akron had contributed to John Brown's abolitionist endeavors only in secret, perhaps to minimize the risk of being charged as fellow conspirators in his crimes. Some worked routes on the Underground Railroad, while others donated money, goods, and services. Lucius V. Bierce was undeterred about any threat of potential prosecution and pridefully spoke about his efforts on behalf of his old friend.

The *Summit County Beacon* quotes Bierce praising John Brown as "the first martyr in the irrepressible conflict of liberty with slavery." He said further, "Thank God, I furnished him with arms and right good use did he make of them. Men like Brown may die, but their acts and principles will live forever." In these words, Bierce describes the considerable supplies given by him to John Brown, likely referencing the broadswords wielded so ferociously at Osawatomie.

Bibliography

Adams, Becky. "Kent and the Underground Railroad." October 4, 2005, Kentwired.com.

Brands, H. W. *The Zealot and the Emancipator: John Brown, Abraham Lincoln and the Struggle for American Freedom*. Doubleday, 2020.

Brown and Oviatt Agreement, Richfield, January 2, 1842. Boyd B. Stutler collection, W.V. State Archives, Stutler Selection, ID No. Ms78-1.

Carton, Evan. *Patriotic Treason: John Brown and the Soul of America*. 2006; University of Nebraska Press, 2009.

Carvalho III, Joseph. "John Brown's Transformation: The Springfield Years, 1846–1849." *The Historical Journal of Massachusetts* (Winter 2020).

DeCaro, Louis A. *Fire From the Midst of You: A Religious Life of John Brown*. New York University Press, 2002.

"December Second in Akron." *Akron Summit Beacon*. December 7, 1859, 2, Newspapers.com.

Douglass, Frederick. *My Bondage and My Freedom*. Ed. John Stauffer, Random House, 1885. Google Books.

Dubois, W. E. B. *John Brown*. 1909; Oxford University Press, 2007.

Dyer, Joyce. *Pursuing John Brown: On the Trail of a Radical Abolitionist*. University of Akron Press, 2022.

Geewax, Marilyn. "Kent Needs $400,000 for Horning Rd. Work." *Akron Beacon Journal*, September 23, 1980, B3, Newspapers.com.

Goodheart, Lawrence B. *Abolitionist, Actuary, Atheist: Elizur Wright and the Reform Impulse*. Kent State University Press, 1990.

Horwitz, Tony. *Midnight Rising: John Brown and the Raid that Sparked the Civil War*. Henry Holt, 2011.

Jackson, James and Margot Y. *At Home on the Hill: The Perkins Family of Akron*. Summit County Historical Society, 1983.

"John Brown Tannery Razed." *Akron Beacon Journal*. June 3, 1976, B2, Newspapers.com.

Kern, Kevin F. and Gregory S. Wilson. *Ohio: A History of the Buckeye State*, second ed. Wiley Blackwell, 2023.

King, William S. *To Raise Up a Nation: John Brown, Frederick Douglass and The Making of a Free Country*. West Holme Publishing, 2013.

Land, Mary. "John Brown's Ohio Environment," *Ohio Archaeological and Historical Quarterly* 62 (January 1948): 24.

Lane, Samuel A. *Fifty Years and Over of Summit County*. Beacon Job Department, 1892.

Mackey, James and Carolyn Mackey, *The Wrights of Tallmadge: Elizur Wright Sr. to Geneva Wright Atwood, 1810 to 1915*. Published by the authors, 1997.

"Memories of John Brown on Sunday." *Akron Beacon Journal*, August 17, 1910, 1, Newspapers.com.

Middleton, Stephen. *The Black Laws in the Old Northwest: A Documentary History*. Greenwood, 1993.

Middleton, Stephen. *The Black Laws: Race and the Legal Process in Early Ohio*. Ohio University Press, 2005.

Obituary of Heman Oviatt. *Cincinnati Inquirer*. December 31, 1854, 1, Newspapers.com.

Reynolds, David S. *John Brown, Abolitionist: The Man Who Killed Slavery, Sparked the Civil War, and Seeded Civil Rights*. Knopf, 2005.

Sanborn, F. B., ed. *The Life and Letters of John Brown, Liberator of Kansas, and Martyr of Virginia*. Roberts Brothers, 1885. Google Books.

Stearns, Frank Preston. *Cambridge Sketches*. Lippincott and Company, 1905. Google Books.

Stutler, Boyd B. Letter to James T. Babb, Yale University, March 18, 1951. W. V. Memory Project, Stutler Collection, ID No. RP10-0070A-D.

Villard, Oswald Garrison. *John Brown, 1800–1859: A Biography Fifty Years After*. Knopf, 1943. Library of Congress.

Webb, Richard D. ed. *The Life and Letters of Captain John Brown*. Smith, Elder, 1861. Google Books.

Whitman, Alden. *American Reformers: An H. W. Wilson Biographical Dictionary*. H. W. Wilson, 1985.

\ **4**

Truth in Between

The Social and Political Environment of the 1851 Woman's Rights Convention in Akron, Ohio

Philathia Bolton

•••

We trust in Truth, and yet shall see
Proud Wrong into Oblivion hurled,
The human race shall *all* be free!

—FROM GEORGE W. PUTNAM'S "A POEM"
FOR THE 1851 WOMAN'S RIGHTS
CONVENTION[1]

We settled into a small community room at Hale Farm and Village large enough to accommodate the crowd expected from surrounding areas.[2] We were diverse in constitution, most ostensibly by age and race, with a few families appearing to be in attendance for the event. Little children dangled from laps of older individuals, and senior citizens with walkers and canes could be seen nearby. Cushioned seats arranged in the stadium-style, sunlit room faced floor-to-ceiling windows.

This would be the focal area where Sojourner Truth, or more accurately, Robin Echols Cooper from Women in History, would stand to represent Truth through reenactment. Women in History, based in Ohio, is comprised of a group of performing artists who provide reenacted histories of notable historical types for the purposes of educating a broad public.

Truth entered from the back of the room singing a spiritual a capella that some in attendance appeared to recognize. A few people hummed along to the melody. She glided by audience members and grabbed a few hands as she sang. Trees that lined the rolling hills could be seen through the windows rustling lightly in the wind, as she continued to walk to the front of the room. Over the next half hour or so, standing in front of that landscape, we would hear from Truth. We would not get the famous, often-recited "Ain't I a Woman" speech delivered at the 1851 Women's Convention. Neither would much time be spent on Frances Gage's controversial representation of the speech, although it was addressed. Instead, we received a dramatic retelling of Truth life's story from Cooper that emphasized Truth's work ethic, bravery, wit, and ingenuity. We found out what it was like to be enslaved in a Dutch colony, work in the suffragist and antislavery movements, and strategize as a businesswoman to secure funds and property without the benefit of literacy.

This chapter takes its inspiration, in part, from approaches to history offered through dramatists like those who comprise Women in History. Much like we were asked to consider aspects of Truth's story that deepen an understanding of her beyond what is afforded through representations of her speech, this chapter invites a consideration of the larger sociopolitical milieu that drew suffragist and abolitionist crowds to Northeast Ohio and, particularly, Akron. Sojourner Truth's extemporaneously delivered "Ain't I a Woman" speech at the 1851 Women's Convention at the Old Stone Church contributes to Akron's national visibility. However, Truth's speech is just part of a larger story of activism that saw much of its activity concentrate in our region.

Northeast Ohio proved an attractive gathering place due to its location near water and because of its activist roots. "When the Chesapeake and Ohio Canal along the Potomac and the Baltimore and Ohio (B&O) Railroad were built in the 1830s, Harpers Ferry became a transportation center as well," informs Mary McNulty.[3] These networked waterways attracted opportunities for employment as industry prospered in the region. As communities flourished, so did the social and political activities joined to their everyday lives, especially those connected with suffragist and abolitionist causes. Antislavery societies existed in Northern parts of the country and had been a vital part of the Underground Railroad system. These areas included Ohio's Western Reserve and "the area that encompassed the banks of Lake Erie on the north, Cleveland and Hudson on the east, Akron on the south, and Sandusky on the west."[4] Simply put, a robust community of nineteenth-century activists committed to sociopolitical change had become established in the region, and it was fairly easy to access places like Akron due to the railroads and canals.

The larger sociocultural context that informed emergent antislavery and suffragist groups who organized, created networks, and held conventions in Northeast Ohio grew out of changes the entire nation saw in the mid-nineteenth century. A rise in industrialization catalyzed by advances made in transportation, along with opportunities made available due to the country expanding further West, "changed the social fabric," argues Dorothy Salem.[5] "Immigrant labor created urban areas and modified gender and class roles. The women's rights movement emerged from this dynamic context," she explains. She also mentions the significance of women gaining experience organizing in the moral purity, temperance, and antislavery movements, crediting such efforts as laying groundwork for the eventual founding of the nineteenth-century women's movement. Many of the women who played key roles in these movements would go on to assume leadership in the women's movement, such as Frances D. Gage. Before Gage helped orchestrate the 1851 Woman's Convention in Akron, Ohio, she would be among several who gathered in Seneca Falls, New York, to formalize a movement to improve the lives of women. By this convention's end, one hundred signatures—from sixty-eight women and thirty-two men—endorsed the "Declaration of Sentiments." It was a document detailing gender inequalities and the actions deemed necessary to take to rectify them.

Momentum from the 1848 Seneca Convention, particularly the effects of female leadership demonstrated at the meeting, factored into setting the stage for the 1851 Woman's Convention in Akron. Leaders of the nascent women's movement, in concert with influential Ohio residents, organized to bring the convention to Akron. Gage was elected as the convention's president. She and others had continued to work after the 1848 Seneca Falls Convention in New York, holding several meetings in their home state during 1850. Gage presided over the meeting held in McConnelsville the year before the 1851 Woman's Rights Convention and before the state constitutional convention the same year. Petitions were collected at the conference in McConnelsville to give women the right to vote.[6] The fact that Ohio's constitution would be ratified in 1851 weighed significantly into decisions to hold the convention in Akron, Ohio, that May. The hope was that extending women the right to vote would be included.

Ohio's rich history of civil rights engagement across genders and between races suggests support could be garnered at this juncture. Such alliances were indicative of nineteenth-century civil rights activity. By 1854, northern abolitionist organizations, like the Maine Anti-Slavery Society, would hire women such as the African American poet Frances E. W. Harper to lecture for them. Frederick Douglass—who delivered his famous "What to the Slave is the Fourth of July?" speech (1852) in Rochester, New York—was also enlisted to advance abolitionist efforts. William Lloyd Garrison invited him to play a central role in advancing their causes after hearing Douglass speak in the years prior. Figures of the era such as Frances E. W. Harper, Frederick Douglass, Sojourner Truth, Susan B. Anthony, Elizabeth Cady Stanton, Robert and Harriet Purvis, and Lucretia Mott joined forces to work for change in the American Equal Rights Association founded in the decade following the 1851 Woman's Rights Convention.[7] Harper was living in Ohio during this time and found it beneficial to get involved in lecturing again due to financial strains brought on by the passing of her husband. With such alliances in place regardless of race or gender, the upcoming ratification of the state's constitution, and given Akron's opportune location among waterways and railroads, the 1851 Woman's Rights Convention was set to take place in the city. Its proceedings show efforts between men and women to bring the event to fruition, with most of the leadership at the officer and committee levels concentrated among women.[8] People from Akron were involved at all levels. Mrs. Martha J. Tilden, from Akron, served on the nominating committee, and of the eight vice presidents seated in office at the convention, three of them— Mrs. A. Akley, Mrs. Sarah F. Swift, and Miss (*first name not printed*) Webb—were from Akron.

The Anti-Slavery Bugle, founded in 1845 and the official publication of the Ohio American Anti-Slavery Society, famously covered the speech Sojourner Truth delivered at the convention in its June 21, 1851, issue. Along with its report of her speech, one finds a published declaration against slavery from the American Unitarian Association's meeting in Boston, *The Princeton Review* on slavery, letters to the *Bugle* and the Western Anti-Slavery Society, and a couple of legal cases that involve the enslaved, such as Clarissa's. After having been detained in the non-slave-holding state of Pennsylvania for several months, Clarissa successfully petitioned for freedom once her master returned and attempted to take her back to Kentucky. All of these news items are on the front page of a four-page newspaper that provides some coverage of the convention.

At first glance, encountering details about the 1851 women's convention on the last page of this edition of the *Anti-Slavery Bugle* may lead one to believe the event proved less significant than other content featured. In fact, issues that ran in the weeks prior, and the issue directly following the June 21, issue, label the last page "miscellaneous." A review of this page in select issues typically shows short stories, poetry, and advertisements that have little if anything to do with antislavery causes. The exception would be the edition that contains a summary of Sojourner Truth's speech at the 1851 Woman's Convention and the poem by George W. Putnam read at the convention and mentioned, but not published, in its proceedings. *The Anti-Slavery Bugle* published the poem in its entirety.[9] In lieu of the typical heading "miscellaneous" in the upper right-hand corner, one sees "The Bugle." The last page yet contains miscellaneous items, but most seem women-oriented in topic. There are a couple of sections on fashion, a religious reposting from *The Independent*, and advertisements. A column bearing the title "Woman's Rights Convention" in bold print stands out prominently among these pieces. "Sojourner Truth" accompanies as a byline of sorts in a font size that rivals what is used for the title and that is noticeably larger than the print chosen to feature names of other authors on the page. Absent is the name of the reporter who contributed the piece and any names of individuals who organized the convention, expressly, the convention's president Frances Gage. The newspaper provides complete deference to Sojourner Truth, which perhaps makes sense considering the *Anti-Slavery Bugle's* cause. "One of the most unique and interesting speeches of the Convention was made by Sojourner Truth, an emancipated slave," the write-up begins. "It is impossible to transfer it to paper, or convey any adequate idea of the effect it produced upon the audience. Those only can appreciate it who saw her powerful form, her whole-souled, earnest gestures, and listened to her strong and truthful tones."[10] The writer lends agency to Truth while speaking about her words and their impact. If "miscellaneous" historically had been perceived as the fragmented, superfluous elements of the paper, then breaking from habit to title the last page "The Bugle" would have proven significant as a gesture. Readers, particularly faithful subscribers, could have seen the aberration as intentional reframing. Although still relegated to the last page, the content there—particularly the metonymic representation of the Woman's Convention through Truth—gains weight.

The newspaper's approach to covering the convention could have been influenced by what Truth would contribute to the *Anti-Slavery Bugle's* cause. She, after all, by fact of her past experiences of enslavement and her current displays of courage and conviction, is a living testament against slavery. If the 1851 Woman's Convention were to be covered, since Truth spoke, she would be the likely person to feature. However, by privileging her and simultaneously omitting the names of others, a veiled statement could have been made, also, about a Woman's Convention that sought equality for the lives of women without acknowledging how such a pursuit involves the enslaved woman differently.

In certain cases, the enslaved woman's experiences became displaced in the context of the convention and outside of Truth's being allowed space to speak. A letter shared at the convention, for example, drew from slavery to characterize,

Cabinet card of Sojourner Truth sold by Truth at speaking engagements, circa 1870, printed with the caption "I sell the shadow to support the substance." \ Wikimedia Commons.

Truth in Between

assumedly, a white woman's experience of suffering at the hands of a patriarchal system. A letter from P. W. Davis to a Mrs. McMillan in support of the convention sought to show how women bore responsibility for shaping the male-governed society they deemed oppressive, stating, "In one family you will find mother and sister toiling like southern slaves, early and late, for a son who sleeps on the downiest couch, wears the finest linen, and spends his hundreds of dollars in wild college life." She adds, "How should he not feel that women were made purposefully to minister to his happiness?" In such a scenario, the gravity of an enslaved woman's experience becomes lost in what accounts to false equivalency. "Can man be free if woman be a slave?" the writer of the letter goes on to question.[11]

Given such a conflation, one could see how someone like Marius R. Robinson, the editor of *The Anti-Slavery Bugle*, might take offense. He was directly involved with the Underground Railroad, helped to found a school to educate African Americans, and was subjected to several violent encounters, including a tar and feathering, due to his work for abolition. Some of the women with whom he worked most closely stood bravely against pro-slavery mobs, risking bodily harm. Mrs. Garretson was one such person. She came to his aid when he was being beaten during the 1837 attack that left him tarred and feathered. Emily Rakestraw also became a significant partner. She helped with his educational efforts and eventually married him.[12] Both examples of womanhood differ from how P. W. Davis portrays it. These women committed their lives to more than the men in their households, and their close proximity to challenges had by enslaved individuals likely evoked nuance in how they viewed their lives by comparison. It makes one wonder if either would have used the word "slave" or "slavery" to characterize their lived experiences, given that slavery had yet to be abolished, and people like Truth could speak so heart-wrenchingly about life as an enslaved person.

Understanding the social and political climate of the 1851 Women's Convention in Akron, then, involves a consideration of certain intersections and departures related to what it means to recognize shared womanhood and also challenges associated with building and sustaining effective alliances comprised of diverse individuals. On one hand, the conference arguably legitimated Truth by providing her room to speak, although she was not originally on the program. She contributed during the second day of the convention at their morning session and is reflected in the proceedings as giving remarks on education. On the other hand, women who looked like Truth still suffered as enslaved individuals in many parts of the country. They could not freely travel to organize for such conventions, be welcomed into many of the homes and families of the host

Local artist Woodrow Nash created this bronze statue of Sojourner Truth standing at the Sojourner Truth Legacy Plaza outside the United Way on High Street. \ Photo by Matthew Brown, *Akron Beacon Journal*.

cities, or experience other taken-for-granted freedoms the conference organizers enjoyed or expressed gratitude for in their resolutions. And yet, women, regardless of race, struggled in various ways to realize the best expressions of freedom in a country that disenfranchised them. How this freedom could be understood as meaning something different based on context, be advocated for, and supported across racial and gender alliances was the challenge of the day. In many ways, such challenges continue. Nevertheless, Akron drew the crowd that held these tensions in place, as those working for change pressed towards something better.

Truth in Between

As the poet Putnam articulated, "We trust in Truth ... the human race shall *all* be free."

In the years that followed, Akron would continue to be a magnet for civil rights activity. Most notably, historical figures such as Booker T. Washington, W. E. B. Du Bois, and Martin Luther King, Jr. would speak in the city. Washington delivered a speech at First Congregational Church in 1909, with Du Bois delivering an address at the same church several years later in 1921. Martin Luther King Jr. would address his audience at The University of Akron in Memorial Hall in 1962.[13] Before any of these events occurred, Truth made her mark, first, at the Universalist Stone Church. As recorded in *The Anti-Slavery Bugle*, she opened by saying "I want to say a few words about this matter. I am a woman's rights. I have as much muscle as any man, and can do as much work as any man." Lending both her figurative body and intellect to the cause, she challenged listeners to consider the validity of arguments made to exclude others based on assumptions tied to appearance, whether it be gender or race. As a Christian minister, she challenged them further to consider what God would think about the treatment of women, considering He trusted his Son to be born through a woman without the aid of a man. As a sovereign individual, she stood in the certainty of her personhood by suggesting equality with man. She aligned "I am a woman's rights" with "I have as much muscle as any man," denying values such as strength and fortitude to men alone. To be woman is to be strong. Her story, along with the stories of other notable women in history, lives on through dramatists like Robin Echols Cooper. In May 2024, a statue of Sojourner Truth by internationally acclaimed Akron artist Woodrow Nash was unveiled and dedicated at the site where she delivered her speech at the 1851 Woman's Convention.[14]

Notes

1. George W. Putnam, "A Poem," *Anti-Slavery Bugle*, June 21, 1851, 160, Chronicling America.

2. Hale Farm and Village is a museum and historical site in the township of Bath, Ohio. The reenactment was part of a Black History Celebration event that took place on February 11, 2023.

3. Mary McNulty, "Harpers Ferry," *Salem Press Encyclopedia*, May 2022.

4. McNulty.

5. Dorothy C. Salem, "Akron Woman's Rights Convention." *Salem Press Encyclopedia*, July 31, 2021.

6. Ellen Carol Dubois, *Feminism and Suffrage: The Emergence of an Independent Women's Movement in America, 1848–1869* (Cornell University Press, 1978), 68.

7. "Frances E. W. Harper," *The Norton Anthology of African American Literature*, second edition, ed. Henry Louis Gates and Nellie McKay (Norton, 2004), 492.

8. Of note is the solitary male vice president among the cohort of female officers for the convention. Among the secretaries and business committee, one sees a comparable mix, with their being a two-to-one ratio of women to men among secretaries and with their being eleven women on the seventeen-person business committee.

9. An excerpt from the poem serves as an epigraph for this chapter.

10. "The Woman's Right's Convention," *Anti-Slavery Bugle*, June 21, 1851, 157–60, Chronicling America.

11. "The Proceedings of the Woman's Rights Convention, Held at Akron, Ohio, May 28 and 29, 1851." Library of Congress, https://tile.loc.gov/storage-services/service/rbc/rbnawsa/n8317/n8317.pdf.

12. Stacey M. Robertson, *Hearts Beating for Liberty: Women Abolitionists in the Old Northwest* (University of North Carolina Press, 2010).

13. Mark J. Price, "Akron Landmarks in Black History," *Akron Beacon Journal*, February 28, 2022, beaconjournal.com.

14. Gari Estwick and Kassi Filkins, "Hundreds on Hand for Unveiling of Sojourner Truth Statue in Akron," *Signal Akron*, May 29, 2024, https://signalakron.org; Isabella Schrek, "'Mother, Activist, Suffragist': Plaza Honoring Sojourner Truth Opens Wednesday in Akron," *Akron Beacon Journal*, May 30, 2024, http://beaconjournal.com.

\\ **5**

An International City

Charlotte Gintert

From its beginning, Akron has been home to new Americans. When the Ohio & Erie Canal (O & E Canal) cut into the landscape that would become Akron, most of the labor was conducted by immigrants. The majority were from Ireland. Approximately one million Irish immigrants arrived in the United States between 1815–1845.[1] Although conditions in Ireland were not as dire as they were during the later and more well-known potato blight, small family farms were already experiencing economic downturns. The British government encouraged emigration to prevent economic and environmental collapse in Ireland, while the United States desperately needed laborers for building projects like canals.[2]

Akron's first immigrant neighborhood, "Dublin," sprang up in the Little Cuyahoga River valley along Furnace and Howard streets. The location made sense, having easy access to both water at the river and the construction site of Cascade Locks, which took longer than other sections of the canal to build. The neighborhood remained after the canal was completed.[3] Once the O & E Canal work ended, many of these immigrant "canawlers" turned to the construction of the Pennsylvania & Ohio Canal, quarried stone, dug the Cascade and Chuckery races, harvested clay for Middlebury potteries, or, later, constructed railroads.[4] A second Irish neighborhood of mostly railroad and foundry workers, flamboyantly known as "Hell's Half Acre," sprang up in the 1840s near Thornton, High, South, Miami, and Washington (now Wolf Ledges) streets.[5]

Akron's Northside District in 2023. During the canal days this was part of the Dublin neighborhood and home to Irish laborers. \ Photo by Charlotte Gintert

One of the most prominent Irish families in Akron history is the O'Neil family. Michael O'Neil, originally from County Cork, opened a dry goods store with fellow Irishman Isaac Dyas in 1877. What they started would go on to become the O'Neil's department store on South Main Street. His son, William F. O'Neil, founded The General Tire & Rubber Company in 1915.[6]

By 1870, as much as 26 percent of Akron's population was foreign-born and claimed mostly Irish or German ancestry.[7] Although some Germans worked digging the O & E canal, most arrived in Akron after it was completed. They came from many backgrounds, from the upper middle to working class, and fled economic, political, and social upheaval back home. They were the largest immigrant group from 1840–1880.[8] In Akron, the German working-class neighborhood was located just east of Hell's Half Acre. To non-Germans, the neighborhood was derogatorily known as Goosetown, referring to the residents' geese.[9]

Many wealthy and middle-class Germans went on to found some of Akron's most important industries and businesses. Ferdinand Schumacher's Akron oatmeal business was the first in the United States. Fellow German Erhard Steinbacher arranged for Schumacher to supply oatmeal to the Union

An International City

2023 view of Allyn Street in Akron's old German neighborhood of Goosetown. \ Photo by Charlotte Gintert

Army during the Civil War, a contract that led to Schumacher becoming "The Oatmeal King."[10] Akron history is filled with German last names. These include, but are certainly not limited to, the Albrechts, Billows, Buchholzers, Burkhardts, Pfluegers, Seiberlings, and Werners.

New Arrivals of the Early Twentieth Century

Around the turn of the twentieth century, immigration patterns changed. In Europe, railroads were built connecting rural communities to industrial centers, agricultural patterns shifted due to transatlantic trade, and the last remnants of the old feudal system finally ended.[11] Eastern Europe experienced a dramatic increase in population at this time, so many nations encouraged emigration as a solution to overpopulation.[12] At the same time, the industrial age was in full swing, and demand for laborers in the United States was higher than ever.

Jews were one of the largest groups to leave for the United States. The Jewish community was the most isolated and oppressed minority in Russia and what is now Poland, Latvia, Lithuania, and Ukraine. From 1880 to 1924, about three million Jews relocated to the United States, and over one-third of the Jewish population of Russia had fled.[13]

Jewish arrivals to Akron in the nineteenth century settled along Howard Street. In Akron's commercial district, many worked in retail or in their own stores, such as kosher groceries and services, which catered to the Jewish community. Others were self-employed as doctors and lawyers.[14] By the 1920s, Akron's largest Jewish neighborhood was along Wooster Ave. The following decade the Jewish community moved north into what is now West Hill and Highland Square. In addition to synagogues and temples, they opened schools.[15] One of the most recognizable downtown landmarks is Polsky's department store, now a part of The University of Akron. Abraham Polsky, a Jewish immigrant from Poland, and his business partner, Samuel Myers, opened the original store in 1885. The South Main Street location was opened by his sons Bert and Harry in 1930 and sat directly across the street from O'Neil's.[16] It would be a favorite shopping destination for Akronites until it closed in 1978.[17]

Akron attracted approximately seventy thousand immigrants during the "Rubber Boom" years of 1890 to 1920. The largest non-Jewish group from Eastern Europe were Hungarians, reflecting the national trend, followed by Slovenians, Slovaks, and Croatians. Many settled in South Akron, in and around the old German Goosetown neighborhood.[18] Just like Eastern Europe, Italy also experienced a change in its economy and began to encourage the poor to emigrate. During the early twentieth century, Akron's Italians landed in the old "Dublin" neighborhood, changing its nickname to Akron's "Little Rome" or "Little Italy."[19] After the North Hill Viaduct opened in 1922, they migrated to the North Hill neighborhood.[20] North Hill became a center of Italian culture and has been associated with the Italian American community ever since. Italian Americans employed in the rubber industry also settled in South Akron.[21]

Societies and Clubs

Ethnic societies and clubs were a fixture in Akron. In 1871, the first German organizations were listed in city directories. That year there were three: the Akron Liedertafel, Akron Harmonie, and Harmonie Fraternell; all of these were singing clubs.[22] The Germans had the largest number of societies and clubs in Akron for much of its history. The Irish started a chapter of the Ancient Order of Hibernians sometime in the 1870s. After a dormant period, the organization was restarted in 1953 and continues today.[23] Italian clubs were organized according to the region of Italy from which the clubs' founders originated. Akron was home

An International City

Polsky's department store as it appeared in the late 1930s. \ *Akron Beacon Journal* Collection, Summit Memory, Akron-Summit County Public Library

to the Sicilian Club, the Unione Abruzzese, the Carolvillese, the Casanese, and Castel DiSangro clubs.[24] The Akron Jewish Center opened on Balch Street in 1929.[25] Other ethnic clubs started in Akron during this time were the Hungarian Kozmuvelodesi Society, the Polish American Club, the Croatian American Club, and the Slovak Jednota Club.[26]

Ethnic organizations were often sponsored by wealthy immigrants to serve their respective communities. In addition to churches, these clubs provided a necessary place to celebrate and gather. While sponsors genuinely desired to

Plate 5: The Slovak Jednota Club and bowling alley on Morgan Avenue in South Akron still operates as a club. It is also open to the public. \ Photo by Charlotte Gintert

An International City

The Carovillese Club in North Hill is one of the remaining Italian Clubs of North Hill. \ Photo by Charlotte Gintert

assist their less wealthy countrymen, they also had a shared interest in their success. The more their group avoided the pitfalls and struggles of failed assimilation, such as crime and poverty, the less likely they all would be targeted by bigotry.[27] These clubs, for a reasonable annual fee, would provide medical and death benefits that were not available from employers.[28] Many clubs organized presentations and published native language newspapers that shared news from back home as well as immigrant success stories to encourage the community and counter anti-immigration bias in the American press.[29]

In the 1930s, the clubs began offering native language classes to children of immigrants and their descendants and to transition from mutual aid to social clubs. Many held traditional dance and craft classes to attract membership from the younger generations. As memberships dwindled from ethnic populations, most of the clubs loosened membership requirements and opened the club bars to the public. Bar revenues were used to maintain benevolent funds and club properties.

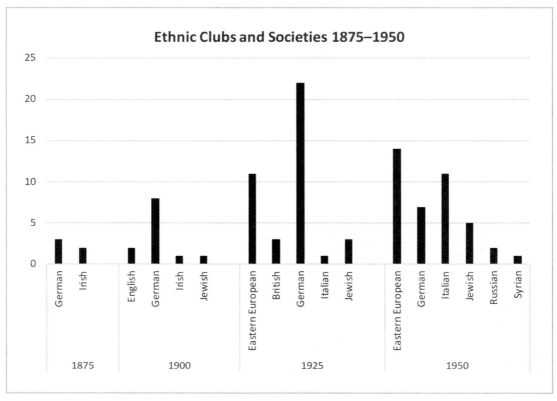

Ethnic Societies and Clubs listed in the Akron City Directories every 25 years from 1875–1950 (N. H. Burch & Co. 1875; The Burch Directory Company 1900, 1925, 1950)

Oppression and Support: The Ku Klux Klan and The International Institute of Akron

While xenophobia, nativism, and bigotry have been a serious problem in the United States from its beginning, this dramatically increased in the early twentieth century. The peak of anti-German prejudice across America took place from 1914 to 1920, during and after World War I. Akron was no exception. The Board of Education banned the teaching of German in high schools, and Paul E. Werner went bankrupt after local investors pulled out of financial agreements with the prominent German publisher.[30]

After World War I, antisemitism increased. American lawmakers, working with eugenicists and the legal foundation laid by the Chinese Exclusion Act of 1882, began crafting restrictions that would curtail immigration from "undesirable" places.[31] In 1924, Congress passed the Johnson-Reed Act, which banned immigrants from Asia and restricted immigration from Eastern Europe to prevent immigration of Jews.[32] United States Border Control was established shortly afterward.[33] The law, more commonly known as the Immigration Act of 1924, was supported by the Ku Klux Klan and the labor movement, which feared workers would lose jobs to recent immigrants.[34]

The Ku Klux Klan (KKK) was revived in 1915 and popularized nationwide with the release of the movie *The Birth of a Nation* that same year. The twentieth-century version of the Klan gained a foothold in northern cities with the arrival of migrants from Appalachia, promoting anti-immigrant, anti-Catholic, and anti-Semitic views.[35] In Akron, the popularity of the Klan took off in the 1920s when Akron reached the zenith of the rubber boom.[36]

The Akron KKK began regularly organizing meetings and membership drives in 1922. It disingenuously presented itself as a white Protestant ethnic club, no different from the other immigrant clubs and societies in the city.[37] The qualifications for membership were to be a "native-born American and a Gentile."[38]

Klan activities were met with strong resistance from Akron's Jewish, Catholic, and Black organizations.[39] The first KKK public meeting at Calvary Baptist Church was shut down due to an injunction filed by the secretary of the Akron Black YMCA.[40] The *Akron Beacon Journal* also denounced their activities.[41] However, the general population was divided on its views. Akron councilman Edward C. Rose was quoted in the *Akron Beacon Journal* on May 24, 1922: "I think some principles of the Klan are mighty good. For example, that one about 100 percent Americanism. I stand for that." He was immediately rebutted by Councilman E. L. Marting with, "We have no place in Akron for that kind of organization."[42]

Over the next few years, the KKK gained acceptance in Akron. Much of the white Protestant community resented the influx of Black laborers during the boom years, and they were also prejudiced against Jewish and Catholic people.[43] Jews were not welcome in the rubber factories, and it was difficult for Irish Americans to get work in the public schools.[44] Klan events were held at Masonic lodges, Springfield Center, Goodyear Hall, the Akron Fairgrounds, and the Akron Armory. The Klan also received support from numerous Protestant churches around the city.[45] The appeal of the Klan to Protestants was not only tied to anti-Semitism but also to longstanding hatred of the Catholic church.[46] From 1901 to 1920 Akron went from having three Catholic churches to nineteen.[47] This rapid increase was just the fuel the KKK needed to reignite old conspiracy theories about Catholic political takeovers.[48] In addition to exploiting cultural and racial tensions, the Klan also appealed to capitalist concerns about the rising labor movement. A letter to the editor in the *Beacon* mentions the author had been approached by his foreman for membership and that the Klan was supported by the company superintendent.[49] As an example of Akron's feelings about the Klan, the accounting department of The Goodyear Tire & Rubber Company hosted a Halloween party in 1921 that closed with a mock KKK initiation ceremony. The *Akron Beacon Journal* reported this party in the society pages as "one of the merriest parties of the week."[50]

The Klan quickly took over city politics through the Republican ticket, and they gained the majority of the School Board, despite resistance by the anti-Klan minority. The Akron chapter of the KKK eventually claimed to be the largest in the country. However, due to internal corruption, scandals, and consistent resistance from citizens and minority advocacy groups, the KKK's power in Akron collapsed by 1928.[51]

Although the organized Akron Klan was short-lived, immigrants to Akron continued to experience discrimination and prejudice. The 1939 Home Owners Loan Corporation Residential Security Map, more commonly known as the "Redlining Map," designated neighborhoods with "foreign elements" and Black residents as low-grade neighborhoods and areas not to invest in.[52]

However, one of the city's oldest institutions supports immigrants: the International Institute of Akron. It began with the Akron YWCA, which had been hosting English language classes for immigrant women since 1904. In 1916 its new International Center expanded the support offered to include healthcare assistance, childcare, and family counseling.[53] When the United States entered World War I, they extended services to men.[54]

The Center also offered citizenship classes and assisted with residency paperwork, the draft, and other legal issues encountered by new Akronites. At the time this was the only organization that assisted these communities outside of their own clubs and societies. The management committee was composed of wealthy YWCA board members and, crucially, women who were immigrants themselves or daughters of immigrants. While the American half of the committee wanted the Center to focus on helping with assimilation, the immigrant members also wanted the Center to be a safe place for new arrivals to adjust while retaining their traditional cultures. The Center was served by paid staff and volunteers who could communicate in all the different languages spoken by clients.[55]

The Center officially split from the YWCA in the 1930s and began receiving its funding from United Way precursor the Better Akron Foundation's Community Chest. During World War II, it again expanded and began assisting entire families.[56] Although the Klan was gone, there were still anti-immigrant sentiments in the city. In 1950, the Center came under investigation due to accusations it

An International City

A citizenship class being taught by Carlo Maltempi at the International Institute in 1972. \ Photo by Bill Hunter. Akron Beacon *Journal* Collection, Summit Memory, Akron-Summit County Public Library

was overfunded and had been spending too much to advocate for individuals fighting deportation. Foundation budget committee member William Mettler accused the center of being "a glorified country club for foreign people," according to an *Akron Beacon Journal* article. The Center was also accused of poor management and of neglecting some nationality groups.[57] An investigative subcommittee cleared it of all charges the following year.[58]

After the war, it assisted with reuniting families who had been separated during the conflict, filing asylum paperwork for individuals fleeing Soviet harassment, and connecting recent arrivals to much-needed healthcare.[59] It was reorganized into the International Institute of Akron (IIA) in 1958. In 1979, the IIA established its Refugee Resettlement program.[60]

The IIA continues to support immigrant and refugee communities today, much in the same ways it always has. The success of the IIA can be directly tied to the fact that from the beginning, immigrants were partners in its founding and management.[61] In addition to citizenship and English classes, it assists refugees and immigrants with finding employment, applying for unemployment assistance, accessing legal counsel, opening businesses, and acquiring social services. It also works with partnership organizations to promote cross-cultural experiences. In 2021, the IIA helped to resettle 424 individuals. It also helped 77 people achieve United States citizenship and 122 people receive permanent residency status.[62]

More than Europeans: Asian, Latin American, and Middle Eastern Akronites

During the nineteenth century, Chinese immigrants were exploited, targeted for violence, and restricted from entering the United States. Most immigrated to port cities of the West Coast—first during the California Gold Rush and later to build the transcontinental railroad.[63] The Chinese Exclusion Act of 1882 barred all Chinese laborers from entering the country after anti-Chinese hysteria gripped the nation. With the passing of the Johnson-Reed Act in 1924, all Asian immigrants were barred from entering the country.

Chinese men, stereotyped as effeminate, were not welcome in most industries. They were able to own and operate successful laundry services because this was considered "women's work." By 1920, thirty percent of the employed individuals who identified as Chinese worked in laundries in the United States.[64] In nineteenth-century Akron, the Asian population was not large in number. In 1875, the city's first Chinese laundry service was opened on Market Street by Hop Sing.[65] Later, two more laundries were opened on Howard Street, and a fourth opened on South Main Street.[66]

Another opportunity for Chinese immigrants was family restaurants. The first Chinese restaurant in Akron was opened in July 1902 by Loie Hong Low, Sam Chong, Hong Hing, and Jo Toi. It was located on Market Street above a plumber's shop. The review of the restaurant in *The Beacon Journal* was rife with racist language, on par with the anti-Chinese vitriol that appeared in American literature and other newspapers of the period.[67] The restaurant was only open for a year. It wasn't until 1920 that another Chinese restaurant would appear in the city directories. "The New China Restaurant" was located on South Main Street. In 1925, "The Oriental" opened on East Market. The *Akron Beacon Journal* praised it as "one of the leading eating places in Akron," popular for its special noon lunches and "much favored by after-theater parties." It was the first Chinese restaurant in Akron to offer carryout.[68]

An International City

During the Korean War and the Vietnam War, immigration patterns to the United States began to shift from Europe to Southeast Asia. By the 1970s, the IIA was mostly assisting arrivals from Vietnam, Laos, and Cambodia. Asian communities also established their own mutual aid clubs and organizations. The Indian Community Association of Greater Akron was founded in 1968, and in 1985 Akron had a Vietnamese Association and the Greater Akron Laos Association.[69] In 1995, the Laotian community opened the Wat Lao Siriwathanaram Buddhist Temple in an old Church of Latter-Day Saints near Summit Lake.[70]

Also in 1995, May Chen and three other women of Asian descent founded Asia Services in Action (ASIA Inc.) in Akron. Their goal was to create an organization dedicated to the needs of Asian Americans and Pacific Islanders in Northeast Ohio.[71] The organization now serves over 58,000 clients in Akron and Cleveland annually. ASIA Inc. provides services for children and families, aging adults, physical health, interpretation and translation, legal aid, mental health, economic development, and community engagement.[72]

In 2018, the Akron Mon Community Temple opened the Theravada Buddhist pagoda on Sherman Street. It is the only Buddhist temple in Ohio to contain authentic relics from Sri Lanka.[73] The temple is the religious center for the Mon community of University Park, the old German neighborhood once known as Goosetown. A Mon Buddhist temple is also located on Palmetto Avenue in East Akron. In June 2022, the Cleveland Buddhist Vihara and Meditation Center opened on Vernon Odom Boulevard. It is the first temple and meditation center for the region's Sri Lankan Buddhist community.[74]

Today, North Hill carries on its legacy of being a place for new Americans to start their lives in Akron. In the twenty-first century it has become the central neighborhood for several Asian communities. While some of the Italian landmarks remain, like Dontino's Restaurant, DeVitis Italian Market, and the Carovillese Club, many storefronts now house Asian grocery stores, clothing shops, and restaurants. In February 2022, the Unione Abruzzese Italian Center was sold to Bhutanese refugees to transform into an event center for the Nepali community. Former Italian Center president, Fred Strebicki called the sale "a rebirth" of the old Italian club and made note that it was once again filling a void for immigrants.[75]

Many Latin American families and individuals have also settled in the North Hill neighborhood, alongside immigrants from Asia and Africa, where they have opened groceries and restaurants. The growth of its economic center caused by the investment of the neighborhood's international communities has made North Hill the multicultural center of Akron in the early twenty-first century.[76]

Unlike much of the rest of the country, Ohio has historically had a low population of immigrants from Latin America. In 2017, only 21% of the foreign-born

Pagoda (dhatu cetiya) in the backyard of the Akron Mon Community Temple on Sherman Street, 2023.
\ Photo by Charlotte Gintert

Symbolic of the changing demographics of Akron's largest immigrant neighborhood, the former Unione Abruzzese Italian Center in North Hill was sold to Bhutanese refugees. The Royal Palace restaurant and event center now serves Akron's Nepali community. \ Photo by Charlotte Gintert, 2023

George's Tangier shortly after closing in 2020. \ Photo by Charlotte Gintert

population were Latin American, compared to 28% from Asian nations.[77] However, from 2010 to 2020 the population grew by 45.6%.[78] Many have fled instability caused by political and social unrest, seeking asylum for the safety of themselves and their loved ones. In 1998, individuals from Akron's Latino community founded Proyecto RAICES, which stands for Recognizing and Integrating Culture, Education, and Service. The organization provides services for children ages four to fourteen and their families. In addition to providing academic assistance, they also provide physical and mental health counseling. RAICES also has a strong alliance with St. Bernard Church, which conducts a weekly Sunday mass in Spanish and maintains the Our Lady of Guadalupe Committee, which brings Latin peoples together.[79]

Akron also became home to populations of immigrants and refugees from the Middle East, as conflicts from the late nineteenth century onward displaced thousands from the region. The first documented Syrian was Joseph Azar, who arrived in 1878. By 1938, more than three thousand Syrians called Akron home, and the city had multiple Syrian social, political, and athletic clubs.[80] Edward A. George, who opened the famous George's Tangier restaurant and nightclub,

An International City

was the son of a Syrian immigrant. He came to Akron in 1929 to study engineering but ended up in the music and restaurant business. He opened the Tangier in 1954 on East Exchange Street, offering Middle Eastern cuisine. After the first location burned down in 1958, he relocated it to West Market Street and over the years transformed it into a lavish entertainment center. The blue arabesque domes were landmarks of the West Hill neighborhood until 2020 when the Tangier closed and was sold to the LeBron James Family Foundation.[81]

Lebanese immigrants began arriving during the early 1900s.[82] Many have opened some of Akron's favorite eateries. The Hamad family has owned and operated numerous restaurants such as Hamad's on Main and the Rockne's on Merriman Road.[83] Norma Touma opened the beloved Sanabel Middle East Bakery on South Street in 2018.[84] The Nemer/Nemr family owns and manages multiple night spots and eateries such as Manny's Pub and Mr. Zub's.[85]

Today, Akron's Middle Eastern, Asian, and Latin American immigrants and their descendants are helping to drive the economic development of the city. They are professionals in Akron's largest industries, healthcare providers, lawyers, and community leaders. In January 2024, Shammas Malik was sworn in as Akron's 63rd mayor. The son of a Pakistani immigrant and an Irish American, Malik is the first person of color and Muslim American to serve as mayor.[86]

Akron has always been a multiethnic city. Recent years have seen an increase of immigration from Africa.[87] As Akron enters its 200th year, it continues to be a place for refugees and immigrants to start their new lives in the United States (Figure 3; Table 1). New Americans have carried Akron through its booms and struggles from the canal days to the post-Rubber Age. Akron will not have a future without the support of its new residents from Asia, Africa, Latin America, and the Middle East. As the history shows, the city is at its best when new arrivals are embraced as neighbors, for it is only together that Akron can stride into the next one hundred years.

Countries of Origin of Akron's Immigrant and Refugee Community 2010–2021

Afghanistan	Dominican Republic	Iran	Nepal	Ukraine
Bhutan	El Salvador	Iraq	Nicaragua	Uzbekistan
Burundi	Guatemala	Lebanon	Pakistan	Vietnam
Democratic Republic of Congo	Honduras	Liberia	Syria	
Cuba	India	Myanmar	Thailand	

Table 1. IIA 2018, 2019, 2020, 2021; Bayram and Mills 2021

Mayor Shammas Malik, the first person of color and Muslim American to hold the office, began his first term in January 2024. \ Photo courtesy of the City of Akron Mayor's Office

An International City

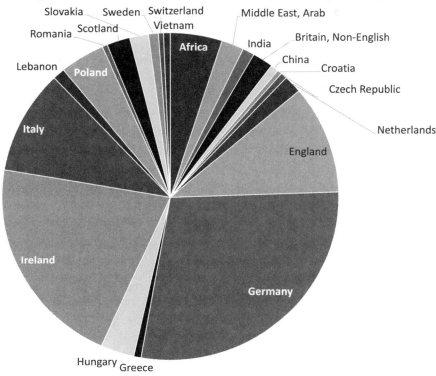

Chart showing the claimed ancestry for Akron's population born in the United States. \ (Source: United States Census Bureau, "American Community Survey," 2011–2015, https://data.census.gov/table?q=Akron+city,+Ohio)

Notes

1. Peter Way, *Common Labour: Workers and the Digging of North American Canals* (Cambridge University Press, 1993); John A. Tully, "Akron's First Proletarians," chap. 1 in *Labor in Akron, 1825–1945* (University of Akron Press, 2020); Sean Connolly, *On Every Tide: The Making and Remaking of the Irish World* (Basic Books, 2022), 19.

2. Connolly, *Every Tide*, 22.

3. Samuel A. Lane, *Fifty Years and Over of Akron and Summit County* (Beacon Job Department, 1892), 39. By the 1880s the "Little Dublin" neighborhood was full of German immigrants. "A Bit of Local Geography," *The Akron Daily Beacon*, April 7, 1888, Saturday supplement. Unless otherwise noted, newspapers are cited from digital versions through Newspapers.com.

4. Tully, *Labor in Akron*, 17; Kenneth Nichols, "History of Cascade Full of Mystery, Intrigue." *Akron Beacon Journal*, June 25, 1970.

5. Oscar Smith, "20,000 Sons of Erin Include City's Most Prominent," *Akron Beacon Journal*, July 2, 1938; Charles Buffum, "A Bit of Blarney About the Irish," *Akron Beacon Journal*, April 17, 1972.

6. Karl H. Grismer, *Akron and Summit County* (The Summit County Historical Society, 1952), 430; 711–712.

7. Catherine Anderson, "Accent On the Ethnics," *Akron Beacon Journal*, March 24, 1985, *Beacon* Sunday supplement.

8. Carl Wittke, *Refugees of Revolution: The German Forty-Eighters in America* (Philadelphia: The University of Pennsylvania Press, 1952), 161–202; National Museum of American History Behring Center. n.d. "Germans in the Midwest." Accessed May 26, 2023. https://americanhistory.si.edu/many-voices-exhibition/peopling-expanding-nation-1776%E2%80%931900/pushed-and-pulled-european-immigration-0.

9. Grismer, *Akron and Summit*, 250; Joyce Dyer, *Goosetown: Reconstructing an Akron Neighborhood* (University of Akron Press, 2010), 15–16.

10. Grismer, *Akron and Summit*, 174–176

11. Tara Zahra, *The Great Departure: Mass Migration from Eastern Europe and the Making of the Free World* (W. W. Norton & Company, 2016), 5.

12. Zahra, *Great Departure*, 71; Carl J. Bon Tempo and Hasia R. Diner, *Immigration: An American History* (Yale University Press, 2022), 122.

13. Zahra, *Great Departure*, 17.

14. Anderson, "Accent."

15. Judy Orr James, *Akron Family Recipes: History and Traditions from Sauerkraut Balls to Sweet Potato Pie* (American Palate, 2022), 143–145.

16. Grismer, *Akron and Summit*, 431.

17. Reginald Stuart, "Closings of Store and Plants Mark Decline in Akron." *New York Times*, December 10, 1978, https://www.nytimes.com/1978/12/10/archives/closings-of-store-and-plants-mark-decline-in-akron-bad-news-from.html

18. Anderson, "Accent."

19. Kenneth Nichols, "Our Gang ... Furnace Street's Past Comes to Life." *Akron Beacon Journal*, April 4, 1980; Josephine van der Grift, "Akron's Little Italy Fittingly Celebrates Night of Maria, Patron Saint of Bari," *Akron Beacon Journal*, August 7, 1922.

20. Anderson, "Accent."

21. James, *Akron Family Recipes*, 120.

22. *Akron City Directory* (NH. Burch & Co, 1871), 13.

23. James, Family Recipes, 104; Buffum, "Blarney," 25.

24. Anderson, "Accent."

25. Charlotte Gintert, "Balch Street Community Center," *The Devil Strip*, February 2021, 12, https://issuu.com/thedevilstrip/docs/feb-2021-final.

26. Anderson, "Accent."

27. Bon Tempo and Diner, *Immigration*, 46.

28. Anderson, "Accent."

29. Bon Tempo and Diner, *Immigration*, 126, 133.

30. Grismer, *Akron and Summit*, 382.

31. Erika Lee, *The Making of Asian America: A History* (New York: Simon & Schuster, 2015), 89.

32. Reece Jones, *White Borders: The History of Race and Immigration in the United States from Chinese Exclusion to the Border Wall* (Beacon Press, 2021), 77–78.

33. Jones, *White Borders*, 195.

34. Jones, *White Borders*, 78.

35. Erika Lee, *America for Americans: A History of Xenophobia in the United States* (Basic Books, 2019), 122; Jones, White Borders, 70.

36. John Lee Maples, "The Akron, Ohio Ku Klux Klan 1921–1928" (master's thesis, University of Akron, 1974), 13.

37. "Governor Closes Armory to Klan." *Akron Beacon Journal*, May 23, 1922; "Hundreds Jam Church as Court Order Halts Meeting of Klan." *Akron Beacon Journal*, May 25, 1922.

38. "One Thousand Klan Members Meet Here." *Akron Beacon Journal*, July 20, 1922; Maples, "Ku Klux Klan," 24–34.

39. "Governor Closes Armory to Klan." *Akron Beacon Journal*, May 23, 1922.

An International City

40. "Hundreds Jam Church as Court Order Halts Meeting of Klan." *Akron Beacon Journal*, May 25, 1922.

41. Maples, "Ku Klux Klan," 20.

42. "To Hold Meeting, Is Word of Klan." *Akron Beacon Journal*, May 24, 1922.

43. Maples, "Ku Klux Klan," 15–17; Embrey Bernard Howson, "The Ku Klux Klan in Ohio After World War I" (master's thesis, The Ohio State University, 1951), 21.

44. Anderson, "Accent"; Buffum, "Blarney."

45. "One Thousand Klan Members Meet Here." *Akron Beacon Journal*, July 20, 1922; Maples, "Ku Klux Klan," 24–34.

46. Lee, *Xenophobia*, 132; "Remember the Pilgrims." *Akron Beacon Journal*, February 2, 1924, News papers.com; "The Motive Back of It." *Akron Beacon Journal*, February 2, 1924.

47. Kathleen L. Endres, *Akron's "Better Half:" Women's Clubs and the Humanization of the City, 1825–1925* (University of Akron Press, 2006), 98.

48. Robert E. Batholomew and Anja E. Reumschüssel, *American Intolerance: Our Dark History of Demonizing Immigrants* (Prometheus Books, 2018), 44; Maples "Ku Klux Klan," 16–17.

49. Howson, "Ku Klux Klan in Ohio," 22; "The Motive Back of It." *Akron Beacon Journal*, February 2.

50. "Goodyearites Make Merry," *Akron Beacon Journal*, October 28, 1921.

51. Maples, "Ku Klux Klan," 36; 74; 1; 109.

52. The summary of the map includes a percentage of "foreign families" as an evaluative variable on the area descriptions. Area descriptions of grade C and D would mention immigrant presence, singling out Hungarians and Italians in particular. Home Owners Loan Corporation, Residential Security Map, Ohio State University, 1939, 6, 22–23, 27–28, 34–35, 37, 51, 53, 60, 62–63, https://guides.osu.edu/maps/redlining.

53. International Institute of Akron (IIA), "History of the International Institute of Akron," n.d., https://www.iiakron.org/history-2; Endres, *Akron's Better Half*, 174.

54. IIA, "History."

55. Endres, *Akron's Better Half*, 174–175.

56. IIA, "History."

57. Keith Spriggel, "Budget Committee Questions Fund Use in Deportation Cases," *Akron Beacon Journal*, December 6, 1950.

58. Robert H. Stopher and James S. Jackson, "Behind the Front Page." *Akron Beacon Journal*, January 1951.

59. Helen Waterhouse, "Akronite Meets Brother She Never Saw," *Akron Beacon Journal*, April 27, 1950; Helen Waterhouse, "Comes from Yugoslavia to Join Father Here," *Akron Beacon Journal*, February 2, 1951; Helen Waterhouse, "Poland Seeks News of Akron Resident," *Akron Beacon Journal*, February 16, 1960; Helen Waterhouse, "Polish Visitor Aided Here," *Akron Beacon Journal*, September 23, 1960.

60. IIA, "History."

61. Endres, *Akron's Better Half*, 174–75.

62. International Institute of Akron, "Annual Report 2021," 2021, 1, https://static1.squarespace.com/static/59244a7fe3df285163464984/t/637276c9495f2d2d48f60d04/1668445900587/IIA+2021+Annual+Report+%281%29.pdf.

63. Lee, *Asian America*, 68–108.

64. Hanna Park, "'A Sad and Glorious History': One of NYC's Last Chinese Hand Laundries Closes," October 2020, NBC News, https://www.nbcnews.com/specials/one-of-new-york-city-last-chinese-hand-laundries-closes/; Eveline Chao, "How Childhoods Spent in Chinese Laundries Tell the Story of America," January 3, 2018, https://www.atlasobscura.com/articles/chinese-laundry-kids-new-york.

65. "Fragments," *Summit County Beacon*, October 27, 1875.

66. *Akron City Directory* (Akron: N. H. Burch & Co., 1879–80), 308; "Rakings," *Akron City Times*, August 29, 1888; "Incendiarism Perhaps," *Akron City Times*, August 25, 1886.

67. William B. Baldwin, "Heathen Chinee: He Has Started Restaurant in Akron," *Beacon Journal*, July 29, 1902.

68. *Akron Official City Directory* (Burch Directory Company, 1920), 1001; *Akron Official City Directory* (Burch Directory Company, 1925), 233; "Make Specialty of All Chinese Foods," *Akron Beacon Journal*, July 21, 1925.

69. Anderson, "Accent."

70. Jim Carney, "Diversity on Rise," *Akron Beacon Journal*, July 31, 1999; *Akron Official City Directory* (Burch Directory Co., 1953), 1217.

71. Asian Services in Action (ASIA Inc.), "About," 2021, https://asiaohio.org/about/; Betty Lin-Fisher, "Lending Circles Fulfill Dreams," *Akron Beacon Journal*, February 17, 2018.

72. ASIA Inc., "About."

73. Theresa Cottom, "Akron Mon Community Celebrates New Pagoda," *Akron Beacon Journal*, August 27, 2018.

74. Alan Ashworth, "Sri Lankan Buddhists Dedicate Akron Temple," *Akron Beacon Journal*, June 27, 2022.

75. Seyma Bayram, "Former Italian Center in North Hill to Now Serve Bhutanese Immigrants," *Akron Beacon Journal*, February 15, 2022.

76. Doug Livingston, "Unwanted in Bhutan, Man Finds Belonging in America," *Akron Beacon Journal*, February 5, 2017.

77. "Immigrant Facts in Ohio," *Akron Beacon Journal*, February 5, 2017.

78. Seyma Bayram and Emily Mills, "Asian and Latino Populations See Growth in Summit," *Akron Beacon Journal*, August 15, 2021, A16.

79. Anthony Thompson, "Path to Future: Proyecto RAICES Helps Akron's Hispanic Youths," *Akron Beacon Journal*, September 21, 2022; St. Bernard Parish, stbernardakron.org.

80. Oscar Smith, "Many Akron Syrians Fled from Cruelty of Turks," *Akron Beacon Journal*, May 20, 1938.

81. Charles Lally, "Rags-to-Riches Tangier Owner Dies at 70," *Akron Beacon Journal*, December 18, 1976, A3; Charlotte Gintert, "George's Tangier," *Devil Strip*, January 2021, https://issuu.com/thedevilstrip/docs/jan-2021-final.

82. Diane Paparone, "Ethnic Communities," *Akron Beacon Journal*, June 28, 1981.

83. Katie Byard, "Rockne's Owner Dies at 59." *Akron Beacon Journal*, January 27, 2016.

84. Phil Masturzo, "Home Cooking: Sanabel Middle East Bakery Brings Authentic Lebanese Dishes to Akron," *Akron Beacon Journal*, December 15, 2021.

85. Carol Biliczky, "UA to Pay $1.8 million for Exchange Street Land," *Akron Beacon Journal*, December 3, 2008; Doug Livingston, "Sticking to Hometown Roots: Highland Square's Quirky Businesses Seek Success, Individuality Amid an Uncertain Future," *Akron Beacon Journal*, February 5, 2018.

86. Doug Livingston, "How Shammas Malik's 'Most Amazing' Mom, 'Very Dishonest' Dad Shaped Akron's Future Mayor," *Akron Beacon Journal*, May 11, 2023.

87. International Institute of Akron, "Annual Report 2021," 2021, https://static1.squarespace.com/static/59244a7fe3df285163464984/t/637276c9495f2d2d48f60d04/1668445900587/IIA+2021+Annual+Report+%281%29.pdf.

\ **6**

The Christian Churches of Akron

From the Gore to the Globe

Jane Gramlich

Tightly woven into the lives of many city residents, American churches not only provide an anchor for personal life but also contribute toward social cohesion and serve as a strong catalyst for community development. The churches of Akron have admirably fulfilled that role and have also gone much further. Powerful and significant trends took root here and flourished, eventually spreading worldwide. We can truly say that Akron stands out as a vanguard in America's larger religious story.[1]

By the time of Akron's founding, a variety of cultural influences were already set to make the city a hotbed of religious thought and action. Even within the confines of Protestant Christianity, the earliest settlers were still broadly affected by two competing religious and philosophical approaches of the early nineteenth century, the Second Great Awakening and the Enlightenment. Evidenced by the presence of a strong early Universalist Church and its effects through the years, Enlightenment and humanist ideals have played a significant role in Akron's efforts toward religious progressivism and ecumenism. But the Second Great

Awakening, with its emphasis on evangelism, spiritual fervor, and personal salvation, would prove to be the dominant force putting Akron on the world map.

Demographics and geography were an early harbinger of this trajectory. For much of the nineteenth century, Ohio was a funnel for countless people moving from New England and Pennsylvania to the western frontier and as a destination for those in the bordering southern states of Virginia, West Virginia, and Kentucky, eventually concentrating within Ohio's northeast corner, the Western Reserve. Centrally located within the Western Reserve and easily accessible by canals from the north, east, and south, early Akron was well-situated to draw residents from a wide variety of US states, Canada, and many European countries. If the Western Reserve was "a microcosm of America," as George Knepper asserted, then in the middle of that microcosm stood Akron, whose melting-pot population coalesced to a large degree in its churches.[2]

Newly arrived residents imported religious traditions as varied as the places they left behind. New England transplants came with two hundred years' worth of Calvinist doctrine and polity as well as Episcopal leanings. The first Germans brought Lutheran and Reformed faiths. The earliest Roman Catholics, Irish immigrant canal laborers, established a strong base of ethnic Catholicism that solidified and broadened over time.

Yet the 1850 US census of Akron shows one significant demographic characteristic that heavily shaped the city's religious landscape. By far, New York State was the most common place of birth for residents born outside Ohio, and the 556 New York natives outnumbered residents from the next three highest places of origin combined: Germany (233), Pennsylvania (190), and Connecticut (124).[3] Between the 1820s and 1840s, central and western New York witnessed such a strong wave of revivalism and social reform that the area became known as the "burned-over district."[4] Protestant evangelism, New York State-style, landed in Akron long before the Appalachian influences of the early twentieth century.

Easily accessible information on the city's churches, especially the earliest ones, is scanty. Primary source records and contemporary publications, if they survive, are likely scattered in a wide variety of repositories and aren't yet fully studied. Standard published histories, commemorative books, and newspaper articles are still the best sources we have. While it's necessary to read between the lines to get a sense of the religious atmosphere in early Akron, it's easy to spot the theme of division and conflict, as well as cooperation and goodwill, forging the path ahead.

During the first few decades of settlement, it was work enough to get congregations gathered and churches built. Religion's most basic impact was primarily felt in the development of the churches themselves, and especially in the role of

The Christian Churches of Akron

their leading clergy who helped shepherd the young community. Both Protestant and Catholic pastors brought a level of education and experience that would have influenced their congregations and kept them connected to the world beyond. In addition, Akron took a very active part in the larger religious and social reform movements of the era.

According to Rev. John J. Scullen, pastor of St. Vincent Church, a hundred log cabins housed the first itinerant Irish laborers who made south Akron their home while working on the Ohio and Erie Canal. For two decades, with no church building or resident priest, sporadic visits from Catholic clergy outside the area had to suffice. St. Vincent de Paul parish was established in 1837, but it was not until 1844 that a small frame building and an established pastor were available for Akron's Roman Catholics.[5] The development of the Catholic Church in Akron would remain slow for much of the rest of the nineteenth century, with just three churches in existence in 1900.[6]

The standard histories of Akron disagree on the identity of its earliest Protestant church. William Henry Perrin credited the formation of the First Methodist Episcopal Church in 1830, while Samuel Lane claimed it was "undoubtedly" the First Presbyterian Church organized in 1831. Later histories sided with Lane, except Karl Grismer, who thought it was an Episcopal congregation but didn't claim any certainty.[7] What is certain is that the 1830s witnessed a burst of new Protestant congregations, and soon after, a burst of divisions. One dispute seems comically trivial, yet illustrative of universal human nature. The contentious geography of North and South Akron led the churches to build in the neutral center known as the Gore, only to spark conflict over which way the church faced. To face north or south was anathema; west was best.[8]

Schisms erupted in the Protestant churches over more serious social and doctrinal matters as well. A rare surviving issue of the early Akron newspaper *American Balance* may be the earliest evidence we have for the existence of an Akron Anti-Slavery Society and clergy involvement in it. At a meeting on December 18, 1837, this group appointed Rev. J. B. Walker to draft resolutions and listened to an address by Rev. Thomas Graham.[9] By the mid-1840s, First Presbyterian Church split over the issue of slavery, though it later reconciled.[10] This decade also saw the phenomenon of Second Adventism, a movement growing out of the Second Great Awakening that prophesied the end of the world about 1843–1844. Followers of this teaching, known as "Millerites" after the movement's founder William Miller, caused members of the First Congregational Church to form a Second Congregational Church.[11]

The *Summit County Beacon* of the 1840s and early 1850s focused on economic, political, and legislative news, with very little reporting on town churches. During

Erected in 1835.

A drawing of the first church in Akron by Samuel Lane, from *Fifty Years and Over of Summit County* (Beacon Job Department, 1892), p. 500.

these years, the Summit County Bible Society and the Universalist Church seem to get the most press. The Bible Society was not an established church, but a branch of the American Bible Society whose primary purpose was Bible distribution. However, the group was organized in the Methodist Church, and meeting reports show the participation of "different clergy," making it a good example of the cooperative nature of Akron's denominations.[12] In 1842, the Universalist Church hosted a day-long political meeting of two opposing parties, the abolitionist Liberty Convention and a group of conservative supporters of President John Tyler. The meetings overlapped peacefully, to the astonishment of the reporter:

> The facility with which a Liberty meeting can be … amalgamated into a Tyler meeting is surprising to those who have witnessed it. — The President and Secretaries of the Liberty meeting left the stand and presto! chango! The man who not only holds blacks as slaves, but is using his best endeavors to make every white man a slave also, had a convention ready formed, to sustain him. O Consistency![13]

As a historically progressive faith with broad doctrine and members who were often politically active, the Universalists' sponsorship may have been the defining factor that allowed this meeting to unfold as it did.

Increased church activity becomes more evident throughout the years bracketing the Civil War, with the Beacon reporting on fairs, fundraisers, revivals, and indications of communication between congregations. By 1852, the Universalist Church was thriving enough to hold a concert described as a "Juvenile Cantata"

FOR THE AMERICAN BALANCE.

At a meeting of the Akron anti-Slavery Society, held at Akron, Dec. 18, 1837; the meeting was called to order by T. E. Botsford, Vice President, and opened with prayer by Rev. Thomas Graham; when on motion, J. F. Fenn, Rev. J. B. Walker and D. F. Bruner, were appointed a committee to draft Resolutions—after which a lengthy and interesting address was delivered by Rev. T. Graham.

As early as 1837, some of Akron's clergy were active in the local anti-slavery movement. \ Special Collections, Akron-Summit County Public Library.

that was open to the public. A few years later, pastors of the Methodist, Episcopal, Baptist, and Congregational churches banded together to present a series of public lectures.[14] The sacred and the secular seem to overlap in Akron during this time, perhaps out of a lack of adequate meeting space. For example, "Union Prayer Meetings" attracting different denominations were held every morning in the public Tappan Hall for a time in 1858, while St. Vincent held a benefit fair in Empire Hall in 1860. At the beginning of 1863, as the war dragged on with no signs of an end, area churches united to observe a week of prayer.[15]

As evidenced by the earlier Millerite phenomenon, Akron was always subject to larger religious trends, and in turn contributed to them. Spiritualism, another outgrowth of New York State's singular religious environment, found its way to Akron by the 1850s. Margaretta Fox and Leah Fox Fish, two of the three sisters who spearheaded the movement, visited Akron in July 1851. "Their rooms were thronged" with people seeking their metaphysical services. Not long after, *Summit Beacon* articles describe Spiritualist meetings, lectures, and even noteworthy Spiritualist occurrences in other states.[16]

Akron was also drawing the attention of out-of-towners as a place to meet. By 1860, local German Protestants were numerous enough that the German Reformed Synod, "a large ecclesiastical assembly" of one hundred ministers, held its session in Akron that year.[17] Around the same time, German-speaking Catholic immigrants also mobilized to create change. A small group asked the Catholic Diocese of Cleveland to assist them in establishing a new parish apart from English-speaking St. Vincent. The cornerstone of the new St. Bernard's Church was set the following year.[18] The formation of the city's first deliberately ethnic Catholic church highlighted the fact that St. Vincent was founded as, and still was, a predominantly Irish congregation. This dichotomy may be partly the reason why reporting of its celebration of St. Patrick's Day doesn't seem to occur before 1865.[19]

As the city emerged from the Civil War, Akron's small Black population of less than two hundred began to develop a distinct congregation. Sources conflict on their early story. Though one source mentions integration among local Methodists in 1864, separate accommodations for Black worshippers was the norm. They met in rented halls, local homes, and an abandoned school for several years. By the early 1880s, they purchased a lot on South High Street and were able to acquire four solid walls to call their own with assistance from the Ladies' Home Missionary Society and Akron businessman George W. Crouse. They were part of the African Methodist Episcopal Zion Church, a denomination formed in 1821 and eventually took the name Wesley Temple AME Zion Church in honor of Mrs. Bell Smith Wesley, who had contributed the most to its funding. The church would go on to have an integral role in its community. In addition to being the place of origin for the Akron chapter of the NAACP, many members have been active in local government, politics, and businesses.[20]

Post-Civil War Akron also saw new developments with religious underpinnings that generated significant effects beyond the city. First Methodist Episcopal Church (now First United Methodist) had long held a large, active congregation, with industrialist Lewis Miller as one of its prominent members. As supervisor of its Sunday School, Miller sought a new, pragmatic architecture for the new church building in the works that would be more useful for students and teachers. The result was the Akron Plan, a Sunday School design popular with churches all over the country throughout the nineteenth century.[21] A few years later in 1874, Miller teamed up with Bishop John Heyl Vincent to form a "Sunday School Teachers' Assembly" on Chautauqua Lake in New York State. Originally emphasizing more comprehensive Christian education through art, literature, and recreation, the assembly went on to become the Chautauqua Institution.[22]

Miller's business partner John R. Buchtel, one of the few Universalists in the city at the time, had designs of his own. By 1870, almost a half-century after its founding, Akron was ripe for a college or a theological seminary. The early church had declined over the years, and there was no longer an organized congregation. It didn't seem like the ideal place for a Universalist school, but with Buchtel's backing and significant funding, the Ohio Universalist Convention selected Akron as the location for Buchtel College. Interestingly, its founders' original goal was to provide Universalist youth with a place to receive higher education "where their religious opinions would be no cause—as was often the case

The Christian Churches of Akron

in those days—for social ostracism and unkind treatment." Eventually evolving into The University of Akron, this institution has had an immeasurable impact locally, regionally, nationally, and globally.[23]

Clergy communication and cooperation solidified in the 1870s and 1880s with the formation of the Akron Ministerial Association. Apparently in existence by 1876 as a gathering of Protestant clerics, by 1885, they resolved to amend their constitution to allow Catholic clergy as members. This was timely, for the Catholic population of Akron had increased enough that a third church, St. Mary, was established in 1887.[24] Over the next several decades, the association involved itself in countless activities, including listening to local educators, supporting radio programs, and by 1945, sponsoring the city's first interfaith Thanksgiving Day service that included Jewish clergy and congregations.[25] This organization was instrumental in bringing Akron's citizens together.

The primary social and political issues of the early twentieth century, prohibition and women's suffrage, garnered a great deal of attention from Akron's churches, especially Protestant ones. A large number of clergy continued their crusade against alcohol until Prohibition was finally enacted in 1920. At the turn of the century, the city's Prohibition Party benefitted from the talents of Akron resident and Universalist minister William Frost Crispin. Crispin never held a regular church post, preferring to devote his time to the temperance cause. He was the editor of *Solid Facts*, a local prohibition newsletter published by the party, from December 1896 until April 1900.[26] On Universalism, Crispin wrote baroquely that it "inspires the human heart with courage and fortitude to do and dare for the uplifting of the race." On Prohibition, he thundered, "it is treason to Jesus Christ and humanity not to oppose the saloon."[27] Fortitude and daring were indeed his modus operandi.

While some clergy and church members may have been openly against extending the vote to women, it is notable that the opposite was the case as well. In 1914, a debate society at St. Paul's Episcopal Church concluded the issue in the affirmative. A year earlier, the pastor of High Street Church of Christ, Rev. L. N. D. Wells, skirted his opinion on the subject by saying that he didn't believe most women wanted the vote. After the Nineteenth Amendment was passed, however, he urged them to go to the polls because it was now their duty.[28]

In addition to these momentous changes in Akron's society, the first two decades of the twentieth century also saw increased immigration, which led to a marked uptick in ethnic Roman Catholic and Orthodox Catholic congregations. In another example of civic space given over to religious and ethnic activities, the German American Hall was a popular venue for several congregations that didn't have sufficient space of their own. This included non-immigrant congregations

Akron's Prohibition Party published a newsletter called *Solid Facts*, which contained a great deal of rhetoric from its editor, Universalist minister Rev. William Frost Crispin. \ Special Collections, Akron-Summit County Public Library.

like First Church of Christ, Scientist, which met there for nearly two years, but it was a significant destination for Akron's ethnic groups. Newly arrived Serbians used it for their services, and in 1913 the Hungarian community gathered at the Hall for Independence Day, celebrating both their adopted nation and the nation of their birth.[29]

The circumstances that led to the founding of St. Bernard's Church eventually repeated themselves decades later, with one congregation forming out of another. These were "national" parishes, founded on ethnic identity and custom, separate from "territorial" parishes established by geographic boundaries.[30] Though the national parishes themselves were also separated by language and ethnicity, they found many ways to work together. Most notably, older established churches frequently shepherded new congregations. Recently arrived Polish and Slovak immigrants attending St. Bernard were restless for their own parish and church of their own. By 1907, St. John the Baptist parish had been formed. As it happened, St. Bernard was preparing to build a new church, so they sold their old building to the new parish the following year.[31] After that, it didn't take long for the Polish attendees to break off from the Slovak worshippers to form St. Hedwig parish, whose church was dedicated in 1915.[32]

For the earliest Serbians of Akron prior to World War I, "church and religious life was only a glimmer ... because the immigrants thought that their stay in America would be temporary."[33] With difficult financial circumstances, it wasn't until 1932 that St. Demetrius's Serbian Orthodox Church held a dedication ceremony for its first church building.[34] The struggle didn't end there. In 1940, a women's auxiliary, Ženska Zadruga, was credited with the funding needed to keep the church from being closed due to court receivership.[35] The church surmounted these challenges and quickly became known for the vocal musical talent of the Isidor Bajich Serbian Choir. Over the years, the nationally acclaimed choir performed for Akron residents in several venues, including Liedertafel Hall, Goodyear Theater, and the Central High School Auditorium.[36]

Similarly, the congregation of Annunciation Greek Orthodox Church overcame early difficulties to become a flourishing congregation. In a mere six years between 1912 and 1918, Akron's Greek population skyrocketed from about 150 to 2500. However, many were young unmarried men with few resources to spend on church development. In 1920, while still gathering in rented halls for services, the congregation purchased land for a future building and started a Greek school. A second Greek school, begun in 1938, benefitted from community

First Methodist Episcopal Church about 1920. Later renamed First Methodist and First United Methodist, it was one of the earliest congregations in Akron. \ Carl Pockrandt Collection, Summit County Historical Society.

St. Bernard's Catholic Church about 1930. The congregation was formed in the early 1860s by Akron's growing German population. \ Carl Pockrandt Collection, Summit County Historical Society.

The Christian Churches of Akron

collaboration when the East Akron Community House allowed the school to use its facilities rent-free. Increasingly embedded in Akron's culture, at its fiftieth anniversary Annunciation members could say that they had reached a period of "smooth sailing for our church and community."[37]

By 1925, there were several ethnic Catholic congregations, including St. Joseph Syrian, Holy Ghost Ukrainian, and St. Peter Lithuanian. Whereas there had only been three Roman Catholic churches in the city in 1900, in 1925 there were nineteen, both Roman and Orthodox. In addition, a number of ethnic Protestant churches emerged, such as German Apostolic, Scandinavian Methodist, Slovak Lutheran, Romanian Baptist, and Hungarian Reformed. Akron's Christian immigrants seem to have been well-served that year, but there was one new ethnic group on the formidable hill north of the city that had yet to establish a church.[38]

North Hill was known as a neighborhood bordering Akron as early as 1885. However, the opening of the North Hill Viaduct in 1922 firmly connected the area to downtown Akron and allowed it to mushroom. St. Martha's Catholic Church, an outgrowth of St. Vincent, first occupied its new building on Christmas Day 1923, but St. Martha's alone wasn't sufficient. North Hill's Italian community needed a national parish. Between 1910 and 1920, Akron's Italian-born population had more than quadrupled.[39] This time, St. Hedwig's predominantly Polish parishioners found themselves in the role of foster congregation. In 1922, Akron Italians ended a weekend celebration of the feast of St. Anthony of Padua with a service in St. Hedwig. As late as 1931, St. Anthony's parish was still meeting at St. Hedwig until its own church building was constructed.[40]

Despite the preference for separate places of worship, there is evidence of the national parishes' assimilation into Akron's civic life. Perhaps this was most apparent in local sports, which boasted a plethora of church leagues, both Catholic and Protestant, for baseball, basketball, and bowling. Church leagues played not only each other but also local businesses and organizations, yet again bringing the sacred and secular together. The *Akron Beacon Journal*'s sports pages are full of examples. St. Hedwig appears to have had an impressive baseball season in 1922, remaining undefeated in late May and then going on to rout the Akron Police team in June. In 1927, the Hungarian Sacred Hearts baseball team played Klein Realtors, while in 1931 they lost a basketball game to Tichenor Cleaners.[41]

Tightly layered interaction such as this may have helped pave the way for the ambitious project of St. Thomas Hospital, which was a collaborative effort across many strata of Akron's citizens and heavily promoted as such. It was significantly funded by Catholics, including Akron's department store magnate Michael O'Neil, yet it was operated by a secular board of directors and nonsectarian staff with the supervision of the Catholic Sisters of Charity of St. Augustine.

This institution represented a momentous step forward in the cooperation of Akron's Catholic, Protestant, and civic contingents. Even its cornerstone ceremony, though expected to draw a large gathering of Catholics, was presented as a nonparochial event. Located just at the doorstep of North Hill, the hospital's main entrance facing the neighborhood spoke volumes to its ethnic ethos, but its southern-facing windows over the Little Cuyahoga River valley gazed squarely at the larger city it served.[42]

Firmly settled in the United States, the ethnic Catholic congregations of Akron looked homeward with dismay. For almost the entire first half of the twentieth century, they witnessed war and political strife cripple their homelands and wreck the lives of relatives left behind. Across the board, the response was to organize support for their native countries. But in doing so, they also had a significant effect on Akron. St. Demetrius' women's auxiliary, Ženska Zadruga, was formed to aid the Serbian people after the Balkan War of 1912. Though their focus after World War I shifted to "strengthening and preserving church life in Akron," they marshalled resources again during World War II to assist the Red Cross.[43] Annunciation Greek Orthodox Church partnered with the Akron Business Men's Association in 1919 and 1922 to hold large rallies in support of Greece's people during difficult times for the nation. Held at the Akron Armory and Perkins School respectively, these events were endorsed by the Akron Ministerial Association. They also attracted well-known speakers such as Rev. Lloyd C. Douglas, pastor of First Congregational Church, and future presidential candidate Wendell Wilkie.[44]

Though early-twentieth-century Catholicism has left a rich imprint on Akron, it has also been described as "comparatively weak" next to the effects of the larger Protestant population. But this was probably primarily due to the city's unique history of attracting a hefty number of migrants from Ohio's bordering Appalachian regions to work in its flourishing rubber industry. This community, as George Knepper observed, was "overwhelmingly Protestant" and thus boosted Akron's Protestant majority. While some of these new arrivals blended in with mainline Protestant denominations, the influx happened so quickly "that there was not adequate time for the established Akron churches to absorb the newcomers." In addition, many sought to recreate the evangelical, fundamentalist, and Pentecostal congregations of the rural South they left. As Knepper wrote, "This element gave rise to more huge, independent congregations than existed perhaps in any other city, certainly any city of Akron's size."[45]

Before the larger congregations were formed, smaller ones broke ground. For some time during the 1920s and early 1930s, the evangelist team of J. Lyle Shaw, John W. Sproul, and A. B. Hobbs conducted revivals and faith-healing services at

The Christian Churches of Akron

Rev. W. D. Herrstrom and the Akron Bible Church, formerly the Tire Town Tabernacle. Independent congregations such as this, often incorporating southern and Appalachian influences, were numerous in Akron during the pre-World War II era. \ *Akron Beacon Journal* Photograph Collection, Summit Memory, Akron-Summit County Public Library.

the interdenominational Glory Barn. Prayer over the ill and infirm and anointing them with oil led to several testimonials of healing. At one point it was claimed that 7,000 Akronites "have been brought to grace by conversions" at the Barn. Yet the mission seemed to flounder, with several announcements of closings and reopenings under new leadership. Running this concern was a decidedly symbiotic effort. The name alone appealed directly to Akron's Appalachian population with its imagery of rural, back-country old-time religion. Visiting preachers included Miss Elizabeth Miller, "mountaineer evangelist," in 1926, and an assistant of Aimee Semple McPherson in 1930. Another revival meeting that year featured music by the local City Mission Mandolin Club. This group was its own interdenominational and civic attraction, providing entertainment for the local Kiwanis Club and even finding its way to the Episcopal Church in Hudson.[46] At some point in the mid-1930s, the Glory Barn closed permanently.

Another group of worshippers, the Tire Town Tabernacle, developed in a much different manner. Its existence was entirely due to the "fiery" Rev. W. D. Herrstrom, pastor of the North Akron Baptist Church, "a fundamentalist of the strictest sort." Ousted by trustees over his preaching style and church finances, he and a group of followers decided to form their own congregation on Spicer Street. Classified as "independent fundamentalist" in the *Akron Beacon Journal*, the Tire Town Tabernacle later changed its name to Akron Bible Church. On Sundays in the early 1930s, Herrstrom delivered his doctrine over the airwaves on WADC and WJW, appearing very near Rev. Dallas Billington in the Beacon's radio listings. While Billington went on to form the prominent Akron Baptist Temple, Herrstrom quit his post in 1935 to go on a nationwide speaking tour. The Akron Bible Church never quite gained steam. By 1942, with Herrstrom long gone, it was down to eighteen members. When Rev. Dean Henry arrived that year to help close the church, to his surprise, it began growing again. Henry went on to shepherd the fledgling new congregation, and it eventually became Brown Street Baptist Church.[47]

Both the Glory Barn and the Tire Town Tabernacle demonstrate the sheer fluidity of Akron's independent Protestant congregations during this time. As these congregations ebbed and flowed, the more stable mainline denominations were facing their own challenges adapting to modernity. Mirroring national trends, Akron saw rapid changes in the religious atmosphere of the 1920s. Scientific advancements gave pause for thought, and progressivism frequently clashed with conservative tenets. In the Beacon's reporting on local religion, it wasn't uncommon to see these tussle symbolically on the same page. The September 18, 1926, issue featured a column describing an upcoming sermon at First Methodist Church based on the questions of "human nature," while next to it, the Christian and Missionary Alliance Gospel Tabernacle announced an extended revival meeting and a sermon on the "Second Coming of Christ."[48]

Human nature was a subject never out of bounds for Rev. Lloyd C. Douglas, who served as pastor of First Congregational Church from 1921–1926. He had succeeded Dr. Howard S. MacAyeal, described as a "spirited community builder" with "an active interest in municipal problems."[49] Douglas reinforced First Congregational's progressive character and significantly added to it. He was a frequent speaker for local organizations such as the Social Workers Club, and he served in several public capacities including chairing a special committee formed by Akron's Mayor Rybolt to ease local unemployment.[50] His heavily advertised sermons, once they were delivered, were also frequently recorded in the Beacon's religion columns. Douglas argued, for instance, that a common imposed Sabbath day made no sense "in an urban civilization where ... so large a majority is utterly dependent on others for comforts and necessities." One evening program at the church featured discussions on topics as varied as "Will the Russo-German Alliance Seriously Postpone an Amicable Settlement of European Problems?" to "Does the Miracle at Cana Indicate That Jesus Sanctioned the Use of Wine?" In 1925, close to the end of his Akron tenure, Douglas asked frankly, "Do Americans Want Bibles in the Public Schools?"[51]

Douglas was also known for his vehement opposition to the Ku Klux Klan, whose strong presence in Akron at the time sparked unease and hot debate.

Local church reaction to the Klan was mixed. One pastor, Rev. John I. Wean of Woodland Methodist Church, had come from a "Klan church" in Niles and had no problem speaking at an Akron Klan meeting.[52] Rev. D. Emmet Snyder of the South Akron Church of Christ asserted that the Klan had strayed from its original purpose, but that purpose was needed more than ever. "If the Klan is headed for hell, its members are sending it there," he claimed, but "I for one stand ready to stop it on its downward trend and pull it back to its original plan."[53] Douglas, on the other hand, took several opportunities to denounce the Klan outright both from the pulpit and in public. Commenting on the Klan's practices, he implored, "We must not permit this sad method of presenting such causes to bring us to a disesteem of the institutions which really mean more to our welfare than any other facts in life."[54]

Despite contentious divisions during those years, in some circles, idealism and a positive outlook toward change prevailed. In 1925, Rev. George P. Atwater, rector at the Episcopal Church of Our Saviour, commented on the rich mix of religious communities in Akron: "With this diversity there is an increasing spirit of service, a civic spirit of helpfulness, a profound emphasis on righteousness, and among all enlightened people the noble spirit of religious tolerance."[55] To some degree, what Atwater was seeing was ultimately an effect of the progressive movement. The ancient concept of Christian love and charity, in an industrial, post-Enlightenment democracy, was being translated into tolerance and social service as modern Christian duties. One way Atwater lived this out was by his involvement in the Better Akron Federation, an outgrowth of Akron's War Chest.[56]

The cultural challenges of the 1920s gave way to pressing economic and political challenges during the Depression and World War II, causing many churches to refocus efforts inward. For example, the effects of the Depression were "nowhere ... more keenly felt than in highly industrial South Akron," and in response, St. Mary's Catholic Church operated a soup kitchen from its school, feeding hundreds of people in a day at the height of the downturn.[57] The need to boost morale, and perhaps nostalgia, during this difficult era was also apparent. One response by St. John the Baptist was to hold a Slovak Day, a celebration of a cherished shared culture that was conceivably already diminishing. On July 23, 1933, Slovaks throughout northeast Ohio gathered in Akron for a festival offering Mass, sermons and speeches, games, music, and folk dancing.[58]

Despite the push to preserve cultural heritage, Catholic churches were also adapting to modern society. In 1939, one initiative of Annunciation Catholic Church demonstrated greater tolerance, attention to the secular leanings of young people, and adaptation to technology. Rev. Fr. Richard Dowed, a "priest turned radio technician," discovered a high-fidelity recorder that could transmit radio programs onto transcription discs. After recording dance programs featuring popular bands on these discs, he used them to hold weekly dances for teenagers in the church's parish hall. This "guardian angel" didn't care that only about ten percent of the attending youth were Catholic. The more important objective was to get them "safe and off the streets and having a good time, in a place where their parents do not have to worry about them."[59] Dowed's ecumenical achievements caused him to be remembered as Akron's "greatest civic-minded priest."[60]

As early as 1927, the Akron Ministerial Association proposed to expand further by creating a separate cooperative group of both clergy and lay church members called the Akron Council of Churches. The plan didn't seem to catch on, perhaps waylaid by the challenges of the Depression and war years. It was revived in 1947 to supply churches "with an agency for cooperation in educational work, social service, and united worship and evangelism." Throughout the 1950s, the group created, sponsored, and participated in many local initiatives. These included broadcasting Christmas services over local radio station WAKR, bringing in a notable Presbyterian clergyman from Japan, and distributing a county-wide questionnaire to gauge residents' involvement in area churches.[61] In 1959, when the City of Akron held public hearings on a proposed downtown Civic Center, the Council was among a long list of organizations that gave input.[62]

As the stability of the postwar years turned into the social upheaval of the 1960s, Akron's churches responded in a variety of ways. Race relations and civil rights reached priority in dialogue and action. As early as 1922, the Federal Council of Churches established a "Race Relations Sunday," an annual event still in existence in which Akron's congregations took part for decades.[63] In 1945, the Akron Ministerial Association conducted a two-year-long Interracial Clinic consisting of several community studies, and this was followed by the Akron Community Audit, a study of discrimination done in 1952. Among Catholic churches, there was "no discrimination," most likely due to Catholic policy of imposed church attendance in territorial parishes based on residence. Among predominantly white Protestant churches, the study noted that there was no detectable codified policy on discrimination, but there was significant ambivalence toward Black participation. The result was de facto segregation.[64]

Akron's Black churches had expanded significantly in the decades since the founding of Wesley Temple AME Zion. As with predominantly white evangelical churches, membership was boosted by migrants from Appalachian regions in search of work in the rubber industry. One of these was George W. Suddeth, who was born in Alabama about 1870. After several years of farming, Suddeth set out for Akron, arriving by 1917. Though census records describe him as a rubber worker, his calling was clearly the church, and he built the foundation for what

Mrs. Cordia E. Wheeler leads the congregation in song at The Miracle Lighthouse Apostolic Church about 1964. Along with the white community, Akron's Black residents formed independent congregations flavored with southern and Appalachian culture.

later became one of Akron's best-known Black congregations. After his death in 1945, Robert Street Church of God found a dedicated pastor in Rev. Robert L. Fowler, who took an active part in city affairs and served for twenty-three years. His son Ronald, who as a child "had no intentions of becoming a preacher," continued his legacy. Later renamed Arlington Church of God, it reached a membership of about seven hundred and has left an indelible effect on Akron.[65]

Local Black churches mobilized their community in several ways and helped to fill in gaps left by discrimination. One example of this is the Negro Business Directory of Akron, which appeared in the late 1960s and early 1970s. The publisher was a nonprofit organization called The Christian Home. The directory included a great deal of information on Black-owned businesses, but it was also heavily focused on churches, including photos of pastors and buildings. *The Reporter*, a newspaper serving Akron's Black community, regularly published news of the churches that numbered nearly ninety by the mid-1970s. In an *Akron Beacon Journal* interview with local clergy on the rise of fundamentalism, Rev. Eugene E. Morgan of Wesley Temple AME Zion said, "We exist at the level of man's inhumanity to man. Black churches are the outgrowth of racial segregation, not of theology. And we've kept the fire in our temple."[66]

Perhaps more than any other local clergyperson during this era, Rev. Lyle Schaller had his finger on the challenges that mainline Protestant denominations faced. As director of the Regional Church Planning Office serving Cleveland and Akron, Schaller closely studied social patterns and trends affecting local churches. Exodus from the cities to suburbia had left the inner-city churches and their needs behind. Urban renewal was at questionable cost. Integration was "easier said than done."[67] In an especially prescient observation in 1961, Schaller asked:

> Can main-line Protestantism, with its traditional orientation to the middle-class, white, home-owning family, minister to the lower-class residents of low-rent housing, a majority of whom are Negroes? Can Protestantism, with its family-centered approach, reach those people who are not part of a "family" in the normal definition of the word?[68]

In 1963, Schaller and the Regional Church Planning Office produced a detailed study titled *The Church in Akron: An Interpretive Analysis*, which posited that Protestants "can plan effectively for the future of their churches only if they do so within the general framework of secular forces [and] the work of other churches."[69] This is exactly what both Protestant and Catholic local churches have done. As urban society became more complex during the late twentieth century, church involvement in area social service initiatives and organizations continued to grow. In fact, in many instances, these organizations were founded by individuals with religious motivations.

The Christian Churches of Akron

Volunteer Webster Anderson packs groceries purchased from the Akron-Canton Regional Foodbank at St. John's Christian Methodist Episcopal Church in 1990. Many of Akron's social service agencies have grown out of church initiatives and their cooperation continues today. \ Photo by Susan Kirman. *Akron Beacon Journal* Collection, Summit Memory, Akron-Summit County Public Library.

The list of these groups is long and collaboration has been the vital element. Haven of Rest began in 1941, superintended by a member of the Ellet Brethren Church. Good Neighbors began at the North Hill Methodist Church about 1958. OPEN-M was the 1969 brainchild of Rev. Bob Ralph of the Church of the Good Shepherd, and Father Sam Ciccolini established the Interval Brotherhood Home a year later. Both the Akron-Canton Regional Foodbank and ACCESS were formed in the early 1980s by individuals with strong ties to the Akron Catholic Commission. In more recent years, Heart to Heart has sought to bring "spiritual values into the workplace." Love Akron, a nonprofit organization co-founded in 1994 by pastors Mark Ford, Knute Larson, and Ron Fowler, works "to unify the colors, cultures and congregations to see greater Akron thrive" with a focus on clergy fellowship, collaborative ministries, and bridging racial divides.[70]

Perhaps one organization stands out as a culmination—though not an end—of efforts that began long ago. The Akron Area Interfaith Council, founded in 1980, has sought to foster increased goodwill among residents of all faiths while promoting "freedom of religion, equality, and understanding."[71] As an outgrowth of the Akron Council of Churches, it is also in turn an outgrowth of the Akron Ministerial Association of the 1870s and the earliest attempts at church cooperation Akron ever witnessed. There is no doubt that these organizations have become an intrinsic part of the city's life.

While these organizations wove themselves into Akron's collective consciousness, individual clergy continued to have profound effects on their congregants and their community. Though Dallas Billington, Rex Humbard, and Ernest Angley have loomed as larger-than-life figures, other, lesser-known clergy deserve credit for shaping the city's religious character. At First Congregational Church, Lloyd Douglas's successors maintained the church's progressive focus. Noble Elderkin was already well-known for his pacifism and efforts toward social reform when he arrived at the church, while Gabe Campbell and George Murphy fearlessly brought science to the pulpit.[72] Father-and-son teams like the Fowlers and Carl and David Burnham at The Chapel took small congregations and built them into arguably the most stable and successful legacies of Akron's early twentieth-century evangelism. Though not without struggle or failings, numerous contemporary local clergy continue to teach, lead, and work for the betterment of their parishioners, neighborhoods, and city.

Akron's Protestant and Catholic churches planted a bedrock foundation for much of the city's religious life. Like daub to wattle, they also helped connect the complex structures of civic life. From education and recreation to social service and even urban planning, Akron's churches and their clergy and laity influenced their community in a multitude of ways. In the 1960s, that influence was still primarily local. Yet this was set to change because of the abundance of nondenominational, independent, evangelical Protestant congregations and the dynamic personalities who led them. These forces, combined with contemporary communication technology, would soon catapult Akron's unique religious culture onto the world stage.

The Christian Churches of Akron

105

Notes

1. Due to the limited space of this anthology, this chapter is broadly illustrative of Akron's church history and selective in the number of churches discussed.

2. George W. Knepper in Harlan Hatcher, *The Western Reserve: The Story of New Connecticut in Ohio* (Kent State University Press, 1991), xii.

3. Population figures calculated by using the 1850 US census for Akron. See "1850 Census," United States Census Bureau, https://www.census.gov/library/publications/1853/dec/1850a.html.

4. Whitney R. Cross, *The Burned-Over District: The Social and Intellectual History of Enthusiastic Religion in Western New York, 1800–1850* (Cornell University Press, 1950).

5. *Story of the First One Hundred Years, 1837–1937, of St. Vincent de Paul Church, Akron, Ohio* (n.p., 1937?), not paginated.

6. *Akron Official City Directory: Supplemented by a Directory of the Villages of Barberton and Cuyahoga Falls* (Burch Directory Co., 1900), 30.

7. William Henry Perrin, ed., *History of Summit County, With an Outline Sketch of Ohio* (Baskin & Battey, 1881), 366; Samuel A. Lane, *Fifty Years and Over of Ohio and Summit County* (Beacon Job Department, 1892), 188; Karl H. Grismer, *Akron and Summit County* (Summit County Historical Society, 1952), 144.

8. Grismer, 106.

9. "For the American Balance," *American Balance*, December 28, 1837, 3. Special Collections Division, Akron-Summit County Public Library.

10. Lane, 188.

11. Lane, 605.

12. "Summit County Bible Society," *Summit Beacon*, March 19, 1845, 1.

13. "Liberty Convention and Tyler Meeting," *Summit Beacon*, September 28, 1842, 2.

14. "Flora's Festival," *Summit Beacon*, September 29, 1852, 3; "Lectures," January 16, 1856, 2.

15. "Religious," *Summit Beacon*, April 7, 1858, 3; "Fair for the Benefit of St. Vincent's Church," *Summit County Beacon*, December 13, 1860, 3; "The Week of Prayer," *Summit County Beacon*, January 1, 1863, 3.

16. "The Rapping Spirits," *Summit Beacon*, July 2, 1851, 3; February 28, 1855, 1; "Lecture on Thursday Evening," *Summit Beacon*, January 9, 1856, 3; "Spiritualism in Ellsworth, Me.," *Summit County Beacon*, April 22, 1857, 1.

17. "Synod of the German Reformed Church," *Summit County Beacon*, June 7, 1860, 3.

18. [N.a.], *Saint Bernard's Church, Akron, Ohio: Renewing our Legacy* (Tappan, New York: Custombook, ca. 1978), not paginated.

19. "St Patrick's Day," *Summit County Beacon*, March 23, 1865, 3.

20. Theodore R. Wilson, ed., *Negro Business Directory of Akron* (The Christian Home, 1971), 2; Shirla Robinson McClain, *The Contributions of Blacks in Akron 1825–1975*, PhD diss., University of Akron, 1975, 96–98; Iris Bolar, "Wesley Temple African Methodist Episcopal Zion Church," *Past Pursuits* 8, no. 1 (Spring 2009): Special Collections Division, Akron-Summit County Public Library, 5–6.

21. John Thomas McFarland and Benjamin Severance Winchester, *The Encyclopedia of Sunday Schools and Religious Education* (Thomas Nelson and Sons, 1915), 29–30.

22. Ellwood Hendrick, *Lewis Miller: A Biographical Essay* (G. P. Putnam's Sons, 1925), 167; "Chautauqua Leader to be Honored," *Akron Beacon Journal*, October 11, 1997, A10.

23. A. I. Spanton, *Fifty Years of Buchtel (1870–1920)* (n.p., 1922), 1, 4–7.

24. "The Departure of Rev. C. A. Hayden," *Summit County Beacon*, July 12, 1876, 3; "Sabbath Desecration," *Summit County Beacon*, July 29, 1885, p. 6; *Golden Jubilee, St. Mary's Parish, Akron, Ohio* (The Church, 1947), 5–6.

25. "Ministerial Association," *Akron Beacon Journal*, March 7, 1908, 6; "Plan Special Music, Talk for Broadcast," *Akron Beacon Journal*, January 25, 1930, 22; "Set Holiday Church Rites," *Akron Beacon Journal*, November 21, 1945, 13.

26. "The New Prohibition Organ," *Akron Beacon and Republican*, 15 February 1897, 1; "W. F. Crispin, Aged Foe of Liquor, Dies," *Akron Times*, 21 January 1916, 1; W. F. Crispin, ed., *Solid Facts* (bound newsletter), Special Collections, Akron-Summit County Public Library.

27. William Frost Crispin, ed., *Universalism and Problems of the Universalist Church*: Or, a Statement of Our Doctrines (Beacon Publishing Company, 1888), 11; *Solid Facts*, no. 2 (December 1896), not paginated.

28. "Young People Will Debate on Suffrage," *Akron Beacon Journal*, March 10, 1914, 9; "Women at Church Vote on Suffrage Question," *Akron Beacon Journal*, April 14, 1913, 2; "Urges Women to Vote," *Akron Beacon Journal*, October 4, 1920, 2.

29. "Akron Church Announcements," *Akron Beacon Journal*, November 13, 1915, 5; "Hungarians to Celebrate Fourth," *Akron Beacon Journal*, July 3, 1913, 3; St. Demetrius Church (Akron, Ohio), *50th Anniversary, 1919–1969: Serbian American Community, Akron, Ohio* (n.p., 1969), not paginated.

30. "Parish," *The Catholic Encyclopedia: An International Work of Reference*, vol. 11 (Robert Appleton Company, 1911), 499.

31. [N.a.], *St. John the Baptist Roman Catholic Church, Akron, Ohio* (n.p., ca. 1982), not paginated; "Old St. Bernard's Church Sold to Slavonians," *Akron Beacon Journal*, June 22, 1908, 3.

32. "Bishop to Dedicate Akron's New Church," *Akron Beacon Journal*, July 23, 1915, 10.

33. *50th Anniversary, 1919–1969: Serbian American Community, Akron, Ohio*.

34. *50th Anniversary, 1919–1969;* "Ceremony Planned at Serbian Church," *Akron Beacon Journal*, May 6, 1932, p. 34.

35. *50th Anniversary, 1919–1969*.

36. "DeLeone to Direct at Concert Sunday," *Akron Beacon Journal*, November 19, 1938, 15; "Annual Bajich Recital Today," *Akron Beacon Journal*, May 21, 1944, 8D; "Choral Festival," *Akron Beacon Journal*, May 13, 1951, 8B.

37. Greek Orthodox Church of the Annunciation (Akron, Ohio), *Fiftieth Anniversary, 1917–1967* (Akron Greek-American Community, 1967), 23–25, 30.

38. Historical Committee (Akron, Ohio), *A Centennial History of Akron* (Summit County Historical Society, 1925), 278–293; *Akron Official City Directory, Supplemented by Directories of Kenmore, Barberton, Cuyahoga Falls, etc.* (Burch Directory Company, 1925), 24–25.

39. "Local Notes," *The Summit County Beacon*, July 1, 1885, 4; "Church Closings and Mergers," *Akron Beacon Journal*, March 15, 2009, A12; population figures calculated using the 1910 and 1920 US censuses. See "1910 Census," United States Census Bureau, https://www.census.gov/library/publications/1913/dec/vol-1-population.html and "1920 Census," United States Census Bureau, https://www.census.gov/library/publications/1921/dec/vol-01-population.html.

40. "Italians Celebrate," *Akron Beacon Journal*, June 19, 1922, 12; "Directory of Church Services," *Akron Beacon Journal*, September 26, 1931, 2.

41. "Crowds Flock to See Class A Games," *Akron Beacon Journal*, May 25, 1922, 19; "Hedwigs Stop Cops," *Akron Beacon Journal*, June 19, 1922, 11; "Sunday's Games," *Akron Beacon Journal*, May 21, 1927, 16; "Tichenor Cleaners Top Sacred Hearts," *Akron Beacon Journal*, December 16, 1931, 22.

42. "A Hospital for Rich and Poor Alike! For Any Race or Creed!", *Akron Beacon Journal*, June 14, 1926, 18; "The O'Neil Gift," *Akron Beacon Journal*, June 23, 1926, 4; "Bishop to Preside as Stone is Placed," *Akron Beacon Journal*, September 22, 1927, 19.

43. St. Demetrius Church, *50th Anniversary, 1919–1969;* "Serbian Women's Group Knits for Red Cross," *Akron Beacon Journal*, January 25, 1942, 6C.

44. *Fiftieth Anniversary, 1917–1967*, 25.

45. N.a., *The Church in Akron: An Interpretive Analysis* (Published by the Regional Church Planning Office in Cooperation with the Council of Churches of Greater Akron, 1963), 13–14; George W. Knepper, *A Brief History of Religion in Northeast Ohio* (Center for Sacred Landmarks, Cleveland State University, 2002), 13–14.

46. "Signs and Wonders at the 'Glory Barn,'" *Akron Beacon Journal*, May 27, 1924, 18; "Report Healings at Tabernacle Services," *Akron Beacon Journal*, June 5, 1924, 23; "Our Seven Thousand," *Akron Beacon Journal*, July 16, 1924, 4; "Glory Barn Mission to Be Again Reopened," *Akron Beacon Journal*, March 20,

1926, 12; "Adams Conducting Revival at Mission," *Akron Beacon Journal*, April 19, 1930, 10; "Minister, Wife Plan Revival Campaign," *Akron Beacon Journal*, January 4, 1930, 2; "Club Entertained by Mission Girls," *Akron Beacon Journal*, September 26, 1930, 27; "City Mission Group Will Go To Hudson," *Akron Beacon Journal*, December 16, 1930, 25.

47. "Oust Herrstrom from Pastorate in Church Fight," *Akron Beacon Journal*, March 7, 1930, 23; "Tabernacles Will Be Built in Akron," *Akron Beacon Journal,* April 17, 1930, 11; "Directory of Church Services," *Akron Beacon Journal*, January 3, 1931, 10; "Beacon Journal Radio Time Table," *Akron Beacon Journal*, January 27, 1934, 22; "Rev. Mr. Herrstrom, Fiery, Fundamentalist, Quits Post," *Akron Beacon Journal*, April 22, 1935, 17; "Pastor Gets A-OK After 40-Year Wait," *Akron Beacon Journal*, July 12, 1982, A1.

48. "Human Nature Basis for Sunday Sermon," "New York Minister to Conduct Revival," *Akron Beacon Journal*, September 18, 1926, 12.

49. "Dr. MacAyeal, Former Akron Minister, Dies," *Akron Beacon Journal*, May 19, 1946, 11-A.

50. "Social Events," *Akron Beacon Journal*, November 15, 1921, 6; "Mayor Adds New Members to Aid the Unemployed," *Akron Beacon Journal*, January 18, 1922, 1.

51."Says Blue Laws Not Applicable to Modern Life," *Akron Beacon Journal*, February 2, 1925, 5; "First Congregational Church," *Akron Beacon Journal*, April 22, 1922, 5; "Do Americans Want Bibles in the Public Schools," *Akron Beacon Journal*, February 7, 1925. 5.

52. "Rev. Mr. Lewis is Ordered to Steubenville," *Akron Beacon Journal*, September 25, 1928, 1; "M. E. Pastor to Make Address at Service," *Akron Beacon Journal*, March 14, 1925, 8.

53. "Asserts America Needs Klan More Than Ever Before," *Akron Beacon Journal*, August 10, 1925, 15.

54. "Scores Forcing of Bible Upon Public Schools," *Akron Beacon Journal*, February 9, 1925, 9.

55. *A Centennial History of Akron*, 281.

56. Ethan J. Larrick, comp., *A Brief History of the Better Akron Federation* (unpublished typescript, Special Collections Division, Akron-Summit County Public Library, 1936), 2.

57. *Golden Jubilee, St. Mary's Parish, Akron, Ohio* (Akron, Ohio: The Church, 1947), 17.

58. *St. John the Baptist Roman Catholic Church, Akron, Ohio.*

59. "Priest Gets an Idea, and Younger Generation Benefits," *Akron Beacon Journal*, November 12, 1939, 4A.

60. Murray Powers, *History of the Catholic Church in Summit County From Origin to '76*, (n.p., 1976), 31.

61. "Start Organization of Church Council," *Akron Beacon Journal*, July 2, 1927, 18; "Four More Organizations Vote to Join in Forming Akron Council of Churches," *Akron Beacon Journal*, January 18, 1947, 9; "Here's Schedule of Yule Church Services," *Akron Beacon Journal*, December 23, 1953, 15; "Toyohiko Kagawa, Noted Japanese, to Preach Here," *Akron Beacon Journal*, September 11, 1954, 4; "Religious Census Card," *Akron Beacon Journal*, January 16, 1955, 9.

62. Akron Chamber of Commerce, *Civic Center Project Public Hearings* (unpublished typescript, Special Collections Division, Akron-Summit County Public Library, 1959), 5.

63. The Martin Luther King Jr. Research and Education Institute, Stanford University, "National Council of the Churches of Christ in America (NCC)," https://kinginstitute.stanford.edu/encyclopedia/national-council-churches-christ-america-ncc, accessed April 1, 2023; "To Observe 'Race Relations Sunday,'" *Akron Beacon Journal*, February 5, 1924, 13.

64.Akron Committee for a Community Audit, *The Akron Community Audit: A Study of Discrimination in the City of Akron, Ohio, 1952* (Special Collections Division, Akron-Summit County Public Library), https://archive.org/details/the-akron-community-audit.

65. United States Federal Census records 1880–1940 for George Suddeth, United States Census Bureau, census.gov; *Akron Official City Directory, 1917* (Burch Directory Company), vol. 2, 1734; "Rev. George Suddeth," (obituary), *Akron Beacon Journal*, January 5, 1945, 21; "Rev. Fowler is Speaker for EACH," *Akron Beacon Journal*, February 17, 1961, 16; "For One Minister's Son, the Label Was Far from True," *Akron Beacon Journal*, December 15, 1980, A7; "Akron School Board Race Draws Six for Two Seats," *Akron Beacon Journal*, October 29, 1987, D11.

66. Wilson, ed., *Negro Business Directory of Akron*, 1969, 1971, 1973–74; *The Reporter*, December 21–28, 1974, 14; "Clergymen See Move Toward Fundamentalism," *Akron Beacon Journal*, October 2, 1971, A7.

67. Lyle E. Schaller, "The Cost of Urban Renewal," *Church Management* XXXVII, no. 12 (September 1961), "Integration: Easier Said Than Done?" *Church Management* XXXVIII, no. 4 (January 1962), both reprinted in Regional Church Planning Office, *Annual Report*, 1961 (Special Collections Division, Akron-Summit County Public Library).

68. Schaller, "The Cost of Urban Renewal."

69. *The Church in Akron*, 13.

70. "'Haven of Rest,' New Mission, To Be Opened Downtown Soon," *Akron Beacon Journal*, August 2, 1941, 4; "Akron Good Neighbors Club Just That," *Akron Beacon Journal*, November 8, 1958, 7; "Rev. Bob Ralph Dies at 50; Founded Inner-City Project," *Akron Beacon Journal*, April 12, 1978, B4; "Shifts from Monks to Former Drunks," *Akron Beacon Journal*, May 20, 1971, D1; "Out of Hunger Scandal, Food Bank is Born," *Akron Beacon Journal*, July 23, 1982, D1; "Forum to Focus on Homeless Women," *Akron Beacon Journal*, August 28, 1984, C3; "Bottom Line of Ethics is Respect, Says Banker," *Akron Beacon Journal*, April 27, 1994, D1; Love Akron, "About Us," https://www.loveakron.org/about-us, accessed April 1, 2023, "Pastor to Exit Love Akron," *Akron Beacon Journal*, October 3, 2018, A1.

71. Akron Area Interfaith Council, https://www.akroninterfaith.org/#, "History and Vision," https://www.akroninterfaith.org/history-vision/; accessed April 1, 2023.

72. M. Zlonis, "Noble Elderkin Comes to Pilgrim Church," 17, accessed from https://www.pilgrim duluth.org/history April 1, 2023; "Again, Where Did We Come From?," *Akron Beacon Journal*, July 18, 1986, B1; "Former Pastor Let Others Know They Mattered," *Akron Beacon Journal*, February 3, 2012, B1.

\ **7**

Akron's Servants, 1900 to 1940

Christi Blythin

When considering the people who shaped Akron's history, the famous rubber barons and other wealthy capitalists are likely the first people who come to mind. They are the ones who have local streets and buildings named after them, books written about them, and their personal papers preserved as historically significant documents. Yet there were other, uncelebrated Akronites who also supported the city's growth in important ways, though their contributions were much less visible. The people employed as domestic workers are one of the unsung populations who helped build the city through the strenuous and necessary work they performed in people's homes.

Servants lived their lives largely out of public view, as their duties included being noticed as little as possible. This invisibility is reflected by their infrequent appearances in historical records.[1] Most of what we know about servant life comes not from the workers themselves but rather from the records of the wealthy people who employed them.[2] Domestic workers have left behind few personal records, perhaps because they didn't have the education and leisure necessary for writing or the money to buy stationery supplies. Servants also tended to move frequently, pursuing higher pay or a better situation,[3] and the lack of permanent addresses makes them very difficult to trace in historical records. Yet we can still learn something about Akron servants' lives by searching for mentions of them in the preserved papers of their employers, reading old newspapers, and touring what remains of their living and working quarters in historic homes.

It's easy to imagine uniformed maids bustling around a mansion like Stan Hywet, but into the early 1900s, even more modest homes in Akron relied on the assistance of servants due to the physically demanding nature of housework at the time. As one 1911 *Akron Beacon Journal* article noted, "Women need help in the typical city houses which have kitchen and laundry in the basement and three stories above, making almost literally a house on end."[4] Technological innovations such as washing machines, gas stoves, and electric carpet sweepers were starting to make housework easier, but it was still very difficult for one person to do everything necessary to keep a house in order. Families who were able to employ live-in servants typically kept just one or two general maids to assist with the housework and cooking,[5] but most households that could afford help employed live-out workers who could be hired for full- or part-time work. Those who could not afford or secure regular help could still hire occasional temporary help or outsource specific tasks, such as laundry. Looking at US Census data can give us a sense of how many people were working as servants in Akron at a given time:[6]

As the numbers show, while there were always more women than men working as servants, the percentage of women working as servants compared to other occupations was also significantly higher. In other words, male servants made up a tiny percentage of men who were working, whereas women who worked were

Year	Men working as servants in Akron	Women working as servants in Akron	Total men working in Akron	Total women working in Akron	Total dwellings in Akron
1900[7]	82	650	13,864	3,393	8649
1910[8]	129	728	26, 297	6,090	15,851
1920[9]	664	1340	92,082	16,021	44,195
1930[10]	88 (58 servants, 30 cooks)	2555 (2423 servants, 132 cooks)	82,574	23,826	61,174 (31,707 owned nonfarm, 29,467 rented nonfarm)
1940[11]	106	2,734	77,184	26,307	57,898

more likely to be employed as servants. For instance, in 1900, about 19 percent of working women were servants, and even in 1940, servants still made up about 10 percent of the female workforce. Note that early census reports counted working people as those "10 years of age and older," so a number of the people working as servants in Akron were children. The 1920 census even published a volume on "Children in Gainful Occupations," which included data on employed children ages 10–15.[12] According to the data, 4,123 children worked as servants in Ohio in 1910, but by 1920, this number had dropped to 1,410, likely due to the implementation of tougher child labor laws and extended compulsory schooling.[13]

Including the number of dwellings in Akron for each year gives a sense of how many households there were compared to the number of people working as domestic servants. For instance, in 1900, approximately 732 people worked as servants, while there were 8649 dwellings, which suggests that roughly 8 percent of Akronites employed servants. (This estimate does not account for households that employed multiple servants or for domestics who worked for multiple households.) By 1940, that percentage slipped to about 4 percent. Although these estimates don't give us specific information about where domestic workers were employed, they do suggest that the majority of Akron homes did not have servants, likely because many of those living in the boomtown city had moved there to find work in the factories.[14]

While most people who had domestic help had to make do with one or two general maids, Akron's wealthiest families had their housework done by a mostly female staff of full-time, specialized workers. Maids trained in specific duties were needed to do various kinds of housework and assist the women of the family, and nurses or nannies cared for the children. Laundresses took care of the heavy work of washing and ironing the family's clothing and linens. Cooks oversaw the preparation of all the meals, often with separate menus for family and staff, and were also expected to produce fancier fare when the family entertained. Putting meals on the table was much more difficult to orchestrate in the days before innovations such as home refrigerators and freezers, hot and cold running water from the tap, gas ovens with temperature controls, and well-stocked supermarkets cut down on time spent in the kitchen.[15] While women servants handled the indoor work, the outdoor work was done by men who served as chauffeurs, coachmen, gardeners, and general handymen. Indoor male servants, such as butlers, footmen, and chefs, were found only in the wealthiest, showiest homes as they performed work light enough for women to handle but required higher salaries to do so, thus making them more of a luxury service.[16]

Domestic workers tended to be European immigrants or African Americans, as few native white Americans were willing to take on what was seen as a position of subservience in another person's house.[17] The title of "servant" itself, with its seemingly un-American implications of subordination and required deference to the employer, was enough to deter many people from entering domestic service even if they didn't mind the work.[18] Moreover, the pay was very low: in 1872, Akron servants made around $2.00 a week, which was considered a "scanty sum" even back then,[19] but by 1935, some housemaids still earned only $2.00–$4.00 per week.[20]

Despite these disadvantages, immigrants and Black people often took on domestic work because, due to discrimination, they had few other options for employment in Akron; this was especially true for women workers.[21] Many were unable to read or write, and some newer immigrants could barely speak English.[22] Another reason people turned to domestic work was that no special training was required to become a servant, even for people advertising themselves as cooks. However, cultural differences made it difficult for some workers to understand what was expected of them.[23] Employers were often unpleasantly surprised when their new cook had no idea how to make breakfast or their just-hired maid had never seen, let alone cleaned, a carpet.

Before World War I, it was common for servants to live in their employer's home as domestic help was wanted almost around the clock.[24] With few labor-saving devices available, the basic work of keeping a house in order took much longer and required a lot more physical effort than it does today. Servants typically worked twelve to sixteen hours a day for six to seven days a week, with duties that started before sunrise and ended only once the family was settled for the evening. Even then, live-in servants were expected to be on call.[25] Domestic workers were supposed to receive scheduled breaks for meals and rest during their long days, as well as regular days and afternoons off, but a common complaint among servants was that employers did not respect their free time.[26] Servants could even be summoned to cook and serve during the night: one former maid told the *Akron Beacon Journal* that the reason she had left service was she disliked being roused "out of bed at night to whip up a lunch for unexpected company."[27]

Living in the employer's house also meant that servants did not get to choose their own food or lodgings, and the quality of both varied widely. Some employers made sure that their domestic workers were well-fed with hearty, nourishing food appropriate for the physically demanding work required of them. Other employers skimped on their workers' food, giving them essentially table scraps of the family meals or inadequate portions of simpler fare.[28] One maid complained to an *Akron Beacon Journal* columnist that she received only a tin of sardines and some crackers for her lunch after a morning of heavy scrubbing and washing.[29]

Akron's Servants, 1900 to 1940

Lodging for live-in domestic employees ranged from simple, comfortable rooms to makeshift spaces unfit for habitation. Servant quarters were frequently located in a house's attic with minimal insulation and poor air circulation, making the bedrooms stifling in the summer and freezing in the winter.[30] The rooms tended to be furnished with castoffs from the family that were broken, worn-out, or otherwise unappealing. Even in the most opulent houses, there was no thoughtful decor in servant areas to make the spaces inviting. In surviving historic mansions, it is easy to tell where the servants lived and worked, as the spartan surroundings make a sharp visual contrast to the sumptuous rooms inhabited by the family. However, due to the population boom in Akron between 1900 and 1925, housing was scarce—particularly safe, clean housing suitable for a young woman living alone—so domestic workers might have been grateful to have a room at all.[31]

Living under the employer's roof also meant living by their rules, so domestic workers had very little autonomy, even in their free time. Employers dictated whether a maid could have visitors, what she was allowed to eat and drink, what she wore, whether she attended church, when she could leave the house, if she could smoke, and what time she had to be home when she was permitted to go out.[32] Some of these rules were motivated by the employers' genuine, if self-interested, desire to protect what was seen as an unfortunate class of people, particularly when the domestic worker was a vulnerable young woman living away from her family.[33] As Kathleen Endres discusses in her history of Akron women's clubs, it was common for affluent women to impose their own traditions and values onto working-class women as part of their charitable work.[34] However, the rules for domestics were mostly implemented to benefit the employers: as one *Akron Beacon Journal* article noted, many employers expected a servant "to live in a cage, have little or no personal life, be absolutely sexless if possible, and simply curl up and sleep when not called upon to serve."[35]

These objectionable working conditions made it difficult to attract people to service, leading to a demand for domestic workers that far outstripped the number of people willing to do the work. In 1907, Fannie Steizerwald, who worked as a maid at an Adolph Avenue home, attempted to end her life rather than continue working in service: the *Beacon Journal* reported that after Steizerwald's fiancé postponed their wedding, she swallowed carbolic acid because she "was tired of doing housework" and dreaded "another winter's work."[36] While domestic work was unappealing in its own right, factories were also luring young women away from service. This was especially a problem in a growing town like Akron, where new factories were opening all the time, and the abundance of lucrative jobs made service even less attractive.[37] The ensuing lack of available, competent domestic workers was known as "the servant problem," which had been a problem for as long as anyone could remember.[38] Nevertheless, the news media frequently addressed this topic as different groups tried to find a permanent solution to the shortage of domestic workers.

In 1903, *Harper's Bazar* published an article titled "The Factory Girl and Domestic Service" that explored why fewer and fewer women were willing to work as maids and cooks.[39] When asked why they preferred dirty, monotonous factory work to the relative coziness of housework, almost three-fourths of the respondents said it was because working in a factory offered more freedom than being in service.[40] While the base pay was about the same, factory women enjoyed having regular and predictable working hours (and overtime pay for extra hours), uninterrupted time off, and privacy in their lives away from work.[41] They also preferred the treatment they received in factories.[42] It is telling that one of the most frequent tips given for attracting and retaining domestic help was to "make the 'hired girl' feel that she was at least human."[43]

As people became more desperate for increasingly scarce household help, various organizations attempted to solve "the servant problem" by trying to rebrand and retool domestic service to make it more attractive. One approach established service schools to professionalize and standardize domestic work, thus giving it "the dignity of a calling."[44] In March of 1937, the Akron YWCA announced its first class of graduates from their new school for domestic workers.[45] The project was greeted with enthusiasm by the community, but the school was ultimately unsuccessful.[46]

Unions were also proposed as a way to ensure better working conditions for servants. Pockets of domestic workers across the country attempted to organize to bargain for minimum standards in their working conditions. Their demands typically included a competitive minimum wage, an eight- or nine-hour maximum workday, overtime pay for extra hours, a full day off each week, reasonable portions for meals, and a proper bedroom.[47] However, unlike factory employees working in a central location, domestic workers were too isolated from each other to form strong unions.[48] In 1903, union representatives tried to organize Akron domestic workers, but the attempt failed, ostensibly because local servants were happy with their work conditions and pay.[49] Domestic workers in Akron tried to organize again in the 1930s[50] while also pushing for a national code of workplace and wage standards similar to those being implemented with the National Recovery Act, part of Franklin D. Roosevelt's New Deal program.[51] (While domestic work was not included in the National Recovery Act, Eleanor Roosevelt nevertheless encouraged domestic employers to abide by its principles, as many had been taking advantage of the widespread unemployment and desperation caused by the Depression to "use sweatshop methods in the home.")[52] However, household employers vehemently resisted any attempts to regulate the work done and wages paid in their private homes[53] and claimed that Akron servants were "satisfied" with the going rate of $3.00 per sixty-hour work week for live-in workers and $5.00 a week for live-out workers.[54]

Yet the domestic employees' supposed satisfaction with their position was rooted in "the servant problem" itself: because so few people were willing to work as servants, good domestics had some leverage with employers who did not want to lose them. But this leverage was limited. With no union, servants had almost no workplace protections and were at the mercy of their employers for fair treatment. If an employer withheld wages, reneged on agreed time off, or even abused a servant, the servant had almost no recourse against the employer, especially if the employer was an important person in the community.[55] Domestic workers were also especially vulnerable to sexual harassment and assault: if a servant was assaulted by her employer's husband or son and chose to report the incident, it would be her word against the man's, and she would likely be fired regardless.[56] For this reason, some domestic workers protected themselves by refusing to work in homes where men were present.[57] Otherwise, the only other way a servant could improve their situation was to leave it, often without warning. Many of them did, causing employers to complain about their general fickleness and unreliability.[58]

The "servant problem" was not as much of a problem for the wealthiest households, which could always offer higher wages and better accommodations than their more modestly situated neighbors.[59] These advantages in pay and working conditions were important incentives because Akron's most massive homes, such as the Seiberlings' Stan Hywet and the Firestones' Harbel Manor, could not have functioned in even the most basic ways without a team of domestic workers behind the scenes. Yet even families with seemingly unlimited resources were inconvenienced by "the servant problem" from time to time. In 1942, F. A. Seiberling wrote to his adult daughter, Irene, about the shortage of servants due to World War II: "We are all having our domestic troubles these days, so you are only sharing the common experience of housewives generally. Ordinarily we have four women helpers in the house but last week for one day we got down to one."[60] To attract domestic workers to Stan Hywet over other avenues of employment, the Seiberlings offered not only competitive pay but also enticing workplace amenities, such as a screened porch for the workers' private use, labor-saving devices to make their work easier, and comfortable bedrooms with views of the grounds.[61]

But no amount of workplace perks would outweigh an employer's poor treatment of a domestic servant, particularly in a city bursting with other job opportunities. It is thus unsurprising that Akron's most prominent families appear

Carrie Ray, a servant who worked for the Hower family. Photo from the personal album of Grace Hower Crawford, circa 1908. \ Hower Family Papers, Series VII-4 (formerly box G4). Hower House Museum via University of Akron Archives and Special Collections, University Libraries, The University of Akron

to have treated their servants very well, if somewhat paternalistically. Perhaps the working-class roots of the city's rubber barons and their fellow capitalists instilled in them more empathy for working people. In any case, numerous anecdotes demonstrate the good relationships between Akron's wealthiest citizens and their domestic workers.

Akron's Servants, 1900 to 1940

For example, the Howers had a special personal relationship with their cook, Valinda Hurley, that lasted well beyond her employment with them. The Hower family also did not hesitate to pitch in when there was more work around the house than their domestics could handle.[62] Similarly, Katharine Knight, first wife of John S. Knight, wrote in her diary about cleaning bathrooms alongside her maids and noted her appreciation for them: "I am certainly lucky with those two nice girls."[63] Harvey Firestone's private chauffeur, Harry Linden, must have been very well treated as he worked for the family for fifty years,[64] and he was rumored to wear silk shirts that were better quality than those worn by his employer.[65] George T. Perkins, son of Simon Perkins, rewarded loyalty in his domestic employees as well: after his death in 1910, his will stipulated that each servant would receive $100 for every year they'd served the Perkins family.[66]

Yet even the families with the best reputations had their moments of treating servants poorly. In a 1938 letter to Willard Seiberling, his wife, Mary, complained about matriarch Gertrude Seiberling's treatment of the family's domestic workers:

> Of course no matter how hard they try the cook and the maids just can't please Mother. She criticizes continually & gets up & takes service dishes back to the kitchen to show them they are al wrong, etc., etc., etc. Well a week ago, Bertha the cook told me she was going to stick it out as long as she could but she didn't think she would last all summer. When she worked at Firestones she almost had a nervous breakdown and had to stop working for a year & up here the nerve strain was so terrible she was getting in just the same state – so nervous & heart pounding etc. I tried to calm her down told her mother was not well and old & her criticism didn't mean anything & not to let it get her down.[67]

High-profile employers who demanded perfection in their domestic workers undoubtedly contributed to "the servant problem" in their own massive homes, but less affluent households were just as likely to mistreat their maids and cooks. Several advice columns counseled housewives to simply be kinder to their domestic workers to keep them around. "You no longer can buy all of a woman's waking hours for the small sum you once could," one *Beacon Journal* article cautioned.[68] Without financial resources that would allow them to pay top dollar to domestic workers, families in need of domestic help had to turn to other solutions for getting their housework done.

One approach was to hire hourly day workers instead of employing live-in servants. Women's advice columns began offering tips and sample schedules for getting by with only eight or nine hours of domestic help. For instance, in an *Akron Evening Times* article, a woman confided that she had begun cooking the family breakfast herself as a way of shortening her maid's workday.[69]

For those Akronites who could not get even hourly help, a slew of products were advertised as being the solution to "the servant problem." These included washing machines powered by Ohio Edison electricity (the "electrical servant"),[70] Marmola prescription diet pills (lose weight and gain the energy to do your own housework),[71] and even Shredded Wheat: "There's no servant problem in the home where Shredded Wheat is known."[72] Others looked to updated home designs with more efficient layouts, thus eliminating the need for household assistance.[73] Technology, including robots, was also touted as the answer. In 1928, Westinghouse Electric took its famous "electrical man" robot, Mr. Televox, to the Goodyear plant to demonstrate how robots could one day replace servants.[74]

As it turns out, the people who imagined that a human-like robot would solve "the servant problem" were not far off. After World War II, the number of women working as domestics decreased by half, and new labor laws, along with the implementation of Social Security for domestic workers in 1951, made it more complicated to employ people in the home.[75] Accordingly, by 1965, the *Mary Worth* comic strip joked about how the servant problem had turned into "the service problem" since it was difficult to find technicians to repair all the new devices in our "push-button homes."[76]

Today, most American homes rely on technology to do the work that used to require live-in servants, from dishwashers and clothes dryers to robotic vacuum cleaners and camera doorbells. But before these automated devices, human beings were hired to do the physically and psychologically grueling work that kept Akron's homes clean and comfortable. Akron's domestic workers have not left behind many records of their own, but it is nevertheless important to acknowledge their contributions to the city's history alongside those of the better-known families they served. Without domestic workers, the historic mansions we still admire today could not have functioned, and even more modest houses would have collapsed under the sheer amount of labor required to maintain basic cleanliness. Domestic workers supported Akron's homes, and their story is a crucial component of Akron's history.

Notes

1. Elizabeth L. O'Leary, *At Beck and Call: The Representation of Domestic Servants in Nineteenth–Century American Painting* (Smithsonian Institution Press, 1996), 166–67.

2. Faye Dudden, *Serving Women: Household Service in Nineteenth-Century America* (Wesleyan University Press, 1983), 8.

3. Dudden, 51–53.

4. "With the Up-To-Date Akron Housekeeper," *Akron Beacon Journal,* November 27, 1911. Unless otherwise noted, newspapers are cited from digital versions through Newspapers.com.

Akron's Servants, 1900 to 1940

5. Daniel E. Sutherland, *Americans and Their Servants: Domestic Service in the United States from 1800–1920* (Louisiana State University Press, 1981), 10; David M. Katzman, *Seven Days A Week: Women and Domestic Service in Industrializing America* (University of Illinois Press, 1981), 117.

6. However, it must be considered that the census data is not a perfect representation of who was working from year to year, especially as domestic work was difficult to categorize and track. For example, in the 1910 data, it's not clear whether domestic cooks were included in the tally of people categorized as servants as they are not mentioned, whereas they are specifically included in 1920, and by 1930, they have a separate category. These numbers also may or may not include laundresses and other live-out domestic workers, depending on how they were categorized in a given census year.

7. US Census Bureau. 1900 Census Special Reports: Occupations at the Twelfth Census. Principal Cities, Table 42. 1904. Census.gov. And: 1900 Census, Volume II: Population, Part 2. Table 104. 1902. Census.gov.

8. US Census Bureau. 1910 Census Volume IV: Population, Occupation Statistics. Table IV. 1904. Census.gov. And: 1910 Census Volume 1: Population, General Report and Analysis, Chapter XIV, Table 15. 1913. Census.gov.

9. US Census Bureau. 1920 Census, Volume 4: Population, Occupations. Table 19. 1923. Census.gov. And: 1920 Census Monograph 2: Mortgages on Homes. Table 24. 1923. Census.gov.

10. US Census Bureau. 1930 Census, Volume 4: Occupations, by States. Table 1. 1933. Census.gov. And: 1930 Census, Volume 6: Families: Reports by States. Table 7. 1933. Census.gov.

11. US Census Bureau. 1940 Census of Population. Volume 3: The Labor Force. Table 11. 1943. And: 1940 Census of Housing, Volume I. Table 4. 1943. Census.gov.

12. US Census Bureau. "Detailed Occupation of Employed Persons (Except on Public Emergency Work), by Sex, for the State, and for Cities of 100,000 or More: 1940." Table 11.

13. US Census Bureau. 1920 Census: Children in Gainful Occupations. Table LVIII. 1924. Census.gov; Linda Martin and Kerry Segrave, *The Servant Problem: Domestic Workers in North America.* (McFarland, 1985), vi.

14. In *Labor in Akron, 1825–1945* (University of Akron Press, 2020), John Tully discusses why large numbers of European immigrants and poor Southerners migrated to Akron in search of work. See especially chapter 10, "Labor in a Boomtown."

15. For more on what Akron cooking was like in the days of wood- or coal-burning stoves, water collected by cisterns, and iceboxes, see Jon Miller's introduction to *Recipes by Ladies of St. Paul's Church* by Harriet Angel (University of Akron Press, 2009). The recipes themselves likewise give us an idea of what people in Akron were eating at home in the late 1880s, regardless of whether the meals were cooked by servants or housewives. Compare these dishes to those that appear in *Glenna Snow's Cook Book: Home Tested Recipes by Beacon Journal Readers* (University of Akron Press, 2010), featuring Akron recipes during the 1930s and 1940s, to get a sense of how cooking methods and materials changed over the years. In his introduction to the Snow cookbook, Kevin Kern emphasizes how the influences of immigration, the Great Depression, and World War II shaped cuisine in Akron, and he notes how instructions in the recipes reflect the then-emerging technologies of home refrigeration, access to freezers, and electric appliances.

16. O'Leary, 175–177.

17. Katzman, 44; O'Leary, 164–5.

18. Katzman, 238–241.

19. *Akron Daily Beacon*, October 24, 1872; qtd. in Tully, 31.

20. "Loses Faith in New Deal," *Akron Beacon Journal*, January 31, 1935.

21. There were similar restrictions and "glass ceilings" in factory work for women and Black people in Akron. For instance, see chapter 11, "A War Brings Progress," in *Wheels of Fortune: The Story of Rubber in Akron* by Steve Love and David Giffels (University of Akron Press, 1999).

22. Dudden, 222–223.

23. Dudden, 66–7; Sutherland, 36, 64.

24. Katzman, 48–49, 95.

25. For instance, in 1936, a former maid wrote a letter to the editor of the *Beacon Journal* and enumerated the reasons she would no longer do domestic work, and one of her chief complaints was the hours she'd had to put in: "I worked 15 to 18 hours a day and was told I must remain awake at night in order to answer all telephone calls." *Akron Beacon Journal*, October 2, 1936.

26. Sutherland, 94–100; Dudden, 179–180.

27. French, Betty. "Maid vs. Mistress: Labor Unrest in Kitchen Finds Both Sides Complaining." *Akron Beacon Journal*, February 3, 1946.

28. Dudden, 195–6; Katzman, 108–10; Sutherland, 113–14.

29. French, 15.

30. Katzman, 108–9; Dudden, 196; Sutherland, 114–17.

31. Kathleen Endres, *Akron's "Better Half": Women's Clubs and the Humanization of the City, 1825–1925* (University of Akron Press, 2006), 93; 96; 147. For more information on the housing crisis in Akron through the 1920s, see also John Tully's *Labor in Akron*, especially chapter 10, "Labor in a Boomtown."

32. Katzman, 113–17; Dudden, 195–203.

33. Sutherland, 138–39; 27–28; O'Leary, 163–166.

34. Endres, 131; 165.

35. Harris, Sydney J. "'Servant Problem' to Get Worse." *Akron Beacon Journal*, December 2, 1961,

36. "Takes Poison Because of Postponement of Wedding." *Akron Beacon Journal*, November 5, 1907,

37. "Servant Girls' Union: Effort to Organize Here Has Failed." *Summit County Beacon*, May 14,1903; Katzman, 223–224.

38. Sutherland, 6–7.

39. Ida Jackson, "The Factory Girl and Domestic Service." *Harper's Bazar*, October 1903, 953–957.

40. Jackson, 954.

41. Jackson, 954–957.

42. Gwendolyn Wright, "The 'Servant' Problem." *Akron Evening Times*, March 7, 1914.

43. Ann B. Miller, "How Do You Treat Your 'Hired' Girl?," *Akron Beacon Journal*, June 13, 1913,

44. "Would Have College Women Work as Cooks," *Akron Evening Times*, March 14, 1914.

45. Helen Waterhouse, "Girls Who Know How to Make Bed, Feed Baby, Sweep, Answer Phone, Graduate from Domestic Help School," *Akron Beacon Journal*, March 23, 1937.

46. Kathleen Endres has discussed a similar domestic school that was founded by the Woman's Benevolent Association in 1889. The WBA's school was operated as a charitable institution and aimed to teach low-income women the basics of cooking and housekeeping in order to help them improve their home lives. However, as Endres notes, this schooling also meant "that these young women would be well trained for domestic jobs," giving the WBA women access to a pool of competent maids and cooks for their own homes (83–84).

47. "Servants' Union Asks 9-Hour Day." *Akron Beacon Journal*, January 4, 1917.

48. Sutherland, 132–133.

49. "Servant Girls' Union: Effort to Organize One Here Has Failed," *Summit County Beacon*, May 14, 1903.

50. *Akron Beacon Journal*, September 8, 1933. Referenced in Tully, 186.

51. "Housemaids' Code Object of Study," *Akron Beacon Journal*, November 16, 1933.

52. "NRA in the Home," *Akron Beacon Journal*, September 20, 1933.

53. Hina Shah and Marci Seville, "Domestic Worker Organizing: Building a Contemporary Movement for Dignity and Power," *Albany Law Review*, vol. 75, no. 1 (2012), 413–46, Golden Gate University School of Law Digital Commons, digitalcommons.law.ggu.edu.

54. "'Satisfied' Domestics," *Akron Beacon Journal*, January 27, 1934.

55. Dudden, 87–92; Sutherland, 100–11.

56. Donna L. Van Raaphorst, Union Maids Not Wanted: Organizing Domestic Workers, 1870–1940 (Praeger, 1988), 55.

57. Judith Rollins, *Between Women: Domestics and Their Employers* (Temple UP, 1985), 150–51.

58. Katzman, 212; Dudden, 51–55; Sutherland, 130–32.

Akron's Servants, 1900 to 1940

59. Katzman, 223.

60. Seiberling, F. A. Letter to Irene Seiberling Harrison. October 9, 1942. Transcription. Courtesy of Stan Hywet Hall and Gardens, Akron, Ohio.

61. Information received during the writer's "Nooks and Crannies" tour at Stan Hywet Hall and Gardens, Akron, Ohio, April 2, 2022.

62. Information gathered from various documents in the Hower Family Papers collection in the University of Akron Archives, Akron, Ohio.

63. Katharine Knight, personal diary, January 3, 1924. John S. Knight Papers collection. Series A, Box A1, Folder 54. Transcription by David Lieberth, provided to writer via email.

64. "Harry Lindon, 80, Firestone Chauffeur," *Akron Beacon Journal*, October 30, 1972.

65. "Firestone Offers $200 Reward for Return of Stolen Suitcase," *Akron Beacon Journal*, August 27, 1921.

66. "Two Institutions to Divide $100,000 from Col. Perkins," *Akron Beacon Journal*, September 13, 1910.

67. Mary Gerrish Seiberling, letter to Willard Penfield Seiberling, July 22, 1938. Transcription courtesy of Stan Hywet Hall and Gardens, Akron, Ohio.

68. Jane Eads, "It's Hard to Get a Steak … And Hard to Get Cook to Broil It," *Akron Beacon Journal*, July 4, 1943.

69. "News for the Housewife," *Akron Evening Times*, January 29, 1920.

70. Eden Electric Washing Machine advertisement, *Akron Beacon Journal*, April 9, 1919; Ohio Edison advertisement, *Akron Beacon Journal*, April 1, 1936.

71. "Letters of a Slim-Made Woman to Her Fat Sister," advertisement for Marmola Prescription Tablets, *Akron Beacon Journal*, December 5, 1912.

72. "There's No Servant Problem," advertisement for Shredded Wheat, *Akron Beacon Journal*, August 5, 1908.

73. "West Hill Special," Kelley & Ritchie real estate advertisement, *Akron Evening Times*, March 17, 1920; "Prices Offered for Best Plan and Equipment of Modern Kitchen," *Akron Evening Times*, December 1, 1920.

74. "Joe Televox Visits City," *Akron Beacon Journal*, December 3, 1928.

75. Erin Blakemore, "How America Tried (and Failed) to Solve Its 'Servant Problem,'" *JSTOR Daily*, April 3, 2017, https://daily.jstor.org/how-america-tried-and-failed-to-solve-its-servant-problem. Accessed March 1, 2023.

76. Saunders and Ernst, *Mary Worth*, *Akron Beacon Journal*, November 24, 1965.

\ **8**

Akron—Home of Serial (and Cereal) Entrepreneurs

Christopher C. Esker

So much of Akron's history is built on the lore of rubber. Akron may always be The Rubber Capital of the World, but hundreds of other self-starters began manufacturing companies that impacted the world well beyond Akron.

Manufactured Pottery: Setting the Table for an Industrial Future

The first industry to put Akron on the map was the manufactured pottery industry, which earned worldwide fame for its clay products and sewer pipes. Rich clay deposits and the earnest, hardworking folks who worked them played a major role in the first undertaking that would define early industrial Akron.

In *A Centennial History of Akron 1825–1925*, H. Karl Butler describes the start of Akron's clay products industry. It began when a man named Fiske discovered a clay bed suitable for making stoneware in Springfield Township. He bought the land and began manufacturing crocks and pans. At this time, Butler writes, "no cabin had more than a few such utensils," and "there was an immediate demand

Akron—Home of Serial (and Cereal) Entrepreneurs

for those which Fiske manufactured." He enlarged production with a man named Smith, and together they set up the firm of Fiske and Smith, "the first clay products company in what was to become Summit County." Business was good and two years later, they hired a boy, Edwin H. Merrill, "whose name was to loom as the real founder of the industry which made Akron the center of the clay products trade in America."

Merrill was joined by his father Abijah and his brother Calvin, who all worked for Fiske. By 1835 Merrill bought out Fiske, housed his factory in a shed, and with his father and brother, they worked—*hard*. Merrill invented a machine to make clay smoking pipes, added stoneware beer and ink bottles, and by 1847 established on Bank Street in Middlebury—today's Sixth Ward—Akron's first industrial plant. Hill, Foster & Company started additional Middlebury potteries in 1849; in 1851 the Merrills joined, making it Hill, Merrill & Company. While stoneware utensils for home and farm made the company, the Hills' interests were in developing practical pipe machinery to make sewer pipe. In 1856, Whitmore, Robinson & Company entered the growing pottery business, setting the table for what would become Akron's first *Capital of Everything* industry.

The Buckeye Sewer Pipe Works opened at Exchange and Arlington Streets in 1868, the Akron Sewer Pipe Company opened in 1871, and in 1873, Hill chartered the Hill Sewer Pipe Co. In 1879 Robinson Bros. & Co. built one of the largest plants in the "Old Forge" just east of what would later house Goodyear's massive East Akron campus. In the 1880s the leading competitors created the American Sewer Pipe Co., a trust with each company represented on the board of directors. This trust carved out territories, fixed prices, and winnowed out inferior manufacturers. With an abundance of manufacturers and plants, dominance and wealth were formed and maintained by regulating the flow of manufacturing and distribution. It would be a lesson often reemployed in Akron's industrial history.

By the 1920s the industry had matured into combined firms, and as cities like Akron grew, the demand for better pipes fed Akron's particular and peculiar inventiveness—a trait that would serve it well for two centuries. The Robinson Clay Product Company and the American Vitrified Products Company simply dominated and defined the sewer pipe industry at the turn of the twentieth century, creating the iconic Standard Akron Sewer Pipe, the gold standard of that era serving to make Akron the literal sewer pipe capital of the United States. And Akron was just getting started.[1]

Akron's Oatmeal King: Ferdinand Schumacher

No Akron history is complete without mentioning Ferdinand Schumacher, Akron's Oatmeal King. Born in 1822 in Celle, Germany, he came to the United States with little formal education, clerking in a grocery store and working in a sugar refinery. In 1850, he and his brother, Otto, emigrated, buying forty-six acres of land in Euclid to farm. In 1852 he left Otto in charge and moved to Akron to start a fancy goods, toys, and notions store, later adding groceries.[2] By 1854 he leased rights on Akron's Cascade Mill Race and started manufacturing oatmeal like in his native Germany on North Howard Street.[3] Initially he made just enough to supply his family, but word of it spread through Akron's German community, and the tale of Akron's future Oatmeal King began. He incorporated the German American Oatmeal Company in Akron, Ohio, in 1856.[4]

Until Schumacher's operation oatmeal had been primarily imported. Harnessing Akron's mill race, he was able to produce it at a lower price, developing a lucrative business. His introduction of German techniques at his mill turned oats into a cereal fit for frontier folks and new immigrants alike, making his business thrive. In 1854, he invented a machine to chop oats into small cubes, which he packed into glass jars and sold.[5] He developed a way to make oats cook faster by pre-cooking whole oats in their hard outer shell and passing them under ceramic rollers to produce flakes, or "rolled oats." Contracts to supply the Union Army during the Civil War with his portable, packable, durable, usable oatmeal rations bolstered his business. It would become the F. Schumacher Milling Company, a massive enterprise that would dominate not only downtown Akron's manufacturing centers, but the cereal industry itself. As millrace power gave way to steam, then to electricity, the success of this company earned Ferdinand Schumacher the nickname of "Oatmeal King." For a time, Akron was the unchallenged capital of cereal manufacturing in the United States.

Schumacher's massive, eight-story "Jumbo Mill" was entirely consumed by fire on March 6, 1886, a loss of some $600,000 (the equivalent of about $20 million today).[6] He vowed to rebuild and, in 1888, he joined six other major oat millers to form the American Cereal Company.[7] Headquartered in Chicago, the company soon dominated the cereal industry by carving out territories, fixing prices, and managing manufacturing. While he was the combination's first president, conflicts with others led him to assign his varied financial interests to an executor in 1896, and he was removed by his partners in 1899. Put simply, he may have been too honest for them to tolerate.[8] Two years later it would become the familiar Quaker Oats Company, that name and likeness having come from a Ravenna, Ohio, competitor who was one of the seven in the trust. Its Akron

Akron—Home of Serial (and Cereal) Entrepreneurs

Ferdinand Schumacher's Cascade Mills. \ Summit County Historical Society, David Lieberth collection.

Quaker Oats Company. \ Summit County Historical Society, David Lieberth collection.

locations had operated for decades without Ferdinand Schumacher. He passed away on April 15, 1908, at age eighty-six, in his beloved Akron, Ohio, his final resting place in Glendale Cemetery. So, while in life Ferdinand Schumacher never wore the mantle of Quaker Oats nor labored under the smiling Quaker Man still fronting those familiar cardboard canisters, he will forever be remembered as Akron's Oatmeal King.

Mechanizing Agriculture: Lewis Miller and the Buckeye Reaper

Lewis Miller was born in Greentown, Ohio, in 1829. He started life on the family farm, worked as a plasterer and a teacher between 1846 and 1851, and joined Canton's Ball, Aultman and Company, which manufactured stoves, threshers, reapers, and plows. In 1855 he invented the first combine, a harvesting-reaping machine called the "Buckeye Mower and Reaper." By 1864 he founded Aultman, Miller, and Company to produce mechanized farming machinery. He founded the Buckeye Mower and Reaper Works in Akron with John R. Buchtel, and through those associated industries, the Buckeye Mower and Reaper became the tool that mechanized modern farming in the United States.[9] He served as general superintendent of a branch of Buckeye Works incorporated in Akron as Aultman, Miller and Company. His Buckeye Mower and Reaper was manufactured and produced under licenses across the United States and used throughout the world. Following his untimely death in 1899 at just sixty-nine, the company soldiered on until Chicago's International Harvester Company bought a controlling interest and took over the Buckeye Works.[10] By 1906, the Buckeye line was dropped, and by 1907, Akron began building "auto-buggies and tractors" in the renamed International Harvester Company Akron Works.[11] Akron's leadership in dominating the mechanized farming implements industry opened the door to today's flourishing industrial truck business.

There are more reasons to remember the ever-industrious and inventive—*there's that word again*—Lewis Miller. Closely associated with the Methodist Episcopal Church, in 1867 he co-created the "Akron Plan" for Sunday schools in churches. An "Akron Plan" church was built with a central assembly hall surrounded by small classrooms, conceived by Miller along with Methodist minister John Heyl Vincent and architect Jacob Snyder; from that Akron Plan, an "International Uniform Lesson Plan Curriculum" was devised and, within just a few years, 80 percent of church members were introduced through Sunday Schools.[12] Many such structures still stand bearing this design hallmark, including the former St. Paul's Episcopal Church, badly damaged by fire a few years ago, its sturdy stone walls currently buttressed, awaiting its next reinvention.[13]

Akron—Home of Serial (and Cereal) Entrepreneurs

Thomas and Mina Edison, circa 1908. \
Courtesy of the National Park Service.

By 1874, looking for a way to further improve training, Miller and Vincent collaborated to invent, create, and found the Chautauqua Assembly—what is now known internationally as the Chautauqua Institution—on Chautauqua Lake, New York, continuing to this day to educate and inform.[14]

On February 24, 1886, Miller's daughter, Mina, married celebrated inventor Thomas Edison at Miller's Oak Place mansion, whose red brick walls still overlook downtown Akron from its lofty perch on the hills just above Akron's Glendale Cemetery.[15] Miller was laid to rest there in February 1899. Like so many of Akron's creative, inventive folks, he helped to make Akron the one-time capital of the mechanized farming implement industry, created the Akron Plan that would sweep across the country and the world, and co-founded a celebrated institution of learning whose name is etched in history, still doing good nearly 150 years on.

The Match King: Ohio Columbus Barber and the Power of Trust

Ohio Columbus Barber was born in 1841 in Middlebury and began working for his father's Akron-based match factory at age fifteen.[16] In 1862 he took the reins, later leading its consolidation with many other match factories to create the Diamond Match combination trust which, by the late 1800s, would control 85 percent of the match market in the United States, with plants across the country and in Europe and South America, earning him the moniker of "The Match King."[17] In doing this, he was not unlike his fellow industrialists in the clay, cereal, and agricultural machinery industries, realizing that the power in commerce was the ability to manage every aspect. While the Match King reigned, he and his contemporaries did that through the power of business trusts. Akron was by then the country's undisputed capital of matchmaking.

In 1891, he created Barberton, and in 1894, relocated the company to this new industrial city.[18] In addition to Diamond Match, Barber pursued many other business ventures, including his 3,500-acre model Anna Dean Farm in Barberton, also the site of his fifty-two-room modern mansion.[19] He was a great philanthropist and the primary financial supporter of what would become Akron City Hospital, and a founding member, in 1906, of the Akron Chamber of Commerce.[20]

Barber was invested in many other industries, including the Diamond Rubber Company in Akron, founded in 1894; the Great Western Cereal Company in Akron, founded in 1901; the Stirling Boiler Company, later merged with Babcock & Wilcox; and a planned, but never built, centralized transportation hub in Cleveland, known as the Barber Subways, envisioning a subway system connecting every railroad entering Cleveland, facilitating the handling of freight and the establishment of the great warehouse system on the lake shore—where he owned significant frontage.[21]

A widower for two decades, Barber married his secretary, Mary Orr, in 1915.[22] He died on February 4, 1920, with plans in his will to donate Anna Dean Farm to an educational institution.[23] While Mary had hoped to fulfill his plan for its use as an agricultural college, the indebted estate was sold to pay off creditors. The Match King died at his estate in Barberton, and despite that moniker, some might say that among the pantheon of Akron industrialists, he was indeed matchless.

Akron—Home of Serial (and Cereal) Entrepreneurs

O. C. Barber, portrait from Samuel Lane, *Fifty Years and Over of Summit County* (Beacon Job Department, 1892), p. 533.

Marbles: Aggies, Cat's-Eyes, and the Toy Industry

Akron's Samuel C. Dyke arguably invented the modern toy industry when he developed a method for mass-producing marbles. In 1884, he established the American Marble and Toy Manufacturing Company.[24] By 1892 a small workforce, consisting mainly of teenage girls and young women, turned out four hundred thousand marbles per day.[25]

One of Dyke's factories was located on the grounds of a lumber yard that stood on the site of Lock 3 Park. Mass production caused prices to fall so dramatically that it was said at the time that children could first afford to buy a toy with their own money, a penny being enough for a handful of clay marbles. Dyke's toy company spurred other Akron entrepreneurs into making toys, making Akron yet another capital of industry.

Dyke and his Akron competitors made miniature jugs, pots, boots, shoes, dogs, cats, and more from Akron's rich clay deposits. The nascent rubber industry took notice, turning out mass-produced balloons, balls, dolls, and ducks. Local Akron Ironworks stepped in with mass-produced cast iron and tin toys, bicycles, pedal toys, tops, and more.[26]

The real danger in Akron, as it had been for decades, was fire—and the same fire that helped to create Akron's marble and toy industry also consumed it. In 1904 The American Marble & Toy Manufacturing Company burned to the ground. News reports detailed children converging on the charred remains the next day, eagerly filling pockets with marbles. Akron police secured the ruins and ran off the little looters, and the city ordered the former factory condemned and buried.[27] When Akron's current Lock 3 Park was created by razing the buildings that formerly fronted South Main Street between the Civic Theatre to the O'Neil's department store building, the descendants of those same scrappy marble scavengers may have made their way onto that construction site, again finding treasured commies, aggies, cat's eyes, and even ceramic Blue Santas in the fertile ground that once made Akron the capital of the country's marble and toy industries.

Publishing: Paul Werner, Arthur Saalfield, and Akron's Publishing Empires

Born in May 1850 in Württemberg, Germany, Paul Werner immigrated to Akron in 1867. He worked as a clerk and bookkeeper and, in 1873, became an editorial writer for the Akron *Germania* newspaper, doing so well that he bought it a year later, became its publisher, and founded the *Sunday Gazette* and the Akron *Tribune*. He expanded to include commercial printing and, in 1884, sold his newspaper businesses to concentrate on publishing high-quality books, erecting an enormous printing plant for the Werner Printing & Lithograph Company in 1886, which grew to carry on a very large business in the 1890s.[28] At his death in 1931 the *Akron Beacon Journal* credited him for "the building up of the greatest publishing house—up to that time—the world had known." In Akron he earned a reputation for being a leader in civic affairs; for many years, for example, he welcomed "huge throngs of excited and interested men, women, and children" to visit his West Market Street home for a Fourth of July party, "which cost thousands of dollars" to put on. He "staged big parades, where there were brass bands and fireworks and much ado," wearing "gay uniforms" and "hats with cockades."

In 1908, however, Werner's fortunes fell when the publishers of *Encyclopedia Britannica* filed suit against his companies, claiming trademark violations. Suits were filed in every country where he did business—more than twenty—and although he mounted vigorous defenses and eventually won every suit, the costs of doing so led to his company's demise.[29] In 1910 Werner filed for bankruptcy and the eleven-building Akron complex was sold. (The last remaining building of the Werner empire, known locally as the Werner Castle and located on the northeast corner of Union Street and Perkins Parkway, fell to the wrecking ball in 2020.)[30] After lawsuits were concluded by 1915, he left Akron to open a rubber company in Kansas City but lost both his financial backing and his fortune because of his German sympathies at the outbreak of the First World War. In 1927, impoverished, he returned to Akron, where he edited his old paper, the Akron *Germania*, until 1930.

When he returned to Akron, F. A. Seiberling held a dinner for him with forty guests at Stan Hywet. He passed away in Akron in 1931, with Akron's elite packing his funeral. He was laid to rest in the Werner Family Mausoleum in Akron's Glendale Cemetery.[31]

Another Akron publisher was Arthur J. Saalfield. A native of Leeds, England, he was born in 1863 and emigrated to New York as a small boy. His father soon died, and his family moved to Chicago, where he began selling books at the age of nine. At thirteen he moved to New York, attended school for a year, and then went back to work as a bookseller. At twenty-nine he started his own book jobbing business and at thirty-five he moved to Akron to take charge of the book publishing department at Werner's company.[32] In late 1899 he purchased that department from Werner, forming The Saalfield Publishing Company in 1900, which went on to publish children's books and other products from 1900 to 1977. The Saalfield Publishing Company became the world's largest publisher of children's books and materials, making Akron the world capital of children's book publishing. Arthur passed away in 1919, and his son Albert G. Saalfield took over the company. In 1953 he turned the presidency of the company over to his son, Henry R. Saalfield.[33]

Among the Saalfield Publishing Company's many successes was the development of "royalty properties"—the acquisition of exclusive rights to publications related to motion picture stars and other entertainers. In the depths of the Great Depression A. G. Saalfield secured the printing rights for Shirley Temple after seeing her in one of her first movies. The company sold more than fifty million copies of about forty books by and about Shirley Temple.[34] Many other motion picture personalities, cartoon characters, and television figures were added to the Saalfield lines. It rode that specialization market in books, games, and activity books for children through the rest of its existence, finally ceasing operations in 1977.

E. A. Pflueger, circa 1940. \ Photo courtesy of the *Akron Beacon Journal*

Casting About: Ernest Pflueger and Akron's Fishing Empire

Ernest F. Pflueger was born in 1843 in Baden-Baden, Germany, emigrating at the tender age of five to Buffalo, New York, where he learned the molder's trade. He moved to Erie at age twenty, met and married Julia Dunnebeck, and they moved to Akron with their baby boy, Ernest A. Pflueger, in 1868. Pflueger worked for the Erie Stove Company and then set himself up in the retail grocery business.[35]

An inventor at heart, Ernest had taken out over fifty patents by the 1880s. Fascinated by the way that phosphorous match tips glowed in the dark of his grocery store, he patented a variety of glow-in-the-dark rosettes and harness fittings for horses. He then read a magazine article describing how fish were attracted to phosphorescent prey. This was a virtual light-bulb moment for Ernest, and he set to creating a fishing lure to replicate the prey, eventually landing a patent for luminous fishing lures. Legend has it that he caught a large bass on his first test of a glowing lure at the Portage Lakes with his friend, Dr. B. F. Goodrich.[36]

The Enterprise Manufacturing Company was established in 1881 and incorporated in 1886. The business grew wonderfully. The fishing tackle was soon in demand throughout the country, and other novelties, such as luminous keyhole covers, also sold well. In 1887, President Grover Cleveland wrote a letter to the company praising the merits of their tackle. By the early 1890s, Enterprise Manufacturing, located just south of Ash Street, east of the location of the Akron Ronald McDonald house, was the "most extensive manufacturer" of "flies, floats, luminous and non-luminous fish bait" and "every manner of apparatus which will coax the finny tribe to swallow a hook ... in the world."[37] Pflueger died in 1900 after a fall, and his family continued the business.

In 1943 the company moved from Ash Street to North Union Street into a three-story structure, once occupied by the Werner Printing Company, that looked like a medieval castle. Enterprise remained the world's largest and most diversified producer of fishing tackle into the 1950s, at which point it produced more than 100 million fish hooks and sold tackle through 32,000 dealers and 1,000 wholesalers around the world.[38] In the 1960s the company changed its name to Pflueger Corporation and was soon acquired by its competitor, Shakespeare, who pioneered fiberglass fishing rods in 1946.[39] Pflueger's headquarters moved to Miami, and fishing tackle operations left Akron in 1969. In 1977 a massive fire destroyed the factory.[40]

Today people collect antique Pflueger tackle as well as Enterprise Manufacturing bridal rosettes, admiring them for their build quality and beauty.[41]

Pflueger-branded tackle continues to be manufactured by Pure Fishing, a massive fishing gear conglomerate headquartered in Columbia, South Carolina.[42] So while it's no big fish story, it is the one that got away.

Dum-Dums: Akron, Land of a Million Suckers

As master huckster P. T. Barnum was rumored to say, "There's a sucker born every minute." In Akron, by 1932, that was more truth than fiction. The Akron Candy Company got its start in Akron just after the turn of the twentieth century, with confectioners Lloyd Bader and Peter Heckman opening their candy factory in 1907 in the brand-new Hower Building, a magnificent seven-story multiuse structure located at 31 West Market Street. It went bust the next year. Bader joined with John Schwartz to form a new business, the Akron Candy Company, in 1909, along with Jesse Merriman, Lewis Ott, and Harvey Bachtel—well-known Akron industrialists—and then the Hower Building promptly caught on fire, a thing far too common in early twentieth-century Akron. They later relocated to 244 Sumner Street, offering a variety of confections to a hungry-for-sweets Akron.

Akron's world-famous Dum-Dum lollipops came along in 1924. The confection's name, Dum-Dum, is from a British bullet—the dum dum—used in World War I. Stranger still, Dum Dum was the name of the West Bengal municipality in India where the bullets were manufactured. The Akron Candy Company's sales manager, C. Frederic Bahr, is said to have coined the name because he thought it easy for children—their primary marketing target—to remember and say.[43] In April 1934, the *Akron Beacon Journal* published three photos of boxcars bearing banners that read "ONE MILLION DUM-DUMS." After ten years of steady growth, the company was making half a million Dum Dums a day, distributed to candy stores through five hundred distributors in thirty states.[44] That Akron had become the nation's lollipop-manufacturing capital was undeniable.

However, following the unexpected death of the company's leader, Curt Schwartz, in 1938, new leadership moved the plant to Bellevue, Ohio. Just months later its former long-time factory on Sumner Street burned down.[45] The factory stood on the site of The University of Akron's Auburn Science and Engineering Center, then just across the street from campus. About 1,500 people, mostly college students, gathered to watch it burn.[46] After the Akron City Planning Commission turned down a zoning change requested by the company in 1952 that would have seen it return to Akron—some may argue that was a Dum-Dum move on Akron's part—it was sold to the Spangler Candy Company of Bryan, Ohio in 1953, with all machines and operations moved there. Spangler still turns out twelve million Akron-invented Dum-Dums each day, or about three *billion* every year.[47]

Akron: City of Invention

Wherever you are—whether you're from Akron, left Akron, came back to Akron, or simply have a connection to it—you know this city and its quirky, creative, industrious, inventive citizens have carved from its sandy sediments a role far larger and deeper than its humble roots may have otherwise allowed. It's no surprise to any Akronite that the city is marching into its third century still anchored in community, enamored of research, ready to invent, and eager to embrace its next *Capital of Practically Everything* enterprise. It's just another reason why Akron is Akron.

Akron—Home of Serial (and Cereal) Entrepreneurs

Notes

1. H. Karl Butler, "Clay Products," in *A Centennial History of Akron: 1825–1925*, ed. Oscar E. Olin et al (Summit County Historical Society, 1925), 303–12, Google Books.

2. Samuel Lane, *Fifty Years and Over of Akron and Summit County* (Beacon Job Department, 1892), 155, Google Books.

3. Carl D. Sheppard, "Cereal Mills and Millers," in *A Centennial History of Akron: 1825–1925*, ed. Oscar E. Olin et al (Summit County Historical Society, 1925), 297, Google Books.

4. Lane, 454.

5. Sheppard, 297.

6. Sheppard, 298–99; Lane, 346.

7. Sheppard, 300.

8. "Ferdinand Schumacher," in *Centennial History of Summit County, Ohio, and Representative Citizens*, ed. William B. Doyle (Biographical Publishing Company, 1908), 423, Google Books.

9. Lane, 140, 466.

10. Karl Kendig, "Buckeye and Empire Days," in *A Centennial History of Akron: 1825–1925*, ed. Oscar E. Olin et al (Summit County Historical Society, 1925), 248–49, Google Books.

11. *Report of the International Harvester Company: December 31, 1908*, 11, Wisconsin Historical Society McCormick-International Harvester Collection, https://content.wisconsinhistory.org/digital/collection/ihc.

12. Donald G. Kohrs, *Chautauqua: The Nature Study Movement in Pacific Grove, California* (Pacific Grove: Hopkins Marine Station of Stanford University, 2015), chapter 3, https://seaside.stanford.edu/Chautauqua.

13. "Historic Akron Church Goes Up in Flames; Crews Battle Blaze for Hours," *Akron Beacon Journal*, April 19, 2018, https://www.beaconjournal.com.

14. Kohrs, chapter 3.

15. Lane, 500.

16. Lane, 533.

17. "Ohio Columbus Barber: America's Match King (1841–1920)," Barberton Historical Society, annadeanfarm.com/ocbarber.htm; "The Eighties," in *A Centennial History of Akron: 1825–1925*, ed. Oscar E. Olin et al (Summit County Historical Society, 1925), 102, Google Books.

18. "Founding and Early Growth," City of Barberton, Ohio, https://cityofbarberton.com/282/Part–II-Town-Founding-Early-Growth

19. "Barberton and Kenmore," in *A Centennial History of Akron: 1825–1925*, ed. Oscar E. Olin et al (Summit County Historical Society, 1925), 170, Google Books.

20. "Welfare Work in Akron," in *A Centennial History of Akron: 1825–1925*, ed. Oscar E. Olin et al (Summit County Historical Society, 1925), 406, Google Books.

21. Scott Dix Kenfield, ed., *Akron and Summit County, Ohio, 1825–1928*, vol. 3 (S. J. Clarke, 1928, Chicago, 1928), 696, Google Books.

22. "Barberton and Kenmore," 170.

23. "Ohio C. Barber Provides for Big Agricultural and Industrial School on Anna Dean Farm in his Will," *Akron Evening Times*, February 26, 1920, 3. Unless otherwise noted, newspapers are cited from digital versions through Newspapers.com.

24. H. Karl Butler, "Clay Products," in *A Centennial History of Akron: 1825–1925*, ed. Oscar E. Olin et al (Summit County Historical Society, 1925), 308, Google Books.

25. "Millions of Marbles," *Summit County Beacon*, June 1, 1892, 7; "Clay Workers Strike," *Akron Beacon and Republican*, February 11, 1896, 2.

26. Ingrid Floyd, "Once Upon a Time in Akron: Marbles Make U.S. Toy History." *Kovels Antique Trader*, March 3, 2018, https://www.antiquetrader.com/collectibles/upon-time-akron-marbles-make-u-s-toy-history; "The Original North Pole: The Story of Samuel C. Dyke and the Akron Toy Industry," Ideastream

Public Media Documentaries & Specials, December 15, 2015, video, 27:20, https://www.ideastream.org/show/specials/2015-12-15/the-original-north-pole-the-story-of-samuel-c-dyke-and-the-akron-toy-industry.

27. "Toy Factory Is Entirely Destroyed," *Akron Beacon Journal*, September 6, 1904, 3.

28. Lane, 537; James A. Braden, "Newspapers, Publishers and Printers," in *A Centennial History of Akron: 1825–1925*, ed. Oscar E. Olin et al (Summit County Historical Society, 1925), 241–42, Google Books; Mark J. Price, "Historic Castle Razed at Perkins Union," *Akron Beacon Journal*, September 5, 2020.

29. C. W. Howard, "Death Takes Paul Werner, Civic Leader," *Akron Beacon Journal*, February 7, 1931, 1, 3; "Akron Pays Final Tribute to Paul E. Werner at Rites," *Akron Beacon Journal*, February 10, 1931, 25.

30. Price.

31. Howard, 3; "Akron Pays Final Tribute."

32. "A. J. Saalfield, Akron Publisher, Dies in Florida," *Akron Beacon Journal*, January 13, 1919, 1.

33. "A. G. Saalfield, Publisher in Akron Is Dead at 72," *The Plain Dealer*, February 8, 1959, 26.

34. "Saalfield Chairman Dies at 72," *Akron Beacon Journal*, February 8, 1959, 1.

35. "Ernest Andrew Pflueger," in *Akron and Summit County, Ohio, 1825–1928*, Scott Dix Kenfield, ed.,vol. 3 (Chicago and Akron: S. J. Clarke, 1928, Chicago, 1928), 84, Google Books; "Ernest A. Pflueger, Industrialist, Dies," *Akron Beacon Journal*, January 6, 1944, 19.

36. "Enterprise Top Fishing Tackle Maker As It Observes 90th Year In Business," *Akron Beacon Journal*, December 26, 1954, 48.

37. Lane, 32; "Enlarging the Enterprise Works," *Akron Daily Beacon*, September 11, 1886, 4; "Luminous Goods Lighting Up the East," *Summit County Beacon*, January 23, 1884, 3; "Local Business Notes," *Summit County Beacon*, April 27, 1887, 2; "Akron Products," *Akron Beacon Journal*, May 21, 1892, 5.

38. "Enterprise Top Fishing Tackle Maker."

39. "Fishing Tackle Firm Now Pflueger Corp.," *Akron Beacon Journal*, August 3, 1964, 15; "Competitor Takes Over Pflueger," *Akron Beacon Journal*, July 18, 1966, 17; "Pflueger Hits 'Comeback Trail," *Akron Beacon Journal*, September 26, 1966, B2.

40. "Pflueger to Move to Miami," *Akron Beacon Journal*, June 27, 1969, B3; "Fire Destroys Old Pflueger Building," *Akron Beacon Journal*, January 5, 1977, 1.

41. Mark J. Price, "Reeling in History," *Akron Beacon Journal*, November 6, 2006, E1; Susan Quinn, "History of Bridal Rosettes in America," Horse Bridal Rosettes: Equine Gems of History, accessed July 24, 2024, https://squinn465.wordpress.com/welcome-to-the-world-of-antique-bridle-rosettes-3/history-of-bridle-rosettes-in-america/.

42. "The Pure Fishing Story," Pure Fishing, last accessed July 24, 2024, https://about.purefishing.com/.

43. Mark J. Price, "Yum-Yum: Kids Got First Taste of Dum-Dums," *Akron Beacon Journal*, October 23, 2017.

44. "Shipping Dum Dums by the Carload," *Akron Beacon Journal*, April 28, 1934, 24.

45. Price, "Yum-Yum."

46. "$20,000 Fire Laid to Carelessness," *Akron Beacon Journal*, January 9, 1940, 26.

47. "History," Spangler Candy Company, accessed July 24, 2024, https://www.dumdumpops.com/about/history.

\ **9**

Akron, Home of the World of Make-Believe

Sharon Moreland Myers

Just as Akron was known as the Rubber Capital of the World and the place where multiple industries flourished (oatmeal, sewer pipe, fishing tackle), most people don't appreciate that from about 1900 to about 1965, Greater Akron produced millions of toys and children's books and shipped them all over the world. At least three Akron toy makers still manufacturing in the United States are in Summit County. Akron's many successful toy companies were founded and built on the skills developed in manufacturing and sales of clay and rubber goods.

The previous chapter chronicled the growth and development of our first toy company, the American Marble and Toy Manufacturing Company. But the city's industrial prowess made room for other manufacturers that were oriented to children's world of make-believe.

Saalfield Publishing

While the name Saalfield is most closely associated with publishing, it was also known worldwide as a maker of toys. In the early twentieth century, Saalfield became one of the largest publishers of children's books in the world. They also published picture puzzles, boxed activity items, and paper dolls.[1] They secured licensing rights to all paper-doll likenesses of Shirley Temple and English princesses Elizabeth and Margaret. In three months in 1935, they printed 3.5 million Shirley Temple paper dolls. In 1958, when Shirley Temple Black was doing well on television, she called Saalfield with a request to revive the books, puzzles, and cut-out dolls.[2] In 1953, Marilyn Monroe refused to approve Saalfield paper dolls of her image until artists revised the shape of her figure to better reflect her measurements of 37-23-34.[3]

Saalfield also manufactured games such as "Blockheads."[4] This popular mid-century game consisted of twenty-six blocks of many colors and shapes. A player tries to build a tower of blocks, and the one who causes the tower to topple loses.[5]

The 1960s were good years for Saalfield. In 1964, Saalfield sold more copies of a Beatles' coloring book in the first three days than it had ever done in a month's time with any other book it had ever published.[6] Saalfield distributed popular Peanuts for President buttons at the 1968 New York Toy Convention. They also introduced two games of a more physical nature. One was a volleyball-sized lump of rubber called a Bump Ball that two people would press between them while they danced. The second was called Tight Squeeze, which brought young people together inside a plastic hoop.[7] The firm tripled the sales force and made additions and improvements to the facilities in 1967. They also installed a third-generation high-speed computer to expedite customer service and control inventories. Saalfield retired all shares of the company's stock held by people outside the company, turning it into an employee-owned business.[8] Nineteen days after the July 20, 1969, moonwalk by astronauts Neil Armstrong and Buzz Aldrin, two million copies of an Apollo coloring book were sold. The book depicted the Apollo 11 story from before takeoff to after splashdown. Saalfield's "Man on the Moon" puzzles, created from photos taken by the astronauts during the moonwalk, also sold exceptionally well.[9]

Saalfield collapsed in the 1970s. In 1976 five banks foreclosed on unpaid loans and the firm was placed in receivership. The Rand McNally Company purchased $500,000 of Saalfield's inventory and Artcraft Publishing bought an additional $100,000 of inventory.[10] Kent State University Libraries acquired the company's archives.[11] Crane-Howard Lithograph Company of Cleveland purchased the buildings, machinery, and furnishings for $951,000 from state receivership in 1977.[12] In 1984 the company filed to reorganize under Chapter 11 of the federal banking law, listing debts of $4.92 million. This was the end of Saalfield.[13]

Actress Shirley Temple at the 1947 Soap Box Derby, with a car built by Hower Vocational students. Photo courtesy of the *Akron Beacon Journal*.

Anderson Rubber

In July 1925, as part of Akron's centennial celebration, the city put on the Centennial Industrial Exposition at the Akron Armory downtown. A large room was filled from end to end with displays of various products produced in Akron. The *Akron Beacon Journal* reporter covering the exposition noted that the display taught citizens much about "the city of the moment," which differed from both "the Akron of yesterday" emphasized by most of the centennial events and publications and the "one-industry town" imagined by many at the time. One of the more interesting displays was that of the Anderson Rubber Company. This featured "out of the ordinary rubber toys and balloons" including "rubber dumb bells" and "oddly designed and amusing rubber balloons."[14]

The fourth rubber company to be organized in Akron, Anderson Rubber, was founded in 1907 by Selden William Anderson III.[15] By the 1920s, the business was thriving, turning out one thousand balloons per day. They were one of the largest originators and manufacturers of toys, balloons, and rubber novelties in the world. Their rubber toys, balloons, basketballs, footballs, and punching bags were sold worldwide. Their line of imprinted balloons for advertising was very popular.[16] Anderson Rubber gave away toys to the Akron community at *Beacon Journal* Santa Claus parties held in places like Loew's and the Palace Theaters.[17]

The company also manufactured larger inflatable items, such as lifeboats. One of their most famous larger inflatables was a translucent, person-size rubber ball or balloon, which they made for exotic dancer Sally Rand. Rand paid for the mold and patented them as "bubbles" for use in burlesque dancing during the 1930s. She would plaster flesh-colored pieces of cloth to her body and do a "fan dance" with two large fans. To the viewer, she appeared to be naked during the brief glimpses afforded by the shifting of her large fans. This dance led to repeated arrests for indecent exposure in the 1930s, beginning with performances at the Century of Progress International Exposition (the Chicago World's Fair) in 1933.[18] In her "bubble dance" she replaced the fans with a large, Anderson-made balloon, through which, with the help of powerful backlighting, viewers could see her figure in silhouette. When the Navy and US Weather Bureau began ordering the "bubbles" for use in target practice and as weather balloons, Rand earned a commission on each sale.[19]

The original Anderson Rubber factory was located at 124 Union Street. In the 1940s they expanded with the construction of a two-story modern building at 644 Tallmadge Avenue.[20]

Anderson stopped making balloons in the early 1970s, but they continued to print on them and package them for many years.[21] In the shop office at 83 Cuyahoga Street, there was an exceptionally sturdy balloon in the shape of a pig that had been inflated fifteen years prior. In the 1980s their plant was located at 312 North Howard Street. In 1985, the company moved to Hudson.[22]

Sun Rubber

Sun Rubber Company began business on April 4, 1923, in a small building at Fairview Avenue and Van Buren in Barberton that had belonged to the bankrupt Avalon Rubber Company. The company originally was going to manufacture hard rubber radio panels, but when that didn't pan out, they went into manufacturing toy hot water bottles and soon moved on to producing dolls and squeak toys. By 1950, they were the largest producer of rubber dolls in the world. They held licensing agreements with companies like Disney and Gerber, producing a line of Gerber doll babies and Disney crib and wheeled toys featuring Disney characters. They also made a full line of basketballs and footballs. During World War II they produced gas marks and rubber protective clothing.[23]

They became a giant of the rubber toy world mainly because Sun Rubber president Tom Smith believed in the sales potential for a toy hot water bottle. A worker made a little hot water bottle for his daughter and told Smith how happy she was with it. Smith took the toy to Woolworths. The store buyers were convinced, and Sun was in the toy business! Sun Rubber soon made rubber cars and squeaky toys.[24]

In the early years of World War II, the company invested $10,000 to develop Mickey Mouse gas masks for children. In England, people told the company that "children were more afrightened by their elders sporting gas masks than they were by Nazi bombs." Seeing other children wearing masks frightened them even more. So, Sun thought the children would feel better seeing a mask with Mickey Mouse on it. The company manufactured about one thousand of these masks and gave them away to politicians and other influential people in the hopes for large orders. Apparently Americans feared they might need them in the course of the war. The government declined to purchase them and banned private sales of gas masks, so the entire project was shelved.[25]

Toy production stopped for a few years so Sun Rubber could manufacture airplane parts and other goods for the US military. They got back to making baby dolls, animal dolls, and dolls of a range of cartoon and Disney characters. In the 1930s, the Seiberling Latex Products Company had held exclusive rights to manufacture Disney characters in rubber. War-time collaboration with Disney led to Sun Rubber getting a license to make Disney character toys after the war. Sun Rubber also made rubber cars and trucks, bathtub toys, and crib toys. To capitalize on the birth of the Dionne quintuplets in 1934—they were the first set of quintuplets known to have survived infancy—Sun Rubber sold Quintuplet dolls, sets of five baby dolls packaged in a basket or carrying case.[26]

Dolls were their best sellers. "Sunbabe" was the first post-war doll made by Sun Rubber. It had a hard rubber head, a white skin-colored, jointed body, metal sleeping eyes, and painted mouth and hair. It came with a glass nursing bottle and a flannel diaper for the "wetting" function. For the 1947 holiday season, these dolls were produced at the rate of twenty thousand per day.[27]

A very popular radio show that originated in Chicago in 1928 featured Freeman Gosden and Charles Correll, who were both white actors who portrayed African American characters, Amos Jones and Andrew Hogg Brown, better known as "Amos 'n' Andy." The actors wore blackface when posing for publicity photos. The radio show turned into a television series, which featured Black actors and was popular into the 1960s.[28]

Mark Price tells the story of "Amosandra" in his November 30, 2020, local history column for the *Akron Beacon Journal*. The Sun Rubber Company had been bombarded for years with requests for a "Negro doll." Sun's general manager,

Thomas W. Smith, flew to Hollywood in 1948. He met with CBS executives and with Gosden and Correll and proposed that Amos and his wife, Ruby, have a girl baby on the show. Sun Rubber would produce the doll in celebration of the birth.

Sun Rubber invested a great deal of money and boosted employment to manufacture Amosandra, the first mass-produced, Black-skinned rubber doll. To design the doll, they hired a photographer to take pictures of Black children in Harlem, where Amosandra was born on the show. These photos were then turned over to an artist by the name of Ruth Newton, who was a children's book illustrator. Her sketches were then given to six sculptors and a model of a dimpled, smiling, wide-eyed baby was selected. The ten-inch doll was readied for production by Sun Rubber artist Bernard McDermott. The doll was packaged in a colorful box and came with a nursing bottle, a flannel diaper, a teething ring, a bell rattle, soap, a soap dish, a hot-water bottle, and a framed birth certificate.

On February 20, 1949, baby Amosandra debuted on the comedy show. Amosandra dolls were soon on shelves around the country, and Sun Rubber produced twelve thousand dolls a day for weeks to keep up with demand.

Ebony magazine called the Amosandra doll one of "the most beautiful Negro dolls America ever produced." Before Amosandra, the magazine noted, always "the Negro doll was presented as a ridiculous, calico-garmented, handkerchief-headed servant." Amosandra is now a collectors' item, bringing more than $500 at auctions for dolls in mint condition in the original box with all of the accessories.[29]

An *Akron Beacon Journal* editorial expressed great pride in the Amosandra doll as something "mighty important to the Akron area." It praised Sun Rubber for "new ideas, new business and more jobs," and it expressed hope that the doll might "have a constructive influence in the cause of brotherhood." "Little children don't know prejudice," it noted, and if children find it "natural" for "dark and white dolls to associate together, they may grow up with minds that are more open than their elders'.[30] Sun Rubber stopped making the doll by 1958, and foreign competition drove the company out of the doll business in the 1960s.[31]

In the early 1950s, Sun entered the vinyl plastic field and produced plastic dolls, toys, and balls along with its traditional rubber products. They also made rubber molding and other products for automobiles, refrigerators, and various appliances. Vinyl is soft, permits better detail in molding, lasts longer, and endures any climate. By 1964 they were making toys from polyethylene plastic, which enabled them to make larger "ride-a-way" products like its Mark III racer that was more than thirty inches long.[32]

Akron, Home of the World of Make-Believe

In 1968 Sun came out with the popular Hoppity Hops. These large inflatable balls, molded from rugged plastic vinyl and colored red and blue, were inflatable to twenty-five inches in diameter and had a ring handle for gripping. The company sold more than 300,000 in the first three months and more than four million in the first five years. Talley Industries acquired Sun Rubber in 1969 for more than $6 million. After their United Rubber Workers employees went on strike for better wages and benefits at the end of 1973, Talley Industries shut down the Barberton factory and moved operations to Georgia.[33]

B. F. Goodrich

The big tire companies also made toys as a sideline. At the start of the century, B. F. Goodrich manufactured Rubber Brownies, six-inch-tall gnomes with funny faces made out of red rubber. There were a variety of representations of specific Brownie characters in Palmer Cox's popular children's book series that began with *The Brownies, Their Book* (1887). Their stories were told in long poems. His Brownies were mischievous little men who went on adventures together. Sold individually and in sets of ten, the Goodrich Brownie toys were advertised as "lifelike" and "durable" and were sold around the country. They might remind us today of Brownie the Elf, the mascot of the Cleveland Browns, who looks a great deal like a Brownie by Palmer Cox. In Akron the red rubber Brownies were available at the Akron Rubber Store at 223 South Howard Street.[34]

General Tire and Goodyear

At the age of two, Akronite Carol Achberger Freeland was hired by the Miller Division of B. F. Goodrich to star in its national print ad for My Dolly, the company's biggest offering for the 1930 Christmas season. Small and pretty with blonde curls, she was the daughter of a man who worked in the tire division for fifty-five years.[35]

In the middle of the twentieth century, General Tire made and exhibited "Arctic rubber balls," which would still bounce in below-zero temperatures. One of their subsidiaries, the Pennsylvania Rubber Company of Jeannette, Pennsylvania, made tennis balls, basketballs, baseballs, and footballs out of rubber.[36]

Goodyear made tires for toys in the 1930s and sold "Goodyear Toys" at their service stores in the 1950s. These toys were likely not all manufactured by Goodyear. In the 1950s the company put their branding on a wide variety of products.[37]

Seiberling Latex

The Seiberling Latex Products Company, located on Fifth Street in Barberton, was founded in 1928 by F. A. Seiberling and his brother Charles.[38]

In February 1938 there was an "Akron Industrial Week" which began with fireworks, a radio show, and industrial exhibits in the shop windows of forty Main Street businesses. Over the radio, Mayor Lee D. Schroy told the shivering crowd that the exhibits prove that Akron was "not a one-industry town." Exhibits showcased children's books, stoves, mattresses, ice cream, ornamental iron, packaged fuel, metal products, furnaces, casting, electrical devices, salt, cereals, candy, and dairy products. But most of all, exhibits featured rubber. Seiberling Latex Products Company featured inflated rubber toys of Snow White and the Seven Dwarfs and Mickey Mouse.[39] The largest toy maker in Akron in the 1930s, Seiberling Latex also produced Ferdinand the Bull (the pacifist star of the 1936 children's book), Cleo the goldfish, Jiminy Cricket, and Figaro the cat. In advance of Disney's 1940 film *Pinocchio*, they produced one thousand Pinocchio toys a day. They produced four new bounce toys—rubber balls with a comic face molded into them—at a rate of twelve thousand per day. For the Christmas season they also produced a new rubber panda bear and a new rubber clown. Rubber toy sales were growing in the late 1930s, and so was employment at Seiberling Latex.[40]

World War II brought rationing and restrictions on the use of rubber for nonmilitary purposes. Rubber toy production and sales rebounded after the war. The 44th annual American Toy Fair in New York in 1947 felt like the "good old days" to attendees. At least six area companies attended. Sun Rubber brought forty-six different toys. Oak Rubber of Ravenna brought squeaky squeeze toys in happy animal shapes, perhaps in collaboration with Rempel Manufacturing, the subject of the next section. Karman Rubber of Akron brought kids' bike tires, handlebar grips, and pedal pads. The Jim Brown Toy Company of Akron brought scooters. Saalfield brought children's books. Anderson Rubber brought balloons. Seiberling Latex brought back the natural rubber balls that they were making before the war.[41] The rubber toy business thrived in the late 1940s as many millions were born in the postwar baby boom.[42] As Joseph Kuebler, the business and industrial writer for the *Akron Beacon Journal*, wrote in 1949: "There seems to be little doubt that Akron is the capital of the rubber toy industry just as it is the center of the tire world."[43]

In the early 1950s there were two Seiberling Latex plants. The Barberton plant went out of business in 1952. In 1953 Sydney Albert, a widely known Akron rubber machinery dealer, bought Seiberling Latex.[44] The second plant, in New

Bremen, Ohio, had opened in 1937. It moved to Oklahoma City in 1967, where it manufactured rubber gloves.[45]

Rempel Manufacturing

Rempel Manufacturing, located at 404 Morgan Avenue in South Akron, was founded by Dietrich and Ruth Rempel. In 1945 Dietrich had an idea to mold a rubber toy without pumping steam under pressure into the molds, which was the common practice of curing rubber products. By June 1946, his idea worked. This method did not require the maintenance of heavy equipment such as boilers, which lowered the cost of production.

Rempel had been a development design engineer for Sun Rubber in Barberton, where he developed a reputation for inventive and lucrative genius.[46] (One of his many inventions for Sun Rubber was the Mickey Mouse gas mask described above.)[47] Born in Russia in 1904 to German and Dutch parents, Rempel fled the Russian Revolution as a Mennonite refuge. He escaped, but his parents and a brother were killed before he was able to immigrate to the United States in 1923 with the help of an uncle. Before coming to Akron to work in the rubber plants, Rempel lived in California and Pennsylvania and graduated from Bluffton College (now Bluffton University) in Bluffton, Ohio, as a sculptor with a degree in art. At Bluffton he studied under John Peter Klassen, another Mennonite refuge from Russia, and while there he sculpted "The Fallen Rider," which depicts a dying young man, said to represent his brother, attended by his horse. The statue remains on display outside Bluffton library's reading room.[48]

Ruth Rempel attended Kent State and The University of Akron and was a cum laude Akron law school graduate. She was admitted to the Ohio State Bar in 1934 and worked in Akron as an attorney before marrying Charles Worster, who moved to Akron from Brooklyn, New York, to work for Goodyear Tire. Worster died in 1940 of an illness contracted while working as the Brazil export manager for the Chrysler Corporation. While married, the Worsters kept a home in Puerto Rico, where Ruth made a hobby of collecting seashells and fashioning them into small dolls, which she exhibited at the International Doll Exhibit in Akron, the Pan American show at Tampa, Florida, and at the New York's World Fair in 1939. Dietrich and Ruth Rempel married in 1941 and lived at 792 West Market Street (now the location of Angel Falls Coffee).[49]

The Rempels organized as Rempel Manufacturing and Rempel Enterprises. The latter business owned the patents and copyrights used in their production of toys. They began with a set of ten barnyard animals. The originals were sculpted in clay by Dietrich. By the spring of 1947, Rempel Manufacturing had forty-three employees who made six thousand toys a day. Rempel licensed Oak Rubber Company of Ravenna to make these toys too. Frisky the Horse, Milky the Cow, and Balky the Mule were some of the first of the barnyard animals.[50]

Another example of Rempel's ingenuity explains the addition of squeakers to his soft, hollow-bodied toys. During production, such toys would collapse unless the temperature and pressure were equalized inside and outside of the toy. Rempel made a hole in the toy with a straw to accomplish this and inserted small squeakers to plug it. Rempel Enterprises secured about fifty patents and registered one hundred copyrights over the nineteen years it was owned by the Rempels.[51]

Frank Ferrin, Hollywood radio producer, visited Akron for a Froggy the Gremlin business promotion. Froggy was introduced on the Smilin' Ed McConnell children's show on NBC during the war and became very popular. Smilin' Ed used a frog-like voice whenever he told stories. Someone remembered Ed's frog voice and Froggy the Gremlin was born. They chose Rempel to produce Froggy, who wore a bright jacket and would stick out his tongue when squeezed.[52]

Another story that brought favorable national attention to Rempel happened in 1953. To answer a dying four-year-old's prayer, Rempel specially manufactured a black duck with a white hat, yellow feet, and bill for a child in Oklahoma who was dying of leukemia. The girl saw another child's toy and cried for it. A local radio station got people around the nation looking for her "right duck." No one was able to find one like she wanted, so Rempel shut down a 450-person production line for three hours to make her one.[53]

Rempel Manufacturing grew rapidly. In 1953 the business and industrial writer for the *Akron Beacon Journal* called it "one of the world's foremost producers of rubber toys" and the company setting "the hottest pace" for progress in Akron. In addition to toys, Rempel also manufactured mattresses for the military, crash pads for tanks, rubber drinking bottles, and pontoons for the Army Corps of Engineers. Rempel had multiple plants in Akron, a subsidiary in Canada, and an affiliate in Mexico. Their toys were being made and sold under licenses in Europe and India, with negotiations ongoing in Asia and South America.[54]

In 1951 a group of Bluffton business majors visited Rempel Manufacturing. Rempel gave them a tour of the plant and afterward discussed startup and business management strategies with them. He explained his profit-sharing policy. At Rempel, 25 percent of all profits, before taxes, were shared with employees. The remainder paid corporation taxes and dividends. He told the students that the profit-sharing plan was so popular, he had more than three hundred people waiting for the 150 positions at the plant.[55] The *Akron Beacon Journal* reported the details of Rempel profit sharing for many years.[56]

Sheep rattle. \ Summit County Historical Society, David Lieberth collection

Cow toy. \ Summit County Historical Society, David Lieberth collection

Pig toy. \ Summit County Historical Society, David Lieberth collection

Santa toy. \ Summit County Historical Society, David Lieberth collection

Santa toy. \ Summit County Historical Society, David Lieberth collection

In a 1954 speech to the Council of Profit-Sharing Industries, D. K. Swartout, president of Swartout Company in Cleveland, noted that unions were suspicious of profit-sharing plans. In 1956, Rempel employees twice voted against joining the United Rubber Workers in close elections.[57] In April 1962, employees voted almost two to one to join the United Rubber Workers.[58] In early 1963, Rempel relocated to West Point, Mississippi, laying off nearly all of its 150 workers. Sixty percent were women.[59] In 1965, a Cuyahoga Falls-based company, Blazon, which made play equipment, bought the former Rempel Manufacturing Company. Dietrich Rempel joined Blazon to do product research and development for both firms.[60] The Rempels never moved to Mississippi. Ruth died on March 20, 1986, and Dietrich followed her on March 22, 1987.[61]

Little Tikes, Step2, and Simplay3

Little Tikes and Step2 are not Akron toy companies, but they are successful toy manufacturing ventures in northern Summit County.

Little Tikes began as Rotadyne, a molded container and auto parts company born in a barn in Aurora around 1968. In 1969 Thomas Murdough Jr. joined the company after working at Wilson Sporting Goods, with a plan to apply their rotational molding process to the toy industry. This process produced unusually durable polyethylene products. From the start, sales of their toy products, marketed for young children under the name Little Tikes, were very strong. Sales of frog-shaped toy chests were so strong, the company had to expand dramatically to meet demand.[62]

Rubbermaid, based in Wooster, acquired Little Tikes in 1984.[63] One very popular product, the Cozy Coupe, is a red foot-powered car with a yellow roof and a door that swings open. In 1991 half a million of these cars were sold, making it the best-selling car in America.[64] By 1995 Little Tikes was the largest rotomolder in the world.[65] In 2006, the Little Tikes brand was acquired by MGA Entertainment, a California-based company that describes itself today as the world's largest private toy company. In the twenty-first century, children's toys have become much more technological and digital, and globalization has seen toy production for American companies move overseas to places with cheap labor, such as China. When Little Tikes was acquired by MGA Entertainment in 2006, all of MGA Entertainment's toys were manufactured in China. A large portion of the smaller and mid-size Little Tikes toys were made in China, but the larger, heavier items were still manufactured in Hudson, making Little Tikes one of the last toy makers manufacturing in the United States.[66] In 2014, Little Tikes employed about eight hundred people at its plant and headquarters in Hudson.[67]

Akron, Home of the World of Make-Believe

Another toy maker still manufacturing in the United States—and in Summit County—is Step2. After leaving Rubbermaid, in 1981 Little Tikes founder Thomas Murdough Jr. founded Step2 Corporation to create toys that rival and go a step beyond the toys sold by Little Tikes.[68] In 2014, Step2 employed about four hundred workers at its Streetsboro plant and another five hundred at its plant in Ashland County.[69]

In 2016 Murdough founded a third toy company, Simplay3, also in Streetsboro. Simplay3 markets its toys as "made in America by an American workforce." In 2019 he was inducted the Toy Industry Hall of Fame.[70]

Notes

1. Grismer, 642.

2. Kenneth Nichols, "Town Crier," *Akron Beacon Journal*, March 31, 1958, 18. Unless otherwise noted, newspapers are cited from digital versions through Newspapers.com.

3. Mark J. Price, "Tales of Love, Longing," *Akron Beacon Journal*, August 27, 2015, B3.

4. Carl Chancellor, "Better Times for Children," *Akron Beacon Journal*, June 20, 1999, C3.

5. Kenneth Nichols, "Movie Star a Blockhead," *Akron Beacon Journal*, November 3, 1965, D18.

6. Joseph E. Kuebler, "Cost Stability Ending?" *Akron Beacon Journal*, August 28, 1964, 32.

7. Mickey Porter, "Sex by Another Name," *Akron Beacon Journal*, March 14, 1968. C1.

8. "Saalfield Publishing's Sales Show a 15 Percent Gain," *Akron Beacon Journal*, February 5, 1967, 16.

9. "2 Million Moonwalk Books Sold," *Akron Beacon Journal*, January 11, 1970, G9.

10. "Banks Foreclosing on Saalfield Loan," *Akron Beacon Journal*, May 4, 1976, 1; Bob Downing, " 120 Workers Lose Pensions at Saalfield," *Akron Beacon Journal*, September 19, 1976, 1.

11. Dottie McGrew, "Expert Tells How to Choose Children's Books," *Akron Beacon Journal*, December 6, 1992, B10.

12. "Old Saalfield Publishing Sold," *Akron Beacon Journal*, February 18, 1977, B1.

13. Greg Gardner, "Akron's Crane-Howard Lithograph Files to Reorganize," *Akron Beacon Journal*, March 28, 1984, C7 ; Greg Gardner, "Bankruptcy Fight Fails," *Akron Beacon Journal*, June 29, 1984, 5 ; Rick Reiff, "Ex-Boss Owes Lithograph Firm Almost $1 Million," *Akron Beacon Journal*, September 19, 1984, 6.

14. "Industries of Akron Display Their Products," *Akron Beacon Journal*, July 20, 1925, 1, 21.

15. "Anderson Rubber Head Dies," *Akron Beacon Journal*, December 10, 1962, 9.

16. Grismer, 619; "Heavy Demand for Rubber Novelties," *Akron Beacon Journal*, May 18, 1922. 11 ; "Anderson Co. Makes Rubber Novelties," *Akron Beacon Journal*, July 21, 1925. C26.

17. "Plan More Surprises at Old Santa's Party." *Akron Beacon Journal*. December 21, 1926. 26; "Doors Open at 9:30 for Christmas Party," *Akron Beacon Journal*, December 19, 1929, 26.

18. "Sally Rand to Continue Fan Dances Despite Sentence to Year in Pen; Wins Support," *Great Falls Leader*, September 25, 1933, 7; "Fan Dancer May Do Year in Cell," *Knoxville News-Sentinel*, September 24, 1938, 1.

19. "Farmer's Candid Shot of Sally's Dance May Hit Navy's Budget For Her Bubbles," *Akron Beacon Journal*, November 10, 1938, 21.

20. "Anderson Rubber to Build Plant," *Akron Beacon Journal*, March 3, 1931, 21.

21. Nancy Peacock, "Some Surprises Found in Summit Old Toy Exhibit," *Akron Beacon Journal*, December 1, 1981, 45.

22. "Toying with Inflation," *Akron Beacon Journal*, October 26, 1975, 195 ; Marilyn Geewax, "For Venerable Akron Firm, Cheap Toys Spell Solvency," *Akron Beacon Journal*, July 6, 1982, 10; Katie Byard, "Anderson Chooses Hudson," *Akron Beacon Journal*, January 8, 1985, 29.

23. Grismer, 643–44; Barberton Historical Society, "The Sun Rubber Company," Facebook, August 16, 2014, accessed July 29, 2024.

24. Hal Fry, "Biography in Brief – Thomas William Smith, Jr.," *Akron Beacon Journal*, April 15, 1951, 27; "Sun Rubber," Fabtintoys: Vintage Toys, Dolls, Model Cars, Trains & Collectibles, http://fabtintoys.com/sun-rubber, accessed July 29, 2024.

25. Kenneth Nichols, "The Town Crier," *Akron Beacon Journal,* March 9, 1942, 13; Harry Rinker, "The End of the Sun Rubber Story," *Morning Call* (Allenstown, PA), April 22, 1990, G2.

26. Oscar Smith, "Toys, Not War Products Now Roll at Sun Rubber," *Akron Beacon Journal*, September 2, 1945, 5; Harry Rinker, "A Definitive Book on Sun Rubber," April 8, 1990, *Morning Call* (Allentown, PA), G12.

27. Rinker, "The End."

28. Wikipedia, s.v., "Amos 'n' Andy," accessed July 29, 2024.

29. Mark Price, "Remembering Amosandra," *Akron Beacon Journal*, November 30, 2020, 1B.

30. "Akron's Amosandra," *Akron Beacon Journal*, March 3, 1949, 6.

31. Price, "Remembering," 4B.

32. Joseph E. Kuebler, "Sun Rubber Turns to Plastics as Toy Material," *Akron Beacon Journal*, March 1, 1953, 11; Joseph E. Kuebler, "Sun Rubber Heads for Biggest Year," *Akron Beacon Journal*, August 19, 1953, 27; Joseph E. Kuebler, "Big Plastic Toys Open New Era for Sun Rubber." *Akron Beacon Journal,* May 3, 1964, 38A.

33. Mark Price, "Hoppity Hop Put Bounce in Barberton," *Akron Beacon Journal*, October 1, 2018, B1.

34. "Brownies!," advertisement, *Akron Evening Times*, December 21, 1900, 9.

35. Mary Ethridge, "Doll of the Toy World," *Akron Beacon Journal*, November 12, 1998, B1.

36. James Haswell, "General Tire Stages Exhibition in Capital," *Akron Beacon Journal*, April 5, 1952, 14.

37. S. Victor Fleischer, *The Goodyear Tire and Rubber Company: A Photographic History, 1898–1951* (University of Akron Press, 2020), 46n16; Advertisement for Goodyear Service Store, *News-Star* (Monroe, LA), December 16, 1955, 5; Advertisement for Snow's service station, *Sun-Journal* (Lewiston, ME), December 19, 1956, 17; Advertisement of Goodyear Service Store, *Bryan Daily Eagle* (Bryan, TX), November 27, 1958, 16.

38. Joseph Kuebler, "Albert Bids $565,000 for Latex Firm," *Akron Beacon Journal,* January 13, 1953, 1.

39. "Crowds See City's Exhibit," *Akron Beacon Journal,* February 19, 1938. 10.

40. "New Disney Characters to Feature Toys," *Akron Beacon Journal*, October 10, 1939, 33.

41. Joseph Kuebler, "Akron Area Products Displayed in New York," *Akron Beacon Journal*, March 10, 1947, 9.

42. Joseph Kuebler, "Akron Built Toys Going to Exhibit," *Akron Beacon Journal*, March 7, 1948, 35.

43. Joseph Kuebler, "Toys are Big Business for Akron Area Plants," *Akron Beacon Journal,* December 18, 1949, 25.

44. Joseph Kuebler, "Albert Bids $565,000 for Latex Firm." *Akron Beacon Journal,* January 13, 1953, 1; Joseph Kuebler, "Nearly All Shares Are Turned In." *Akron Beacon Journal,* February 6, 1953, 27.

45. "Action Line," *Akron Beacon Journal*, August 5, 1968, 3.

46. "Dietrich G. Rempel," *Akron Beacon Journal*, October 20, 1944, 30; "Biography in Brief: Dietrich G. Rempel," *Akron Beacon Journal*, April 1, 1945, 3D.

47. Nancy Peacock, "Some Surprises Found in Summit Old Toy Exhibit," *Akron Beacon Journal*, December 1, 1981, 45.

48. Grismer, 817; "The Fallen Rider," Blufton Forever, September 29, 2023, accessed July 31, 2024, https://www.blufftonforever.com/post/the-fallen-rider.

49. "Miss Ruth Fogle Passes Bar Test," *Akron Beacon Journal*, July 31, 1934, 8; "Charles Worster Succumbs in East," *Akron Beacon Journal*, March 12, 1940, 26; "She Shows Sea Shells," *Akron Beacon Journal*, February 5, 1939, 4B; "Akron Attorney Weds," *Akron Beacon Journal*, May 18, 1941, 7B.

50. Joseph Kuebler, "New Idea Pays in Rubber Toys," *Akron Beacon Journal*, May 11, 1947, 19.

51. Peacock.

52. Bee Offineer, "'Froggy' Creator Visits Akron," *Akron Beacon Journal*, July 18, 1948, A12.

Akron, Home of the World of Make-Believe

53. "Firm Shuts Down to Make Toy for Dying Girl," *Frederick Leader* (Frederick, OK), June 12, 1953, 1; "Duck Helps Cheer Dying Girl," *Akron Beacon Journal*. June 12, 1953, 15.

54. Joseph E. Kuebler, "Hottest Pace in Akron Industry is Set by Rempel Manufacturing," *Akron Beacon Journal*, October 11, 1953, 10B.

55. Mary Margaret Soldner, "Bluffton Students Visit Rempel Toy Company," *Mennonite Weekly Review* (Newton, KS), May 31, 1951, 3.

56. For example, see Joseph E. Kuebler, "3-Year-Old Firm Here Splits $12,000 Melon," *Akron Beacon Journal*, July 3, 1949, 1; "Rempel Santa Splits $24,000 Profit," *Akron Beacon Journal*, December 21, 1949, 40; "Rempel Stockholders, Employees Split Melon," *Akron Beacon Journal*, December 25, 1950, 10.

57. "Says Unions Resist Profit Sharing Plan," *Akron Beacon Journal*, April 2, 1954, 39; "Reject URW by 26 Votes at Rempel," *Akron Beacon Journal*, October 25, 1956, 51.

58. "Vote In URW at Rempel," *Akron Beacon Journal*, April 20, 1962, 16.

59. "Will Move Rempel Toy Plant South," *Akron Beacon Journal*, January 6, 1963, 33.

60. Joseph Kuebler, "Ex-Akron Toy Firm Bought by Blazon," *Akron Beacon Journal*, May 18, 1965, B9.

61. "Dietrich Rempel, Toy Maker," *Akron Beacon Journal*, March 24, 1987, E2.

62. Larry Froelich, "This Frog Explosion Nearly Made Toy Company 'Croak,'" *Akron Beacon Journal*, March 30, 1973, 11; Joseph Kuebler, "Toymaker's Bonanza Includes Second Plant," *Akron Beacon Journal*, November 26, 1975, 9.

63. Greg Gardner, "Rubbermaid Wins Bid to Acquire Toymaker Little Tikes," *Akron Beacon Journal*, April 19, 1984, 6.

64. "Hottest-Selling Auto Runs on Foot Power," *Akron Beacon Journal*, November 29, 1992, 17.

65. Peter J. Mooney, "Rotomolding on a Roll," *Plastics Engineering*, September 2014, 6, OhioLINK Electronic Journal Center.

66. "Little Tikes Ready to Cast New Mold," *Akron Beacon Journal*, December 10, 2006, D1; "About Us," MGA Entertainment, accessed July 31, 2024, https://www.mgae.com/about.

67. Betty Lin-Fisher, "Toys Roll Out for the Holidays," *Akron Beacon Journal*, November 23, 2014, D1.

68. Robert Fernandez, "Battling His Own Goliath," *Akron Beacon Journal*, October 14, 1991, D1.

69. Betty Lin-Fisher, "Toys Roll Out for the Holidays," *Akron Beacon Journal*, November 23, 2014, D1.

70. "About," Simplay3, accessed July 31, 2024, https://simplay3.com/our-story; Bob Gaetjens, "Little Tikes Founder Gets Hall of Fame Nod," *Akron Beacon Journal*, June 24, 2019, B1.

Wendell Willkie, Republican presidential nominee, head-and-shoulders portrait, facing slightly right, circa 1940. \ Photo by Bachrach; copyright not renewed. Library of Congress.

\ **10**

Wendell Willkie

Akron's Favorite (Adopted) Son

Clair Dickinson

A young man moved to Akron in the spring of 1919, convinced that the city held more opportunities for success than his hometown of Elwood, Indiana.[1] Elwood had a population of about eleven thousand and was slowly shrinking.[2] Akron would soon have 208,435 residents, most of whom had arrived since 1910, when it had a population of 69,687.[3] That young man, Wendell Willkie, like so many of the newcomers, had come to work for one of the city's rubber companies. But he had not come to build tires. He had come to build a legal career and a life as an active member of the community. And that's exactly what he did. Over the next ten years he became a leader in the city's political, legal, and social lives. People in Akron soon came to recognize that there was something special about Willkie.

According to Willkie, he didn't know anyone when he arrived. But when he left ten years later in the fall of 1929, 125 members of the Akron Bar Association turned out to wish him well.[4] And when he passed through the city in October 1940 as the Republican nominee for president of the United States, more than twenty-five thousand people came out to hear him speak.[5] Among other things, he told them that he had formed some of his finest friendships and had had the most stimulating experiences of his life in Akron.[6]

Willkie was born in 1892, the fourth of six children of Herman and Henrietta Willkie.[7] Herman had been the Superintendent of Schools in Elwood but, by the time Wendell was born, had become a lawyer and was practicing law. Henrietta became a lawyer in 1897, perhaps the first woman admitted to the Indiana bar. Both of Wendell's parents were "persons of extraordinary ability and character." They read widely and viewed exposure to intellect as an important part of raising their children. Herman read to them every night and recited Shakespeare to wake them in the morning. Mealtimes were marked by debates about such things as economics, politics, history, or literature, and all members of the family participated.[8]

Willkie received his AB degree from Indiana University in 1913. He then taught high school history for a year in Kansas. He was "a remarkable teacher who made history come vividly alive to his students." But he left teaching for a better-paying job working with his brother in Puerto Rico. He returned to Indiana University in the fall of 1915 to study law and received his LLB degree in the spring of 1916.[9] Upon receiving his law degree, he was admitted to practice in Ohio, Indiana, and New York.[10]

He returned to Elwood and began practicing law with his father and brother Robert. But less than a year later, on April 2, 1917, the United States entered World War I, and Willkie enlisted in the army. He spent time at various bases in the United States, finally leaving for Europe in September 1918. Upon arrival in France, his regiment was ordered to the Western Front, but the armistice was announced before they got there. He spent a few months representing soldiers accused of violations of the military code before returning to Elwood and civilian life.[11]

Willkie married Edith Wilk in January 1918 while he was on leave from the army. She was from Rushville, Indiana, and Willkie had met her when she had been a bridesmaid at a friend's wedding.[12]

Back in Elwood, Willkie considered becoming the Democratic candidate against a Republican Congressman who appeared vulnerable. But a family friend who was a Democratic leader in Indianapolis told him that, while he could probably beat the incumbent in 1920, he would have a hard time holding the seat because it was a Republican district. The friend suggested that Willkie's long-term prospects would be better in a growing industrial area and offered to help him get a job in Akron with Firestone Tire and Rubber Company.[13]

Willkie was hired by Firestone at a salary of $2500 a year. A number of sources indicate that he started his new job on April 1, 1919, but he actually started in the middle of May.[14] There were a number of conventions in Akron around the time of his arrival: secretaries of Ohio chambers of commerce began a convention on May 16th; the Gideons held a convention on May 17th and 18th; and the Ohio Christian Missionary Society and Ohio Christian Women's Missionary Society held a convention on May 19th through May 22. No doubt because of all the conventioneers, Willkie spent his first night in Akron on a cot in a hallway of the Howe Hotel at 11 South Main Street.[15]

Edith, who was pregnant, had stayed behind in Indiana, and Willkie rented a room in a boarding house at 157 South Balch Street.[16] His arrival in the city was marked by an announcement in the *Akron Beacon Journal*: "Firestone has established an employee's legal department with Wendell L. Willkie in charge where employees may get legal advice, have wills drawn, or other legal questions taken care of."[17] According to the announcement, Willkie had practiced law in Indiana for six years, which wasn't true, and also had become "prosecuting attorney of Madison county, Ind.," which doesn't appear to be true.

Willkie later said that the first task he was put to at Firestone was writing wills for employees. According to him, he "wrote several thousand wills." He joked that he was glad that none had "ever come into contest, because I have worried about my immaturity about such matters at that time." He said that during the year and a half he stayed at Firestone, "hundreds and hundreds of people who were employed by the [company] individually consulted me about their various problems, and I tried their simpler cases in the courts of [Summit] county."[18]

The Willkies' son Philip was born in December 1919, and Edith, or "Billie" as she was known, and Philip soon joined Wendell in Akron.[19] They moved into an apartment at 238 Rhodes Avenue, which they may have shared with another couple.[20] By the time the 1922 City Directory was published, they were living at 67 Rhodes Avenue, the southern side of a side-by-side duplex.[21] By the 1924 Directory, they were living at 180 Beck Avenue, where they stayed for the remainder of their time in Akron.[22]

Willkie made an impression on Akron. When he visited the city in July 1940 during his presidential campaign, an article in the *Akron Beacon Journal* described what Willkie was like during his years here. The author spoke with "more than a score of people," including "attorneys who fought with him, liked him, and were afraid of him" and "people with whom he lived, drank, and ate." He learned that Willkie was an incredibly hard worker and effective lawyer:

> The Wendell Willkie that Akron knew was the hardest-working, fastest-thinking, most dangerous lawyer ever to practice before the local bar. He was a man of almost superhuman energy who could read until two a.m., sleep for two hours, get up and read until breakfast, then go to the office for a fifteen- to eighteen-hour working day.

He would bring cheese sandwiches and beans to the office so he wouldn't have to break for lunch.[23] Al Blinn, who had been president of Northern Ohio

Traction & Light Company, a client of the firm Willkie joined after he left Firestone, described him as a "bull dog for work" and "the best trial lawyer in town."[24] Perhaps because of those debates around his family's dinner table growing up, he loved to argue. When he arrived at a party, he "would look around to see who was there, decide how they stood on a certain issue, and start the argument on the opposite side."[25] According to John S. Knight, Willkie "had a booming voice, waived his arms a great deal and was indeed an impressive figure of a man."[26] But, he was a sloppy dresser: "He was constantly in need of a hair-cut, his shoes were never shined, his suits were unpressed and his straw hat was a disgrace." He didn't own a car, saying he could not think and drive at the same time. Instead, he depended on buses and friends for his transportation needs. He bought books by the box load.[27] He was a member of Portage Country Club but didn't play golf, preferring to sit on the patio and kid his friends as they finished their rounds.[28] According to Blinn, "His job was his hobby."[29]

Willkie's grandson, who was born after Willkie's death, described him, apparently based on information from family members who knew him, as "a cardiologist's worst case: He smoked three packs of Camels daily, clearly enjoyed his scotch, ate more than he should, and never exercised."[30] It's unclear whether he had acquired all of those habits by the time he was in Akron, but the beginnings of some of them were probably already present. (Photographs of him during his time here reveal someone who weighed considerably less than he did in photographs from later years.)

Willkie, Robert Guinther, and other young lawyers in Akron joined the local Democratic Club.[31] According to Guinther, he and Willkie "cover[ed] the area, backing Democrats" in 1920.[32] Willkie also campaigned that year for the League of Nations. He would speak in favor of the League "whenever and wherever he could get an audience," including "from trucks parked on Akron street corners." Once when he was introduced as a guest at a Kiwanis Club luncheon, he startled everyone by making a speech in favor of the League.[33] According to Guinther, Willkie was "a fine speaker, having an excellent voice and mechanically perfect delivery.... His forte was just talking."[34] He was a delegate to the 1920 Democratic National Convention because he won a coin toss over Guinther.[35]

Willkie was in great demand as a speaker. Perhaps because of his time as a history teacher, he often spoke to groups about Washington or Lincoln.[36] On July 4, 1923, he played Lincoln, complete with whiskers, in a pageant at Perkins Woods attended by five thousand people.[37] Part of the pageant showed the separation of the states during the Civil War. Willkie, as Lincoln, depicted the reuniting of the states by reciting the Emancipation Proclamation and striking "the shackles from the arms of a slave."[38] On Memorial Day 1927, Willkie was among the speakers at Glendale Cemetery. However, the crowd drew a disappointing three hundred, as it coincided with the start of the national balloon race at the Akron Cleveland Speedway, which attracted twenty-five thousand people.[39]

When Hammel Business University organized the Akron Law School in 1921, Willkie was one of the fourteen "leading lawyers now engaged in legal practice at the Akron bar" announced as faculty members.[40] He taught at the school for two years.[41] His photograph was among those of "Citizens Prominent in Development of Akron," published in July 1925 by the *Akron Beacon Journal* as part of the celebration of the city's centennial.[42]

When Willkie first came to Akron, he joined Firestone Park Memorial Post No. 301 of the American Legion.[43] By February 1921, there were ten American Legion Posts in Akron.[44] Although Akron was booming when Willkie arrived, between the spring of 1920 and the spring of 1921, a recession caused 45,000 employees of Akron's rubber plants to lose their jobs. This meant that thousands of men who had come to Akron to work, many of whom were veterans, were now jobless. Many looked to the American Legion for assistance.[45]

Nine of the ten Akron posts decided to consolidate to solve the "Legion problem in the city."[46] Since Summit Post 19 had the lowest post number and there was "an advantage in a low number," it was chosen to survive the consolidation.[47] An election of officers for the consolidated post was held on May 2, 1921, in which 690 votes were cast. O. D. Hollenbeck was elected post commander, and Willkie, who at the time had been in Akron for a little less than two years, was elected first vice commander.[48] Speaking to the YWCA in July 1921, Willkie described the importance of the Legion: "No organization in the United States has such possibilities for good or evil as the American Legion."[49] When Hollenbeck resigned four months later to take a job in Indiana, Willkie succeeded him as commander.[50]

Post 19 struggled to find money to provide the help veterans needed. Among other things, it launched a "Help-a-Buddy fund" to raise $10,000 by Armistice Day 1921 "to furnish meals, beds, an employment bureau and incidental expenses necessary to bring the men in contact with employers."[51] Willkie said, "We are after funds simply because we must have them if we are to help out those unemployed ex-service men who come to us, out of work, without a place to sleep, and oftentimes hungry."[52] The post struggled to meet the goal, extended the deadline, and eventually ended the campaign without reaching the goal.[53]

When it came time to elect new officers in January 1922, Willkie was elected commander in his own right.[54] But the post's struggles to raise money continued. Ernestine Schumann-Heink, an operatic singer known as the "Mother of American Legion," agreed to do a benefit concert at the Akron Armory "as an outright gift."[55] Still, the tickets weren't selling as quickly as had been hoped. Someone came up with the idea of selling tickets to students at Kent State. The story goes that Willkie went to campus and spent ten minutes talking about "the charm of Mme. Schumann-Heink" and how the post needed money to help veterans. He left some tickets behind, and the next day the dean's office called for more. When the concert was finally held, the armory was full, and the post cleared a profit of either three or four thousand dollars, depending on the report.[56] The esteem in which members of Post 19 held Willkie is clear from the fact that, in 1945, they changed its name to Wendell L. Willkie Post No. 19.[57]

Willkie didn't like the limitations of his work at Firestone but loved the drama of the courtroom.[58] By December 1920, his annual salary at Firestone had risen to $5,400 and, when he told Harvey Firestone he intended to leave, Firestone supposedly offered to raise his salary to $10,000.[59] Willkie, however, turned down the offer, leaving Firestone on December 31, 1920. Firestone reputedly told him he would "never amount to much" because he was a Democrat.[60]

The next day, Willkie joined the firm of Mather and Nesbitt at an annual salary of $3,600 and a promise of a future partnership.[61] When Willkie first started with the firm, he didn't even have an office and worked in the firm's library.[62] By the time the 1922 City Directory was published, the firm's name had been changed to Mather, Nesbitt and Willkie.[63]

Nation O. Mather, the senior member of the firm, had been a Republican member of the Ohio Senate and was a corporate lawyer and "rainmaker."[64] Roy Nesbitt was a trial lawyer.[65] Willkie started out helping Nesbitt, but soon was trying cases on his own.[66]

The Northern Ohio Traction and Light Company was among the firm's important clients. In fact, the firm's offices were in the company's Terminal Building at 47 North Main Street.[67] Willkie was soon busy trying cases on its behalf, usually opposing people who had been injured by its streetcars.[68] When a former Republican mayor of Akron, who had supported a candidate other than Willkie for the 1940 Republican nomination, wrote a "hit piece" aimed at helping to keep him from again being nominated in 1944, he damned his trial skills with faint praise: "I knew him and saw him over the years devote his superlative talents to preventing poor people who had lost their eyes, arms or legs from wringing a just compensation from his employing corporation."[69]

But Willkie didn't only defend personal injury cases. In June 1923, he won a jury verdict of $20,000 against East Ohio Gas Company on behalf of an employee of Northern Ohio Traction and Light Company for serious injuries he suffered in an explosion in a manhole in which he and others were working.[70] It was, at that time, the largest verdict ever awarded in Summit County.[71]

In 1925, he represented a former city councilman in a lawsuit filed against him by Willkie's former employer, Firestone Tire and Rubber Company.[72] According to Firestone, Willkie's client, who had previously been employed by a subsidiary of Firestone, had sold stock in the *Akron Times Press* to Scripps Publishing Company and kept the proceeds when he should have turned them over to Firestone. Although the shares were held in Willkie's client's name, they had been bought by Firestone and were held by the client in trust for the company. Firestone sought judgment for $60,000. The parties settled the case, and, when asked about the terms, Willkie would only say that they were confidential and satisfactory to both parties. When asked about a rumor that the settlement was a complete victory for his client, he refused to comment.[73]

In 1926, he defended Northern Ohio Traction and Light Company in a lawsuit brought by one of its preferred stockholders seeking $5 million for alleged illegal payments for services and as dividends. Willkie obtained a "sweeping victory" for the company.[74]

In 1927, he and E. W. Brouse obtained an injunction in a taxpayer's suit preventing a construction company from carrying out a contract to build the 13,000-foot interceptor link in the Botsum sewage disposal system. That judgment, however, was reversed by the Court of Appeals.

He also represented Northern Ohio Traction and Light Company in negotiating streetcar franchises with governmental entities, including Akron. When, in 1933, after Willkie had moved to New York, difficulties arose between Northern Ohio and Akron during franchise negotiations of a rate for electric lights, the *Beacon Journal* suggested that maybe they should bring Willkie back to "lead the boys around by the hand." "You always could count on a fairly decent show, at least, when Willkie negotiated the franchise."[75]

Willkie was unanimously elected president of the Akron Bar Association in March 1925. In remarks after his election, he said, among other things, that he knew it was customary for newly elected Bar presidents to promise to do as well as his predecessor: "I say to you that I will endeavor to be, as the *Beacon Journal* said of my predecessor, 'handsome and clean cut.'"[76]

Willkie was an opponent of the Ku Klux Klan. By May 1922, the Klan had several thousand members in Akron.[77] In November 1923, three Klan members were elected to the Akron Board of Education.[78] At the end of 1924, one of the non-Klan members of the Board resigned.[79] At the next meeting, a member of the Klan was chosen by the Board as his replacement, giving the Klan a four-person majority on the seven-member Board.[80] In June 1925 the three non-Klan members resigned after the Klan members hired a former superintendent of the schools in Springfield, Ohio, who had aligned with the Klan when he held that position, as the new superintendent. Three new members were chosen as their replacements.[81] A Committee of 100 was formed to recruit candidates for the four seats that would be elected to the Board in November of that year, hoping to present candidates "responsible solely to the electorate of Akron and not to any political or fraternal organization, group or bloc." Willkie's friend Robert Guinther and six others led the committee. Willkie was listed as one of the 100 members.[82] No further mentions of Willkie appear in the *Beacon Journal* during that campaign. The author of the previously mentioned article, who had talked to "more than a score of people" who knew Willkie in Akron, suggested that his role in the campaign may have later been overstated by some: "Although Willkie's opposition to the Ku Klux Klan was unquestioned, the part he played in breaking the Klan's control of Akron schools has been greatly exaggerated by uninformed biographers."[83]

Regardless, three of the four committee-supported candidates were elected, and the Klan's hold on the Board was broken.[84]

Willkie was a delegate to the 1924 Democratic Convention at which John W. Davis was nominated for president on the 103rd ballot. A proposed plank in the party platform condemning the Ku Klux Klan by name was defeated at the convention by a single vote.[85] Back in Akron after the convention, Willkie explained that the Ohio delegation had been instrumental in breaking the deadlock and enabling Davis's nomination. New York Governor Al Smith agreed that, if the Ohio delegation would switch its support from favorite son candidate Ohio Governor James Cox to him, giving him the lead, he would then withdraw in favor of Davis. Willkie moved that the delegation switch its support to Smith, and his motion passed by a vote of twenty-two to fifteen. According to Willkie, the twenty-two delegates who supported his motion were those who were not afraid of what the Ku Klux Klan and its allies back home would say about them.[86] (Smith was a Catholic, one of the groups targeted by the Klan.)

Willkie's work for Northern Ohio Power and Light Company brought him to the attention of that company's parent company, Allied Power & Light Corporation. In August 1929, he announced that he would be leaving Akron on October 1 to join Allied's general counsel Weadock & Weadock in New York City.[87] One hundred twenty-five members of the Akron Bar Association attended a dinner in his honor to mark his departure. Willkie told them that leaving Akron was the "most difficult thing I have ever had to do," and that he "never would have considered leaving Akron if [he] had realized it would be so hard to sever [his] associations here.[88]

By January 1933, Willkie had become president of Commonwealth & Southern Corporation, one of the five largest electric utilities in the country.[89] Soon he was battling with the Roosevelt Administration over The Tennessee Valley Authority's competition with private suppliers of electricity like Commonwealth & Southern.[90]

In 1940, Willkie sought the Republican nomination for president of the United States, despite having been a Democrat until shortly before becoming a candidate. John S. Knight, an old friend from Willkie's Akron days, wrote an editorial in the *Akron Beacon Journal* stating that he regarded Willkie "as admirably equipped for the highest office in the land." But he didn't think the Republicans would nominate him: "His conversion to the party of Lincoln and McKinley is much too recent for them to admit him into their hallowed lodge as a full-fledged member of the Grand Old Party.... Politics 'just ain't' run that way."[91]

But Willkie proved his old friend wrong. He won the nomination but went on to lose the election to Franklin Roosevelt. (Knight was in Willkie's suite at the Philadelphia convention the night he cinched the nomination and participated in discussions about who should be his running mate.[92]) Despite the esteem in which many in Akron held Willkie, Roosevelt carried Summit County 89,305 to 63,027.[93]

In 1942, Willkie took a seven-week world tour of inspection and goodwill with the approval and assistance of President Roosevelt.[94] After his return, he wrote "One World," in which he talked about the trip and his vision for the world after the war. Among other things, he argued for "the creation of a world in which there shall be an equality of opportunity for every race and every nation."[95]

Willkie again sought the Republican nomination in 1944 but dropped out of the race after losing the Wisconsin primary.[96] Six months later he died of a heart attack.[97]

The City of Akron celebrated Willkie and his time here with the unveiling of a plaque in his honor at the Akron Jewish Center on Balch Street on December 10, 1953.[98] Among the speakers that evening was Henry Cabot Lodge, the US Ambassador to the United Nations. Among other things, Lodge said that, without Willkie's 1940 presidential campaign, "there might never have been a United Nations."[99]

The plaque was later hung on the first floor of the Summit County Courthouse, where it remains today, across from the Probate Courtroom.[100] It includes a low relief sculpture of Willkie and describes him as a "distinguished citizen of our county, and of our country.... lawyer, soldier, industrialist and author." It also includes a Willkie quote: "I believe in America because in it we are free—free to choose our government and speak our minds, to observe our different religions because we hate no people and covet no peoples' lands; because we have great dreams and because we have the opportunity to make those dreams come true."

Notes

1. Letter of application from Wendell L. Willkie to Firestone Tire and Rubber Company, quoted in Ellsworth Barnard, *Wendell Willkie Fighter for Freedom* (Northern Michigan University Press, 1966), 57–58.

2. "Population—Indiana," *Fourteenth Census of the United States: 1920 Bulletin*, Bureau of the Census, Department of Commerce, 15, census.gov.

3. "Population—Ohio," *Fourteenth Census of the United States: 1920 Bulletin*, Bureau of the Census, Department of Commerce, 2, census.gov.

4. "Willkie Honored with Dinner by Bar Association." *Akron Beacon Journal*, September 24, 1929, 33. Unless otherwise noted, newspapers are cited from digital versions through Newspapers.com.

5. H. H. Harriman, "25,000 Hear Willkie's Plea to Labor." *Akron Beacon Journal*, October 25, 1940, 1.

6. "Text of Willkie's 'Homecoming' Address on Collective Bargaining." *Akron Beacon Journal*, October 25, 1940, 8.

7. Steve Neal, *Dark Horse, A Biography of Wendell Willkie* (Doubleday & Company, 1984), 1–2.

8. Barnard, 9–20.

9. Barnard, 39; Neal, 11–12; Barnard, 44; "Wendell Lewis Willkie," *Maurer Notable Alumni*, Maurer School of Law Digital Repository, https://www.repository.law.indiana.edu.

10. "We congratulate—W. L. Willkie," *Akron Beacon Journal*, February 18, 1928, 11.

11. Barnard, 46; Neal, 14–16; Barnard, 54.

12. Barnard, 50, 47.

13. Neal, 16; Barnard, 57.

14. Barnard, 57–58; "We congratulate—W. L. Willkie;" "Akron Attorney to New York," *Akron Times Press*, August 8, 1929; C. Nelson Sparks, *One Man—Wendell Willkie* (Rayner Publishing Company 1943), 30. "Text of Willkie's 'Homecoming' Address," 8; Neal, 17.

15. "C. of C. Secretaries of Ohio Meet Here," *Akron Beacon Journal*, May 16, 1919, 1; "Gideons Meet Here Saturday and Sunday," *Akron Beacon Journal*, May 15, 1919, 23; "Churches." *Akron Beacon Journal*, May 17, 1919,6; Anthony Weitzel, "Willkie's Days Here Recalled," *Akron Beacon Journal*, June 28, 1940, 1; "Text of Willkie's 'Homecoming' Address," 8.

16. Keyes Beech, "Here is Wendell Willkie as Akronites Knew Him." *Akron Beacon Journal*, July 7, 1940, 1.

17. "Will Give Legal Advice to Firestone Workers." *Akron Beacon Journal*, August 16, 1919, 2.

18. "Text of Willkie's 'Homecoming' Address," 8.

19. Barnard, 59; Neal, 17; Helen Waterhouse, "'Billie' Beside Husband 'Every Step of the Way." *Akron Beacon Journal*, October 25, 1940, 1.

20. Akron 1920 Directory, 1299; Neal, 17; Barnard, 59.

21. Akron 1922 Directory, 1137.

22. Akron 1924 Directory, 1208.

23. Beech, 4.

24. Parker La Moore, "Indianian, Wendell Willkie, Is 'Favorite Son' in Akron," *Akron Beacon Journal*, June 10, 1940, 16; "Wendell Willkie—He Grew Up in Akron." *Akron Beacon Journal*, November 27, 1953, 29.

25. Beech, 4.

26. John S. Knight, letter to Steve Neal, January 17, 1978.

27. Beech, 4.

28. "We congratulate—W. L. Willkie," 11; "City, County Honor Willkie Tonight," *Akron Beacon Journal*, December 10, 1953, 1.

29. La Moore, 16.

30. Wendell L. Willkie II, "My Grandfather Was a Republican Nominee Who Put Country First." *The Atlantic*, October 6, 2018.

31. Barnard, 64.

32. "Wendell Willkie—He 'Grew Up' in Akron," 29.

33. Beech, 4.

Wendell Willkie

34. "Wendell Willkie—He 'Grew Up' in Akron," 29.

35. Ben James, "'He Made U.S. Safer'—Lausche." *Akron Beacon Journal*, December 11, 1953, 2.

36. "Speaker on Lincoln," *Akron Beacon Journal*, February 10, 1926, 2; "Realtors Will Hear Talk on Presidents," *Akron Beacon Journal*, February 18, 1928, 24; "Washington, Lincoln Greater as Humans," *Akron Beacon Journal*, February 22, 1928, 18.

37. "Prominent Akron Citizens to be Seen as Historical Characters in July Fourth Pageant," *Akron Beacon Journal*, July 4, 1923, 1; "1000 Citizens Take Part In Patriotic Pageant on Fourth," *Akron Beacon Journal*, July 5, 1923, 20.

38. "1000 Citizens," 20.

39. "With Akron Veterans," *Akron Beacon Journal*, June 4, 1927, 13; Herman Fetzer, "Throng Thrills as Balloons Take Off," *Akron Beacon Journal*, May 31, 1927, 20.

40. "Judge Grant Will Be School Dean," *Akron Beacon Journal*, June 10, 1921, 22.

41. Stanley A. Samad, *Legal Education in Akron, Ohio: A Concise History of the Akron Law School and the University of Akron School of Law* (Akron: Stanley A. Samad, 1990), 60.

42. "Citizens Prominent In Development of Akron," *Akron Beacon Journal*, July 21, 1925, C11.

43. Barnard, 60; "Three Legion Posts Hold Meetings and Vote for Consolidation Plan," *Akron Beacon Journal*, January 18, 1921, 14.

44. "New Legion Post," *Akron Beacon Journal*, February 3, 1921, 14.

45. Barnard, 60.

46. "Would Amalgamate All Legion Posts," *Akron Beacon Journal*, December 22, 1920, 18.

47. "Summit Legion Post Would Put Large Sum into Building Fund. *Akron Beacon Journal,* January 11, 1921, 14.

48. "Hollenbeck Named Post Commander at First Election," *Akron Beacon Journal*, May 3, 1921, 15.

49. "Asks Recognition of American Legion," *Akron Beacon Journal*, July 13, 1921, 10.

50. "Legion Post Holds Spirited Meeting; Delegates Elected," *Akron Beacon Journal*, September 14, 1921,14.

51. "Legion to Launch Campaign for $10,000 to Aid Ex-Service Men Who Are Now Seeking Employment," *Akron Beacon Journal*, October 4, 1921, 5.

52. "Legion Post's Drive for Funds Meeting with Success Here," *Akron Beacon Journal*, October 11, 1921, 5.

53. "Legion Extends 'Help A Buddy' Campaign," *Akron Beacon Journal*, November 12, 1921, 2; "Legion Workers to Have Big Tag Day," *Akron Beacon Journal*, December 7, 1921, 16.

54. "Willkie Reelected Post President," *Akron Beacon Journal*, January 11, 1922, 8.

55. "Legion Members of Summit Post Will Present Madame Schumann-Heink with Rare Cameo," *Akron Beacon Journal*, September 29, 1922, 28; "Schumann-Heink, 'Mother of American Legion,' Touches Heart of Audience," *Akron Beacon Journal*, October 2, 1922, 1.

56. "Willkie's Work for the Legion Is Recalled on Eve of Visit," *Akron Beacon Journal*, May 26, 1940, 14; "As We Remember," *Akron Beacon Journal*, December 6, 1953, 17.

57. "Post Honors Willkie in Name Change Today," *Akron Beacon Journal*, June 18, 1945, D7.

58. Ben James, "'He Made U.S. Safer'—Lausche," *Akron Beacon Journal*, December 11, 1953, 1.

59. Barnard, 59.

60. Neal, 18.

61. Barnard, 59.

62. Keyes Beech, "Here is Wendell Willkie as Akronites Knew Him," *Akron Beacon Journal*, July 7, 1940, 1.

63. Akron 1922 Directory, 1137.

64. "Nation O. Mather," *Akron Beacon Journal*, November 10, 1938, 4; Barnard, 67.

65. Barnard, 67–68.

66. Barnard, 68.

67. Akron 1920 Directory, 945.

68. Barnard, 69.

69. Sparks, 31.

70. "Court of Appeals Affirms $20,000 Judgment Award," *Akron Beacon Journal*, April 15, 1924, 12.

71. Keyes Beech, "Here Is Wendell Willkie," 1.

72. "Newspaper Suit of Wm. Kroeger, Firestone Ends," *Akron Beacon Journal*, September 2, 1926, 1.

73. "Newspaper Suit."

74. "Kenfield Gives Ruling in N.O.P. Finance Action," *Akron Beacon Journal*, December 31, 1926, 13.

75. "Council's Majority Taking Poor Advice," *Akron Beacon Journal*, March 25, 1933, 5.

76. "Attorneys Select Willkie President," *Akron Beacon Journal*, March 7, 1925, 1.

77. Steve Viglio, "The Ku Klux Klan in Northeast Ohio: The Crusade of White Supremacy in the 1920s" (master's thesis, Youngstown State University, 2021), 22; "Ku Klux Gets Warning," *Akron Beacon Journal*, May 22, 1922, 1.

78. Viglio, 26; "Rybolt Victor by 13,802 Votes: Akron Republicans Score Great Victory," *Akron Beacon Journal*, November 7, 1923, 1.

79. Viglio, 30; "Board of Education Member Quits Post," *Akron Beacon Journal*, December 31, 1924, 1.

80. Viglio, 30; "Charles Sweeny Picked for Place on School Board," *Akron Beacon Journal*, January 6, 1925, 1.

81. Viglio, 34; "M'Cord School Chief; 3 Board Members Quit," *Akron Beacon Journal*, June 9, 1925, 1.

82. "Plan Struggle for Control of School Affairs," *Akron Beacon Journal*, August 8, 1925, 1.

83. Keyes Beech, "Here Is Wendell Willkie."

84. "Will Not Contest School Ballot: Anti-Klan Body Decides Policy On Grant Hyde," *Akron Beacon Journal*, November 4, 1925, 1.

85. "Tired, But Cheerful, Akron Delegates Home From Democratic Convention Predict Success," *Akron Beacon Journal*, July 11, 1924, 1.

86. "Ohio Delegation's Part in Selecting Davis Is Related," *Akron Beacon Journal*, July 17, 1925.

87. "Wendell Willkie Becomes Partner in Gotham Firm," *Akron Beacon Journal*, August 8, 1929, 21.

88. "Willkie Honored With Dinner by Bar Association," *Akron Beacon Journal*, September 24, 1929, 33.

89. "First Delegates Are Due in City for Convention," *Akron Beacon Journal*, January 25, 1933, 13.

90. "Willkie Endorses Tennessee Project," *Akron Beacon Journal*, May 19, 1933, 11.

91. "The Editor's Notebook," *Akron Beacon Journal*, May 19, 1940, 2D.

92. John S. Knight, letter to Steve Neal, January 17, 1978.

93. "Presidential Vote in State," *Akron Beacon Journal*, November 6, 1940, 13.

94. Arthur Krock, "Willkie Spoke For Self in Second-Front Calls; and He Was Free to Express His Views in Moscow and Chungking by an Understanding with the President." *New York Times*, October 18, 1942, E3, nytimes.com.

95. Wendell L. Willkie, *One World* (Simon and Shuster, 1943), 84.

96. Lyle C. Wilson, "Willkie Quits Race, May Bolt G.O.P. As Dewey's Star Brightens in Nation," *Akron Beacon Journal*, April 6, 1944, 1.

97. "Wendell Willkie Dies," *Akron Beacon Journal*, October 8, 1944, 1.

98. James, "'He Made U.S. Safer'—Lausche."

99. George Scriven, "Lodge Hails Willkie as UN 'Father.'" *Akron Beacon Journal*, December 11, 1953, 1.

100. "A Bronze Plaque," *Akron Beacon Journal*, December 19, 1953, 9.

\ **11**

The Wingfoots and Nonskids

Kings of Akron Baseball

Jeffrey Smith

The *Akron Beacon Journal* reported that it was "just an ordinary ball game." Except that it wasn't, and sports editor Jim Schlemmer knew it.[1] So did everyone else in the stands, for that matter. Hometown hero George Sisler, among the greatest hitters at the time (or ever, for that matter) and now playing for the Boston Braves, was playing in the Rubber City against the General Tires for the first time since he left for the University of Michigan some seventeen years ago. In late August of 1928, the player dubbed "Gorgeous George" by the Akron press all those years ago was back in town, and it was big news.

Akron had evolved into a real baseball town in his absence—thanks to the rise of company teams like General Tire. Nationally, baseball attendance skyrocketed in the 1920s, with an average of about nine million people attending big-league games a year. Annual attendance the year Sisler came back to Akron had grown some twenty-eightfold from when he left.[2] In Akron, baseball fans read the coverage of the big leaguers in their newspapers, and local games grabbed big headlines. Teams organized by companies starting in Sisler's teenage days were the main attraction, organized primarily by local tire manufacturers. They didn't do so out of love for the game. The Goodyear Wingfoots, the Firestone Nonskids, and the other teams playing around the city were part of a broader management philosophy called "welfare work," designed to reduce turnover and build loyalty to companies. An unintended outcome of this welfarism was the creation of a citywide community of baseball fans who followed and rooted for these companies and made their players into local heroes. Local baseball fans knew the names of infielder Glenn "Speed" Bosworth, outfielder Frank Stefko, and pitchers Dutch Raabe and Jimmy Vaughn as well as they knew the names of big-league players. In this way, industrial teams perhaps did more to build interest in baseball spectatorship in cities without professional baseball teams than anything else. Akron wasn't alone, either; such programs promoted baseball in manufacturing cities such as Flint, Battle Creek, Dayton, and Pittsburgh.

Akron and its baseball world became very different places in just a few years, and it involved more than just the national pastime. When Sisler left town for the University of Michigan in 1911, Akron was in the throes of burgeoning growth. In the first two decades of the twentieth century the city tripled its population, largely by growing the workforce required to supply tires and rubber products to meet the needs of World War I and the mushrooming auto industry. All those cars rolling off the assembly lines in cities like Detroit needed tires and tubes and hoses, and Akron was the leading manufacturer of them. Sprawling factories sprouted all around the city—Goodyear to the east of downtown, B. F. Goodrich just south of it, and Firestone southward beyond that. Thousands of workers crowded streets and streetcars in a smoke-clogged city that reeked of burning rubber and coal smoke—the smell of money, some joked.

The *Akron Beacon Journal* made quite the deal of Sisler's coming back, even though at thirty-five years old he was in the twilight of his playing days. "Sisler's our own," the paper bragged. "It is unnecessary to review in detail Sisler's youth and connection with Akron baseball. Every old-timer here lived through it. Every boy in Akron has memorized it."[3]

On August 23, 1928, the Braves were in town on their way to a series with the Chicago Cubs and took the opportunity to make some extra cash on an off-day by playing the General Tires. Heaven knew they needed it, too. The Braves were a terrible team that year, finishing near the cellar with a dismal 50–103 record. The Braves won the game 11–4 (and took $1,300 as their share with them), which was no surprise.[4] The surprise, though, was that the Braves found two Generals players that looked to manager Rogers Hornsby like big-league material. By the time the Braves boarded the seven o'clock train for an overnight ride to Chicago, they had two extra players, centerfielder Chuck Hostettler and third baseman Mike Bosco, who signed contracts after the game.[5]

The Wingfoots and Nonskids

But where did teams like the Generals, the Goodyear Wingfoots, and the Firestone Nonskids come from? Despite local urban legends that the likes of Goodyear founder F. A. Seiberling and his crosstown counterpart Harvey Firestone were simply baseball fans (for which there exists no evidence), these teams emerged in the early 1910s in Akron as part of a broader management philosophy called "employee welfare work" that focused on work environment, safety, and loyalty to reduce turnover and keep unionization efforts at bay.

Starting in 1912, the Goodyear Tire & Rubber Company was at the forefront of the "employee welfare work" movement nationally, followed a year later by the Firestone Tire & Rubber Company and, to a lesser extent, General Tire. Welfare work started in the 1890s in Dayton, Ohio, at National Cash Register and spread rapidly across the country. The oft-told story of its origins involved a London buyer who returned a huge shipment of defective cash registers. Company owner John H. Patterson moved his desk to the factory floor to figure out why. His factory was like most others at the time—dimly lit, smoky, steaming hot, deafeningly loud from clattering machinery and belts, and dangerous. This led Patterson to introduce a sweeping program to make his factories more productive by focusing on workers and their environment, maintaining workers much the same way he maintained equipment and machinery. He built factories with better lighting and ventilation. He then added "perks," from lunchrooms and employee housing to an employee magazine, social activities, and sports teams. It might sound paternalistic to us today, but Patterson repeated over and over that it made NCR more profitable. He posted signs all over the factory stating simply, "It Pays." Goodyear echoed those sentiments in 1920, telling employees that "The Labor Division ... is governed by no paternalistic 'welfare' motive. All its activities are devised on business-like, self-supporting bases, the idea being to help those who help themselves."[6]

Goodyear president F. A. Seiberling was the first in Akron to adopt the idea and started a full-fledged program that included lunchrooms, safer conditions, a housing development just north of the factory complex called Goodyear Heights, and an employee newspaper called *The Wingfoot Clan*.

Goodyear workers first donned their company-sponsored Wingfoots baseball uniforms in 1912. They played home games at League Park; the company rented it for $25 a game.[7] At the end of the 1912 season *The Wingfoot Clan* lamented that "a large part of the factory is ignorant that there is such a thing as a Goodyear baseball team." The company moved the city's wood-frame baseball grandstand from League Park closer to the factory on the city's east side for the Wingfoots and expanded seating.

By 1920, employees knew all about the ball team—and so did every other potential fan in Akron—when Goodyear boasted that Seiberling Field was

General Tire dedicated its new baseball field in 1925 with ceremonies and a multi-page souvenir program with photos of the players, including Glenn "Speed" Bosworth, seen here. \ Glenn V. Bosworth Collection, Glenn V. Bosworth Collection, Archives and Special Collections, University Libraries, The University of Akron

SOUVENIR PROGRAM AND SCORE CARD

DEDICATION

of the New

GENERAL TIRE ATHLETIC FIELD

and

GRAND STAND

"a model recreational field conveniently located midway between the great Goodyear plant and Goodyear Heights, the model city of 'Goodyearites.'" Seiberling Field included six tennis courts and four ball diamonds. Men played ball on evenings and weekends, and women played ball on Wednesdays. The baseball field was the centerpiece.[8] The company situated it just a short walk from Goodyear Heights but clearly intended the new Seiberling Field to attract more than its own workers alone.

The *Akron Beacon Journal* gushed over the new location when it opened in May 1916, noting that it was "just three minutes' walk from the East Market streetcar line ... and is accessible by all main car lines." Seiberling Field included seating for one thousand people under a wooden roof that stretched beyond both first and third bases. Company officials figured they could add bleachers when the crowds outgrew the stands, and they did.[9] After sharing the field with the company soccer team, Goodyear replaced the old park in 1929 with a new one dedicated to baseball alone.[10]

By the time Goodyear inaugurated its new Seiberling Field, two crosstown rivals already played in larger, nicer fields which had been expanded during the 1920s. Firestone replaced its old field with a larger brick edifice in front of the factory in 1925 at a cost of some $50,000—about $900,000 in today's dollars. Firestone Stadium remains an active recreational facility today. Its location near the factory buildings a few minutes' walk away suggests the close relationship between the workplace and the baseball field.[11]

The new ballpark emulated big-league parks such as Yankee Stadium, "The House That Ruth Built," constructed in 1922 and 1923. Several more teams expanded stadiums to accommodate swelling crowds and growing popularity. At Firestone, two brick ticket booths flanked the main entrance, so workers could proceed straight into the park. As soon as they walked up the steps inside, they had a magnificent view of a verdant baseball field framed by seats and fellow workers. It really was a stadium instead of merely a ballpark. Today, the City of Akron owns the stadium and uses it for softball tournaments.

While Firestone followed close behind with employee welfare programs, it was slow to join the city's league of industrial powerhouses. It created an Industrial Service Department in mid-1913, focused on safety and working conditions. It expanded two years later, apparently to keep up with Goodyear, to include services including barbers, lounges, a library, and even on-site medical and dental care to complement the employee stock plans, life insurance, and housing developments.

Creators of two short-lived leagues tried to organize the popularity of baseball in the mid-1910s, the Auto Tire League in 1913 (the first year both Firestone and Goodyear had fields close to the factories) and the Akron Amateur Baseball Association (usually called the "city league") in 1916 and 1917. The loftily named

American Industrial Athletic Association (AIAA), created by athletic directors at several rubber companies, replaced the city league in 1918. To most fans of any spectator sport, the behind-the-scenes work of organizing the leagues is invisible, but some person or entity had to make all sorts of decisions about the games we watch. Who can play, or be an umpire? And where? What are the rules, and what about rules specific to a particular field? What's the schedule? Most of the people making those decisions and myriad others were athletic directors at the companies who formed the association, and those athletic directors were part of the employee welfare programs. Since all of them handled AIAA business as part of their regular jobs rather than as volunteers, the league lasted longer than its predecessors.

Through the AIAA, company officials agreed on rules, schedules, umpires, and other details, but the biggest sticking point centered on the amateur nature of the players. The athletic directors at Goodyear, Goodrich, Firestone, and General Tire were the driving figures, which made the AIAA unusual among industrial leagues with companies creating and monitoring the league. Eligibility was a central problem. Writings about employee welfare work were clear that players should be employees so that the folks in stands felt a particular kinship to the players as fellow workers, guys they knew from the plant.

For most of the AIAA's history, players had to be employed for at least three months to be eligible to play so that no one hired "ringers" for a particular game. By 1924 eligibility requirements for the AIAA were the subject of intense debate.[12] Before they withdrew from the league, the representatives from Goodyear and Firestone both decried the rule. Goodyear Athletic Director Ed Connor said the rule "makes for a better team balance all around," but Firestone's athletic director Paul "Pep" Sheeks was less diplomatic, fuming that "the six-day rule is really no rule at all for it would enable any team to import players regardless of their employment status."[13]

Bringing people together in ways to increase morale and, thereby, productivity was the essence of employee welfare work, and that included baseball. Company newsletters were filled with articles that couched welfarism in terms of concern for workers rather than paternalism. "It all comes down to this," trumpeted the Goodyear *Wingfoot Clan* in its first issue in June 1912, when it rolled out its program to employees. "Welfare Work in its fullest meaning if successful should make the employee more useful to himself and to the company."[14]

The very nature of baseball served management's objectives. The values on the playing field that workers picked up while watching from the stands mirrored those management wished to instill—fair play, teamwork, loyalty to the team over individual achievement, adherence to the rules, and respect for authority figures. More than anything, companies focused on baseball as a team sport and spoke about "teamwork." Baseball is a game that acknowledges that when individuals perform their best, it benefits the whole team, and that's exactly what management wanted from its workforce. Harvey Firestone drew the parallel clearly in his 1925 address to employees, noting that "wholesome athletics is a boon to work."[15]

Employees could only receive the messages of the ball field if they attended, though. Companies used their employee papers to promote games and encourage attendance in ways to make workers feel like part of the team, as if winning the game was partly their responsibility. When the Goodyear Wingfoots found themselves in a tight pennant race in 1920, the company turned to its fans. With two games coming up, The Wingfoot Clan promised that "fans and rooters can gain some of the glory by attending both frays and giving 100 per cent support."[16]

The following year, as the Nonskids chased the AIAA pennant, Firestone placed responsibility squarely on the shoulders of ball fans, suggesting that "with your help, by your pressure and your rooting for the home team, they're going to really make you proud of them."[17] Management made it easy for workers to attend, too. The fields were nearby, and tickets were cheap. Nationally, experts on employee welfarism warned against even a whiff of paternalism, and that included free baseball tickets, so Akron companies charged nominal fees for tickets. The pricing system mirrored professional teams, in that good seats in the grandstands carried higher prices. Most games with seats in the bleachers down the first- and third-base lines were twenty-five cents until 1924, when the price rose to thirty cents. Grandstand seats, which cost an extra dime, were under cover and close to home plate. Since these fields had such modest foul territory, spectators were close enough to the game to hear the umpire's calls and the banter between players. The AIAA ran cartoons in both company papers promoting season tickets for just $1.10.[18] And it worked. Industrial team games routinely attracted as many as four thousand or more fans. Some six thousand attended the season opener between Goodyear and Miller Rubber in 1920, and eight thousand came to the game that followed the dedication of Goodyear's Seiberling Stadium in 1929.[19]

To build spectatorship even more, company teams played big leaguers as well. These exhibition games, like the one in 1928 that featured George Sisler, drew well. It's hard for us to imagine today's major league teams traveling to a smaller city to play an extra game so the team could make a few extra dollars, but that's precisely what happened in the 1910s and 1920s. Akron rubber teams routinely played teams such as the Pittsburgh Pirates, Brooklyn Dodgers, Boston Braves, and Homestead Grays. Contracts generally required that the regular starting lineup play in the games, since promotional articles noted that the "regular nine" would start.

That was the case toward the end of the 1919 season when the Cincinnati Reds came to town en route to Chicago to play the Chicago White Sox in the World Series. The Reds were riding high, having clinched their first National League championship. One year later, sports fans read that as many as eight of the Sox

The Wingfoots and Nonskids

Undated clipping of a newspaper cartoon encouraging the General Tires to not feel so bad about a recent game against the New York Yankees. Industrial teams like General, Firestone, and Goodyear played major league teams a handful of times every year. \ Glenn V. Bosworth Collection, Archives and Special Collections, University Libraries, The University of Akron

players (including "Shoeless" Joe Jackson) accepted bribes from gambling interests to throw the series, for which all eight were banned for life from baseball.[20] But in late September, just over a week before playing the Sox at Redland Field in Cincinnati, the Reds made a stop at Liberty Field in Akron to play the Firestone Nonskids. It was big news, too. The headline across the front page of the *Akron Evening Times* blared "Reds Play Here Tomorrow." The Reds signed a contract listing their regular starting nine and guaranteeing that they would take the field.

Writers for the *Firestone Non-Skid* were ecstatic and wasted no time reinforcing company values in their admiration for the Reds. "Year after year, with everything in the baseball world against them, they have fought doggedly," noted the company paper. "After repeated failures they have finally won their way to a championship." The game was expensive, too—fifty cents for general admission, a dollar for grandstand seats close enough to the dugout and home plate to see the players sweat.[21] The Reds arrived around nine thirty and had a full day of meetings with city leaders, a factory tour at Firestone, a lavish luncheon, and a

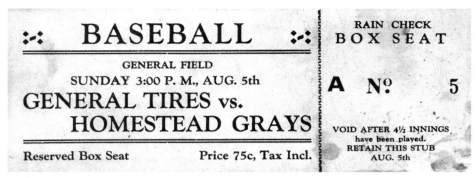

The Homestead Grays were regulars in Akron, especially on Sundays, when Pennsylvania blue laws forbade baseball exhibitions. Despite comments in newspapers and company publications about his "advanced age," none were ever able to defeat the Grays' Hall of Fame pitchers Smokey Joe Williams and Satchel Paige. \ Glenn V. Bosworth Collection, Archives and Special Collections, University Libraries, The University of Akron

parade "in machines"—that is, automobiles—in downtown Akron culminating with a game at four thirty "so that every employee on the day shift may have the opportunity of seeing the National entry in the world's series in action." Not unexpectedly, Cincinnati won 3–0. Firestone got just one hit, a double in the seventh.[22] Even the New York Yankees played Firestone at least twice, both times promising that Babe Ruth himself would play.

More often, tire teams hosted Negro League teams. With baseball segregated from 1887 until 1947, African Americans were forced to create their own teams and leagues. In 1920 former pitcher Rube Foster created the Negro National League (NNL), which included teams that came to Akron. NNL teams played more than two hundred games a season, almost half of which were on "barnstorming" tours to places like Akron.

The Homestead Grays from the Pittsburgh area were the most popular African American team to play in Akron. It included future Hall-of-Famers catcher Josh Gibson and pitchers Smokey Joe Williams and Satchel Paige. When the Grays came to play General Tire in 1925, advertisements in the local papers noted they were the "Famous Colored Champs."[23] The Goodyear Wingfoot Clan boasted that the arrival of the Grays in late April 1926 as "the real opening of the season at Wingfoot Stadium" since "this team has been playing in Akron for many years and their popularity grows greater each year."[24]

The Grays joined a number of major league teams playing Goodyear, Firestone, and General Tire through the 1920s, so Akron fans could see Babe Ruth, Lou Gehrig, Rogers Hornsby, and "Pie" Traynor along with Sisler.

Once in a while, the local teams even won. For example, General Tire beat the Pittsburgh Pirates 6–0 in 1926. Winners of the World Series in 1925, the Pirates

The Wingfoots and Nonskids

were 65–47 and in first place in the National League. General Tire pitcher Charlie Ketchum threw a no-hitter—his second no-hitter in eight days—before what looked to many to be the largest crowd ever assembled in Akron for a baseball game.[25] And sometimes, players signed professional contracts. Goodyear infielder Ralph Shafer came to Goodyear mid-season in 1919 after getting hurt and being released by the Cincinnati Reds but was back in Cincinnati briefly in 1921.[26] Pitcher Pat "Lefty" McKinstry signed with the New York Yankees, but two years later was back on the south side pitching, now hailed by the Nonskid as an ex-Yankee.[27] A few came from the minor league ranks, too, but for the most part Akron baseball players came to the company as either regular employees or as former semi-pro players. Frank Stefko moved to Akron after World War I when Glenn "Speed" Bosworth wrote him that Goodyear was hiring ball players. The company hired him when he mentioned Bosworth and his baseball background in Europe. Even though he played for other teams after the AIAA folded and they became semi-pro teams, Stefko stayed at Goodyear and retired from the company.

Unlike professional baseball, working and playing ball for a rubber company had long-term benefits. These teams had benefits for both workers and management. Employees did benefit from welfare programs, and management accomplished its goals of increased productivity and keeping unionization efforts out until the Great Depression, when welfare programs were cut along with workers' hours. But for a lot of folks in Akron who came to see players like Gorgeous George Sisler, it was about baseball.

Notes

1. James W. Schlemmer, "Fans Watch Sisler As Braves Triumph, *Akron Beacon Journal*, August 24, 1928, 30 Unless otherwise noted, newspapers are cited from digital versions through Newspapers.com.

2. "1920–1929 MLB Attendance," Ballparks of Baseball, https://www.ballparksofbaseball.com/1920-1929-mlb-attendance/; "1910–1919 MLB Attendance," Ballparks of Baseball, https://www.ballparksofbaseball.com/1910-1919-mlb-attendance/.

3. James W. Schlemmer, "Sisler Whole Show in Exhibition Here," *Akron Beacon Journal*, August 22, 1928, 23. Sisler was a high school star at Akron High School; the first article recognizing his pitching prowess is "Akron High Defeats Central of Cleveland," *Akron Beacon Journal*, April 30, 1910, 10. Also see Rick Huhn, *The Sizzler: George Sisler, Baseball's Forgotten Great* (University of Missouri Press, 2004), 9–10.

4. The Braves organization made exactly $1,300, for its portion of the gate receipts. Receipt, General Tires B. B. Club to Boston National League Club, August 23, 1928, Glenn Bosworth Collection, Box 3, Folder 1. It is unknown what percentage each team kept of the gate receipts.

5. In his early forties, Hostettler (1903–1971) ended up playing two years for the Detroit Tigers in 1944 and 1945. The Braves released Austrian-born Bosco to Providence almost immediately, then called him back for the rest of the season. He played for Providence again until May 1929 and left professional baseball. "Michael Bosco," Sporting News Player Contract Cards, Digital Library Collections, LA84 Foundation.

6. Goodyear Tire and Rubber Company, *The Work of the Labor Division* (Goodyear Tire & Rubber Company, 1920), 9.

7. "This is the First Organized Baseball Club Goodyear Ever Had," *Wingfoot Clan*, October 25, 1925, 8.

8. Goodyear Tire and Rubber Company, 37.

9. Leo Neufield, "Seiberling Field Will Be Popular With Athletes," *Akron Beacon Journal*, May 1, 1916, 10.

10. "Goodyear Stadium Under Construction," *Akron Beacon Journal*, May 7, 1929, 33.

11. "Building Activities Display Steadiness," *Akron Beacon Journal*, July 18, 1925, 13.

12. "Industrial League to Decide Eligibility Rule at Meeting Thursday," *Akron Beacon Journal*, April 22, 1924, 21.

13. "Firestone Not to Join Industrial Baseball League. Declare for Amateur Status Based on Three-Month Employment Rule," *Firestone Non-Skid*, May 7, 1924, 1.

14. All Together," *Wingfoot Clan*, June 1, 1912, 3.

15. "Mr. Firestone Addresses Athletes," *Firestone Non-Skid*, April 22, 1925, 1.

16. "Wingfoots Put Up Game Battle For Ball Bunting: Organized Rooting Needed on Last Leg of Pennant Chase," *Wingfoot Clan*, August 12, 1920, 4.

17. "Good Chance Yet to Cop Pennant," *Firestone Non-Skid*, August 17, 1921, 4.

18. "Get Yours Today," *Wingfoot Clan*, June 3, 1919, 6. Adjusted for inflation, the $1.10 season tickets would cost about twenty dollars today.

19. "6,000 Fans Watch Flag Raising Sunday as Goodyear Opens 1920 Baseball Season," *Wingfoot Clan*, May 13, 1920, 4; "Thousands See New Seiberling Field Stadium Dedicated," *Wingfoot Clan*, July 17, 1929, 1.

20. For a full discussion of the Black Sox scandal, see Eliot Asinof, *Eight Men Out: The Black Sox and the 1919 World Series*, Holt, Rinehart, and Winston, 1963.

21. "Cincinnati Plays Here Sept. 23. Contract Stipulates That Regular Lineup Shall Appear at Liberty Park," *Firestone Non-Skid*, September 12, 1919. The *Non-Skid* was right: the Reds had not finished above third place since the 1900s, and their championship was considered something of a phenomenon. Before rumors of gamblers fixing the game emerged, the White Sox were favored 5:1 to win the series.

22. "Reds Play Here Tomorrow," *Akron Evening Times*, September 22, 1919, 11; Eddie Francis, "Firestone Collect One Hit Against Reuther and Eller," *Akron Beacon Journal*, September 24, 1919, 17.

23. Advertisement, *Akron Beacon Journal*, June 5, 1925, 32. The ad promoted an extra enticement for the Sunday game: a performance by the 35-piece Elks Delta Band, "Pride of the Colored Folks."

24. "Homestead Grays, Colored Stars, Play Goodyear Sunday; Fastest Outfit of Kind in Country," *Wingfoot Clan*, June 2, 1926, 4.

25. "Pirates Go Hitless Before Sensational Hurling by Ketchum," *Akron Beacon Journal*, August 23, 1926, 20. Ketchum was a minor-league and semi-pro player before signing with General Tire. Bob Nold, "Ketchum, Addis Leaders of Latest Greater Akron Class," *Akron Beacon Journal*, April 21, 1995, D4; "Non-skids to Meet Grays," *Akron Beacon Journal*, June 15, 1926, 27. The Pirates' first-base coach later recalled how they stole all the General Tire signs and "bore down with everything [they] had" in that game. Jim Schlemmer, "Diamond Dust," *Akron Beacon Journal*, December 14, 1948, 43.

26. Shafer spent almost his entire career in the minor leagues, although he was "in industrial ball after war until 192—when had trial with Cincinnati, Ohio." "Ralph Shafer," Sporting News Player Contract Cards, Digital Library Collections, LA84 Foundation.

27. In February 1923, the New York *Daily News* reported that the Yankees, desperate for left-handed pitching, signed McKinstry. The paper reported that he earned notice from the Yankees after "a whale of a trick he turned last summer. He was working for a tire company out in Akron, O., last summer and incidentally pitching for the company baseball team." He pitched twenty innings to defeat former major leaguer Jim Vaughn with a barnstorming team from Beloit, Wisconsin. He injured his hands while at the Yankees' training field in New Orleans in March then was released to Albany at the end of the month before returning to Firestone. James Crusinberry, "Another Leftie Strays Too Far; Yanks Grab Him," *New York Daily News* February 6, 1923, 21; Marshall Hunt, "Back Luck Trails M'Kinstry, Likely Yank Hurler," *New York Daily News*, March 15, 1923, 23; James Crusinberry, "Huggins Keeps Another Brace of Kid Hurlers," *New York Daily News*, March 29, 1923, 58.

\ **12**

The Brightest Spot in the Underworld

Akron's Furnace Street Mission

Bill Hauser

Introduction

The City of Akron, Ohio, has been blessed with a wide range of churches, businesses, and social organizations that have labored hard to protect and enhance the social well-being of its citizens. All are worthy of recognition! So, what makes a little chapel on Furnace Street in the northern part of downtown Akron so unique? The Furnace Street Mission (FSM) has been a part of Akron's history for one hundred years and, most importantly, it is the wellspring of other churches, radio ministries, halfway houses, women's shelters, the national victim assistance movement, and the Safety Forces Support Center. Whether you speak to police officers (especially retired ones) and their families, or crime victims who have been supported by the mission and the Victim Assistance Program it created, you quickly hear favorable and grateful comments about this local institution.

The following pages look at the development and growth of this community treasure from its beginnings in the roughest section of Akron to its work

Furnace Street Mission in the 1930s. \ Furnace Street Mission (FSM) Archives—Akron Postcards

supporting the social and emotional needs of our safety forces today. At the heart of the Furnace Street Mission is the ongoing legacy of a father and son, as the adjacent chapter on the history of Akron congregations chronicles.

In the 1960s the baton was passed from the Reverend Bill Denton to his son Bob, who led the mission to an even greater level of assistance to the community and to those residents that need it the most. Victims, historically viewed as an afterthought, now became the focus of attention as the concept of the Victim Assistance Movement arose from a collaboration of Bob Denton with three local safety forces and court officers. It would eventually become the international movement that it is today. In recent years the mission under Bob's direction has further focused its concentration to minister to the needs of the area's safety forces (police, fire, EMS, dispatchers) through its chaplaincy services and especially with the creation of the Bob Denton Safety Forces Support Center. The future of the mission continues to emerge as it finds ways to meet its original mission of "promoting the religious welfare of the public."

Furnace Street in the Early 1920s

The best way to view the Furnace Street Mission is to understand the physical and social environment from which it emerged. In 2017, Mark J. Price (local reporter, Akron historian, and a community treasure) published a book that described what life was like in Akron in the early twentieth century, when Akron was very quickly emerging from a small town on the Ohio Canal to a modern city with an ever-growing population that, according to the US Census, had grown from 69,067 in 1910 to 208,435 in 1920. Americans from other parts of the United States and immigrants, especially from Europe, moved to Akron looking for opportunities at the fast-growing rubber companies and other affiliated industries drove this mass immigration into the area. As Price so aptly described it, "the sulfur-infused stench of smoking factories was hailed as 'the smell of jobs.'"

But as history has repeatedly shown, rampant urban growth can also bring challenges that negatively impact a community. The population growth of the 1910–1920 decade left the city unprepared for many challenges. Housing, along with utilities, sanitation, and other urban necessities, was either scarce or nonexistent. To meet needs, residents rented out spare rooms. Cheap housing was quickly constructed, and shanty villages were haphazardly assembled on the outskirts of town. The situation became so bad that rooming houses regularly rented out beds to factory workers on eight-hour shifts aligned with shifts at the local factories. Like those local factories, when your bed shift was up, the person on the next shift took your place.

Population growth caused an increase in crime, especially related to drinking, gambling, and prostitution. After all, the factory workers now had money and were looking for ways to spend it. On top of this, living in close areas was further complicated by racial and ethnic differences among tightly crowded, distrustful enclaves unfamiliar with each other's cultures and languages. Entry into World War I further compounded the situation with the increased production needs of the local factories, the factory workers going off to war, and more immigrants and family members having to take over the roles of those who were now serving in the military.

As these different cultures moved into Akron, it was common for different ethnic groups to congregate in different parts of the community. It was also common for young members in these groups to come together to support each other in the form of gangs. These gangs may have sought to govern particular neighborhoods and made money in a variety of sometimes illicit ways. One neighborhood of Akron that became a hot spot was around Furnace Street near the Little Cuyahoga River in the northernmost part of downtown Akron. The street, originally named after the Cuyahoga Furnace plant that did smelting for local industries, quickly grew as more and more people moved into the neighborhood around it. This in turn brought new housing, businesses, restaurants, bars, pool halls, and other good and not-so-good establishments into the area. The neighborhood changed with an influx of Italian immigrant families looking for work in the rubber industries in the early part of the twentieth century.

As the Furnace Street neighborhood grew and gradually changed to being predominantly Italian, it also brought with it activities and behaviors from the old country. Mafia-type "family" arrangements took hold with groups of young men looking to game the system and make money in less than socially accepted ways. With a small, understaffed Akron Police Department unable to be everywhere all the time, crimes like gambling and prostitution increased. Neighborhood gang warfare was a way of life. This chapter of Akron history is documented in the 2017 book by Mark Price, *Mafia Cop Killers in Akron*.

The Furnace Street neighborhood was in dire need of religion and social reform. A young minister, Bill Denton, took on this battle. Crime and poverty were abundant, and a bright light was needed to show the way. The Furnace Street Mission became that beacon. The mission's work created strong collaborations with the police, the courts, and community social service groups. One hundred years later these collaborations are strong and continue to brighten the community.

The most ironic connection was that the Furnace Street Gang actually hung out at Joe Congena's pool hall on Furnace Street, where they plotted the murder of the Akron police officers. A decade later, the Reverend Bill Denton purchased the now-empty building from the railroad and with the help of a bunch of young men physically moved it across Furnace Street and re-opened the building as the Furnace Street Mission. This reimagined facility remained the home base for the Furnace Street Mission programs until 1962, when it was torn down and a new structure built in its place. The den of racketeers and murderers had become a place to save souls and serve the community. What would Borgia and the Furnace Street Gang think today?

The latter part of the nineteenth century and the early twentieth century brought about the resurgence of revivalism in the United States. *Revivalism*, or spiritual reawakening, was a Protestant way to meet the spiritual needs of a society that was transitioning from rural to urban. Poor people in urban areas would freely gather on a street corner or in an open space to listen to a fire-and-brimstone preacher. From this sprang the Tabernacle Movement of the twentieth century. Based on the original tabernacles of the Old Testament Bible, a tabernacle or tent of the congregation was a portable dwelling that the Israelites

The Brightest Spot in the Underworld

took with them as they journeyed about. These tents were set up as dwellings in which the Israelites could commune with Yahweh.

The late 1920s and early 1930s evidenced the dramatic growth of tabernacles or tent meetings. Large crowds flowed to these events. Many were converted and baptized. The popularity of this evangelism encouraged the Furnace Street Mission to seek out additional space to hold these very popular meetings. A tabernacle was set up on Perkins Street, but this was not sufficient to handle the

Furnace Street in the 1930s. \ FSM Archives—*Akron Beacon Journal*-FSM 1987 60th Anniversary Calendar

Tabernacle revival meeting. \ FSM Archives—FSM 1987 60th Anniversary Calendar

ever-growing crowds. In 1932 a new Akron Gospel Tabernacle was opened on West Exchange Street. Shortly after that, the old Summit Buick Building was converted into another tabernacle. In 1932 the Furnace Street Mission took over the Miles Royal Theater, a former speakeasy and burlesque house, and changed it to a tabernacle to further expand the reach of the ministry. Bill Denton paid unemployed workers to help construct the tabernacles and sent them home each day with a basket of food for their families. Reverend Bill Denton served as the superintendent with Pastor Carl Burnham as the assistant superintendent.

At the same time, the prison ministry continued to grow. Bill Denton regularly visited and counseled inmates. He also provided intervention and counselling after a deadly fire that broke out at the Ohio Penitentiary in 1930 that killed 322 inmates.

The radio ministry started in 1926 on radio station WFJC and moved over to WADC in 1928. The ministry continued to grow and expand. In the following years the "good news" was spread around the country through such radio stations as KDKA, COCO, and CMCK in Cuba. Also, at this time missionary work was expanding across the United States and internationally to Cuba and China. Other ministers and missionaries who had their beginnings at the Furnace Street Mission went out into the world.

During the World War II years of the 1940s the Furnace Street Mission continued to grow, spreading its evangelism. A key emphasis was supporting the soldiers fighting in the war. The mission created and provided spiritual literature to the soldiers. They also corresponded with soldiers from the Akron area. One of the items sent to the soldiers was a copper-covered Bible created to withstand the harsh environments in which the soldiers daily carried them. Thousands of metal-jacketed Bibles were provided. One was returned to the mission with a bullet hole partway through the copper cover. At the end of the war the mission continued to sponsor missionaries in Japan, China, and South America.

Furnace Street Mission—1950s and 1960s

During the 1950s, the mission programs continued to evolve and grow. Literature and correspondence continued with members of the armed services now serving in the Korean Conflict. The Furnace Street Mission also sponsored a missionary who would set up twenty-eight churches in Japan. Similarly, an orphanage and widow's home were purchased and sponsored in Korea. Radio broadcasts remained popular and expanded the mission's reach. Prison work also continued, with more work done with death row inmates. Programs were created to sponsor parolees and the mission strongly advocated against capital punishment.

The Brightest Spot in the Underworld

This parking lot is full for Furnace Street Mission service. \ FSM Archives—FSM 1987 60th Anniversary Calendar

Furnace Street Mission in 1962. \ It looks the same today. FSM Archives

  The initial renovation of the Furnace Street Mission's facilities and property started with older buildings being brought down in the 1950s and culminated with the original mission building being torn down and a new one built in 1962. More changes were to come. The leadership of the mission transitioned from Bill Denton to his son Bob. The radio ministry expanded to two local stations. The mission's staff and services provided were formalized. For the first time

The Reverend Bill Denton with Judge Emmons at the dedication of a halfway house in 1965. \ Photo courtesy of the *Akron Beacon Journal*

grants were applied for, such as the Omnibus Crime Bill, and received. To distribute the ever-expanding workload, Bob Denton handed over policy development to the board, which was enlarged to both gain larger community representation and to further spread awareness of the mission and its programs.

During the 1960s, the mission created programs to intervene in the drug epidemic ravaging the city and the country. Importantly, the mission increased its work with convicts on probation as it became more and more disenchanted with the current state of correctional policies on rehabilitation. As an outcome, the mission became a part of the Ohio Halfway House movement and in 1964, Bill Denton broke ground behind the mission on a three-story, $70,000 building to serve as Ohio's first halfway house for former convicts. The Denton House opened in 1965, welcoming parolees until they found sponsors and jobs. The building had seven bedrooms, a living room, a dining room, and a kitchen. The first floor served as a welfare department for the distribution of food and clothing. Through the use of Law Enforcement Assistance Administration funds, the halfway house grew into three facilities with up to seventy residents.

And the good works continued.

Bob Denton's Akron

William (Bill) Denton and Gladys Isaac Denton had four children. Gladys died in 1932. Bill then married Phyllis May Hamilton Denton in 1942. Phyllis bore two children, Bob in 1943 and his sister Donnell in 1952. Bob was the fifth of six siblings. Allan Robert "Bob" Denton was born in Akron, where he learned firsthand from his father about crime, violence, and its victims. He graduated from Buchtel High School in Akron and then attended Asbury College, where he earned his BA in Philosophy and Religion. Bob then attended the Wheaton Graduate School of Theology, where he earned his MA in Theology and was ordained as a minister. Finally, he received his PhD in Social Welfare from the School of Applied Social Sciences at Case Western Reserve University. In 1970, Bob graduated from the Akron Police Academy and was sworn in as a reserve officer in 1971. During this time, he also received his license as an Independent Social Worker (Supervisory Designation) from the State of Ohio. This diverse background would serve as a strong foundation for Bob's "calling" and career.

The Reverend Dr. Bob Denton has served as the chaplain for the Akron Police Department and more recently the Akron Fire Department since the 1980s. Bob served as chair for the joint Akron Police Department/Summit County Sheriff's Department Critical Incidence Stress Management team. He taught Victim's Rights and Crisis Intervention with Victims in numerous policy academies in Ohio. From this he created the mandated five-hour victim curriculum used by departments throughout the state. He also taught Crisis Intervention,

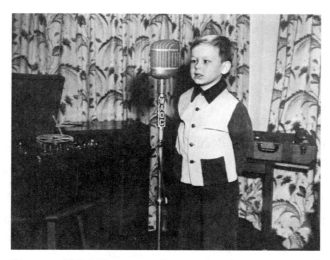

Five-year-old Bob Denton preaching on the radio. Denton started his radio ministry at the age of five. A story has been passed down over the years that the award-winning novelist Kurt Vonnegut was driving through Akron and heard Bob, as a child, preaching on the radio. Vonnegut then went on to create an evangelical preacher in his book, *The Sirens of Titan* (1959), and called the character the Reverend Bobby Denton. \ Courtesy of the Denton family. FSM Archives—FSM 1987 60th Anniversary Calendar

Young Reverend Robert Denton doing a radio broadcast. \ From the Furnace Street Mission Archives

Domestic Violence, Victim's Rights for the Ohio Police Officer's Training Academy, Death Notification, and Bridging the Gap Between Law Enforcement and Ethics for Victim Advocates for both the Ohio Attorney General and the Michigan Attorney General's office.

In 1972 Dr. Denton began teaching courses in sociology at The University of Akron, including one he created called Victim in Society and another called Rednecks and Golden Ghettos. In 1986 he was promoted to Adjunct Full Professor in Sociology. Concurrent with this, Bob created and taught courses on Crisis Intervention, Advanced Crisis, Disaster Intervention, and Intervention Models for the Department of Social Work's Masters of Social Work.

In 1974 Bob Denton was elected as the founding president of the National Organization for Victim Assistance (NOVA) in Washington, DC. Thirty-five years later in 2008–2009, he was again elected president of the organization. For his leadership Dr. Denton was awarded the Margery Fry Outstanding Advocate by NOVA. In 1994 he was also honored with the Outstanding National Victim Advocate by the Department of Justice with then-Attorney General Janet Reno and President Bill Clinton presenting him with the award. In 2013, Ohio's Attorney General, Mike DeWine, renamed Ohio's meritorious award for victim advocacy the Rev. Dr. Robert Denton Outstanding Victim Service Award. This award is presented annually to the outstanding victim advocate in Ohio.

The Furnace Street Mission at the Millennium (1980s to the Present)

Under the leadership of the Reverend Bob Denton, the mission has been able to grow its programs and expand its reach dramatically since the 1980s. As the victim ministry continued to grow so did the ministry to the police. During his regular shifts with police officers riding their beats, Denton heard about the problems the officers were facing and saw the need to provide similar aid and comfort to officers and their families. He strongly believed that they shared the trauma and experienced post-traumatic stress with the victims. However, he felt their trauma was magnified by the sheer number of events that occurred, sometimes on the same day. He saw them as different victims in different situations. Because of the confidentiality needed, officers could not speak to their colleagues about their pain and had nowhere to go to seek help. In many cases the cruiser the Reverend Bob Denton was riding in became the confidential pastor's office. Since traditional ministers were not trained or prepared to counsel officers and their families, programs handled by specially trained counsellors and therapists were needed. As Denton was already serving as the trusted Chaplain (performing weddings and funerals) and a reserve officer for the Akron Police Department, the officers were willing to confide in him. This was the beginning of the mission's focus on safety forces, which led to enhanced, ongoing chaplaincy services and the creation of the Bob Denton Safety Forces Support Center that is the major emphasis of the mission today.

All the while the Furnace Street Mission continued to grow. With the numerous programs and services already in existence and the new ones initiated in the 1960s and 1970s, the number of people served rapidly expanded. In 1983, the mission initiated the Timeout Program as a court-ordered treatment program for domestic offenders. This was the first program of its type in Ohio. With the creation of the Battered Women's Shelter as a separate sister organization, the mission would eventually close its shelter and focus its attention on crisis intervention and court advocacy. The relationship with the Battered Women's Shelter and its iconic director, Terri Heckman, continued to strengthen and grow over the years. Both organizations initiated ways to aid and support victims of abuse, especially domestic abuse. In 1997, working with the Akron Police Department, the Furnace Street Mission, and the Battered Women's Shelter created the Early Intervention Program to intervene in domestic disturbances.

By the 1990s, the Furnace Street Mission had increased its staff to thirteen individuals with two therapists. It continued the radio broadcasts for five nights

Battered Women Shelter President and CEO Terri Heckman. \ Courtesy of Victim Assistance Program

per week, now on WHLO and later on WAKR. Finally, in 1994 the mission obtained separate nonprofit status for the Victim Assistance Program under the same Furnace Street Mission Board leadership.

Victim Advocacy expanded greatly over the years. With a specialized staff, the mission was able to create and formalize a victim advocacy program with the courts and negotiate for a victim witness advocate in the Juvenile Court. Following the Restorative Justice Model that focused on the victim, it created community advocate positions. Additionally, the mission created the first state Victim Rights Vigil in Columbus and, locally, instituted the National Victim Rights Week Luncheons featuring Attorneys General and Ohio Supreme Court Justices.

The Rise of Victimology

Throughout the 1960s, the mission's primary focus was building a halfway house to temporarily house up to seventy residents. During the process, it quickly became apparent that something was missing from correctional programs: there was no sense of remorse for damage done to the other person. Crime was on the increase and the prison population continued to rise sharply. New, innovative correctional programs were being initiated to cut the incarcerated population. But the focus remained on the offender with little or no concern being shown for those individuals and families that had been victims of the crime. The rise in violent crimes, a drug epidemic, and other recidivism set the stage for a newfound concern for victims. The prevailing philosophy by those in criminal justice was only that offenders must be apprehended and must "pay" the state for their crimes. However, attitudes were changing. Forward thinkers began to

The Brightest Spot in the Underworld

view rehabilitation, in addition to making restitution to the state, as requiring reconciliation and responsibility to the people who were victimized.

While the community provided thirty-five free services for offenders, it provided absolutely nothing for the victims. Bob Denton, at that time a PhD student at the School of Applied Social Sciences at Case Western Reserve University, decided to use his doctoral studies and research to lay the foundation for the initial concept of a victim assistance program. His PhD work was used to build the infrastructure including policies, services, research/evaluation, and crisis intervention of what would become the Victim's Assistance Program.

In 1972, Bob Denton convened a small group of police, corrections, and probation officers that included Captain John Cunningham, Chairman of the FSM board; Stella Long, Supervisor, Adult Probation, Common Pleas Court; Richard Kinsinger, Chief Probation Officer, Common Pleas Court; and Bob Denton, Furnace Street Mission Director. They were asked to analyze recent brutal crimes in the Akron area and the impact they were having on the victims. The discussion identified the need for early crisis intervention. Using Bob Denton's doctoral research as the framework, this group created the structure, literally on the back of a napkin, for what is widely considered to be the first Victim Assistance Program in the country.

One hundred and three victims were referred to the program by the Akron Police Department during its first year of operation. Victim advocates responded to the crime scenes to provide immediate crisis intervention. Concurrent with this, a confidential crisis hotline was also created and implemented. Eager to advance victim's rights, the Victim Assistance Program focused on identifying and understanding the needs of the victims and their families in the community. This enabled them to further advocate for victims and victim compensation legislation at the state level.

As the community, especially victims and social agencies, became aware of the services provided by the program, the Furnace Street Mission closed its halfway houses in 1976 and reopened the Denton House as the first Domestic Violence Shelter in the country. The domestic violence shelter at the mission remained a place of refuge for victims until 1985 when a sister agency, the Battered Women's Shelter, opened a new shelter. This enabled the Furnace Street Mission to refocus its efforts once again. First, the Victim Assistance Program created the Time Out Program, a batterer's intervention program that accepted Akron Municipal Court-remanded participants to receive education on the cause and effect of domestic violence. At about the same time, Victim Assistance created a supervised visitation program for the Domestic Relations Court. Finally, services were extended to the Juvenile Court dedicated to assisting victims of youth

Akron Police Department Captain Sylvia Trundle and St. Vincent-St. Mary student Erik Hauser loading a cruiser. \ FSM Archives—Christmas Flyer

violence. In 1992, the Akron Police Department provided an office in their detective bureau which is still used by victim advocates today. It was one of the first such programs in the United States.

In 1973, mission board members implemented a program of formal victim services as part of its ministry. The results of this endeavor grew quickly as the word spread. In 1974 the Victim Assistance Program worked with 103 cases. By 1975 cases had jumped to 906. As the number of people seeking help continued to grow, so did the number of services, with the programs becoming more formalized and more staff hired. In 1975, the mission partnered with The University of Akron to cosponsor one of the earliest victim symposiums. In 1976, Denton was instrumental in founding the National Organization for Victim Assistance (NOVA) in Washington DC. The Reverend Dr. Bob Denton served as founding president. In 1977, the mission, through its Victim Assistance Program, hosted the NOVA national conference at The University of Akron. While this was going on Dr. Denton created the first victimology course in the Department of Sociology at The University of Akron. In conjunction with the victimology course, a course on family violence was created by the author of this article, also in the Sociology Department.

By the turn of the century the focus began to change toward children who were impacted by violence. Once again, the organization identified a silent, underserved group who carried the aftereffects of the violence throughout their lives. In 2003, the Victim Assistance Program, Battered Women's Shelter, and Akron Children's Hospital partnered to create the innovative and well-received Children Who Witness Violence program. This in turn led to Akron Children's

Hospital opening a new unit called the Child Advocacy Center, which provided forensic exams and interviews to children who had been victimized. A victim assistance advocate was stationed in the unit to provide crisis intervention to the non-offending guardian.

In 2006, additional staff was added to meet the victims' needs as requests for services continued to grow. The Juvenile Court requested advocacy support for victims completing victim impact statements, and the Summit County Sheriff's Department requested victim advocacy services. Because of the growing requests the program began using interns from The University of Akron to help with impact statements. Thus, the internship program started through Bob Denton's classes in the Social Work Department at The University of Akron was formalized.

A longstanding tradition of the Furnace Street Mission continued by the Victim Assistance Program was the delivery of food baskets and toys each year to victimized families. The names of victim families were selected along with the ages and genders of the children. Local businesses donated the food, which was then parceled out according to the size of the families. Toys were then donated, wrapped, and identified by the age and gender of the child. Volunteers would meet at the mission and sort the food baskets and gifts by family. Police officers from the Akron, University of Akron, Barberton, Bath, and Copley police departments, as well as from the Summit County Sheriff's Office, with high school student volunteers would load up the cruisers and deliver the food baskets to the families. Imagine a police cruiser pulling up in a neighborhood, guaranteed to attract attention, especially if it was in a high-crime area. The officers and their student helpers would get out and carry the food baskets and gifts to the selected families. This was a great way to aid the victims and demonstrate the positive roles of the police to the community.

Victim Assistance Program—A Change in Leadership

Denton was the Victim Assistance Program's first executive director and served in that role from 1972 to 2012. In 1994, due to its ever-expanding role in the community, the Victim Assistance Program became its own standalone agency and was incorporated as a separate 501(c)(3) organization. After forty years of leading the program, in 2013 Denton handed the leadership to Leanne Graham (M.A., CA), who had worked closely for years with Bob and whose husband is a police officer. Prior to taking on this responsibility, Graham held various positions with the Battered Women's Shelter and the Rape Crisis Center and was the Associate Director of the Victim Assistance Program.

One of the first things the program expanded was the use of AmeriCorps volunteers to research the scope of human trafficking in Ohio. This work led to the creation of the Summit County Collaborative Against Human Trafficking. The next year (2014) the organization developed and offered the Victim Assistance Academy. This provides forty hours of training and has been certified by the National Organization for Victim Assistance. This training is required of all staff and interns and is open to the community. Over the years this has expanded into workshops and both online and on-site training for professionals.

Among its services to the victims, the Victim Assistance Program provides other special programs for the community. For many years, each December the Victim Assistance Program has offered the Angel Tree Ceremony where family members of homicide victims, friends, and community members come together to honor the memory of the victims in Summit County who lost their lives to violence. Family members honor their departed loved ones by placing a specially designed angel Christmas ornament on a Christmas tree. The victim's name is attached to the angel ornament. Angel ornaments from previous years are placed on a special Wall of Remembrance that accompanies the Angel Tree.

Victim Assistance offers its services on a 24/7 basis, and filing a police report is not required. Their goal is to have an advocate meet with the victim within thirty minutes of the incident. That advocate stays with the victim to lead and support them throughout the process.

In 2015, additional staff was hired as the community needs continued to grow. The program collaborated with the Battered Women's Shelter to expand their combined reach and to make sure that services were not being duplicated between the sister organizations. The next year the Victim Assistance Program partnered with Cleveland Clinic Akron General to work with patients who were victims of domestic violence, human trafficking, and elder abuse.

It became apparent that additional space was needed to handle the increasing number of cases and the need for space for confidential and safe victim

The Victim Assistance Program has served victims since 1972. \ Courtesy of Victim Assistance Program

The Brightest Spot in the Underworld

Leanne Graham, CEO, Victim Assistance Program, with Reverend Bob Denton. \ Courtesy of Victim Assistance Program. Leanne Graham & Bob Denton Victim Assistance Program Website

Angel Tree Victim Ornaments. \ Angel Tree Victim Assistance Program

counselling. In 2019, the Victim Assistance Program moved from the Furnace Street Mission to Main Street. Not only did the new facility provide more space, but it was also on main bus routes and this made it easier for victims to get there. It was also closer to the police department, the courts, and the prosecutor's office.

The Victim Assistance Program currently maintains offices in the municipal courts in Akron, Barberton, Stow, the Akron Police Department, the detective bureau, and the Summit County Domestic Relations Court. In 2022, the Victim Assistance Program celebrated its fiftieth anniversary. It had come a long way from the back of a napkin to the beacon of hope that it is today.

National Crisis Intervention Work

Bob Denton's crisis intervention work soon gained national significance. Starting in the 1980s, with mass murders and natural disasters occurring all too frequently, Denton was asked to serve on the National Crisis Response Team. Tasked by the US president, the team evaluated and assessed emergency situations and, most importantly, provided aid and counselling as needed. Reverend Denton focused on pastoral intervention, particularly in his work with the police and clergy.

Many of the national events Denton worked on occurred in the 1980s and 1990s. Among these were the shooting of the mayor of Mt. Pleasant, Iowa (1986), the aftermath of a devastating tornado in West Memphis, Arkansas (1987), the deaths of college students at Ole Miss University (1987), the massacre of six individuals, including two police officers, in Palm Bay, Florida (1987) and the deaths of twenty-four children and three adults in Radcliff, Kentucky by a drunk driver going the wrong way on I-71 (1988).

The 1990s required more of Denton's expertise and compassion. In 1990, he was summoned as the team leader to Gainesville, Florida, in response to the serial killings of five college students. In 1992 Denton provided counselling in Florida after the devastation caused by Hurricane Andrew. In 1993 Bob was involved in the aftermath of an inmate riot at the Lucasville Correctional Facility where nine inmates and two prison guards were murdered by the rioting prisoners. The 1990s ended with Denton being the national crisis liaison in Littleton, Colorado, with the student shootings at Columbine High School.

The new millennium did not start out much better. Denton was part of a team in New York City working in the aftermath of the terrorist attacks on the World Trade Center. More recently in 2008, he provided counselling to numerous local police officers and their families following the killing of Twinsburg, Ohio police officer, Joshua Miktarian, who was shot and killed during a normal traffic stop. In 2011, he led a team dealing with neighborhood and community fear, confusion, and grief, when an individual killed seven people in Copley, Ohio, before being shot by a Copley police officer himself. It is important to remember this national crisis intervention occurred while Denton was also serving as the executive director of the Furnace Street Mission and the expanding Victim Assistance Program.

The Chaplaincy and the Safety Forces Chaplaincy Center

Denton began to focus on the social and emotional needs of first responders. In many ways they too are victims of the trauma, stress, and mental problems that are part and parcel of dealing with crimes (especially violent ones) and disasters. "first responders are usually the first on the scene to face challenging, dangerous, and draining situations. These duties, although essential to the entire community, are strenuous to first responders and ... put them at an increased risk of trauma" (2018 SAMHSA Research Bulletin).

Law enforcement, fire personnel, EMS, and dispatchers experience intense, unique job stressors that impact their physical, mental, and emotional health, requiring specialized support. These well-documented, ongoing stressors and conditions result in a high level of divorce, alcoholism, domestic disturbances, and, especially, suicide.

Out of respect for others, many suicides may not be classified as such to protect family members from the associated stigma, making it impossible to identify the actual rate of suicidal behaviors. But years of tracking data show that safety forces suffer suicide at a rate at least twice the general population. In a similar vein, dispatchers are in a unique environment. Being a major part of a critical incident, but not being physically there, oftentimes leaves them wondering what happened at the event and what was the outcome. National and local safety forces personnel have noted the recent added stressors of a rising distrust of first responders in many neighborhoods and greater scrutiny than ever before as police officers are subjected to accusations of misuse of force. Departments have also found that the increased number of returning veterans joining law enforcement and fire departments, many of whom—especially those who did multiple tours—need additional or more in-depth general and substance abuse counseling encounters.

Safety forces personnel have found that seeking out needed help is further complicated given their unique population. In addition to a general stigma attached to admitting mental health issues, first responders are especially reluctant to admit that they need help. They fear that it may create the perception that they are showing weakness and unable to perform required duties. This instills in them a fear of possible consequences, such as being overlooked for a promotion. Most departments do not provide any training on the subject.

Retirement presents additional unique challenges to many members of the safety forces. Most safety force members retire at a relatively early age by completing the required years of active duty, or they must retire early due to injury or illness, usually related to their job. After years of being the person whose major reason for being was to help others, it may become very difficult to change roles from providing help to needing help.

Psychologically, this is an unknown and uncomfortable territory for most recent retirees. They do not know how to act in this relatively new, unknown environment and do not want to be viewed as a nuisance by active colleagues. The retirees now have time on their hands while those all around are going on with their normal routine life. Financially, if the retiree took the time to plan for retirement, they begin to think about how to manage financial resources over many years of retirement. If the retiree has no financial plan the anxiety begins to grow.

The board commissioned the author of this essay to complete a feasibility study with area clergy, community leaders, and safety forces members. The outcome was unanimous in feeling that such a center was needed. The clergy recognized that they were not trained to handle the very unique situations that members of the safety forces had to deal with. Community and safety force leadership realized that the structure and policies were not conducive for troubled officers to seek help, especially in a public arena. The forces were looking for ways to get the help needed that would help them mentally and emotionally without jeopardizing their careers. All agreed that a special set of services was needed.

Bob Denton Safety Forces Support Center

In 2012, Reverend Denton made the decision to dedicate his focus solely to the needs of safety forces, recognizing that first responders were an underserved population with intense and unique job stresses that required specialized support. Unfortunately, in 2017, Denton suffered major health issues impacting his ability to work. In response, the board of directors and staff worked hard to ensure that all client counseling and emergency response needs continued to be met in a professional, high-quality manner. To that end, today the Bob Denton Safety Forces Support Center provides critical incident stress management (CISM) to all safety forces and their families with no out-of-pocket charges to

Providing support to those who serve us. \ Courtesy of the Safety Forces Support Center.

them. This includes, for individuals and couples, confidential counseling for mental health, PTSD, anxiety, depression, and suicide prevention. The Center also provides substance abuse intervention; emergency response and intervention for critical incidents; professional education for departmental peer support; training through the Ohio Peace Officer Training Academy; chaplaincy services for visitation, funerals, and weddings; limited material assistance; outreach to retirees; and year-end holiday activities such as a Christmas Eve dinner for safety forces on duty and Christmas baskets for retirees.

With Reverend Denton's illness, the board immediately jumped into action to ensure that services would continue to be provided to first responders. In 2019 the organization was renamed and incorporated as the Bob Denton Safety Forces Support Center under its own 501(c)(3) designation and relocated to its new home in the American Red Cross building at 501 West Market Street. Once again larger space was needed for confidential safety forces counselling and other programs to support the forces and their families.

Because of the exponential increase in demand for services throughout this period, coupled with the workload John Balash was facing with both the counselling and operations components of the Center, the Board of Directors hired a permanent Executive Director to oversee the operations of the Center. This enabled Bob Denton to become the emeritus executive director and let John Balash serve exclusively as Director of Behavioral Health Services, focusing on counseling, mental health programs, and peer support training.

On January 1, 2020, Safety Forces Support Center Board Member, Cameron Mosley, assumed the role of Executive Director. Cameron has over two decades of experience in the nonprofit sector, where she still serves as the Executive Director of Bluecoats, Inc., an organization dedicated to supporting first responders in Summit County who have been injured or killed in the line of duty or face catastrophic needs beyond their control. The board also decided that it needed to create a governing structure where the different safety forces constituencies are represented as well as the overall community. It was decided that the president and vice president positions would be held by active members of the respective forces. Thus, the Safety Forces Support Center continues to be governed by a Board of Directors who represent all areas of the first responder community, both current and retired, as well as key professional sectors throughout Summit County.

The Furnace Street Mission in its Second Century

As the Furnace Street Mission enters its second century it is still finding innovative ways to meet the changing needs of the community. During the COVID-19 pandemic many businesses were forced to close down to hinder the spread of the virus. While many individuals could work or go to school from home, safety forces, first responders, and essential workers could not. Accidents, emergencies, crime, and violence continued despite the pandemic. With the closing of business establishments, especially restaurants, safety force members who spent their shifts out on the streets were left with very few places to go for a meal, a break, or even use the facilities.

The mission quickly became aware of this need and reimagined the mission facility as a safe and secluded place where officers could go for respite and a quick meal. Officers are provided with 24-hour access to the building through a special key code. On a self-service basis coffee, tea, water, and microwave ovens are available. The board also provides, free of charge to the officers, small convenience food items such as health bars, jerky, microwavable snacks, and so on that the officers can avail themselves of at their discretion. This service has worked so well that it has become a mainstay of the Furnace Street Missions programs. When local businesses, such as the Billows Company, heard of this service they decided to furnish the officers with "real" meals at least once each month.

For decades Bob Denton prepared short (a minute or two) inspirational pieces or parables for officers that were distributed through the Signal 1 column in the bulletins of the police departments of Akron, Barberton, Tallmadge, The University of Akron, and the sheriff's office of Summit and Medina Counties. Safety forces and their families looked forward to these comforting pieces. Individuals, especially retirees, remembered these inspirational pieces and asked Bob to consider collating and publishing them as a book. As Bob was recuperating from his stroke Bill Hauser volunteered to gather the parables and publish them in a book format. As expected, there were over one thousand parables that had accumulated over the years. To make these accessible and readable by the officers and their families, a three-volume set was published under the title of *Black Coffee for a Blue Soul* (2022). The mission board decided that these volumes would best be made available to the safety forces and the community free of charge. To date, these volumes have been well received and accepted in the community. (Copies can be obtained from the Mission.)

Today the Reverend Dr. Sandra Selby is the associate pastor at the Furnace Street Mission and is the on-call chaplain at Akron Children's Hospital. After spending eighteen years in strategic management at B. F. Goodrich, Selby,

The Brightest Spot in the Underworld

Reverend Dr. Bob Denton and Marian, his spouse and soulmate. \
Courtesy of Safety Forces Support Center

a member of the Furnace Street Mission board of directors for over twenty years, decided that she wanted to follow her passion and administer the spiritual and social needs of others full time. Under the tutelage of Bob Denton, she became a chaplain and then went on to become an ordained minister and to earn a Doctor of Philosophy. Interestingly, her dissertation was on addressing compassion fatigue in individuals working with people in crisis. This continues to be her focus. The Reverend Dr. Selby currently ministers to the community and corporations and leads monthly services at the mission.

The community of Akron, Ohio has been well served by the Furnace Street Mission over the past one hundred years. Our journey that started with a young evangelist preaching from the back of the Gospel Truck in the roughest part of town has consistently seen the mission reinvent itself to meet the needs of the community and its people. Under the leadership of Bill and Bob Denton, the Furnace Street Mission has created a number of firsts whether it be helping convicts, advocating for the victims, or supporting the safety forces. The Furnace Street Mission has come a long way in the past one hundred years and the citizens of Akron are the better for it. It has gone from a bright spot in the Akron underworld to a true beacon of light and hope for all the world.

Bibliography

Carloss, Tracy. "Local Organization on a Mission to Help First Responders." News5Cleveland.com. September 16, 2020.

Carney, Jim. "Robert Denton, Victims' Advocate to Step Down—Akron." *Akron Beacon Journal*. October 24, 2012.

Conn, Jennifer. "Akron's 50 Year-Old Victim Assistance Program: A Model." Spectrum News. March 5, 2022.

Conn, Jennifer. "Victim Assistance Program to Provide Mental-Health Support for Summit County Schools During Crisis." Cleveland.com. September 13, 2018.

Denton, Robert, and Bill Hauser. *Black Coffee for a Blue Soul*. Three vols. Akron, 2020.

Dyer, Bob. "Helper Bob Denton Needs Some Help." *Akron Beacon Journal*, September 3, 2017, beaconjournal.com.

Furnace Street Mission Archives housed at the Akron Public Library, Akron, Ohio.

Green, Jay D. "Lost Soul, Get Right with God. The Akron Gospel Tabernacle and the Plight of Urban Revivalism, 1924–1934," 1995, https:/www.akronlibrary.org/images/SpecCol/Lost Soul Get Right with God.

Price, Mark J. *Mafia Cop Killers: The Gang War Before Prohibition*. The History Press, 2017.

Price, Mark J. "Preacher was on a Mission in 1920." *Akron Beacon Journal*, October 13, 2018.

"First Responders: Behavioral Health Concerns, Emergency Response and Trauma." SAMSHA (Disaster Technical Assistance Center) Supplemental Research Bulletin, May 2018, p. 3.

Safety Forces Support Center Website: https://safetyforcescenter.org.

Victim Assistance Program Website: https://victimassistanceprogram.org/

\ **13**

The Evangelists

From the Tenderloin to Television

Jody Miller Konstand

Many Appalachians migrated to Akron in search of work between 1910 and 1920 when the rubber industry was booming and factories needed more employees to keep running. Advertisements, labor scouts sent south, and word of mouth drew unemployed and underemployed farmers, laborers, lumbermen, and miners, making Akron the fastest-growing city in the United States. A population of 69,067 in 1910 expanded to 208,435 by 1920 and grew again to 255,000 in 1930. Many were deeply religious and brought a wide range of values and practices with them.[1]

About 75 percent of the newcomers to Akron during this time were from south of the Ohio River, with the majority of those coming from West Virginia. Between 1910 and 1920, more than 100,000 white Appalachians and 50,000 Southern Black Appalachians came to Akron to stay. Along with their need for better-paying jobs and their willingness to work, these migrants brought their Bible-belt religious culture with them.[2]

Appalachians were typically Protestants, and many were Bible-centric fundamentalists. When they got to Akron, they were hungry for a church with that down-home, revivalist-type service with which they were familiar. That hunger

201

was filled with an urban revivalism approach and the "tabernacle" strategy, perhaps best demonstrated by the 1924 crusade at Goodyear Field, headlined by the up-and-coming evangelist Bob Jones. As Jay O. Green summarizes it, "Twelve east Akron churches, representing seven different mainline denominations" hosted a five-week, city-wide preaching campaign "orchestrated to achieve renown as one of the most important religious events in the city's history."[3]

The semi-permanent wooden "tabernacle" built for the campaign had seating for five thousand, room for a six-hundred-voice choir, and a nursery for children under three. The Bob Jones Union Evangelistic Campaign held daily services and meetings attended by thousands, led by the young, flamboyant preacher imported from Alabama. Jones preached the gospel, saved lost sinners, and as was typical for urban revivalist campaigns, condemned Akron's rampant "lawlessness, drunkenness, gambling, prostitution, dancing and motion pictures on Sunday."[4]

A common theme of urban revivalist preachers of those days was the pairing of civic leadership, patriotism, and duty with Christian responsibility. Akron's members of the Ku Klux Klan (whose membership in Northern cities during this time was often accepted by white Protestants) found common ground with Jones. At one point during the weeks-long preaching campaign, the local chapter of the Klan was featured. During this service, twenty members of the women's auxiliary of the Klan gifted Jones with a Bible. Robed and masked, they marched up the aisle to him carrying the Bible, an American flag, the Klan banner, and an electrically lighted cross, all to the accompaniment of the Klan's women's glee club singing a Klan hymn. Jones thanked Klan members for their assistance, calling them the "best people of a community."[5] In the 1920s, Klan members in Akron included prominent citizens such as a mayor, the sheriff, business executives, judges, Protestant clergymen, and school board members.[6]

By 1928, the power of the Klan was diminished in Akron and much of the United States, and the same was true of the shrinking affinity between mainline Protestantism and urban revivalism. The political and cultural climate gave way to new evangelistic approaches and a "new breed of independent revivalists ... determined to forge ahead with [their] own spiritual, moral and political agenda." No one in Akron typified that new breed of independent revivalists better than Bill Denton.[7]

Denton was as colorful and charismatic a character as any found in Akron's history. A 5-foot-4-inch-tall immigrant from Cornwall, England, Denton was described over the years as "Crazy Bill Denton" and "a drunk turned preacher ... with the showmanship of a carnival operator with the radio message to open the door to Jesus."[8]

He came to the United States in 1911 at sixteen, landing in Akron a year later to work in the rubber shops. When World War I broke out, he returned to England, enlisted in the British Army, and fought the Germans for three years, during which time he was wounded twice. He returned to Akron after the war, spending the next seven years as a rubber worker "with a fondness for the less spiritual side of life."[9] Visiting every dive in the underworld on payday, he called himself "a hardened young man," gambling, drinking, and gaining acquaintance with the unsavory nature of Furnace Street.[10]

When his young son, Tom, needed an operation, Denton prayed for the first time in his life, promising to follow God while pleading, "Save my boy!" The operation saved Tom's life, and shortly after, Denton wandered into a revival meeting at the Madison Avenue Evangelical Church. The third night of the revival, Denton claimed God spoke to him, saying, "You promised me, keep your promise." That was 1926 and "the beginning of the new Bill Denton."[11]

The Reverend Bill Denton

For the next three years, Denton, ordained through the Wesleyan Tabernacle Association, preached anywhere he could, from the City Mission on South Main Street to the North Akron Baptist Church, from Sunday jail services to street revivals in neighborhoods around town. The latter was possible with "Calvary's Traveling Gospel Car," a gaudy blue bus he bought and outfitted with a donated set of electric bells, signage that urged "Get Right With God" and "Prepare to Meet Thy God," and a drop-down balcony on the back from which he and his assistant in those early years, Carl Burnham, could preach the gospel of Jesus Christ.[12]

Recognizing the potential for reaching the masses through radio, Denton was one of the first fundamentalist preachers to proselytize through that medium beginning in 1926. His gospel broadcasts over WADC started in April 1928 and continued for more than five decades.[13] When he found an abandoned building on Furnace Street—the reputed hangout in years past for notorious cop killers and local gangs—in Akron's "tenderloin district" north of the growing downtown, Denton cleaned it up and opened Furnace Street Mission on Sunday, April 28, 1929. This fire-and-brimstone preacher made it his home for the next thirty-three years.[14]

That first year at his "little mission in the slums," Denton conducted three services on Sunday and themed nightly services the rest of the week. For example, Monday night was for Black people, Tuesday night was for men only, and Friday was "Bible Teaching" night.[15]

Denton installed an amplifying system on the tiny building, and on Sundays, he would speak to an estimated one thousand people. This included nearby neighbors, even those across the North Hill Viaduct who couldn't help but hear the sermonizing. He also attracted two to three hundred cars throughout the day "belonging to both rich and poor."[16]

Always from Furnace Street Mission—and for three short years in the early 1930s from the larger Akron Gospel Tabernacle—Denton "delivered an unyielding message of moral and spiritual reform, seasoned with blatantly patriotic overtones," a message that in those years appealed to "Akron's nebulous radio audience, 'marginal' peoples, and disillusioned mainline Protestants."[17] This "little one-horse local preacher with a great passion for lost souls," as he referred to himself,[18] converted between two to three thousand souls in the Mission's first two years while caring for an average of 1,300 families a month at the mission where "Old, Young, Black, White, Destitute, Discouraged Find Help, Food There."[19]

The city's rapid urbanization and the onset of the Great Depression exacerbated the poverty many in the community faced, particularly with housing and food shortages in the expanding city. During this time, Denton "provided for 900 Souls" and even gave away his own shoes. "Changed by the gospel whose ministry needed no embellishment to appear larger than life," he housed homeless boys, secured land for a forty-acre garden to grow food for the hungry, provided sleeping quarters for the destitute, opened a charity store for the needy, and delivered thousands of meals with baskets of food at Thanksgiving and Christmas.[20]

Denton could not separate words preached from actions taken. He denounced some of Akron's Protestant churches for "their abandonment of the city's economically strapped" as they built great churches with fine kitchens while people went hungry. Nor did his fundamentalist peers escape admonishment as he noted, "You can't expect a man to listen to talk about spiritual food when he's physically hungry."[21]

His ministry over the years included not only daily services and weekly radio broadcasts, but also the printing and distribution of pamphlets and sermons, including editions of the *Gospel Tabernacle News* that urged readers to "Buy your gas at our Service Station," with the Johnston and Arlington Street locations advertised, to help with "feeding the poor and preaching the gospel."[22] Denton preached around the country and in Korea, Japan, and South America; he broadcast his gospel message from a station in Havana, Cuba; and he sat in a model of an electric chair to preach his opposition to capital punishment. He opened missions in Japan, the first halfway house in Akron for ex-convicts, and a house of refuge for battered women, their children, and victims of rape.

The Evangelists

But Denton was also a study in contrasts. A fervent believer committed to saving souls for Jesus Christ, he put his faith into action by feeding the hungry, clothing the destitute, providing beds for the homeless, and walking that last mile to the electric chair with eleven convicted felons. Yet he could be an impetuous zealot, burning a Bible page by page with a blowtorch because its translator, with alleged communist affiliations, substituted the words "young woman" for "virgin." He tried to talk notorious bank robber Pretty Boy Floyd out of a shoot-to-the-death ambush with police; he made enemies of gamblers, bootleggers, and law enforcement when he used a sledgehammer to smash slot machines; and his social commentary alienated striking laborers, the World Council of Churches, local ministers, and even some of his fervent followers.[23]

He was a man of prophetic expedience, understanding the far-reaching power of print, radio, and film to spread the gospel message. Yet he entangled religion with politics, expounding against the Bolshevik influence and organized labor, railing at the too-liberal policies and unchristian principles of President Franklin Roosevelt, and admonishing right-wing Father Charles Coughlin for being too soft. He was also a flamboyant showman and self-promoter. Grainy and flickering copies of his 1930s' silent movie, *The Secrets of Akron Revealed*, contrasted the good works of the mission with scenes—some obviously staged—of nefarious and illegal activities in the seedy neighborhood. He was not averse to relying on the enticement of the unusual to entertain and attract potential souls, whether by promoting a converted Persian priest garbed in exotic clothing or a ukulele-playing evangelist accompanied by her monkey in defiance of evolutionary science.[24]

Furnace Street Mission still stands, and another chapter in this anthology tells the story of Bill's son, the Reverend Bob Denton.

The seeds Denton planted in Akron reached far beyond the confines of the former speakeasy turned into the little mission in the slums. It was a reach that led to religious impacts that would resonate around the world because he set in motion the paths of three of Akron's most prominent and influential religious figures in Akron's history—Dallas Billington, Carl Burnham, and Rex Humbard. Include Ernest Angley with those three, and what resulted was the emergence and exponential growth of four huge, independent congregations not typically found in cities of Akron's size—Akron Baptist Temple, The Chapel (initially at Five Points, then Brown and Vine, then on Fir Hill), Cathedral of Tomorrow, and Grace Cathedral.[25]

The Big Four

In the early to mid-years of the twentieth century, revivalism dominated Akron's Protestant landscape. According to historians, the peculiarities of revivalism included overly simple answers to complex problems; the importance of free will; the joyful experience of conversion for the sinner; and little to no interest in or responsibility for social reforms. The number of converts won—souls saved—was a measure of success, no matter the methods employed. Revivalist leaders differed from dignified, educated clergymen because they were "close to the people and speak their language and rouse their emotions" and could attract the more traditional church members by employing flamboyance and showmanship.[26] Combine those tendencies with the Bible-belt religious culture of so many of the migrants settling in Akron in those years, and the dominance of revivalism was understandable.

Akron's four dominant, independent churches—Akron Baptist Temple, The Chapel, Cathedral of Tomorrow, and Grace Cathedral—flourished outside the mainstream of American Protestantism. The commonality among these four behemoths was one strong, central personality at the head; a family dynasty within their ministries; financial assets accrued in the building of temples, chapels, cathedrals; and a nondenominational, welcoming structure trending theologically toward conservatism to fundamentalism to evangelism. Additionally, the leaders of these churches pioneered the use of radio and television to spread their messages, much of which were "highly moralistic in content and extremely authoritarian in tone."[27] Finally, at the start of their ministries, pastors at three of these churches—Akron Baptist Temple, The Chapel, and Cathedral of Tomorrow—received a helping hand from the Reverend Bill Denton.

Akron Baptist Temple – the World's Largest Sunday School

The man responsible for founding Akron Baptist Temple was born in 1903 in a log house in western Kentucky, the tenth of thirteen children. Dallas Billington's formal schooling—in a one-room schoolhouse—ended at twelve, when he went to work on a large farm once operated with the labor of enslaved people. At seventeen, he moved to Paducah, Kentucky, got a job in a shoe factory, took correspondence courses, and met his future wife. In 1924, he went with her to a tent revival where "God's great love and mercy came into my soul," and he was saved.[28]

Another Southern transplant hungry for a better-paying job, Billington arrived in Akron in 1925 and was hired at Goodyear Tire and Rubber Company.

Sunday School Superintendent J. Stanley Bond and Dallas Billingham (right) outside the Akron Baptist Temple in 1970. \ Photo courtesy of the *Akron Beacon Journal*

He searched, unsuccessfully, for a church home and continued to read the Bible, convinced he was being called by God. He preached anywhere he could, even at the factory, declaring, "Akron is the wickedest place this side of hell." He told his fiancée, Nell, "When we're married, we'll have to start a church of our own" because the churches in Akron "were not like the ones back home."[29]

In circumstances eerily reminiscent of Denton's, Billington's one-year-old son, Charles, needed surgery, during which Billington made this covenant with God. "Dear Lord, if you let my dear baby Chuckie live, I promise ... I'll do my best to preach the Gospel of the Lord Jesus Christ."[30]

Billington began ushering at Denton's Furnace Street Mission, and one October evening in 1930 when Denton was too hoarse to speak, he insisted Billington preach. That first sermon "to less than twenty customers, mostly derelicts, prostitutes and others from the neighborhood" was about the Prodigal Son, and Billington "saved three fine men that Wednesday evening."[31]

Billington honed his preaching, both as a roaming lay evangelist and on Akron's WJW radio—he claimed the call letters meant "Watch Jesus Win." Billed as the "Southern Evangelist" because he had no church affiliation and used the Bible as his script, Billington paid $7.50 for weekly airtime until listeners sent donations to keep him on the air. Within two years, his radio broadcast was heard by nearly 100,000 listeners.[32]

Believing God would help him build his church, Billington and Nell decided on the name. "We chose Baptist, for the Bible speaks of Baptists," he explained. "And we chose the word 'temple' because the first building that was built for God was called a temple, not a church. Our body is called a temple wherein the soul and God live."[33]

Billington held his first church service in a rented space at Rimer School on Manchester Road in the spring of 1934. Fourteen people attended (including the custodian), one person was saved, and an offering of $1.18 was collected. Within a month, there were eighty-one people at his weekly service. In July, Billington traveled to the Sugarcreek Baptist Church in Kentucky to be ordained—no one in Akron would ordain him, he wrote. He returned to town to preach and build his church and the following year, he left Goodyear to become a full-time minister. On Easter Sunday 1935, Akron Baptist Temple was officially born.[34]

The growth of Akron Baptist Temple was meteoric during the thirty-seven-year ministry of Billington. It became one of the country's first megachurches.

The first church building, located on Manchester Road, was 80 by 105 feet and was largely constructed by Billington and church members with their "picks, shovels, and wheelbarrows." Dedicated on Easter Sunday 1938, it seated sixteen hundred people and was debt free in a year. A two-story adjacent building was

The Evangelists

dedicated and debt free by 1940. The third and most iconic Akron Baptist Temple building was a 21,000-square-foot structure, seating up to ten thousand with twelve acres of parking on the 29-acre site. Behind the pulpit there was space for a 250-voice choir, broadcasting and transcription studios, and an immersion baptismal font with a River Jordan backdrop. The scroll over the entrance read "Upon This Rock I Will Build My Church" and beneath it, "Dr. Dallas F. Billington, Pastor and Founder." The *Akron Beacon Journal* reported that 38,000 people attended the dedication that first Sunday of April 1949, and more than 75,000 toured the facility in twelve hours.[35]

During the 1940s and 1950s, Billington's radio sermons aired in every state. In the 1960s, he was featured on thirty television stations. Under his guidance, Akron Baptist Temple developed a worldwide missionary outreach, pioneered Vacation Bible School, dispatched a fleet of buses every Sunday to bring congregants to the services free of charge, and helped establish hundreds of independent Baptist congregations across the country. It was noted as being "one of the very few churches in Akron which spends as much or more money on others as it does on its own local operations." He oversaw the church's several million dollars of physical assets, earned $140 a week, and tithed 18 percent back to the church while living modestly in Firestone Park. When well-meaning congregants proposed a mansion for their minister, Billington said he liked his house and wouldn't move. As a fellow pastor once said of him, millions of dollars passed through his hands over the decades "but none of [those dollars] stuck" to him.[36]

Akron Baptist Temple became known as the largest Sunday School in the world—a four-story, $400,000 Sunday School wing was added in 1958 to accommodate this growth—and at its peak, was considered the largest church in North America. *Time* magazine reported in 1962 that Akron Baptist Temple had 17,000 parishioners, with Sunday church and school attendance figures numbering 10,000-plus, an annual budget of $620,000, and weekly collections of more than $10,000.[37]

Billington's preaching style appealed to the Southerners who migrated north, initially attracting blue-collar workers and families, but as his message spread, the number of white-collar congregants increased. For Akron Baptist Temple's 25th anniversary, 50,000 people came to Akron to hear "The Preacher" preach.[38]

In his autobiography *God is Real*, Billington explained that "if you attend one of our services, you will find that we are old-fashioned, as far as believing every word of the Bible. You will find us God-fearing as well as God-loving people, like the prophets of old."[39] For Billington, this meant that worshippers would find a preacher who opposed smoking, movies, dancing, strong drink, and mixed-race swimming. He campaigned, unsuccessfully, to have the Bible read daily in local public schools; he harangued Akron City Council in 1943 into approving an eleven p.m. curfew for those under sixteen; and he criticized women working during World War II, especially women who frequented bars and dressed scantily. He persuaded a parishioner guilty of murder to reveal the location of the murder weapon, and he railed against the Community Chest (the precursor to United Way) for not having petty cash available for groceries, emergencies, and the homeless.[40] He also crossed horns with Rex Humbard when faith healer Katherine Kuhlman headlined a Humbard Family tent revival in 1952. Billington offered $5,000 "to anyone who could prove he could heal a person through prayer," a blatant denunciation of Kuhlman and the first confrontation in a years-long, uneasy peace between the two rival preachers.[41]

The lack of racial diversity at Akron Baptist Temple was hardly an anomaly in Akron during the decades following World War II. Only twelve of approximately two hundred white Protestant churches in town had Black members in 1963. *The Church in Akron* describes it as "an all-white congregation." And it further notes that "while a very effective effort has been made to reach people from all of the various social, economic, and cultural categories of the white population of Akron, no comparable effort has been made to reach the Negro residents of Akron."[42]

When questioned about racism at Akron Baptist Temple in the early 1970s, Billington described the congregation as predominantly people of Southern heritage. He added, "We have colored folks who come here from time to time, but they usually come once and don't return. They just don't seem to feel as welcome here." Photos in the 1985 Akron Baptist Temple 50th Anniversary album confirm a lack of diversity and give credence to a decades-old incident recounted by Bishop Flanvis Josephus Johnson II of the House of the Lord. Johnson related that an Akron Baptist Temple deacon approached a Black visitor to the church, tapped him on the shoulder and said, "You can stay until the end of the service, but don't come back."[43]

As Billington's outreach beyond Akron paralleled the exponential growth of Akron Baptist Temple, he travelled frequently until his death at sixty-nine of a heart attack on August 26, 1972. During the twenty-four-hour vigil preceding his funeral, more than eighteen thousand people paid their respects, and six thousand people, including ten rows of preachers and their families, attended the funeral of its founder.[44]

His son, Dr. Charles F. Billington, who had served at Akron Baptist Temple since entering the ministry in 1948, took the helm of a 16,500-member congregation, helping Akron Baptist Temple "continue to the glory of God." As the new pastor, he launched a $4.2 million expansion of the sanctuary, dedicated in May

The Evangelists

of 1979, only to watch it go up in flames two years later. The massive fire, one of the largest in Akron's history, destroyed the four-thousand-seat sanctuary. Arson was suspected but never proven. The conflagration did elicit a spirit of ecumenism from two of the city's other megachurches. The Cathedral of Tomorrow loaned them television equipment to enable the continued broadcasting of Akron Baptist Temple's Sunday services. The Rev. David Burnham, pastor of The Chapel in University Park, visited the smoldering ruins and offered Billington equipment, shared space at The Chapel, or anything needed. Calling the fire "the greatest setback in the history of this ministry," Charles Billington nonetheless rallied the congregation, supervised an $8 million reconstruction, and in a week of dedication services in September 1984, celebrated the completion of a five-thousand-seat sanctuary in the 43,000-square-foot main floor.[45]

During his twenty-four-year tenure as pastor, Charles Billington officiated at more than five hundred weddings, three thousand funerals, and he preached countless sermons at tent revivals, missions, schoolhouses, churches, and megachurches. He was credited with starting three hundred churches worldwide and was one of the first pilot missionaries to fly a plane into the jungles of South America.[46]

Like his father, Charles Billington didn't shy away from speaking out. He opposed abortion, lack of prayer in schools, pornography, and homosexuality. He made the front page of the *Akron Beacon Journal* when he refused to marry a couple who had been living together and had been in court about an abortion. He protested a proposed sex convention at a downtown hotel in 1984. In opposition to the Akron Interfaith Council, he favored prayer and Bible discussion groups in Akron Public Schools. In 1992, he was "disgusted" with a television situation comedy when the unmarried Murphy Brown decided to have a baby. "Raising children was the job of a man and a woman," he said.[47]

Charles remained senior pastor until 1996 when his son, the Rev. Dallas R. Billington, the third-generation pastor, succeeded him. Charles died on July 31, 2010.[48]

When Dallas R. Billington became senior pastor, the church was $6 million in debt, and membership numbers had diminished to about six thousand. Over the next ten years, membership and finances rebounded modestly as new programs were initiated. The church added a contemporary service to the traditional service, started a program of small group study for members; expanded the food and clothing ministry, and provided more than two thousand school backpacks to youngsters. When Dallas R. Billington was called to a new chapter in his ministerial life in Florida, the debt at Akron Baptist Temple was less than $1 million.[49] Four years later, this grandson of the church founder returned to Akron to care for his ailing parents. Following the loss of both, a divorce after thirty years, and myriad financial struggles, he started City Church A/C (Akron/Canton) ministering to the broken and hurting.[50]

In 2006, for the first time in seventy-one years, a Billington was not in the pulpit at Akron Baptist Temple. When the Rev. Ed Holland took over as pastor, membership had shrunk exponentially to 1,500, with an average of 1,100 attendees at Sunday services. Eight years later, with membership still in decline, the congregation opted to fund outreach rather than building maintenance and voted to sell the aging, 263,000-square-foot campus of seven buildings for $3.3 million. In June 2018, R. A. Vernon, D. Min., founder and senior pastor of Word Church, negotiated the asking price down to $1.5 million, and Akron Baptist Temple became home to one of the fastest-growing Black churches in Northeast Ohio. Both congregations shared the property until the following year when Akron Baptist Temple "rebooted" as Connect Church in Coventry Township. Word Church put the building and acreage up for sale for $3.9 million.[51]

Three years later, the former Akron Baptist Temple was still for sale. The building—which sixty years previously had been home to what was considered the largest church in North America—sat empty and abandoned, windows smashed, taxes owed, home to looters and squatters, awaiting the wrecking ball.[52]

The Chapel

The founding of the second of Akron's four dominant, independent churches—The Chapel—followed a now familiar pattern. The family of founder Carl Burnham came to Akron from Tennessee by way of Kentucky in 1921, lured by the booming rubber industry. Burnham was twelve. After graduating from West High School, he went to work for B. F. Goodrich Company and became friends with a man finding his way into his own ministry, Bill Denton.[53]

Denton invited Burnham to a revival in February 1928 and soon after, Burnham got down on his knees at Akron's Gorge Park and dedicated his life to Christ. He grew in faith, attended Sunday School, studied the Bible, and began working with Denton, preaching from the back of the "Calvary's Traveling Gospel Car" and at the recently opened Furnace Street Mission.[54]

In the next several years, Burnham shaped and solidified the vision for his ministry and the church he would establish. He spent time in Chicago at the Moody Bible Institute until his money ran out. He returned to Akron and worked as Denton's assistant at Furnace Street Mission and the Akron Gospel Tabernacle. The time spent with Denton allowed Burnham to witness faith in action, especially as the hardship of the Great Depression had a devastating impact on many of the congregants to whom they ministered—often society's

The Evangelists

outcasts and those desperate for the basic necessities in life. Taking the gospel to the streets while providing food, clothing, and hope was a ministry model Burnham would emulate, that of reaching out to the lost and bringing them to Jesus.[55]

Burnham continued preaching and leading evangelistic crusades wherever he could. When he married in 1933, he and his wife Agnes worked at Furnace Street Mission and dreamt of their own storefront church. Travelling home to Akron in a Model A Ford from a series of Oklahoma City revival meetings, they prayed. When a 20-foot-by-50-foot storeroom in a building at Five Points became available, they reached out to friends, asking for "investments for eternity" in $5 and $1 shares. The couple raised enough money for chairs, songbooks, a piano, and the first month's $30 rent. They scrubbed the space and hung a lighted, gold frame in the window to display sermon topics. The Chapel at Five Points—as unassuming as its name—celebrated its first Sunday service on January 15, 1934, preaching the gospel of salvation to between forty and fifty faithful. During that first year, in that "little place where people could get spiritual food," Dallas Billington, who was working to build his own church, was a guest preacher.[56]

"The Chapel had no ties with any denomination and no support from any other church or organization," Bob Schneider writes in his history of the church. "Evangelism was at the heart of everything—and their motto became, 'In the heart of the city, for the heart of the city.' And . . . the church grew."[57]

Two years later, The Chapel's four hundred members left the rented Maple Street storeroom for a lot they purchased on Brown and Vine streets, where volunteers had dug a basement. The congregation met in that basement for four years until the sanctuary, and eventually an annex, was completed. Committed to spreading the gospel while growing his own church, Burnham never passed up the opportunity to preach at other churches and missions. He also established a weekly radio broadcast; radio had become a popular medium for Akron's burgeoning preachers to reach more souls.[58]

Membership and ministries continued to grow at The Chapel at Brown and Vine, as did revivals, frequently featuring guest evangelists. Bill Denton preached for two weeks in February 1945.[59] A typical Sunday morning service at The Chapel was informal, attended by more than seven hundred Bible-carrying men, women, and children. Burnham led the service from the pulpit, "praying, preaching, and singing," dressed in a light gray business suit instead of a clergyman's robe. At the end of the service, new converts would go forward, confess their faith in Jesus, accept Christ with bowed heads, and be welcomed as church members to the accompaniment of an invitational hymn.[60]

Outgrowing their space again, the congregation purchased two and a half acres on Fir Hill, the site of the burned-down Akron Art Institute. It would become The Chapel's third home.[61] In the ensuing six years, church members cleared the site, volunteered their labor, laid the cornerstone, raised the building funds, and on March 27, 1955, marched from Brown and Vine streets to Fir Hill to dedicate the new $400,000 Chapel. With seating for fifteen hundred, stained-glass windows telling the Bible story, radio broadcasting facilities, a blue-tiled baptistry, forty-six Sunday School classrooms and other meeting rooms, The Chapel on Fir Hill was now the second largest church in Akron, surpassed only by Akron Baptist Temple.[62]

The "church with a heart for missions and a passion for evangelism" continued to grow, adding a $200,000 building for education in 1960. The church dedicated one-fourth of its annual budget to "benevolences" and expanded its missionary outreach locally, nationally, and internationally. The demographics of its 2,700 members were at odds with the church's motto "in the heart of the city." Data collated in 1963 described The Chapel on Fir Hill as a drive-in church with a congregation of people who had "walked out of other Akron churches." They were mostly professionals and white-collar workers from all areas of Akron, many from Cuyahoga Falls, many of whom were from the South or had parents born in the South.[63]

Burnham's stature in Akron grew through his parish work, his radio and now television outreach, and his increasing civic involvement. In 1959, he underwent heart surgery in Minnesota for the defective valve that prevented his enlisting during World War II. The 53-year-old "preacher with the big heart ... the minister who grew with his church" died unexpectedly three years later, following a second heart surgery. At his bedside along with his family was Rev. Bill Denton, who conducted the funeral service three days later.[64]

The logical choice as Burnham's successor was his son.

David Burnham was a former all-star athlete from Buchtel High School and Wheaton College, who had declined a potential professional football career to go into the ministry.[65] After graduation, he had returned to The Chapel where he worked side by side with his father for six years before accepting the unanimous call to be pastor of the church founded by his parents.

In the twenty-six years the younger Burnham served as senior pastor, membership at The Chapel expanded to 6,700, due in large part to Burnham's powerful preaching. His innovative leadership expanded Bible studies, the person-to-person ministry, music and campus ministries, and outreach programs for the community at large. The purchase of a former YWCA camp near Ravenna, renamed Camp Carl as a memorial to his father, provided evangelism and spiritual growth programs, especially geared to the young. In 1973, a new 2,500-seat sanctuary was built and connected to the Fir Hill buildings to accommodate the

The Evangelists **215**

congregation, which was adding approximately five hundred members a year. At the May 1973 dedication of the $1.65 million sanctuary, the church, now one of the largest independent churches in the country, again changed its name to better reflect its broader mission, becoming The Chapel in University Park.[66]

Continued rapid growth of the church led to traffic, parking, and zoning issues, prompting Burnham and church officials to consider splitting into congregations throughout the city. The eventual decision to stay in place was confirmation of the church's enduring commitment to the "heart of the city" and triggered an *Akron Beacon Journal* editorial—"Having Faith in Downtown." The most traumatic issue facing the forty-eight-year-old Chapel was Burnham's announcement that he was leaving to pastor a church in Florida. Three thousand packed The Chapel in University Park on a September Sunday in 1982 when Burnham said goodbye.[67]

After a year-long search, Rev. Knute Larson was called to be senior pastor of The Chapel—the geographic designation in the name now gone. Larson, who had served fifteen years at the 1,200-member Grace Brethren Church in Ashland, would lead the second-largest Akron church. He would be responsible for shepherding the 6,800-member congregation, a ministerial staff of thirteen, and scores of volunteers within its ministry and Bible study programs.[68]

It was not smooth sailing for church or pastor; four hundred members left, and Larson struggled to find his footing. "After a beloved leader, there is a time of grief and anger among some of the staff and congregation," Larson told Russell Sibert of *The Akron Beacon Journal.* "Some people were still mad that he left, a wonderful man, Dave Burnham, and with a great heritage here, but they were mad that he left, so they took it out on me."[69] Almost three years later, an hours-long meeting between Larson and some men of the church initiated the healing. Larson not only found a place at The Chapel but in the Greater Akron community.[70]

Church membership increased to eight thousand; three Sunday services were added to accommodate the growth; and community churches in Marlboro, North Canton, Valley View, Wadsworth, and Kent were established to hold weekly services beyond the city.[71] Two building expansions created room for 250-plus activities a week, including support groups for everything from alcoholism, grief, and eating disorders to homosexuality and homelessness. The Chapel presented itself as the downtown Akron church that drew people from everywhere: "everyone is welcome to this church. The fact is we have many people of all incomes and races in our membership."[72]

People were drawn to the church because of Larson. He became known for his wise counsel on boards and community panels. His ubiquitous basketball games in the church's gym were open to all. He achieved a measure of celebrity status because of his catchy, one-minute television and radio spots, broadcast daily, but it was his phone call to Pastor Ron Fowler from the Arlington Church of God and their subsequent friendship that had a far-reaching impact. Starting in 1988, the two ministers—one white and one Black—met once a month and got to know and trust each other as equals. The Chapel was predominantly white, and Arlington Church of God was almost all Black, but Larson and Fowler put together committees from each church to break down barriers. Their "Allies" ministry program linked church to church and person to person to fight prejudice.[73] As Fowler said, "We all have certain racist attitudes. But if we put Jesus Christ at the center of our hearts, we can overcome that. I believe that's what Knute and I have done."[74]

Their work together resulted in thirty partnerships between Black and white churches. With Pastor Mark Ford, they created "Love Akron" in the 1990s, a Christian-based organization that continues advocating for connections to better the community. Their leadership was instrumental during Akron's 1993 *Coming Together* project as more than two hundred community organizations collaborated to improve race relations. Following President Bill Clinton's town meeting on race in Akron, an *Akron Beacon Journal* editorial highlighted the "intentional relationship" between Larson and Fowler as a model of what could be possible. Fittingly, on May 17, 2009, Fowler offered the last prayer at the farewell service celebrating Larson's twenty-six years at The Chapel.[75]

The Chapel was then Summit County's largest church with eight thousand members, six worship services, and three hundred weekly activities. It was also "one church in two locations" after the 2003 establishment of the City of Green campus of The Chapel. Larson left The Chapel "in great shape. The church doesn't owe a cent anywhere, and we've been able to do a lot overseas and in the communities of Akron and Green."[76]

The Rev. Paul Sartarelli, co-pastor for three years with Larson, became the fourth senior pastor. During his 3 ½ year-tenure—brief given the seventy-eight-year history of senior pastors at The Chapel—the discipleship programs grew, and the addition of a Wadsworth campus meant The Chapel was one church, each with its own pastor, in three locations. However, membership by 2012 had declined to 4,500 attendees on Sundays.[77]

During the next year, The Chapel was led by a six-person leadership team, including the three campus pastors. The Rev. Tim Armstrong was installed as senior pastor on August 10, 2014, as part of The Chapel's eightieth anniversary celebration.[78]

The Chapel was not immune to a national decline in church attendance. As the fourth largest of the area's megachurches at that time—Christ Community

The Evangelists

217

Chapel, Grace Church, The Word Church—its approach turned to "planting" churches where people lived. By July of 2019, The Chapel had six campuses—Akron, Green, Hudson, Wadsworth, Kenmore, and Cuyahoga Falls—toward its plan to plant ten churches in ten years.[79]

That plan was upended by a personnel and leadership controversy in 2021 that engulfed the church in crisis and threatened a split between the church and its seven campuses. Ultimately, Armstrong and others resigned; church trustees hired a consulting group; remaining leadership was counselled and coached; town hall meetings for church members took place; and a Transitional Leadership Team was installed. By mid-2021, The Chapel still owned churches in Akron, Green, and Wadsworth and rented or shared space in four other communities. What had been Akron's largest church now had a membership base of between 3,000 and 4,000, with attendance at Sunday services at the seven campuses and through online viewing estimated at 6,000.[80]

As The Chapel's website proclaimed in 2023, this "network of seven church campuses in diverse communities throughout Northeast Ohio" is "connected by a shared commitment to walk in the way of Jesus into the will of God," not unlike what its founder, Carl Burnham, envisioned almost ninety years previously.[81]

Cathedral of Tomorrow and Grace Cathedral

The similarities between the other two independent, nondenominational megachurches in the Akron area during the latter years of the twentieth century are best illustrated by this paragraph in the 1963 analysis, *The Church in Akron*:

> Both the Cathedral of Tomorrow and Grace Cathedral (formerly the Temple of Healing Stripes) were founded by itinerant evangelists who came to Akron temporarily to hold revivals, both were persuaded to stay, both subsequently arranged for temporary quarters in former theaters, both eventually went outside of Akron [city limits] to purchase large parcels of land for development, both claim to be "nondenominational," both went through name changes switching from "Temple" to "Cathedral," both draw the bulk of their people from residents of places other than Akron, both place an unusually heavy emphasis on the use of television and radio, and both emphasize the "camp meeting" revivalistic preaching service, rather than the Sunday School, in attracting people.[82]

The similarities don't end there, especially with the financial, legal, and moral dilemmas that surfaced in the ensuing years, dilemmas often exacerbated by the hubris of the churches' respective founders—Rex Humbard and Ernest Angley.

Humbard was born in 1919 in Little Rock, Arkansas, into the family business of ministry. His parents were Pentecostal evangelists; the first words he heard from them were prayers. When he was eight, he dreamed one night of thousands of people being forced into a great pit of fire. The vision of keeping people from hell with a message of salvation through Jesus Christ became "the driving force of his life."[83] At thirteen, Humbard opened his heart to Jesus Christ and promised to put God on Main Street.

The road became home as the Humbard family grew. Rex was the oldest of six siblings, all musically inclined, and they traveled coast to coast on the evangelistic circuit. Booked into revivals and attracting crowds with the "bait" of "country style gospel music" sung by the children and "down-home gospel preaching" by their father, the Humbard Family gained fame. In every town they visited, this musical family would book themselves on the radio, publicize their evangelical services, and sing to draw larger and larger crowds. Rex managed the family business starting in his teens; he was responsible for the bookings, auditorium rentals, and the scheduling of radio appearances. He also acted as master of ceremonies for church services, leading prayers and inviting people to come forward and receive Christ as their savior. He learned by watching other evangelists fill tents and auditoriums.[84]

Humbard met and married Maude Aimee Jones in 1942; their mutual faith brought them together. They spent the next ten years preaching, praying, and singing with the other members of the Humbard Family, pulling their sixteen-foot Airstream trailer behind them, as they travelled the United States and Canada drawing lost souls to Christ. In Greenville, South Carolina, Rex was ordained a Minister of the Gospel by the International Ministerial Federation and could officially be called Rev. Rex Humbard.[85]

The Humbard Family's fame spread, bolstered by a one-year contract to broadcast their gospel program nationally over NBC's radio network. Because "God's work shouldn't be second best to anything," they raised $21,000 to buy the "Humbard Family Gospel Big Top," home for the travelling revival meetings and a prescient precursor to the Cathedral of Tomorrow. Following a revival in Canton in the summer of 1952, Humbard led a five-week revival in Akron under the Gospel Big Top on the Municipal Airport grounds. Evangelist Kathryn Kuhlman, famed for her Pentecostal healing powers, opened the services. Her appearance attracted the ire of Akron Baptist Temple's Dallas Billington, who vowed to "run the Humbards out of town." The controversy and ensuing publicity attracted even more crowds, drawing some 200,000 people to the Humbard Family Gospel Big Top. By the time the tent came down, the traveling for some of the family ended, and a thirty-year-long, televangelist ministry was about to begin.[86]

Angley, two years younger than Humbard, was born in 1921 in Moores-ville, North Carolina, the fourth of seven children whose parents were devout

Rex Humbard explaining his global plans in 1972. \ Photo courtesy of the *Akron Beacon Journal*

Baptists. Like Humbard, he experienced a vision at eight, a visit with God. As his bed spun out of control into the night sky, he was carried into thousands of stars that would, in time, be revealed to him as the souls he would win for God.[87]

As a youngster, Angley watched as his mother was baptized in a Pentecostal Church, speaking in tongues, and becoming a temple of the Holy Ghost. He was converted at eighteen during a church service when he answered the altar call, accepted Jesus Christ as his Savior, and felt his heart filled with God. Angley spent the next six weeks fasting, praying, and praising the Lord, until he was baptized in the Holy Ghost and received a call from God to preach. At eighteen, he worked as a traveling preacher and attended a liberal arts college where his romantic relationship with Esther Lee "Angel" Sikes grew.[88]

Married in November of 1943, Angley and Angel spent almost a dozen years travelling in a Studebaker pulling a house trailer as he preached the gospel and offered a divine healing service at revivals. The first year of their marriage, Angley nearly died of peptic ulcers, which he claimed were miraculously cured by God. He wrote that he went on "a long fast to receive the Lord's gifts of healing. Then when I came off the long fast ... I knew without a doubt that I had the gifts of healing." They bought a tent to hold their own revivals, continued to travel from town to town, and everywhere they went, "God healed the people. The totally deaf were hearing, the blind receiving sight, cross-eyes were straightening, the crippled were walking, and the Gospel in all its fullness was being preached."[89]

The "divine visitation" happened in 1954, when the Lord carried Angley away in a vision, walked with him, performed miracles, and told him to go to Akron, Ohio, and establish a church for Him.[90]

By June, with the big tent set up just outside city limits on Canton Road, Angley attracted crowds. Newspaper ads promised "Signs! Wonders! Miracles! Healings!" and "A Miracle Service Every Night!" Wednesdays and Saturdays were "Holy Ghost" nights when tongues of flame descend onto followers who "fall on their knees and talk incoherently." Migraine headaches and stomach ulcers were no match for Angley's healing powers as people waited in line for his touch. When the tent folded in August, Angley was in Akron to stay. The first stop was the former Liberty Theater on West Market Street which soon became the Temple of Healing Stripes.[91]

Humbard and Angley set out on parallel paths to establish their places in Akron's church history.

Humbard put the Gospel Big Top in storage, rented the 1,000-seat Copley Theater, hosted nightly meetings, and broadcast a radio program twice a day. His services included a "fair share of emotionalism and dramatics," his way of appealing to those he claimed other churches were not reaching. His next stop

The Evangelists

was the former Ohio Theater on State Road in Cuyahoga Falls. Easter Sunday, April 5, 1953, drew overflow crowds to what was now the interdenominational Calvary Temple. Five services on Sundays, a choir with an eighteen-piece orchestra, three daily radio programs, a twenty-four-hour dial-a-prayer service, and a monthly devotional magazine were just the start for Humbard. With his conviction that "God ought to be on television," he initiated live weekly broadcasts of Calvary Temple's Sunday services on local television. Less than a year later, more than a million people in Ohio, Pennsylvania, and West Virginia were tuning in to his eleven a.m. Sunday services.[92]

Angley's Temple of Healing Stripes, named for the Bible passage in Isaiah starting "With his stripes we are healed," moved to Springfield Township, initially to a framed "Summer Tabernacle" built for good weather until the Cathedral building Angley envisioned was completed. Meanwhile, the church continued to attract congregants lured by twice daily radio broadcasts, promises of miracles and healings, Angley preaching the old-fashioned gospel and strict interpretation of the Bible, and Angel singing and playing the organ. By June 1957 and with a membership of three thousand, the new $1 million Temple of Healing Stripes was dedicated, with a 2,000-seat auditorium, 500-seat chapel, and forty classrooms. Not ten months later, the imaginatively described edifice was renamed Grace Cathedral, signifying the grace of God that brought them to Akron and blessed Angley's ministry to heal the sick and cast out evil spirits.[93]

In parallel to Angley, the exponential growth at Humbard's Calvary Temple led to the purchase of twenty-one acres in Northampton Township as the site of his Cathedral of Tomorrow. This $2.1 million, black granite, round auditorium with a domed roof had 5,400 seats, a six-ton, 100-foot-tall lighted cross suspended from the ceiling, and 154 Sunday school rooms. It was larger than any church in Greater Akron—even the Akron Baptist Temple. Designed for church services and television with its 168-foot stage and state-of-the-art broadcasting facilities, it was unique enough to draw sixty thousand people for its grand opening on May 24, 1958. It heralded the expansion of Humbard's worldwide television ministry and a years-long relationship with Jimmy Hoffa; the Teamster Union Pension Fund provided the building's $1.2 million mortgage loan, the first of several such loans.[94]

Across town, Angley funded a $1 million expansion of Grace Cathedral in 1969 with support from church members, a bi-monthly magazine, books he authored, and radio broadcasts. Guided tours of his completed modern-day "Solomon's Cathedral" showcased the changing colors of the Fountain of Blood, the Living Waters Baptistry, priceless works of art, a 23-karat gold leaf Open Bible pulpit, gold altar chairs, crystal chandeliers, a print shop, and broadcasting equipment. A year later the death of his wife, Angel, devastated Angley. As he wrote in his 2004 autobiography, *Hurry Friday!*, visions he received from Jesus finally convinced him Angel's death was God's will. It was, he wrote, part of God's divine plan for Angley's journey to the nations of the world. While his healing and saving ministry continued at Grace Cathedral, it was national and international crusades and the debut of the *Ernest Angley Television Hour* in 1972 that put Angley's reach beyond Akron. Within a few years, his television program was broadcast nationally on one hundred stations.[95]

The format for Angley's services, whether in person or on television, included singing, preaching, testimonies, prayer requests, blessings, and miracles. Amid Bible quotes at a 1975 North Carolina crusade, Angley proclaimed, "You can't buy miracles, but you can show your faith in God's causes. Close your eyes and ask: God, how much can I give? Remember, I will not use one penny for myself. All of it will go into my ministry ... raise your hands if you can give or pledge $100." Once donations and pledges had been made, prayer cards were passed out. Those afflicted waited in line for Angley's healing prayers and touch, and evil spirits were ousted, and maladies cured.[96]

As Humbard's fame spread, he crisscrossed North America in his 52-passenger Viscount airplane, the fourth plane purchased by the ministry in five years. *Time* magazine's editor-in-chief supposedly coined the term "Tele-Evangelist" in the late 1960s to describe Humbard's roles as pastor, evangelist, and television preacher. By 1972, the Sunday morning *Cathedral of Tomorrow* show was seen on more than 350 television stations in North America by an estimated twenty million viewers; weekly broadcasts could be seen in Australia, the Philippines, and Japan.[97]

"It costs to spread the word of God; and for me to reach as many people as I desired to, it's going to take money," Humbard said in a 1972 *Dayton Daily News* article. Whether renting his tele-production studios for commercial use, buying a Brooklyn girdle factory, Upper Michigan's Mackinac College, or a 23-story office building in downtown Akron, Humbard's business was religion, and religion became his business, as the *Dayton Daily News* observed.[98] He built a twelve-story apartment building on Cathedral of Tomorrow property for the ministry's senior citizens. He opened the Cathedral Buffet restaurant to support the burgeoning television ministry. He spent $225,000 for a twenty-room mansion in West Akron as the church's parsonage. He started construction of a 750-foot-tall Cathedral Tower, which was to be a broadcast transmitter, observation deck, revolving restaurant, and strobe light visible for hundreds of miles. The partially completed tower still stands—construction stopped at 560 feet due to financing—as an enduring symbol of Humbard's hubris, locally known as

The Evangelists

Rex Humbard preaching in the early 1970s. \ Photo courtesy of the *Akron Beacon Journal*

"Rex's Erection." Humbard offered Prayer Key Family memberships to his millions of television viewers—small keys sent as reminders to pray daily, fast one meal a week, and pledge a monthly gift to the evangelistic work of the ministry. The business of religion involved many in the Humbard family, fourteen at one point, children and grandchildren singing the praises of Christ as the Humbard Family Singers; sons involved in video operations and staging rallies around the country; family members in management positions or preaching from the pulpit when Humbard was not in town. When expenses outpaced funding sources, Humbard created a stewardship staff to visit followers throughout the country. Contribution and investment options, including annuity trusts and life estate plans, were a way followers could help in the mission of God's work. As 1972 ended, the business of religion for the Cathedral of Tomorrow was bringing in $8 million annually.[99]

The televangelism of Humbard and Angley far surpassed the outreach efforts of Akron Baptist Temple and The Chapel. They took television to extraordinary lengths to spread the word of the gospel, save lost souls—and in Angley's case, heal the bodies of those souls—and raise millions of dollars from believers. "Once televangelism becomes dependent on viewers response and support, the audience becomes a market, and the gospel is transformed into a product," Quentin J. Schultze writes. "Like an engaging Hollywood film that smoothly moves viewers along with the story, the most popular Pentecostal preachers carry viewers effortlessly from music to sermon to the final appeal for funds."[100]

Cathedral of Tomorrow

On Feb. 12, 1973, the Ohio Department of Commerce and the US Securities and Exchange Commission filed suit against Cathedral of Tomorrow in federal court. The suit effectively froze assets and barred the sale of securities. The Cathedral could no longer solicit donations, borrow funds, mortgage property, or give raises to employees. The defendants (Humbard was listed first in court documents) were charged with violating federal and state laws through the sale of unregistered securities of $12.5 million dating back to 1959 to some four thousand investors around the country.[101]

Humbard claimed his ministry had never defrauded anyone and that the charges were an attempt to shut down his popular televised ministry because evangelists around the country were jealous of his success. "Because I am bigger than the rest of the Evangelists, I was singled out." An agreement was reached with the court for the church to create a trust fund to pay back the bond and note holders. Drastic expense cuts, the divestiture of all commercial enterprises, prayers, fasting, and returning the focus to saving souls were the steps taken to raise funds to pay off the debt. Prohibited by the court from discussing in church or on television the details of the financial emergency, the ministry sent hundreds of thousands of letters to the faithful. On Victory Sunday, December 7, 1975, Humbard celebrated paying off the $12.5 million debt in two-and-a-half years, calling it a miracle and the "most outstanding accomplishment ever accomplished for the glory of God."[102]

Having rebounded from near bankruptcy, Humbard's goal was global evangelism, and in 1978, he stepped aside as pastor of Cathedral of Tomorrow to concentrate on his worldwide television ministry. The countries not visited by the Humbard Family were reached via television with programs broadcast to more than thirty-two million people worldwide in seventy-seven languages with lip-synching translations. At the height of his television ministry, Humbard's program was seen in sixty-one countries on 658 television stations. He employed a staff of eight hundred and acquired a 707 jet to carry the sixty-one tons of equipment needed to stage his rallies.[103]

The Evangelists

Four years after clearing his $12.5 million debt, Humbard was again crying wolf because the ministry was "facing death" with a $3.2 million debt. When 200,000 followers sent in $20 each, that debt was eliminated; however, this second plea to save the ministry with followers' donations became a familiar pattern. Television audiences began to decrease, out-of-town rallies were cancelled, and contributions began to decline. Television production expenses increased, leading to staff layoffs and the cutback of the weekly one-hour television show to thirty minutes; program taping moved from Akron to Georgia. At the same time, the Humbard Family spent $650,000 for three homes in Florida. Citing wife Maude Aimee's health as the reason and denying any misuse of funds, Humbard explained, "My people don't give a hoot what I spend the money for."[104]

The plea for donations was repeated twice in 1982, the year Humbard celebrated fifty years over the airwaves. "Without your help, we will not be able to make it." Then in 1983, Humbard resigned as pastor of Cathedral of Tomorrow; brother-in-law Wayne Jones became pastor. The ministry was $2 million in debt, and the family was purchasing another $1.4 million in Florida property.[105]

The Cathedral of Tomorrow's television studios and office complex were sold to Ernest Angley Ministries. Before long the Humbard Foundation would be sued for money still owed on the incomplete Cathedral Tower, and Humbard would cancel the weekly television show after thirty continuous years. He claimed the Lord was leading him in a new direction, a direction that seldom took him back to Akron.[106] Uncertainty and dissension would plague the Cathedral of Tomorrow for the next ten years.

In 1987, the year Rex Humbard Ministries incorporated in Florida, the ministry was $3.1 million in debt. By year's end, Cathedral of Tomorrow was in turmoil after firing the first pastor who was not a family member. Humbard made a guest appearance, but he spoke to a congregation of less than five hundred. Six months later, Humbard was back at Cathedral of Tomorrow to install another new pastor; this one lasted less than two years before being fired by the board. In 1991, the Humbard Family denied any interest in or influence on the Cathedral of Tomorrow. The following year, the church board sued the Rex Humbard Foundation for, among other things, receiving money that belonged to the church and denying the board the right to sell the church building. On Feb. 28, 1993, Humbard again returned to the Cathedral of Tomorrow when the lawsuit was settled. He reclaimed leadership of the now 200-member congregation for the first time in eight years, saying that God "told me to lend my influence to build this church again so that it'll never be anything but a church." On Sunday, May 30, 1993, Humbard preached to almost four thousand people who came to celebrate the thirty-fifth anniversary of the Cathedral of Tomorrow.[107]

On March 11, 1994, the Cathedral of Tomorrow church building and surrounding property, appraised at almost $7 million, was sold to Ernest Angley Ministries for $2.47 million.[108] Rex Humbard, the Pentecostal preacher turned televangelist who promised to put God on Main Street, and in the process made Akron the home for televangelism for more than thirty years, died in 2007 at eighty-eight in a Florida hospital.[109] The Rex Humbard Foundation had a website as of 2023, but an Internet search for the Cathedral of Tomorrow leads to Angley's Grace Cathedral.

Grace Cathedral

If the opulent Grace Cathedral was the "fortress of the faithful" for Angley's ministry, it was television that was his net for attracting believers.[110]

The Ernest Angley Hour was gaining audiences in more than one hundred markets nationally. That reach expanded exponentially in 1984 with the $2 million purchase by Ernest Angley Ministries of the television studios and office complex of the Rex Humbard Foundation. When the opportunity arose, Angley bought the licensing for a Christian-Family station, and on November 17, 1984, WBNX-Channel 55 began broadcasting from the former Humbard studios in Cuyahoga Falls. The following year, *The Ernest Angley Hour* moved to Channel 55, which also debuted his new daily talk show, *The Ninety and Nine Club*.[111]

By 1986, Ernest Angley Ministry's programs were reaching millions nationally and internationally. The programs delivered miracles to his believers while providing fodder for comedians, who would mimic his emphatically punctuated, Southern drawl, his ill-fitting toupee, and his white suit. "Even nonbelievers find themselves occasionally tuning in to some of the more entertaining televangelists," wrote Quentin J. Schultze, "if for no other reason than to see something new or to chuckle at what seems to be the inanity of it all."[112]

With arms outstretched and eyes looking to heaven, he introduced *The Ernest Angley Hour* with the proclamation, "I believe in miracles because I believe in God!" The programs produced for television catered to his down-home persona. Angley welcomed guests, delivered the gospel message, and encouraged viewers in need to call the Prayer Line. Gospel singing, testimonies, and recorded crusade and personal appearances were preludes to his signature faith healing. The lines were long as each supplicant was led to him. He'd ask what needed to be healed and if they were saved. With eyes closed, he would say, "I have your condition in the vision." Touching the person, he would ask for the miracle in the name of Jesus, praying for as long as he believed the miracle took, and then placing his hand, usually on the person's forehead, push them backward and announce, "You got your miracle!"[113]

The Evangelists

Ernest Angley, 1984. \ Photograph by Paul Tople, courtesy of the *Akron Beacon Journal*

Angley innately understood the value of authenticating his television messages with personal appearances. Crusades and special appearances enabled him to connect with followers beginning in 1974 in St. Louis and internationally six years later. During the next four decades, Angley visited thirty-nine countries on five continents, many to Africa and India, with team members in lime green "Miracle Crusade" shirts passing out Bibles, Angley's books, crusade literature, and invitations to his rallies. In parks, stadiums, and open fields, interpreters stood on stage with Angley as thousands listened to his translated message and witnessed faith healing.[114]

His faith healing was not without controversy. During a 1978 Charlotte, NC, miracle and healing crusade, a woman with a bad heart collapsed on her way back to her seat after Angley had prayed for her. She was left on the floor of the auditorium for fifteen minutes because an Angley usher told those wanting to help her that she was "in the spirit." She died.[115]

In 1984, while on tour in Zurich, Switzerland, a woman with a heart condition collapsed and died during one of his healing services. Three days later in Munich, Angley was arrested after a six-hour service where "souls were saved [and] the sick healed by the loving hand of our God." Charged with suspicion of fraud and the practice of medicine and physical therapy without a license, Angley was held for five hours and released on bond. He continued to France, and the next day a devastating hailstorm pelted Munich. It was God's retribution, according to Angley.[116]

In 2007, Angley claimed to have documented proof that AIDS could be cured by Jesus and the healing power of prayer. He provoked the Guyanese Health Minister, Dr. Leslie Ramsammy, to call Angley's claim "an obscene exploitation of people's vulnerability."[117]

In 1986, seven members of the Committee for the Scientific Examination of Religion came to Akron to investigate Angley's faith healing and expose it as fraudulent. After attending and participating in his Grace Cathedral services, they left town "baffled, with little hard evidence to cite on either side of their questions." Angley claimed he was an instrument of God and the miracles "came only through the power of Jesus Christ," but miracles were offered after asking for donations to keep his programs on the air. Yet, he didn't live lavishly. His yearly salary was $15,000, and he drove a late-model car and lived in a three-bedroom house, both of which were owned by the church. Critics said he never provided proof of curing anyone. Skeptics argued that adrenaline masked symptoms or provided temporary recovery. Believers said he gave them hope.[118]

Angley rode the rising wave of religious television in the 1980s. According to John Green, emeritus director of The University of Akron's Bliss Institute of Applied Politics, Angley had "a big impact on American culture and religiosity." Green described Angley as a charismatic leader who was "not everyone's cup of tea, but he appealed to millions."[119]

When the financial and sex scandals involving nationally known televangelists—most notably Jimmy Swaggart and Jim Bakker—surfaced in the late 1980s, Angley spoke out: "Fallen preachers have caused so many to fall away in disgust." At the same time, he claimed, "I have the authority to speak this Holy Spirit message because I am holy and pure."[120]

On March 11, 1994, what remained of Rex Humbard's Cathedral of Tomorrow properties, appraised at almost $7 million, were sold to Ernest Angley Ministries for $2.47 million. Grace Cathedral's weekly services were moved to Humbard's former properties two weeks later. The Grace Cathedral building and campus on Canton Road were relegated to weddings, funerals, special events, and Angley's Bible College.[121]

The Evangelists

Over the next two decades, Angley would continue his Pentecostal ministry through crusades, television, the launch of a website in 1998, and a YouTube Channel in 2013. His three to four-hour healing services on the Friday nights he was in town would draw two thousand people. His mission to spread the Gospel around the globe was profitable enough for the 2004 purchase of a $26 million Boeing 747, a plane so large there were no facilities to house it at the Akron-Canton Regional Airport.[122]

Angley's profile in Akron during these years was dogged by scandals. There were rumors in 1996 of a homosexual relationship with an employee at the church. A surreptitiously recorded conversation verifying the relationship would not be revealed for almost twenty-five years, but the rumors led to several hundred people leaving Grace Cathedral. In January 1999, a fifteen-year-old volunteer at the Cathedral Buffet Restaurant owned by Angley's ministry was murdered by a twenty-seven-year-old former employee/volunteer whose romantic overtures were rebuffed. Her family was awarded a $100,000 settlement from Ernest Angley Ministries.[123]

Then in July 2014, an assistant pastor at Grace Cathedral quit, accusing Angley, 93, of violating him for years. Recordings of a Sunday service following this incident were sent to the *Akron Beacon Journal*. On the recordings, Angley and two church officials addressed the congregation, denied any sexual abuse, and denied Angley was a homosexual. They accused the former assistant pastor of being a liar, drug addict, and adulterer who wanted to take over the church upon Angley's death. A two-month in-depth investigation followed by reporter Bob Dyer. On October 12, 2014, the *Akron Beacon Journal* published a six-part series revealing explosive revelations from twenty-one former members of Angley's congregation. Denials of those allegations after an interview with Angley and his two defenders from the church were included in the series, but the accusations could not be ignored. Former members described how the church had become "a dangerous cult where pregnant women are encouraged to have abortions, childless men are encouraged to have vasectomies, and Angley—who preached vehemently against homosexuality—was himself a gay man who personally examined the genitals of the male parishioners before and after their surgeries." And "he turned a blind eye to sexual abuse by other members of his church." Less salacious allegations involved misuse of funds, strong-arming donors, and using volunteers to staff the for-profit Cathedral Buffet. When asked by Dyer if his former members were lying, Angley answered, "Most of them are, they really are. Before God they are.... People, they'll just lie and lie and lie. Lying spirits take them over."[124]

The damage was done, especially when the series was reprinted in newspapers around the country. Lawsuits followed, including one that permanently closed the Cathedral Buffet in 2017 following a U. S. Department of Labor court case for damages and back pay for unpaid volunteers. The lawsuit and counter-suit between the assistant pastor and Angley were settled out of court in 2020; had the case gone to trial, Agley, 98, would not have testified due to "age-related maladies."[125]

The final indignity for Angley was the release to the *Akron Beacon Journal* of that 1996 recorded telephone conversation where Angley admitted to a sexual encounter with a male church employee. He did not respond to a request for an interview for the story. The following month, February 2019, Angley resigned from the ministry.[126]

Angley died at age 99, on May 7, 2021, fittingly on a Friday given the title of his autobiography, *Hurry Friday!*[127]

The future of Grace Cathedral—the church started in a tent by an itinerant Pentecostal preacher whose faith-healing ministry became known around the world—will depend on how it transitions after the death of a personality like Angley. According to a co-pastor in 2021, the ministry of Grace Cathedral is bigger than one man. But is it bigger than a man still performing miracles two years after his death on the Ernest Angley YouTube channel?[128]

Epilogue

Rubber brought them—Denton, Burnham, Billington, Humbard, Angley—to Akron. Together and individually, they had an impact on millions of lives—locally, nationally, and even internationally—through ministries they created in the name of God. Humbard and Angley reached far beyond the city, offering faith, hope, and miracles around the world. As of 2023, Humbard's ministry was a website; Angley's ministry was diminished to unknown numbers; Billington's legacy became an empty, abandoned building; and Burnham's Chapel was torn asunder, its recovery undetermined at this time. At Denton's "little mission in the slums," a lighted cross still shines each night, acknowledgment of what was, what is, and what still may be.

Notes

1. George W. Knepper, *A Brief History of Religion in Northeast Ohio*, Center for Sacred Landmarks, Maxine Goodman Levin College of Urban Affairs, Cleveland State University, 2002; Karl H. Grismer, *Akron and Summit County* (Summit County Historical Society, 1952), 16.

2. Grismer, 378; Lyle E. Schaller, *The Church in Akron: An Interpretive Analysis* (Regional Church Planning Office in Cooperation with the Council of Churches of Greater Akron, 1963), 14; Knepper, 16.

3. Jay O. Green, "'Lost Soul, Get Right with God': The Akron Gospel Tabernacle and the Plight of Urban Revivalism, 1924–1934," unpublished manuscript, Kent State University, December 1995, 3.

The Evangelists

4. Green, 3; "Bob Jones to Open Tabernacle Revival Services," *Akron Beacon Journal*, October 4. 1924, 5. Unless otherwise noted, newspaper articles are cited as they appear in Newspapers.com.

5. "Bob Jones Given Bible by Women of Ku Klux Klan." *Akron Beacon Journal*, October 28, 1924, 13.

6. "J. B. Hanan Slated for Ku Klux Post." *Akron Beacon Journal*, October 4, 1924, 1; Jay O. Green, 5.

7. Green, 7–9.

8. Scrapbook 1, Furnace Street Mission/Victim Assistance Program Collection, Special Collections Division, Akron-Summit County Public Library, (hereafter referred to as Furnace Street Mission Collection); Peter Geiger, "Friends to Honor Rev. Bill Denton," *Akron Beacon Journal*, May 11, 1978, B1; Keyes Beech, "Biography in Brief: Soul-Saver," *Akron Beacon Journal*, January 18, 1942, 5D.

9. Scrapbook 1, Furnace Street Mission Collection, Special Collections Division, Akron-Summit County Public Library; Beech, "Biography in Brief: Soul-Saver," 5D.

10. Bill Denton, "For God and Country," pamphlet, 1944. Furnace Street Mission Collection.

11. Denton, "For God and Country."

12. "Akronite Plans Services on Wheels," *Akron Beacon Journal*, April 9, 1929, 22.

13. Booklet in the Blue Binder #1 SC2013-25, Furnace Street Mission Collection; Jay O. Green, 13.

14. "Biography in Brief: Soul-Saver," 5D.

15. *Akron Gospel Tabernacle News*, June 12, 1932. Furnace Street Mission Collection.

16. *Akron Gospel Tabernacle News*.

17. Green, 13, 17.

18. *Akron Times Press*, September 20, 1932, Furnace Street Mission Collection.

19. "We Congratulate William Denton,"*Akron Beacon Journal*, March 11, 1931, 26, Blue Binder No. 1, Furnace Street Mission Collection.

20. *Akron Times Press*, September 20, 1932; "The Furnace Street Mission at 60," 1987 60th Anniversary Historical Calendar, Furnace Street Mission Collection.

21. Green, 15.

22. *Akron Gospel Tabernacle News*.

23. Furnace Street Mission Collection.

24. Film archives, The Bob Denton Safety Forces Support Center; Green, 16.

25. Knepper, 16; Cindy Berry and Pam Cornell, *Upon This Rock I Will Build My Church, and The Gates of Hell Shall Not Prevail Against It: 1934–1984 The Chapel: 50 Years and Building* (Akron, 1984).

26. Schaller, 59.

27. Schaller, 93.

28. Dallas Billington, *God is Real, A Testament in the Form of an Autobiography* (New York: David McKay, 1962), 17.

29. *Akron Baptist Temple, 50 Golden Years, 1935–1985* (Akron Baptist Temple, 1985), 6, Akron Summit County Public Library; Mark J. Price, "Akron Baptist Founder Inspires Book," *Akron Beacon Journal* (April 5, 2021), B1; Billington, 19.

30. Billington, 34.

31. Billington, 40; *Akron Baptist Temple*; Price, "Akron Baptist Founder Inspires Book," 1B; Schaller, 93. History records four different dates for Billington's first sermon. The date used in the text is from his autobiography, *God is Real*.

32. Billington, 58; Price, "Akron Baptist Founder Inspires Book," B1.

33. Billington, 70.

34. Billington, 85; "Dallas Billington," Christian Hall of Fame, Canton Baptist Temple, https:// christianhof.org; *Akron Baptist Temple, 50 Golden Years,* 9.

35. *Akron Baptist Temple*, 20; "Dr. Billington's Life One of Hard Work," *Akron Beacon Journal*, Aug. 28, 1972, A9.

36. "Dr. Billington's Life One of Hard Work," A9; Schaller, 94; "Dallas Billington"; Price, "Akron Baptist Founder Inspires Book," 1B; *Akron Baptist Temple*, 39; Lloyd Stoyer, "'Battling Billy' Still a Fighter," *Akron Beacon Journal*, April 10, 1960, F1; Knepper, 17.

37. *Akron Baptist Temple*, 49; Schaller, 94; Stoyer, F1.

38. "Dr. Billington's Life One of Hard Work," A9; "Akron Baptist Founder Inspires Book," B1; *Akron Baptist Temple*, 44.

39. *God is Real*, 103.

40. "Dr. Billington's Life One of Hard Work," A9; Stoyer, F1.

41. "Dr. Billington's Life One of Hard Work," A9; Stoyer, F1.

42. Schaller, 70, 95, 100.

43. Doug Livingston, "Megachurch Back on Market," *Akron Beacon Journal*, June 11, 2019, A4.

44. *Akron Baptist Temple*, 36, 53; "Dr. Billington's Life One of Hard Work," A9; Billington, 215.

45. "Dad's Gone, Son Depends on God," *Akron Beacon Journal*, Dec. 17, 1972, 1; "Arson Possibility in Temple Blaze," *Akron Beacon Journal*, May 10, 1981, 1; "Baptist Temple Sanctuary Reborn from Ashes," *Akron Beacon Journal*, September 6, 1984, 1; Advertisement for the Akron Baptist Temple, *Akron Beacon Journal*, September 1, 1984, 5.

46. "Beloved Pastor, Known as Faithful, Grounded," *Akron Beacon Journal*, Aug. 2, 2010, B1; *Akron Baptist Temple*, 82.

47. Akron Baptist Temple, 78; "'Principle' ... Billington Won't Wed Abortion Case Couple," *Akron Beacon Journal*, November 18, 1977, 1; Charles Billington, "Schools Should Give God His Rightful Place," *Akron Beacon Journal*, June 11, 1981, 7; Jim Carney and Kathy Spitz, "Locals Take Sides in Debate over 'Murphy Brown,'" *Akron Beacon Journal*, May 21, 1992, 18.

48. "Beloved Pastor, Known as Faithful, Grounded," B1.

49. "Akron Baptist Temple Marks 60th Year," *Akron Beacon Journal*, June 11, 1994, 9; Jim Carney, "Akron Baptist Temple Pastor Will Step Down,"*Akron Beacon Journal*, Feb. 21, 2006, B1, Colette M. Jenkins, "New Church Opening at Musica," *Akron Beacon Journal*, March 29, 2014, 1.

50. "New Church Opening at Musica," 1.

51."Billington is Not in the Pulpit," *Akron Beacon Journal*, January 7, 2007, B1; Colette M. Jenkins, "Having First Visited Akron Baptist Temple at Age 12, Ed Holland Returns as Pastor, Hopes to Add to Its History," *Akron Beacon Journal*, January 27, 2007, A10; Colette M. Jenkins, "Akron Baptist Temple For Sale," *Akron Beacon Journal*, Aug. 10, 2015, 1; Mark J. Price, "Akron Baptist Temple Founder Inspires Book," *Akron Beacon Journal*, April 5, 2021, B1.

52. Doug Livingston, "Empty and Abandoned: Once Among Biggest US Churches, Akron Temple Could Be Razed," *Akron Beacon Journal*, November 18, 2021, A1.

53. Bob Schneider, *Blessed to Be a Blessing: The History of Chapel Missions* (Akron: The Chapel, 2018), 1; Marvin Katz, "Rev. Carl Burnham Dies After Surgery," *Akron Beacon Journal*, July 12, 1962, 2; *Upon This Rock*, 2.

54. *Blessed to Be*, 1; *Upon This Rock*, 2.

55. *Blessed to Be*, 2–3; *Upon This Rock*, 2.

56. *Blessed to Be*, 4, 175; *Upon This Rock*, 3; "thechapel.life," https://akron.thechapel.life.

57. *Blessed to Be*, 4.

58. *Upon This Rock*, 5; Schaller, 96; "thechapel.life"; "Chapel Moves Location," *Akron Beacon Journal*, September 26, 1936, 10; "Akron News Briefly Told," *Akron Beacon Journal*, October 5, 1935, 15; "Youth Council Meets Tuesday," *Akron Beacon Journal*, Dec. 23, 1939, 7; "Speakers Named at City Mission," *Akron Beacon Journal*, Dec. 14, 1940, 4; Church service directory, *Akron Beacon Journal*, March 6, 1937, 6; Church service directory, *Akron Beacon Journal*, April 4, 1936, 11.

59. Advertisement for revival at the Chapel, *Akron Beacon Journal*, Feb. 9, 1945, 9.

60. "Brown, Vine Street Chapel Grows," *Akron Beacon Journal*, April 24, 1950, 17.

61. *Upon This Rock*, 7; "Brown, Vine Street Chapel Grows," 17.

62. Lloyd Stoyer, "Lay Cornerstone Sunday," *Akron Beacon Journal*, April 10, 1954, 11; Lloyd Stoyer, "Chapel on Fir Hill to Dedicate Huge $400,000 Edifice Sunday," *Akron Beacon Journal*, March 26, 1955, 11; *Blessed to Be*, 10; *Upon This Rock*, 7.

63. *Blessed to Be*, 10; Schaller, 96–97.

64. Helen Waterhouse, "Burnham 'Critical' After Surgery," *Akron Beacon Journal*, April 8, 1959, 1; *Upon This Rock*, 9; Marvin Katz, "Rev. Carl Burnham Dies After Surgery,"*Akron Beacon Journal*, July 12, 1962, 2; "Rev. Burnham Rites Scheduled Saturday," *Akron Beacon Journal*, July 13, 1962, 28.

The Evangelists

65. "1965 Inductees," Summit County Sports Hall of Fame, summitcountyshof.org/1965; *Upon This Rock*, 10.

66. https://akron.thechapel.life; *Upon This Rock*, 9–14; J. Curtis Brown, "It's Church Without a Cross," *Akron Beacon Journal*, May 6, 1973, 14.

67. Peter Geiger, "Akron Church Move Possible in Zone Dispute," *Akron Beacon Journal*, July 14, 1979, 23; "Having Faith in Downtown," *Akron Beacon Journal*, September 8, 1980, 4; Tom Ryan, "Minister Considers Florida Post," *Akron Beacon Journal*, May 25, 1982, C1; William Casterbury, "Akron Pastor Bids Tearful Goodbye," *Akron Beacon Journal*, September 13, 1982, D1.

68. Tom Ryan, "New Senior Pastor is Appointed at Chapel," *Akron Beacon Journal*, September 28, 1983, D4; Stuart Warner, "New Pastor at The Chapel is Cut of a Different Mold," *Akron Beacon Journal*, Dec. 3, 1983, p. C5. Note that Ryan describes the congregation of the Chapel in University Park as 3,400 members; Warner describes it as 6,800, which seems more likely given previous membership numbers.

69. Russell D. Sibert, "Getting Out the Word," *Akron Beacon Journal*, July 4, 1993, *Beacon Magazine*, 4–10; Western Reserve Public Media, *NewsNite*, April 10, 2009.

70. "Getting Out the Word," 10.

71. "The Chapel Starts Wadsworth Satellite Church," *Akron Beacon Journal*, January 22, 1994, A16.

72. "Getting Out the Word," 4; Jim Carney, "Pastor of Chapel Wins U.S. Award," *Akron Beacon Journal*, May 24, 1997, C1.

73. Ron Kirksey, "Learning to Love Like Brothers," *Akron Beacon Journal*, May 29, 1994, 1; Terry Pluto, "Pastors Struggle Across Racial Gap," *Akron Beacon Journal*, September 10, 2000, J10; Western Reserve Public Media, *NewsNite*, April 10, 2009.

74. "Pastors Struggle Across Racial Gap," J10.

75. "One America: Coming Together Project," The White House, clintonwhitehouse4.archives.gov; "Learning to Love Like Brothers," 1; "Pastors Struggle Across Racial Gap," J10; Western Reserve Public Media, *NewsNite*, April 10, 2009; Marilyn Miller, "Rev. Larson Says Goodbye to Chapel," *Akron Beacon Journal*, May 18, 2009, 1.

76. Western Reserve Public Media, *NewsNite*, April 10, 2009.

77. Colette M. Jenkins, "Sartarelli to Leave Chapel," *Akron Beacon Journal*, November 19, 2012, B1; https://akron.thechapel.life; Colette M. Jenkins, "Senior Pastor Says Farewell to The Chapel Congregation," *Akron Beacon Journal*, January 21, 2013, B1.

78. Colette M. Jenkins, "Mansfield Pastor, 50, Is Chosen by Chapel," *Akron Beacon Journal*, May 5, 2014, 1; Colette M. Jenkins, "The Pastor to Install Senior Pastor," *Akron Beacon Journal*, Aug. 9, 2014, B3.

79. Colette M. Jenkins, "Sowing Seeds of Faith," *Akron Beacon Journal*, April 5, 2015, 4; Ken Lahmers, "The Chapel Plans Launch in Macedonia Area," *Akron Beacon Journal*, July 30, 2019, B3.

80. Alan Ashworth, "The Chapel Parts Ways With Its Senior Pastor,"*Akron Beacon Journal*, Aug. 7, 2021, 1B; Alan Ashworth, "Petition Seeks to Resolve The Chapel Crisis," *Akron Beacon Journal*, Aug. 19, 2021, 1B; Alan Ashworth, "Summary of Probe Sheds Light on Crisis at The Chapel," *Akron Beacon Journal*, October 8, 2021, 1B; Alan Ashworth, "The Chapel Plans for Local Control of Churches," *Akron Beacon Journal*, May 22, 2022, 1A.

81. https://akron.thechapel.life.

82. Schaller, 97.

83. Rex Humbard, *The Soul-Winning Century, 1906–2006: The Humbard Family Legacy—100 Years of Ministry* (Dallas: Clarion Call Marketing, 2006), 31.

84. Humbard, *The Soul-Winning Century*, 52; Charlotte McMillion, "Humbards Buy Ohio Theater Move to Cuyahoga Falls March 15," *Akron Beacon Journal*, Feb. 28, 1953, 7; Rex Humbard, *Miracles in My Life: Rex Humbard's Own Story* (Old Tappan, NJ: Fleming H. Revell, 1971), 20.

85. Humbard, *Miracles*, 57, 66, 70, 71.

86. Humbard, *Miracles*, 74, 77, 83, 85, 88, 91, 92, 93; "Humbards Buy Ohio Theater Move to Cuyahoga Falls March 15," 7; Humbard, *Miracles*, 90.

87. Ernest Angley, *Hurry Friday! Autobiography of Ernest Angley* (Akron: Winston Press, 2004), 1.

88. Angley, *Hurry Friday!*, 84, 90, 94, 97, 110.

89. Angley, *Hurry Friday!*, 125, 136, 142, 159, 162, 165, 169.

90. Angley, *Hurry Friday!*, 178, 187; Jim Carney, "The Miracle Man," *Akron Beacon Journal*, July 4, 1999, 1.

91. Advertisement for Ernest Angley, *Akron Beacon Journal*, July 17, 1954, 4; Jim Carney, "The Miracle Man," 8; Advertisement for Rev. and Mrs. E. W. Angley, *Akron Beacon Journal*, Aug. 28, 1954, 4.

92. "Humbards Buy Ohio Theater Move to Cuyahoga Falls March 15," 7; Humbard, *The Soul-Winning Century*, 104, 114; Humbard, *Miracles in My Life*, 101.

93. Schaller, 99; "Parade, Services to Open Structure," *Akron Beacon Journal*, June 4, 1955, 5; Carney, "The Miracle Man," 8; Photograph of the new temple, *Akron Beacon Journal*, June 22, 1957, 7; "$1 Million Dollar Temple To Be Called Grace Cathedral," *Akron Beacon Journal*, April 26, 1958, 4; *Hurry Friday!*, 200, 201, 206; Advertisement for Temple of Healing Stripes, *Akron Beacon Journal*, Dec. 14, 1957, 5; "Rev. Ernest Angley," *Akron Beacon Journal*, May 23, 1992, A9.

94. Humbard, *The Soul-Winning Century*, 128, 138; Schaller, 98; "Almost Everything in Cathedral Will Operate by Push Button,"*Akron Beacon Journal*, May 23, 1958, 20; Advertisement for Cathedral of Tomorrow, *Akron Beacon Journal*, Aug. 16, 1962, 23; Laura Haferd, "The Crowds Just Kept Coming," *Akron Beacon Journal*, January 7, 1991, 1.

95. Schaller, 99; "Completed Grace Cathedral on View," *Akron Beacon Journal*, Aug. 1, 1969, 9; *Let Us Go Into The House of The Lord* (Akron: Grace Cathedral, n.d.); *Hurry Friday!*, 319, 330.

96. Darrell Sifford, "The Afflicted See Hope in His Hands," *Akron Beacon Journal*, May 4, 1975, G1; *The Healing Christ* [videos], Ernest Angley Ministries, 2018, YouTube.

97. "182 TV Stations, Weekly Rallies in Rex Humbard's Outreach Ministry" [advertisement], *Akron Beacon Journal*, May 23, 1969, 29; Humbard, *The Soul-Winning Century*, 146; "Pastor Rex Humbard," The Rex Humbard Foundation, www.rexhumbard.org.

98. George Alford, "Rex Humbard's Business is Religion ... and Vice Versa," *Dayton Daily News*, January 16, 1972, B4.

99. Humbard, *The Soul-Winning Century*, 141, 145, 146, 149, 150; Daly Smith, "Cathedral Opening in Red When Security Sales Ended," *Akron Beacon Journal*, January 18, 1973, 1; Laura Haferd, "As Tower Goes Up, Finances Unravel," *Akron Beacon Journal*, January 9, 1991, A1.

100. Quentin J. Schultze, *Televangelism and American Culture, The Business of Popular Religion* (1991; Eugene, OR: Wipf & Stock Publishers, 2003), 16, 18.

101. Daly Smith, "Receiver Asked for Cathedral," *Akron Beacon Journal*, Feb. 13, 1973, 1; Haferd, "As Tower Goes Up, Finances Unravel," 1; Humbard, *The Soul-Winning Century*, 157.

102. *The Soul-Winning Century*, 157, 159, 162, 178, 184; "Humbard Lays Woes To Jealousy of Others," *Akron Beacon Journal*, January 20, 1974, 1, Haferd, "As Tower Goes Up, Finances Unravel," 4; Joan Rice, "Debts Erased, Humbard Will Expand Ministry,"*Akron Beacon Journal*, Dec. 8, 1975, 1.

103. Humbard, *The Soul-Winning Century*, 185, 201; "Pastor Rex Humbard"; Laura Haferd, "Giving the 'Personal' Pitch," *Akron Beacon Journal*, January 10, 1991, 3; Ancella Livers and Peter Geiger, "Who Will Carry On These TV Ministries?," *Akron Beacon Journal*, January 15, 1982, 10.

104. Peter Geiger, "Humbard: I Need a Miracle," *Akron Beacon Journal*, September 23, 1979, 1; "Humbard Buys Florida Home," *The Delaware Gazette*, June 3, 1980, 7; Mary Grace Poidomani, "Fund Pinch Trims Humbard's Show," *Akron Beacon Journal*, Feb. 5, 1981, C2; "Humbard to Resign Pastorate," *Akron Beacon Journal*, January 19, 1983, 1.

105. Debra Stock, "Humbard to Observe 50 Years On The Air," *Akron Beacon Journal*, Aug. 14, 1982, B6; "Humbards Buying Big Despite Ministry Debt," *Akron Beacon Journal*, Feb. 1, 1983, 1; "Humbard to Resign Pastorate," 1.

106. "Humbard TV Studio Being Sold to Angley," *Akron Beacon Journal*, March 25, 1984, D1; Laura Haferd, "Humbard Will Cancel Weekly TV Broadcasts," *Akron Beacon Journal*, May 23, 1985, C1.

107. Laura Haferd, "Cathedral's Future is a Fighting Issue," *Akron Beacon Journal*, January 13, 1991, 1; Laura Haferd, "Humbard's Back in Driver's Seat, But Now What?,"*Akron Beacon Journal*, Feb. 27, 1993, 9; Laura Haferd, "Humbard Gives Cathedral Earful," *Akron Beacon Journal*, March 1, 1993, 1; Laura Haferd, "Himm to Preach at Falls Church," *Akron Beacon Journal*, May 22, 1993, A6; Laura Haferd, "Building Sale to Fund Humbard Reruns," *Akron Beacon Journal*, March 31, 1994, B1.

108. James Quinn and Cindy E. Rodriguez, "Angley Buys from Humbard," *Akron Beacon Journal*, March 14, 1994, 1.

The Evangelists

109. "Humbard Helped to Shape Modern Ministry," *Akron Beacon Journal*, September 23, 2007, 1.

110. *Let Us Go into the House of the Lord*, 1.

111. "Humbard TV Studio Being Sold to Angley," D1; Mark Dawidziak, "Ernest Angley Backs New Christian TV Station," *Akron Beacon Journal*, June 30, 1985, p. C2; Mark Dawidziak, "G-Rated Lineup for Ch. 55," *Akron Beacon Journal*, September 24, 1985, C4; Laura Haferd, "Cathedral's Cash Had Odd Sources," *Akron Beacon Journal*, January 8, 1991, A1; Laura Haferd, "Pitching and Preaching," *Akron Beacon Journal*, April 3, 1987, B1.

112. *Ernest Angley Ministries*, YouTube; Schultze, *Televangelism and American Culture*, 16; Haferd, "Pitching and Preaching," B1.

113. *Ernest Angley Ministries*, YouTube.

114. Bob Dyer, "Televangelist Angley Dies at 99," *Akron Beacon Journal*, May 8, 2021, 1; "Zambia's President to Speak at Grace Cathedral," *Akron Beacon Journal*, April 8, 1995, 10; Haferd, "Pitching and Preaching," B4; Amanda Garrett, "With Angley Gone, What's the Future of Grace Cathedral?," *Akron Beacon Journal*, May 30, 2021, 1; *The Ernest Angley Hour and Ernest Angley Ministries*, YouTube.

115. Al Johnson, "Heart Victim Dies at Rev. Angley Rally," *Akron Beacon Journal*, January 16, 1978, A11.

116. Garrett, "With Angley Gone," 1; *Hurry Friday!*, 363; "W. German Police Arrest Evangelist Angley," *Akron Beacon Journal*, July 12, 1984, 1; "Bondsman Helped Angley From Jail," *Akron Beacon Journal*, Aug. 29, 1984, B5; Carney, "The Miracle Man," 8.

117. "Guyanese Officials Criticize US Preacher," Fox News WBNX-TV (Cleveland, Ohio), April 19, 2007. Retrieved September 1, 2020; Dyer, "Televangelist Angley Dies at 99," 1.

118. Laura Haferd, "Skeptics Train Their Microscopes on Angley," *Akron Beacon Journal*, April 30, 1986, 1; Jane Taber, "Evangelist Takes Care of Business Before 'Healing,'" *The Ottawa Citizen*, September 15, 1986, p. C19.

119. Dyer, "Televangelist Angley Dies at 99," 1.

120. Laura Haferd, "Angley's Hour?," *Akron Beacon Journal*, May 21, 1988, B1; Janice Peck, *The Gods of Televangelism* (Cresskill, N.J.: Hampton Press, 1993), 2, 118.

121. James Quinn and Cindy E. Rodriguez, "Angley Buys from Humbard," *Akron Beacon Journal*, March 14, 1994, A4; " Ernest Winston Angley," Ernest Angley Ministries, www.Ernestangley.org; "Grace Cathedral," thegracecathedral.org; Carney, "The Miracle Man," 8; "Volunteers Staff Buffet Despite Prior Warnings," *Akron Beacon Journal*, October 19, 2014, 6.

122. Carney, "The Miracle Man," 1; https://www.Ernestangley.org, A Lifetime of Service; Garrett, "With Angley Gone," 8; Dyer, 4.

123. Garrett, "With Angley Gone," 8.

124. Bob Dyer, "Ernest Angley's Church Rocked by Accusations," *Akron Beacon Journal*, October 12, 2014, 1; Bob Dyer, "Sexual Abuse Claims Stay in Church Walls," *Akron Beacon Journal*, October 13, 2014, 1; Bob Dyer, "Pastor's Exit Prompts Attacks from Pulpit," *Akron Beacon Journal*, October 14, 2014, 1; Bob Dyer, "'Families Destroyed' by Angley, Ex-Member Says," *Akron Beacon Journal*, October 15, 2014, 1; Bob Dyer, "Huge Jetliner Comes with Sky-High Costs," *Akron Beacon Journal*, October 18, 2014, 1; Dyer, "Volunteers Staff Buffet Despite Prior Warnings," 1; Garrett, "With Angley Gone," 1; Dyer, "Televangelist Angley Dies at 99," 1.

125. Bob Dyer, "Huge Jetliner Comes with Sky-High Costs," 4; Dyer, "Volunteers Staff Buffet Despite Prior Warnings," 1; Garrett, "With Angley Gone," 1; Stephanie Warsmith, "Lawsuit Against Angley Settled," *Akron Beacon Journal*, Feb. 15, 2020, 1.

126. Bob Dyer, "Ernest Angley Admitted Sexual Encounter," *Akron Beacon Journal*, January 20, 2019, 1; Bob Dyer, "Split with Ernest Angley Tough for Assistant," *Akron Beacon Journal*, January 21, 2019, 1; Bob Dyer, "Huge Jetliner Comes with Sky-High Costs," 1; Dyer, "Volunteers Staff Buffet Despite Prior Warnings," 1; Garrett, "With Angley Gone," 1; Alan Ashworth, "Angley Mourned by Church, Faithful," *Akron Beacon Journal*, May 9, 2021, 1; Dyer, "Televangelist Angley Dies at 99," 1.

127. *Hurry Friday!*, p. 443.

128. Garrett, "With Angley Gone," 1; "About Us," Grace Cathedral, thegracecathedral.org; Ernest Angley Ministries, YouTube.

\ **14**

Tees and Greens in the Rubber City

Jane Gramlich

Long before the American Golf Classic and the World Series of Golf, decades before crowds stood in awe of Tiger Woods, Jack Nicklaus, and Arnold Palmer at Firestone Country Club, Akron was a hub of divot diggers.[1] These early players paved the way forward, making it no accident that Akron became a favored location for golf's storied tournaments. The game's local beginnings in the mid-1890s signaled a pioneering approach. Akron was "one of the first cities in this neck of the woods to boast a golf course," claimed the *Akron Beacon Journal* in 1950. By then, the city had become "one of the nation's hotbeds of golf."[2]

How did it all transpire? Across the country, business and leisure travelers from smaller communities discovered the game in larger US cities and abroad. The effort to establish it in their hometowns was the natural next step. "Rumor has it that golf is to become popular," suggested the *Akron Beacon and Republican* on August 1, 1893.[3] The shadowy sources who informed the paper proved correct. Within a couple of years, Charles C. Goodrich, son of B. F. Goodrich, was angling to form a local club. After some resistance, he persuaded George T. Perkins to donate a portion of the property on Perkins Hill for a nine-hole course, with John Brown's home as the clubhouse and the adjoining barn as a

Tees and Greens in the Rubber City

locker room.[4] Were John Brown still alive, it might have come as a shock to the firebrand abolitionist that his former residence was now the headquarters of the Portage Golf Club.

Akron's reputation as a golf destination grew quickly. In 1896, the Portage Club hosted an early tournament against a Cleveland team. In March 1902, the *Beacon* reported, "It is probable that many out-of-town teams will be brought here by the Portage team for match games."[5] It wasn't long before they outgrew the Perkins Hill facility. A change in name and location followed, with Portage Country Club opening at the corner of North Portage Path and Twin Oaks Road in May 1906. In 1909, they had the honor of hosting the Ohio Golf Association's annual tournament. It drew players from twenty Ohio locations, including all major cities and smaller municipalities such as Marietta, Wooster, and Zanesville. Reporting from the four-day tournament merited front-page news, and writers effused at everything. Little was amiss. The visitors were "high in their praises for the grounds and surroundings," and the decorated clubhouse was "one mass of beauty."[6]

During these early years, Akron also made strides in manufacturing golf balls. The use of gutta-percha, which forms an elastomer closely related to natural rubber, made this development perfectly suited to the Rubber City. The B. F. Goodrich Company was one of the first Akron companies to produce golf balls. Their reputation traveled quickly. In 1900, their western US distributor, the Whitman Company of Lincoln, Nebraska, proclaimed in the Nebraska State Journal that Goodrich was the "largest [manufacturer] of high-grade Golf Balls in America."[7] Goodyear Tire & Rubber soon followed suit, and in 1906, the *Beacon* stated that "three-fourths of the golf balls used in the United States are manufactured in Akron."[8]

The Haskell-Match Golf Ball advertisement. \
David Lieberth collection.

The expansive years between World War I and the Depression saw local golf courses and clubs skyrocket. Incorporated by Goodyear and Mohawk Rubber Company executives, Fairlawn Heights Golf Club opened in 1919. Silver Lake Country Club, Rosemont Country Club, and Barberton's Brookside and Anna Dean courses served suburbanites farther out in Summit County. By the time Akron celebrated its centennial in 1925, the *Beacon* noted that golf was the city's "most rapidly growing sport," but that was likely true for much of the country.[9] What was certain was that the boom they had witnessed hadn't yet reached its peak, and the best-known course had yet to be built.

Though late to the party, Harvey Firestone refused to be outdone. Firestone Country Club opened a nine-hole course for the rubber company's employees in 1928, and by 1930, it had completed two eighteen-hole courses. According to the *Beacon*, this was "one of the few 36-hole layouts in Ohio and, as far as can be learned, the only industrial golf course of that length in the country."[10] The magazine *Akron Topics* called it a "conspicuous addition" to area courses, which were becoming increasingly elaborate.[11] As local journalist Helen Waterhouse was famous for saying, "With a million dollars and good taste, you don't need a wand."

Despite the abundance of golf courses at fashionable, private country clubs, there was still room for a public course. In 1925, hardware merchant and philanthropist J. Edward Good donated about 180 acres of land west of Hawkins Avenue to the City of Akron for use as a golf course and park. Akron Municipal Golf Course opened the following year. A mere seven pages of random records from this course give us fascinating snapshots over the 1930s and 40s. In 1934, it cost 60 cents to use the course Tuesday through Friday, while weekends and holidays commanded 90 cents. Both prices included a 10-cent state tax. Monday was "Bargain Day" at 50 cents.

Municipal administrators also observed the city's dominance in the field, noting that there were "24 golf clubs in the Akron district, more per capita than any large city in the U.S." This led to a competitive environment requiring heavy promotion, which, while challenging, also had benefits. It drove a great deal of business and collaboration with other local organizations and enterprises. For example, in 1947, Municipal's special events included local high schools, the Fraternal Order of Police, Akron Liedertafel, and B. F. Goodrich.[12] The cumulative effect over all the clubs showed increased economic activity and broad networking. There can be little doubt that for many years, golf was a significant catalyst that knit the city together.

Though Portage Country Club had dominated the local golf scene for decades, Firestone Country Club gained worldwide recognition as the site of prestigious tournaments. Their challenging course, a favorite among players and

Tees and Greens in the Rubber City

Golfers at Portage Country Club, including F. A. Seiberling (center, fourth from left), cofounder of Goodyear Tire and Rubber, 1920. \ David Lieberth collection

affectionately dubbed "the Monster," was a large part of the appeal. In 1954, the Rubber City Open, a local tournament, received a stamp of approval from the Professional Golfers' Association of America (PGA).[13] Significant funding, support, and the interest of top players followed. The success of the Rubber City Open led to the PGA's American Golf Classic and the World Series of Golf, premiering in 1961 and 1962, respectively. These events were broadcast nationwide, attracted numerous visitors, boosted the local economy, and produced substantial profits bestowed on local charitable organizations. It's easy to see why they were a hit and an immense endorsement for Akron—getting in on the action could only be an advantage. One media director for the World Series of Golf observed an unusual level of cooperation among the rubber companies—"it was Firestone's tournament, but ... Goodyear, General, and B. F. Goodrich helped run it too."[14] There wasn't much room for competition in this particular hustle. Wisely, they left that to the golfers.

As recently as 1998, Akron was still fostering innovation in golf. Edwin Shaw Hospital for Rehabilitation built the Challenge Golf Course for people with differing abilities as part of its rehabilitation program. Internationally recognized as the first facility of its kind, the course provides features such as wheelchair-accessible paths and slopes and adaptive equipment. Classes taught by a PGA professional help boost activity and mental and physical acclimation. Most importantly, the course is an encouraging environment promoting confidence and growth.[15]

By the early 2000s, Akron's role in the larger world of golf had declined. In 2018, the PGA delivered a tough blow to the city when it announced the exit of its signature tournament, the World Golf Championships-Bridgestone Invitational, from Firestone Country Club.[16] The number of local golf courses also dwindled. Some suffered debilitating losses in the summer floods of 2004 and never fully recovered, especially in the Merriman Valley.[17] The former Riverwoods Golf Course transformed into a development of townhomes. Rather than making the news in the form of players and scores, it sparked environmental debate about the fate of land close to the Cuyahoga Valley National Park (CVNP). Just down the road and on the opposite end of the spectrum, two other former courses escaped development. Summit Metro Parks purchased Valley View Golf Course in 2016 to become part of Cascade Metro Park. Similarly, the Conservancy for the CVNP acquired the former Brandywine Country Club near Peninsula in 2019 with the intent to convert it to parkland.[18]

Despite these changes, much remains. Several area courses continue to operate for the swingers and hitters of Akron and beyond, including Portage Country Club, undeniably the oldest, and Firestone Country Club, widely considered the most legendary. Regardless of the future of Akron's golf scene, enthusiasts worldwide will continue to look to our city for many of the game's historic, memorable moments.

Notes

1. An earlier version of this article appeared in *Past Pursuits*, vol. 21, no. 2 (Summer 2022), a newsletter of the Special Collections Division of the Akron-Summit County Public Library.

2. "Golf Pioneers Import Briton," *Akron Beacon Journal*, June 18, 1950, 3C. Unless otherwise noted, newspapers are cited from digital versions through Newspapers.com.

3. "Elegance in August," *Akron Beacon and Republican*, August 1, 1893, 2.

4. Portage Country Club, "History," https://www.portagecc.org/About_Us/History.aspx, accessed March 31, 2023; "Perkins Taboos Play on Sunday," *Akron Beacon Journal*, June 20, 1950, 30; "The Golf Club," *Akron Beacon and Republican*, September 20, 1895, 2.

5. "Golf Tournament," *Akron Beacon and Republican*, September 12, 1896, 1; "A Good Organization," *Akron Beacon Journal*, March 10, 1902, 5.

6. Portage Country Club, "History," "Ohio Gold Tourney in Full Swing," *Akron Beacon Journal*, June 23, 1909, 1.

7. "Golf Repairs!" The Lincoln Evening News, June 7, 1900, 5.

8. "New Golf Ball Being Made Here," *Akron Beacon Journal*, April 12, 1906, 4.

Tees and Greens in the Rubber City

9. "New Golf Club," *Akron Beacon Journal*, April 20, 1917, 20; Fairlawn Country Club, "History," https://www.fairlawncountryclub.org/history, accessed March 31, 2023; "Golf is Akron's Most Rapidly Growing Sport," July 21, 1925, 32.

10. "From Tee to Green," *Akron Beacon Journal*, August 7, 1928, 24; "War Declared Everywhere on Conceding Golf Putts," *Akron Beacon Journal*, April 10, 1930, 33.

11. "Great Drive for '29! FORE!," *Akron Topics*, May 1929, 3.

12. J. Edward Good Park Golf Course Materials, Special Collections Division, Akron-Summit County Public Library.

13. "Akron's Rubber City Open Goes Big Time," *Akron Beacon Journal*, February 14, 1954, 1C.

14. "Akron Steps Up as Player in Pro Sports," *Akron Beacon Journal*, 10 Sep 2000, L10.

15. "When Golf is a Challenge," *Akron Beacon Journal*, April 5, 1998, Golf Ohio (special section), 5; Cleveland Clinic, "Challenge Golf," https://my.clevelandclinic.org/locations/akron-general/specialties/rehabilitation-sports-therapy/challenge-golf, accessed March 31, 2023.

16. "Akron Loses Bridgestone Tournament to Memphis," *Akron Beacon Journal*, April 13, 2018, A1.

17. "Wet Greens May Soon Be In Red," *Akron Beacon Journal*, June 8, 2004, D1.

18. "Park District Finalizes Golf Club Deal," *Akron Beacon Journal*, October 7, 2016, B1; "Peninsula and Woodridge are Against Brandywine Joining CVNP," *Akron Beacon Journal*, September 27, 2021, B1.

Thirteen-year-old Shirley Fry poses with the trophy for her second consecutive city championship at the Portage Country Club. \ Photo courtesy of the *Akron Beacon Journal*

Some of Akron's Olympic Gold Medalists and Hall of Famers

Tim Carroll

Shirley Fry

Girls can do anything! That is how Akron's greatest female athlete Shirley Fry was raised. Fry won the grand slam in tennis in the 1950s by scoring victories in the French Open in 1951, Wimbledon and the US Open in 1956, and the Australian Open in 1957. In 1934 six-year-old Fry is pictured in the *Akron Beacon Journal* on the YWCA swim team with five high-school-aged girls.[1] From the very beginning Fry competed in sports against older athletes both female and male. The youngest of four children, Fry was raised to be athletic and active. She also had the advantage of having five older tennis players to play against in her family, counting her parents. She played in her first tennis tournament at age eight.

Shirley Fry had all the confidence in the world. At age nine she boarded a bus to attend the Great Lakes Exposition in Cleveland all by herself, telling the *Beacon Journal* that she wanted to make the solo trip to prepare herself for traveling alone to future tennis tournaments.[2] When fourteen-year-old Fry played at the US National Championships in 1941, she was the youngest player ever to do so.[3]

Living an active lifestyle, believing in herself, and playing against older opponents molded Shirley Fry into one of the greatest tennis players in the history of the sport. Shirley Fry is one of ten women in history to win all four major tennis championships and one of only six women to accomplish the same feat in women's doubles. She won the last three majors she played in 1956 and 1957 in dominating fashion, not losing a single set. Astonishingly, Shirley Fry was already semi-retired when she made her return to the tennis courts in 1956 after overcoming a nagging elbow injury to play some of the best tennis of her life. Fry and one of her greatest competitors, Doris Hart, won eleven titles together, including US titles 1951–1954, French titles 1950–1953, and Wimbledon 1951–1953. Shirley also combined with Althea Gibson to win doubles at the 1957 Australian Open. Shirley was ranked in the top ten in tennis for thirteen straight years including a number one ranking in 1956 at the tail end of her career. Fry won the Australian Open over Althea Gibson in 1957 the first and only time she competed in it and retired from the game of tennis at the top of her game. She was inducted into the International Tennis Hall of Fame in 1970. Shirley Fry will always be mentioned as one of tennis' greatest players, with Venus and Serena Williams and Billie Jean King.

Nate Thurmond

Hall of Famer Nate Thurmond is one of the greatest basketball players to ever come out of Akron, Ohio. NBA legend Kareem Abdul-Jabbar was once asked who's the toughest center he ever played against, and Abdul-Jabbar, whose name is often mentioned along with Akron's LeBron James as the greatest player in NBA history, replied, "Nate Thurmond"!

Nate Thurmond was a defensive monster, often demoralizing his opponents. "I could look in a guy's eyes and know he's demoralized," Thurmond commented on his career during the Cleveland Cavaliers 1976 Miracle at Richfield playoff run. During the 1976 Eastern Conference finals, Thurmond said, "And blocking shots still turns me on. I wish they were counting blocked shots in my big years. They started keeping track of them too late for me."[4] Thurmond ranked sixth in blocked shots in 1974 when the NBA first started counting them and third during the 1975 season. He recorded a career-high 12 blocked shots against Atlanta in 1974 and recorded 553 blocks in the last six seasons of his fourteen-year career. In that monster performance against Atlanta while playing for the Chicago Bulls, Nate Thurmond became the first player in NBA history with a quadruple double, scoring 22 points and grabbing 14 rebounds and 13 assists with his legendary 12 blocks. He was the third-best rebounder in NBA history at the end of his career,

Some of Akron's Olympic Gold Medalists and Hall of Famers   **245**

Nate Thurmond in early 1976, playing for the Cleveland Cavaliers. \ Photo by Ron Kuner, courtesy of the *Akron Beacon Journal*

behind Wilt Chamberlain and Bill Russell. He is currently ranked eleventh all-time in rebounds. Thurmond was named as one of the NBA's 50 greatest players and was part of the NBA's 75th anniversary team in 2021.[5]

An All-American at Bowling Green State University, Nate Thurmond was drafted by the Golden State Warriors with the number three pick in the 1963 draft. The Warriors retired Thurmond's number 42 jersey in 1978, and he still leads the franchise in rebounds and minutes played. Steph Curry broke Thurmond's minutes-played record in November of 2023, but no Warrior has come close to breaking his rebounding record and likely never will. The Cleveland Cavaliers also retired Nate "the Great" Thurmond's jersey for his contribution to their historic playoff run in 1976 at the end of his career. Thurmond averaged 15 points and 15 rebounds a game in his career highlighted by 20.5 points and 22 rebounds a game in the 1967–1968 season. No player in the NBA has averaged more than 20 rebounds a game since 1969, making Wilt Chamberlain and Nate Thurmond the last to do it. You can find Nate Thurmond's number 42 hanging from the rafters in San Francisco, Cleveland, and the Basketball Hall of Fame. He is the first player to have his number retired by two NBA teams. Bowling Green also retired number 42.

Nate Thurmond died after a short battle with leukemia on July 16, 2016, at age 74. Thurmond, who was one of the toughest players of his era, was also remembered for being one of the kindest individuals and best teammates you could have. Former teammate Al Attles said, "Looking back he was as ferocious as any player in the history of the game on the court, but one of the kindest and nicest souls in his everyday life."[6] LeBron James also tweeted this after Thurmond's passing, "Knowing u played in the same rec league as me growing up gave me hope of making it out! Thanks!"[7] Seven All-Star games, five-time NBA All-Defensive team, and 42 rebounds in a game are just some of the many highlights of Nate Thurmond's run in the NBA.

Gus Johnson

NBA Hall of Famer Gus Johnson was recalled as the Dr. J of his time by the owner of the Baltimore Bullets where Johnson played the majority of his nine-year career.[8] Nicknamed "Honeycomb," Gus Johnson propelled the game forward with backboard-shattering dunks that amazed both crowds and opponents. Johnson recounted the Bullets getting blown out in Milwaukee in 1971 when he shattered the backboard on a fast break in the last minute, earning him a standing ovation from the opposing crowd. "Kareem Abdul-Jabbar told me that was the greatest thing he'd ever seen on a basketball floor, like seeing Niagara Falls for the first time."[9] When asked about Michael Jordan, Charles Barkley, and Dominique Wilkins in 1986, Johnson commented, "I was doing the same things before they were even born. They've got highlight films of me that would make these kids' eyes pop out." Former New York Knick Dave DeBusschere battled Johnson in three straight Eastern Conference finals from 1969 to 1971 and remembered how he was one of the first guys in the league who could bring a crowd to their feet with a dunk or move.[10] Many considered Johnson one of the first to fly, a player who made NBA games more exciting with thundering dunks that electrified crowds! Former Knicks guard and friend Butch Komives recalled how the 6-foot-6 Johnson had the strength to play with Wilt Chamberlain and the quickness to guard Oscar Robertson, saying, "No one played the Big O tougher. In my book, Gus was better than Elgin Baylor, Rick Barry, or Dr. J."[11]

Johnson, who was a Central High School star and teammate with Nate Thurmond, was drafted in 1963 by the Washington Bullets. His number 25 was retired

Some of Akron's Olympic Gold Medalists and Hall of Famers

by Washington before his death. He made the All-Star team five times and the NBA All-Defensive teams four times. Johnson averaged a double-double, an impressive 12.7 rebounds and 17.1 points a game in his NBA career. Johnson also scored an impressive 1,000 points and grabbed 1,000 rebounds in the same season three times in his career. He helped propel the Washington Bullets to five playoff appearances, including a trip to the 1971 NBA Finals. In 1973, after leaving the NBA, Gus helped the Indiana Pacers win a championship in the ABA League. Gus Johnson continued to play basketball and be involved in the Akron community doing what he loved right up until the end of his life. Akron is well known today as the home of LeBron James. Before James, Akron was the home of Thurmond and Johnson, another two of basketball's all-time greats.

Ara Parseghian

Ara Parseghian was an All-City fullback for South High School and was also a member of their star-studded basketball team, which featured players Fritz Nagy and Wyndol Gray as well as Gordon and Ralph Larson, Joe Brown, and Jack Austgen. During World War II Parseghian played football for Coach Paul Brown at Great Lakes Naval Station. Paul Brown, the head coach of Ohio State's football program and father of three boys, was drafted in 1944 and assigned to coach Navy football. Parseghian played for Paul Brown again, as a pro, after being drafted by the Browns in 1948. After a career-ending injury, Ara went on to coach at his alma mater Miami University under Woody Hayes and took over the program there when Hayes departed to Coach Ohio State football in 1951. Parseghian led Miami to a 39-6-1 record in five seasons before taking the reins of Northwestern Football for eight seasons. His time at Northwestern included victories over Notre Dame for four consecutive years from 1959 to 1962. The 35–6 Northwestern win over Notre Dame in 1962 led to Northwestern being ranked number one nationally. Parseghian would go on to be the legendary head coach of Notre Dame football from 1964 to 1974, which included national titles in 1966 and 1973.

He was elected to the College Football Hall of Fame in 1980 and had an extensive sports broadcasting career after he retired from coaching. Parseghian's brilliance led to top-ten rankings for Notre Dame Football in nine out of eleven seasons and All-American honors for his players forty times. In Parseghian's first year at the helm at Notre Dame he took a team that had been losing for five consecutive years to a 9–1 record and the doorstep of a national title. The Football Writers Association of America named him Coach of the Year in 1964 for this dramatic turnaround and return to its gloried past. Notre Dame's Quarterback John Huarte would also win the Heisman Trophy. Parseghian is ranked third all-time in wins at Notre Dame, behind football greats like Knute Rockne and Lou Holtz. Parseghian always wanted a challenge and throughout his time at Notre Dame he tried to get a game with Ohio State on his schedule, but Woody Hayes refused to play him. His willingness to play a tough schedule prepared him to take on anyone, leading Notre Dame to national titles and other historic victories. These victories include Notre Dame's 24–11 victory over Texas in the Cotton Bowl in 1971, which ended Texas's thirty-game winning streak, the longest in college football at the time. After ending USC's 23-game unbeaten streak in the 1973 season, Notre Dame took on number-one-ranked Alabama in the Sugar Bowl, defeating the unbeaten Crimson Tide 24–23 for the national title. Parseghian's last game at Notre Dame in 1975's Orange Bowl was another victory over undefeated Alabama. Notre Dame's record under Parseghian was 95-17-4 as he revived their historic program back into the national spotlight. Not bad for someone who did not play football until his junior year of high school!

Butch Reynolds

On August 17, 1988, Akron track & field star Butch Reynolds raced past Lee Evans's twenty-year-old 400-meter world record from the 1968 Mexico City Olympics with an astounding time of 43.29 seconds. Reynolds' world record was also not aided by altitude or wind, like Evan's 1968 record of 43.86 seconds. A week after his historic performance Reynolds was back in Akron to celebrate his triumph with family before heading to the 1988 Olympics. He told the *Akron Beacon Journal*, "When I looked at the scoreboard and saw the 43.29 I couldn't believe it. I knew I had a chance at the record but not a 43.29. There are some races where everything just feels right. You are excited. You know you can do something special. It's a high. That's how I felt before this race but I never imagined a 43.29." Reynolds' brother Jeff was in Switzerland to celebrate with him and commented, "You should have heard the crowd after the race, they were chanting Rey-nolds, Rey-nolds over and over." As Reynolds did his victory lap the crowd sang with their hands over their heads. He recalled, "I didn't understand the words, but I'll never forget the sound."[12] Ironically, when Reynolds anchored the 4 x 400-meter relay months later at the 1988 Olympics, that team would tie, not break, the world record set in 1968 with their time of 2:56.16. Reynolds was elated with his team's performance and Olympic gold days after the world-record holder was upset by teammate Steve Lewis in the 400-meter dash. The United States swept the 400-meter dash with bronze, silver, and gold medals at the 1988 Olympics with Reynolds capturing the silver medal.

Reynolds' 1988 world record stood for over eleven years and it took one of the greatest sprinters in history, the legendary Michael Johnson, to take it down.

Some of Akron's Olympic Gold Medalists and Hall of Famers **249**

Johnson and his coach Clyde Hart had spent years trying to best Reynolds' 1988 world record and finally did it at the 1999 World Championships in Spain.

Reynolds also won gold in the 4 x 4 three times at the World Championships, in 1987, 1993, and 1995. He also was the 400-meter indoor World Champion in 1993. Reynolds' other medals include silvers in the 400 at the 1993 and 1995 World Championships and bronze at the 1987 World Championships. In 1987, the Archbishop Hoban graduate won the NCAA Championship in the 400-meter dash for the Ohio State University. Reynolds was inducted into the USA Track & Field's Hall of Fame in 2016, a spot well-deserved for the man who was once the fastest person on earth to ever run the 400-meter dash.[13]

The Jenkins Family

In the 1950s two of the best figure skaters in the world were the Jenkins brothers from Akron, Ohio. Iceland, the East Market Street ice skating rink is where the Jenkins brothers got their start wowing the hometown crowds as youngsters. Hayes Alan Jenkins won Olympic gold in 1956 and his little brother crawled out from under his brother's shadow to claim the gold medal at the 1960 Winter Olympics. The 1956 men's figure skating competition was swept by the Americans in thrilling fashion with Hayes Jenkins winning gold and his nineteen-year-old little brother David winning bronze. Hayes jumped out to an early lead in the 1956 competition with perfect execution and was favored to win until eighteen-year-old teammate Ronnie Robertson wowed the crowd with such a dazzling and original performance that the Olympic crowd gave him a standing ovation. David Jenkins was so upset that his brother might not win after his nearly perfect performance that he walked into Hayes' dressing room in tears and told his brother he would quit skating if they robbed him of Olympic gold. Hayes Jenkins smiled and told his brother, "No you won't. If I don't get this gold medal someone in the family has to get one." The judges loved Robertson's performance for its originality but could not ignore perfection. Hayes Jenkins edged Robertson 1,507.7 to 1,492 for gold. Robertson took silver and David Jenkins took bronze with 1,465.3. Hayes had won four World Championships prior to capping his career with an Olympic gold medal.

Hayes retired after the 1956 Olympics, setting the stage for his younger brother David to dominate the sport. David Jenkins won four World Championships in a row from 1957 to 1960. "I'm so happy I could cry" is what David Jenkins said in February 1960 as he received a standing ovation from the crowd when he won Olympic gold in men's figure skating in Squaw Valley, California. "It's nice to keep it in the family."[14]

Hayes Jenkins and his wife, Carol Heiss Jenkins, skating in 1963. \ Photo by John Neitz, courtesy of the *Akron Beacon Journal*

    Hayes went on to practice law at the Goodyear Tire & Rubber Company after graduating from Harvard Law School. David Jenkins became a doctor after graduating from Western Reserve College. On April 30, 1960, Hayes Alan Jenkins fittingly married Olympic figure skating great Carol Heiss in New York. For the record, Carol had five World skating championships to Hayes's four at the time of their marriage. Carol Heiss was a silver medalist at the 1956 Olympics

Some of Akron's Olympic Gold Medalists and Hall of Famers

and dominated the sport for the rest of her career, culminating with Olympic gold in 1960.

The Jenkins boys had athletics in their blood. Their father Hayes R. Jenkins was the only athlete to earn twelve athletic letters at The University of Akron in his time. Hayes R. Jenkins was part of the first graduating class of North High School in 1921. He was an All-City athlete in basketball and football. In addition to football and basketball, Hayes R. Jenkins was also a baseball and track & field star at The University of Akron. He was part of a generation where the greatest athletes competed in as many sports as possible. The talented elder Jenkins was an All-Ohio selection in football and basketball at The University of Akron and certainly passed along much of his talent to his gold medal winning sons.

Notes

1. "Akron Girl Swimmers Ready to Compete," *Akron Beacon Journal*, March 9, 1934, 15. Unless otherwise noted, newspapers are cited from digital versions through Newspapers.com.

2. "Only 9, Inspects Expo All By Herself," *Akron Beacon Journal*, July 30, 1936, 3.

3. "Shirley Fry," International Tennis Hall of Fame, https://www.tennisfame.com/hall-of-famers/inductees/shirley-fry.

4. Dave Anderson, "Nate Thurmond Adds His Touch of Class," *Sunday Missoulian*, May 16, 1976, 13.

5. Richard Goldstein, "Warriors Center and Defensive Wall, Dies at 74," *New York Times*, July 16, 2016, https://www.nytimes.com.

6. "NBA Great Nate Thurmond, Hall of Fame Center, Dies at 74," Rapid City Journal, July 17, 2016, F4.

7. Goldstein.

8. "Ex-Idaho Star Gus Johnson Dies at 48," *The Spokesman-Review*, April 30, 1987, C1.

9. Alan Goldstein, "Cancer Mean Foe for ex-NBA Star Gus Johnson," *Sunday News Journal*, November 16, 1986; D4A.

10. "Gus Johnson Dies: DeBusschere Recalls Battles with Ex-Bullet," *Daily News*, April 30, 1987, 76.

11. Goldstein.

12. Terry Pluto, "Quick to Share: Reynolds Feels Records to Family, Too," *Akron Beacon Journal*, August 24, 1988, D1.

13. "Harry Butch Reynolds," *Olympic Games*, International Olympic Committee, https://olympics.com/en/athletes/harry-butch-reynolds.

14. "Jenkins Earns His Skiing Holiday," *Akron Beacon Journal*, February 27, 1960, 10.

\ **16**

Fritz Pollard

Steve Love

When Fritz Pollard's train chugged into the Akron station in the wee hours of Sunday, November 9, 1919, no one greeted him, much less cheered. He probably wasn't surprised. Strange town but familiar scene. Pollard knew the score.

Akron was like towns near Chicago where Pollard first gained fame running, throwing, and tackling; it was like Providence, Rhode Island, where he became a Brown University legend when Eastern football was king. It was like many places that dotted early-twentieth-century America—and still do.

Akron did not welcome Pollard with open arms. "There wasn't a damn soul there," he said.[1] He knew why.

Fritz Pollard was a Black man in a tough white town.

And Pollard was dark-skinned—unambiguously a Black man.[2] Did Pollard sense peril on that empty train platform? Did he harbor doubt about continuing an All-American career in an upstart, hardscrabble pro game considered inferior to that of colleges? Here's a good bet: Pollard, reared by parents and following siblings, especially brothers, who educated him in the realities of the times, understood not to back down when his dignity was threatened but to choose his fights. The small Pollard listened and learned. A good son, he responded with a brave heart. Seventh of John William and Catherine Amanda Hughes Pollard's eight children, he could also inexplicably contradict family emphasis on practical skills (barbering) *and* education.[3]

Fritz Pollard

Fritz Pollard, circa 1916. \ Wikimedia Commons.

How does a person of a different race and time accurately capture Pollard's moment in Akron history? A century later, NBA star LeBron James ranks as Akron's most famous athletic son. He, too, endured hard times when young, but nothing like Pollard, who for too long was forgotten by the rich National Football League to which he gave credibility when it had little. Even Akron, the NFL's original Title Town, seemed to forget.

By the time Pollard arrived, Akron was gaining a reputation as more than a place where a person from Appalachia, the South, or anywhere could make a living compounding, extruding, and molding rubber products—tires and more. It offered hope but, like Pollard, could be incongruous. It had a dark side. Akron could be inhospitable to Blacks, immigrants—anyone not a native-born white Protestant.

In the years after Pollard joined Akron's football team, the Ku Klux Klan recognized a town fertile for cultivation. The KKK, which gained notoriety for violence against Blacks during Reconstruction, had morphed into an iteration that wallowed in patriotism, nativism, and anti-Catholicism while clinging to prejudice against Black people. It infiltrated the city's power structure, dominating the school board and insinuating itself into city government, even the mayor's office.[4] Frederick Douglass "Fritz" Pollard, named for the abolitionist, may have known nothing of this when he stepped off the train.

The situation could have reminded him of the time when he caught out his coach and unwitting Lane Tech team implicitly discriminating.[5] Pollard had arrived punctually for a train to a game only to discover train and team gone. Determined not to miss the game, Pollard hopped on another train that did not stop at the game site. He rode miles before he could disembark and walk back, too late to play.

"Fritz," his coach said, "our opponents didn't want to play against you because you're Black. I didn't know how to tell you so I just had the entire squad take an earlier train."

Pollard never forgot this transgression. As he faced a lifetime of discrimination, he displayed greater courage than his coach. When he ran from or dodged those who would hurt him, it was not from fear but to win.

Disembarking in Akron was not as fraught. Pollard found a cab driver who had read that the 1916 All-American would be arriving for the remainder of the 1919 Ohio League season to play for the Indians, soon renamed the Pros. The cabbie delivered Pollard to Frank Nied's downtown cigar store.[6] Nied managed the team. Pollard was not what he expected.

Nied knew Pollard's color but not his size. His inflated vision sprang from words of sportswriting giants. They had made Pollard larger than life rather than someone who was about 5' 8" and weighed between 145 and 170 pounds. Inaccuracies such as "burly Negro" crept into the writing.[7] Walter Camp, father of Yale football and then coach, named Pollard to his All-America team, its first Black back. He called him "the most elusive back of the year or any year."[8] No exaggeration, that.

Pollard so enthralled legendary Grantland Rice that he deemed the little wisp of smoke worthy to stand alongside larger, stouter legends Jim Thorpe, Red Grange, and Bronko Nagurski in his Dream Backfield. This fooled Nied.

When he saw Pollard in the flesh—what there was of it—he must have thought he had lying eyes. "You're Fritz Pollard?" Nied asked rhetorically. "Oh, no. Pollard is 6-1 and weighs 190 pounds. You're *not* Fritz Pollard."[9]

Oh, but he was. And the real Pollard proved even more than the imagined. Nied befriended and supported him. Some new teammates had a different response. Many of them were white Southerners or white Appalachian men, and they supplemented their meager football salaries with work in Akron's rubber shops. They were tough without carrying big sticks. Many spoke with a distinctive twang. During the decades when Akron was America's fastest growing city, a jobs magnet to those from surrounding states, especially West Virginia, as well as

Fritz Pollard

foreign counties, Akron became a capital, of sorts. No, not the legendary Rubber Capital of the World; think punchline:

What's the capital of West Virginia?

Charleston?

Nope.

"Ack-ern."[10]

Pollard's teammates hit him with a one-two punch: cold shoulder *and* stiff arm.[11] Quarterback Clair Purdy was an exception. One of Pollard's Brown teammates, he gave Fritz the lay of this new-yet-familiar land of prejudice.

It had been ever thus—in Chicago, in Providence, now Akron. Purdy knew what Pollard had endured at Brown. Because of an odd, peripatetic journey that included football flirtations with several colleges—small (Bates) to famous (Harvard)—that made Pollard look like a walking contradiction to how he was reared, biographer John M. Carroll labeled him a "tramp athlete," one who "wander[ed] from campus to campus, offering their talents to the highest bidder."[12] Finally, on his second try, Pollard settled in at Brown, a Baptist college that his biracial mother, Amanda, had wanted him to attend.[13]

His welcome at Brown wasn't toasty. Whenever he got on the team bus, other players got off. When he went into the shower room, they exited. One new teammate with a Southern drawl greeted Pollard with a racist epithet. Another teammate corrected him: "That's Fritz Pollard." Unimpressed, the Southerner stood his ground: "I don't care what he calls himself."[14]

For the most part, Pollard publicly downplayed the racism he encountered, but in private, with family, he "complained bitterly" about the constant, racialized taunting that he experienced at Yale and Harvard. It was little better, if less imaginative, in Akron. At Yale to open the 1916 season, the Yale students serenaded Pollard with *Bye Bye Blackbird*. Flying into the end zone, Pollard made Yale pay but the tune's echoes lingered.[15]

Though Pollard won over the Brown team, in no small part by taking it to an unimaginable appearance in the first Rose Bowl, his experience of racism did not change. It was not until a return train trip from California that the team that had assaulted him with word and deed became his defender and a *real* team. It presaged the Pros.

Though doubts again turned into acceptance and then respect and support, it did not begin that way in Akron. Teammates could be skeptical to hostile, and spectators were worse, especially those who attended games to cheer on nearby opponents such as Massillon and Canton. They were not neighborly. There were "dire threats."[16] Nied took them seriously enough to have Pollard, who at first commuted to Akron via train from coaching at Lincoln University near

Philadelphia, dress at his cigar store for games. Pollard was driven to Goodrich Field (League Park) at Carroll and Beaver streets; he would climb out of the vehicle and sprint straight away to the *safety* of the field, where only the opponents could assail him. A threat by Massillon to "get Pollard" did not come to fruition or prevent him from flashing his speed and darting cuts and scoring Akron's only touchdown in a 13–6 loss before a crowd of 8,500. Pollard could handle threats.

He had learned self-preservation from brothers Leslie and Hughes. Had it not been for Hughes and Lane Tech's desire to have him on the field, Fritz might never have found his place.[17] When he was a 1909 high school sophomore, 4-foot 11-inch Fritz barely tipped the scales. He weighed 89 pounds. But Hughes, before the first game, approached the coach and principal. "Listen," he said, "if my kid brother can't play, I'm not going to play."

"That did it," Fritz remembered. "I got my first chance. He was just one of those kind of fellows. A man above everybody." Fritz found that love for the game was not measured in pounds but by what he could do with those he had. To Fritz, Hughes was "the biggest and toughest of all of us" but also a person who could be "a big bully." Football was not Hughes's love; music was. After bullying the adults on behalf of Fritz, Hughes left the team to lead the Lane band and orchestra, eventually becoming a jazz musician. (Hughes did return to play for a championship.)

He warned his brother that he would have to protect himself. His brothers had taught him well, especially for pile-ups. Fritz would ball up, roll onto his back like a cat, and lash out with his feet, spikes as sharp as little knives, to discourage late and cheap shots.[18] Decades later, Muhammad Ali conceived his not dissimilar Rope-a-Dope tactic in the ring—only lightning fists replaced feet.

Pollard once told Carl Nesfield, a writer for *Black Sports*, "Throughout my entire career, I had to keep both eyes open, on and off the field. Credit must be given to my father (John) and older brothers. They really prepared me. They taught me to use my fists, elbows, teeth, feet—*everything*. The white players always were trying to hurt me, and I had to be able to protect myself if I was going to stay in the game."[19]

Discretion became as much his game as valor. "I never took ... undue hell-fired chances in a game," he said. "I wasn't one of those fellows who tried to get the last yard." Sidelines and out-of-bounds beyond became friends and protectors. Pollard had not been sure the Indians, whom he joined to help salvage their 1919 season, were either friend or protector. He did not know if they would block for him in that initial Massillon game but "they decided to do their part."[20] Doubters existed.

"In running back punts he was sensational," a *Beacon Journal* writer observed, "while from the backfield position he carried the ball many times for long gains....

Fritz Pollard

Had Pollard been given a cleared way in his end runs he would likely have turned the tide of victory."[21]

In backyard ball games, Pollard discovered he had speed others lacked. Jackrabbit starts, magical elusiveness, flexible hips for directional changes: "I think it was born in me ... just one of those natural things."[22]

When Akron played host to Canton in his second game—it was Natural vs. Natural—Pollard, the game's future, vs. Jim Thorpe, the best, who by then husbanded himself by not playing until second halves. Oops. Too late. Pollard prevailed. The 10–0 outcome attracted rare national attention—though not enough to help the Indians out of a financial quagmire that prompted backers to bail. Nied and Art Ranney recast the team as the Akron Pros and represented it at a seminal gathering of owners in Canton at Ralph Hay's Hupmobile dealership. They founded a stronger if imperfectly constructed American Professional Football Association (APFA) that became the National Football League.[23]

Joe Horrigan, historian of the game and retired executive director of the Pro Football Hall of Fame, has credited the Pros, and specifically Pollard, with helping the NFL establish a foothold at a time when Major League Baseball dominated pro sports.

"The Pros were clearly considered major players in the pro game," Horrigan told the *Beacon Journal*, and Pollard, "marquee player and attraction," contributed broadly. "The Pros gave credibility. Add to that, they went on to capture the NFL's first title in 1920."[24]

Although Nied and Ranney retained the best Indians, they also added players such as Bob "Nasty" Nash, a tough end whose nickname tells a one-word story, and quarterback Harry Harris from West Virginia.[25] Coach Elgie Tobin converted Frank McCormick from tackle to fullback beside Rip King or Pollard, who seemed to play everywhere and do everything. Fronting the backs were center Russ Bailey, guards Al Cobb and Brad Tomlin, tackles Charlie Copley and Frank Johnson, with Al Nesser, youngest of six footballing Nesser brothers, at end opposite Nasty Nash. It was a formidable lineup that outscored opponents 151–7 while compiling 8-0-3 overall and 6-0-3 league records. Their single-wing offense benefitted from Pollard sharing modern plays that he had learned at Brown and coached at Lincoln University, where he had replaced brother Leslie following his accidental death in 1915.[26]

Perhaps the smartest, most humane move made by Nied and Ranney had nothing to do with the game itself. "Nied and Ranney befriended me," Pollard said, "because I was a Negro and they were afraid *for* me." It is why he dressed at Nied's cigar store.[27] "Akron was just like Mississippi in those days," Pollard explained. "A lot of Southerners came there after the war"—some of them not done with fighting. It appears that Pollard moved wife Ada and family to

Cleveland rather than live in Akron—at least there is no documentation of the Pollards living in the city. Horrigan thought they may have but couldn't pinpoint where.[28]

If, as biographer Carroll suggests, "some came to League Park to see [Pollard's] sensational runs while others turned out to abuse the diminutive halfback both verbally and possibly physically," reactions were not limited to the game itself.[29] Jack Gibbons described an Akron restaurant scene in the *Beacon Journal*. When Pollard, accompanied by Nasty Nash, Charley Copley, and other teammates, walked into the establishment, their waiter took every order but Pollard's. Such discrimination occurred often in cities the team visited. But Akron? Pollard was not only the Pros star and one of the league's highest paid players but also, in 1920, the team's co-coach— the NFL's first Black coach. [In the early days, coaches had to sit on the bench and keep their own counsel.] Pollard may have reimagined the offense without recognition, but in 1921 Nied made clear that Pollard was *the* coach. He told the team that if anyone didn't want to listen to Pollard, they could leave. No one did.

In the restaurant it became clear that to his teammates Pollard was not someone who had been forced upon them but a man admired. The team was his community and he was its leader. To Pollard, team was more important than town.

His teammates refused to tolerate the waiter's discrimination. They stood up for Pollard—literally. Gibbons may have overstated the ensuing ruckus—it sounded like a brawl—but the result was that the waiter was *persuaded* to serve the man whom historians indicate would have been league MVP had such an honor existed.[30]

Because two of three tie games occurred at the end of the season and involved championship contenders—the Pros, Buffalo, and the Decatur Staleys—Decatur player-coach George Halas, a league founder, tried to argue that his team deserved to be champion. Before the matter was sorted out by a vote of league owners in spring 1921, two problems were obvious: one, APFA officials had failed to provide sufficient details for deciding a champion, and two, Chicagoans Pollard and Halas had created lifelong enmity.

After their professional teams played to a scoreless tie, the former schoolboy foes—Pollard thought Halas "a good baseball player but not much of a football man"—went at it over the years.[31] By adding a ringer, Chicago Cardinal Paddy Driscoll, to the Staleys' roster to gain advantage over the Pros, Halas defied rules he had helped to write. The ploy failed. Akron controlled the first half and Decatur controlled the second half of their add-on game played in Chicago before 12,000 people, the "largest crowd to see a professional game in the city." It opened the door for the Staleys' move to the big city to become the Bears. Pollard resented it. "He used me to get recognized," Pollard said, "and then Halas refused to

Fritz Pollard

play Akron the next year unless they dropped me." Still angry, Pollard amplified his charge years later for *Chicago Sun-Times* sports columnist Ron Rapoport.[32]

The resentment festered and grew when Akron and other smaller towns lost their teams. The NFL, in 1927, "went through a major reorganization with the intent of focusing on larger markets"—Green Bay, Wisconsin, the notable exception—according to historian Joe Horrigan.[33] Before joining other NFL owners in excluding Black players, Halas refused to play Black all-star teams that Pollard put together. Racial regression began with the 1934 season and continued until 1946. Pollard called Halas "prejudiced as hell."[34] Halas labeled Pollard a "liar" and claimed "at no time did the color of skin matter."

The late Bill Furlong sided with Pollard. Biographer Jeff Davis gave a prominent place among Halas critics to Furlong who described Halas as possessing "all the warmth of breaking bones."[35] Pollard always blamed Halas for raising the "prejudice barrier." If so, he had construction help from the New York Giants' Mara family and especially from George Marshall, whose Washington team was then the NFL's southernmost. Pollard reserved his most vehement condemnation for less-than-cuddly Papa Bear. "Halas," he told Carl Nesfield, "was the greatest foe of the Black football player."[36]

When owners chose Joe Carr, Columbus team manager, AFPA president at an April 1921 reorganization, Halas's arguments that his team deserved the 1920 championship rang hollow.[37] Akron was declared champion and received the Brunswick-Balke-Collender Cup, forerunner of today's Lombardi Trophy. The cup vanished. Though it has been written about and searched for, it remains the missing NFL holy grail. Soon enough the Pros (Indians) were gone, too, diminishing memories and understanding of Pollard's greatness and importance.

After coaching Akron to continued success in 1921 and being recognized as an All-Pro, Pollard's team no longer could afford him. He again became a football nomad, strengthening his coaching resume and playing credentials first in Milwaukee (1922) and then in Hammond, Indiana (1923). Because his coaching role in Akron seems to have been neither fully understood nor appreciated, there is a mistaken belief that it was in Hammond that Pollard became the NFL's first Black head coach. It wasn't. It was in Akron. Despite conflicting locations, time-lines, and memories concerning his coaching ascendancy, there is no argument that Pollard was the first and only Black NFL coach until Raiders' owner Al Davis promoted Art Shell to Oakland head coach in 1989, almost seventy years later.

It remains difficult, one hundred years after Pollard became Akron's coach, for highly qualified Blacks to become NFL head coaches. An organization that identifies potential coaches and raises awareness of them is the Fritz Pollard Alliance Foundation. This organization recognizes Pollard's importance not only in NFL history but also in gaining opportunities for today's Black coaches and front-office executives.[38] Though some seventy percent of NFL players are Black, there were but six Black head coaches of thirty-two as the 2024 season began.

Pollard, I expect, would be disappointed but not surprised. Unlike when he struggled to identify which college and team might best suit him, to prosper in professional football between 1919 and 1926 *required* he again wander and embrace multiple affiliations. In 1923 and 1924, according to material compiled by Pearce Johnson, an early official with the Providence Steam Roller, Pollard coached Hammond in the NFL and played for Gilberton, Pennsylvania, in the Coal League. Akron and the NFL were tough on Black players, and the Coal League may have been worse.

Johnson's records suggest that in 1925, Pollard played for four teams—Akron, Providence, and Hammond in the NFL and Gilberton in the Coal League. If not a pro football record for teams in one season, it was a personal one. In one Gilberton game at Coaldale, a town northwest of Philadelphia that was rife with gambling, an unhappy palooka who had lost a wager challenged Pollard to fight. Pollard accepted and a match ensued before a hostile audience at a brimful venue. At the stadium, police had surrounded the field to protect Pollard; there was no protection, in ring or out.

None was needed—at least not from his opponent. Though Pollard said he was "the only Black man in the whole damn town," he waltzed through six rounds against the "big bully [who] didn't know a lick about fighting." Pollard "didn't try to hurt him seriously" because he feared riotous consequences. He "just boxed him silly."[39]

Back in Akron as player-coach in 1925 and 1926, Pollard found that racial prejudice continued unabated. The going, if anything, had gotten tougher. Twenty years later *Beacon Journal* sports editor Jim Schlemmer reprised in a column what had happened when the 1926 Pros and Pollard visited Buffalo to play the Rangers, a team stocked with former collegians from deep in the heartlessness of Texas.

Shortly before kickoff, Buffalo informed Pros manager John Paul Flanagan that Pollard could not play. "Our Rangers," Flanagan was told, "do not play against Negroes." Flanagan didn't blink. "We have just time enough," he said, "to catch a three o'clock train for Akron." The Rangers *did* blink. "Their 'principles,'" Schlemmer wrote, "were not as important as the dollars they stood to lose."

The Rangers made Pollard pay. "Pollard," Schlemmer wrote, "took a physical beating until carried out, more dead than alive. The Rangers were more intent upon piling on Pollard than in chasing the ball carriers. That was a good Akron Pro team and I have always had high respect for it because of the way the players took care of Pollard."[40]

It may have been sound business for the NFL to focus on larger metropolitan areas: Cleveland survived the purge; Akron and other smaller towns didn't.

Akron's collective memory of Pollard and the 1920 championship to which he contributed so mightily seemed over the seasons to fade, much as the cup had vanished. But if Pollard felt forgotten as years became decades and his race was whitewashed from the NFL, he seemed more intent on eclectic business successes—with the occasional failure—built on an entrepreneurial foundation that impressed even John D. Rockefeller, Jr.[41]

Rockefeller, 1897 Brown alumnus and once manager of its football team, appreciated not only what Pollard did on the gridiron but also his business acumen. When a clothes-pressing operation that Pollard set up in his college room left him too little space, Rockefeller arranged at his expense for more. When his pro career ended with the Pros—Pollard was fired in 1926 because he was too expensive for a fading team—he morphed into coal merchant, booking agent, accountant, film and music producer, and even the publisher of a Black weekly newspaper for which he wrote about sports.

Nearest and dearest to his heart may have been the teams of Black players that he created to prove that many Black players were capable of helping the NFL teams who rejected or banned them. Adding to the animus Pollard felt toward George Halas, the Bears owner refused to play his Chicago Black Hawks, first of his two teams, including the New York Brown Bombers.[42] After Pollard left the Bombers, his legend, real and noteworthy as ever, ebbed to the point of nonexistence.

When Gretchen Atwood in 2016 wrote *Champions: Four Men, Two Teams and the Breaking of Pro Football's Color Line*, she focused on the Cleveland Browns and Los Angeles (née Cleveland) Rams' integration in 1946 of the All-America Football Conference and NFL, respectively. Pollard and those who first integrated pro football—including Paul Robeson—hardly get a nod.[43] They aren't her story. They're Akron's.

The Browns' Marion Motley and Bill Willis and the Rams' Kenny Washington and Woody Strode often are referred to as The Forgotten Four because the attention went to Jackie Robinson for integrating Major League Baseball. Canton native Motley and Willis, Pro Football Hall of Fame members, shared the Hall's 2022 Ralph Hay Pioneer Award with Washington and Strode.[44] Pollard would have been a perfect complement to his successors but he was, unsurprisingly, left out. [The HOF *did* mention that Pollard and Duke Slater were earlier Black NFL pioneers.]

Pollard spent a lifetime being left out of the Pro Football Hall of Fame, though he deserved a bust *and* a statue. In 1963, Pro Football Hall of Fame selectors chose an inaugural class of seventeen critical to NFL success, including Canton Bulldog Jim Thorpe but also owners George Preston Marshall (Washington), Tim Mara (New York Giants), and George Halas, who, like Thorpe, had played against Pollard. Compared to Pollard, Halas was a blocking dummy.

Marshall, Mara, and Halas excluded Black players and then closed the door to them. And Pollard?

"His name never came up in '63," the *Chicago Tribune's* Don Pierson, selector on a later Seniors Committee, told the *Milwaukee Journal Sentinel*, based on Pro Football Hall of Fame notes. "That was before the Civil Rights Act. They weren't looking for historic figures. They wanted guys who would sell the Hall, promote the Hall."[45]

When Pollard wasn't chosen for the second class, *The New York Times* columnist Arthur Daley steamed: "Can the committee continue to skip past such vaunted pioneers from the first-team periods as Paddy Driscoll, Benny Friedman, Joe Guyon, Keith Molesworth, and Fritz Pollard, to name only a few." It could and did.

Driscoll (1965) and Guyon (1966) soon were chosen. Neither were Black.

Year after year, selectors—now 48—ignored Pollard. The historically inclined did not. "It is a shame and a scandal," wrote Jerry Izenberg, Newark, New Jersey, syndicated columnist, "that more young people do not even know his name. He is not a member of the Pro Football Hall of Fame. That is an incredible oversight—almost as incredible as the chain of events which form Pollard's own personal history."

Black writers such as *The New York Times'* William C. Rhoden hammered at Pollard's exclusion. In 2004 Pollard's daughter Leslie told the *Boston Globe*: "This generation doesn't know anything [about her father].... All my younger life, there was mention of my father in his football days almost every time you picked up a newspaper."[46]

Pollard was *The Forgotten ONE*.

John Carroll's 1992 biography should have shamed selectors into embracing Pollard. It didn't. Thirteen more years passed before the Hall of Fame invited Pollard to spend eternity in Canton with other greats. Brett Hoover, researching the "Ivy League at Fifty" in 2004, was shocked to learn Pollard was not in the Pro Football Hall of Fame. He was inducted into others, including the Summit County Sports Hall of Fame (in 1960).[47]

Hoover concluded that this was because "the story of Pollard is not found in statistics." Stats are important to selectors but time and changes in the game made Pollard's statistics less relevant. Hoover compared Pollard with Jackie Robinson, who faced and overcame the kind of abuse that Pollard suffered: "He helped to build the league with his legs, his brain, and his reputation."[48] While acknowledging to the *Beacon Journal* that race could have played a role in his lengthy exclusion from the Pro Football Hall of Fame, Pollard suggested he had been overlooked more because of the passage of time. Selectors, Pollard said, favored recent players, ones they knew—Seniors Committee included.[49]

Joe Horrigan, historian and Pro Football Hall of Fame executive director, recognized that Pollard had had "the ability to rise above the difficulties he must have faced integrating an all-white sport as a player and coach. He was also a great promoter and visionary." Seniors Committee member Pierson got it. "I think it was the historical significance of being the first Black player," Pierson said. [More precisely, *one* of the first Black players—but *the* first Black quarterback—"he was Michael Vick" before Michael Vick—and *the* first Black coach, which he said had meant the most to him.[50]]

"He showed a sense of bravery that's hard for people to relate to," Carroll told the *Baltimore Sun* when Pollard finally was named to the 2005 class of the Pro Football Hall of Fame.

Grandson Steven Towns carried the ball for Grandpa Fritz at his posthumous Hall of Fame induction. Fritz Pollard died in 1986 at age 92 without the totem of a Hall of Famer's Gold Jacket. He had other identifiers. "He had," Towns said, "the speed of Tony Dorsett, the elusiveness of Barry Sanders, and the tenacity of Walter Payton"—Black backs who followed his fleet footsteps, footsteps so swift that Pollard had outrun even the echoes of *Bye Bye Blackbird* and the silence of the empty Akron train platform.

"Grandpa," Towns told him, "the crowds are cheering."[51]

In an *NFL Network* examination on the league's beginnings and the place of African Americans, *USA Today* columnist Jarrett Bell, the first Black writer to receive the Professional Football Writers Association's Bill Nunn Memorial Award for long and distinguished coverage of pro football, summed up Pollard with just a few words.

The NFL's earliest Black standard-bearer had at long last been recognized for what Bell—and perhaps even Akron—realized him to have been: "The Gold Standard."[52]

Notes

1. Carl Nesfield, "Pride Against Prejudice, Part II," *Black Sports*, December 1971.

2. John M. Carroll, *Fritz Pollard: Pioneer in Racial Advancement* (University of Illinois Press, 1992), 16 and 21; Steve Love and David Giffels, *Wheels of Fortune: The Story of Rubber in Akron* (University of Akron Press, 1999), 62.

3. Carroll, 15, 20, and 9.

4. John Lee Maples, "The Akron, Ohio Ku Klux Klan 1921–1928," MA thesis, University of Akron, 1974, 236–237.

5. Carroll, 38.

6. Nesfield, 61.

7. Carroll, 72.

8. Barry.

9. Nesfield, 62.

10. Love and Giffels, 31.

11. Carroll, 131.

12. Carroll, 41.

13. Carroll, 16, 45.

14. Carroll, 61–62.

15. Carroll 4, 72–73, 100–101.

16. Addie Adams, "Tigers Eliminate Indians from Title Race," *Akron Evening Times*, November 10, 1919, 1; "Indians Start Poorly and Lose to Tigers: Big Crowd Sees Game," *Akron Beacon Journal*, November 10, 1919, 15; "Wheeling Expects to Hold Pollard," *Akron Beacon Journal*, November 13, 1919, 24; Carroll, 131–32. Unless otherwise noted, newspapers are cited from digital versions through Newspapers.com.

17. Carroll, 19–20.

18. Tom Reed, "Forgotten Pioneer," *Akron Beacon Journal*, February 5, 2005, C1.

19. Nesfield, 77.

20. Nesfield, 62.

21. "Indians Start Poorly," 15; Carroll, 131–32.

22. Jay Berry, "Fritz Pollard: Breaking the Barrier of Race," Brown Alumni Monthly, 1970; Carroll, 26.

23. "A History of Football in 100 Objects," *Sports Illustrated*, August 28, 2019, si.com.

24. Jim Carney, "Akron NFL Star of 1920s Earns Place in Canton," *Akron Beacon Journal*, August 1, 2005, B1.

25. John Seaburn, "Champions of a Bygone Era," *Akron Beacon Journal*, September 13, 1994, D1.

26. Carroll, 116.

27. Carroll, 137.

28. Carney.

29. Carroll, 137.

30. Jack Gibbons, "Fritz Pollard, Idol of All Both On and Off Football Field," *Akron Beacon Journal*, November 30, 1920, 18; Seaburn.

31. Nesfield, 63.

32. Carroll, 144–145; Ron Rapoport, "Old Pollard Still Senses Prejudice," *Arizona Republic*, July 7, 1976, C5.

33. Carney.

34. Carroll, 145.

35. Jeff Davis, *Papa Bear: The Life and Legacy of George Halas* (McGraw-Hill, 2005), 31.

36. Nesfield, 63.

37. Joe Horrigan, "Joe Carr," *The Coffin Corner*, vol. 6, nos. 5 & 6 (1984).

38. For more, see Fritz Pollard Alliance Foundation, http://fritzpollard.org.

39. Carroll, 161–62; Nesfield, 77.

40. Jim Schlemmer, "Nevada's Move Was Wise One," *Akron Beacon Journal*, November 6, 1946, 20.

41. Carroll, 112–13; Barry.

42. Carroll, 198, 200–205.

43. Gretchen Atwood, *Lost Champions: Four Men, Two Teams, and the Breaking of Pro Football's Color Line* (Bloomsbury, 2016).

44. "Motley Among Forgotten Four Sharing Ralph Hay Pioneer Award," *Akron Beacon Journal*, May 31, 2022, C1.

45. Cliff Christl, "Milwaukee Badgers Star Pollard Joins Hall of Fame," *Green Bay Press-Gazette*, February 9, 2005, C3.

46. William C. Rhoden, "Without Pollard, Football Hall Is a Sham," *The New York Times*, February 5, 2005, nytimes.com; *Third and A Mile: From Fritz Pollard to Michael Vick—An Oral History of the Trials, Tears, and Triumphs of the Black Quarterback*. ESPN, 2007.

47. Paul Dietrich, "Summit Fame for Pollard," *Akron Beacon Journal*, October 9, 1960, 9B.

48. Brett Hoover, "Ivy League at Fifty," IVY@50, ivy50.com.

49. Reed.

50. "Pollard Gets His Due at Last," *Canton Repository*, February 6, 2005, http://cantonrep.com.

51. Tom Reed, "Grandpa ... Crowds Are Cheering," *Akron Beacon Journal*, August 8, 2005, A1.

52. Jarrett Bell of *USA Today*, speaking on the NFL Network Channel, 2016.

\ **17**

Akron in Broadcasting

Mark J. Price

Akron's airwaves crackled with novelty on February 21, 1902, during a simple demonstration of "wireless telegraphy."

Physics teacher Philip E. Graber and student Raymond Foote conducted experiments in a laboratory at Akron High School on South Forge Street between Union and College streets.

"Messages were sent from one end of the building to the other with ease, the waves passing through walls and closed doors," the *Akron Beacon Journal* reported in a front-page article the next day.

Placed on a table, the sending apparatus included a large induction coil, a 22-volt battery, and a sparking circuit breaker. The coil was 7½ inches in diameter, 13 inches long, and contained about 5 miles of wire, with a resistance of 11 million ohms.

The receiver featured a suspended antenna, sheet zinc, coiled wires, a hammer, a telegraph relay, a 2-volt battery, and a glass tube filled with iron filings. With staccato precision, the instrument clicked away with coded messages.

The 20-foot transmission took place two months after Italian inventor Guglielmo Marconi had demonstrated the first transatlantic wireless signal from Cornwall, England, to St. John's, Newfoundland.

A decade later, Akron teenager Jack J. Gritton was credited with owning Akron's first radio, a small crystal set that he purchased in Cleveland and built at home in the summer of 1912. Fellow enthusiasts Paul Derr and Leo Price soon assembled their own sets and formed the Akron Radio Club with Gritton. The youths listened to US weather reports for ships at sea.

By 1913, the club welcomed Donald A. Hoffman, Darley F. Thurnes, Lloyd H. Miller, G. Franklin Dales, and Roland Palmer.

According to Akron historian Karl H. Grismer, Hoffman opened a radio parts store at his home at 56 S. Balch St. and started a 10-watt amateur station, 8UX, where he played Victrola music over the air and, rather amusingly, played checkers by wireless with his friend Alfred Bachtel.

The potential for broadcasting seemed limitless. In a lecture on January 11, 1922, before two hundred members of the Akron Engineering Society at 80 South Main Street, Lewis W. Chubb, radio manager of the Westinghouse Electric Co. in Pittsburgh, gave an upbeat assessment.

"The demand for wireless telephone instruments both for catching news and market reports as well as the catching of music sent out by the powerful sending stations is so great that it seems that almost every owner of a talking machine wants to trade it for this instrument," Chubb told the group. "The wireless telephone, although in its infancy, has a future that no man dares to predict."

In the early 1920s, Akron radios could pick up the signals of commercial stations such as KDKA in Pittsburgh, WWJ in Detroit, KYW in Chicago, WOR in New York, WOC in Davenport, Iowa, and WBZ in Springfield, Massachusetts. Akron soon would have its own station.

WOE

"IT'S AKRON WOE," the *Akron Press* reported April 13, 1922. "Local Radio Station Receives License to Broadcast."

The Buckeye Radio Service Co., a side business of the Buckeye Cycle Co. at 65–67 E. Mill St., believed that the best way to sell radios was to provide local programming. Akron inventor John Gammeter was president of the company and his brother, Emil, served as treasurer.

The US Department of Commerce randomly assigned the Akron station's unfortunate call letters. WOE was permitted to broadcast music and news from 7 to 8:15 p.m. Mondays, Wednesdays, and Fridays, and church services from 10 to 11:15 a.m. Sundays.

The 5-watt station went on the air April 27, 1922. Everything was done live in the studio. Performers that first evening included Campbell's String Quartet, musicians Francisco DeLeone and Robert Reimer, and vocalists Clifford Wilson and Mr. and Mrs. T. Stephen Eichelberger. The *Akron Press* supplied news bulletins and sports scores.

Former checker player Alfred Bachtel served as announcer, H. J. Tucker was program director, and Paul Heasley was station operator.

The studio was initially located at 569 South Main Street across from the B. F. Goodrich Co. but soon moved to the Buckeye Building on Mill Street. For the next two years, the station entertained Akron listeners with a cavalcade of local singers and musicians.

But then, without any explanation, the city's first radio station unexpectedly shut down in July 1924. Perhaps the owners felt it had run its course.

A somber-voiced announcer signed off with the final words: "W-O-E. Goodbye! Forever!"

WADC

It was meant to last a week, but it stayed much longer.

WADC began as a "temporary broadcasting station" to promote the Akron Automobile Show on February 21–28, 1925, at the Central Garage on Ash Street. The call letters stood for "Auto Dealers Company."

The Willard Storage Battery Co. of Cleveland installed the radio equipment for the show, which featured two hundred gleaming automobiles. Among the first performers were Sam Smolin's Orchestra, soprano Bernie Justice, and tenors Leslie Mange and Harry Bloom.

After the car show ended, Allen Theater owner Allen T. Simmons bought the radio equipment for $250 and applied for a permanent broadcasting license. WADC returned April 8, 1925.

"There are a great many who are exceptionally talented in this city and I want to give them an opportunity to get an audience," Simmons explained. "This is going to be an Akron station and therefore it will show what preference it can for Akron."

He turned the station over to such local performers as eleven-year-old Donna Mae Edick, who hosted "Kiddie Kabaret," a fifteen-minute show on Saturdays, until she was fifteen. Banjo and harmonica player Louis Marshall Jones, a West High School student, later created the character of Grandpa Jones, a future star of the national TV variety show *Hee Haw*. Akron singers Helen Jepson, Mary Van Kirk, and Marianne Dunn also rose to fame.

Jack Gritton, owner of the first crystal radio in Akron, grew up to be the station's announcer.

WADC became one of the nation's first thirteen stations to join the Columbia Broadcasting System in 1927. Akron listeners enjoyed national entertainers like Eddie Cantor, Bing Crosby, Red Skelton, Edgar Bergen, and Jack Benny, and tuned in to such series as *Dick Tracy, Our Miss Brooks, Perry Mason, Amos 'n' Andy*, and *The Guiding Light*.

On the AM dial, WADC moved from 1260 to 1320 to 1350. The studio moved, too, broadcasting from the Portage Hotel, Towell Cadillac, and the *Beacon Journal* before relocating in 1935 to Tallmadge. Finally in 1949, the 24-hour station christened a $250,000, two-story building in downtown Akron at Main and Mill streets. WADC occupied 15,700 square feet on the top floor. An aluminum and neon sign, seventy feet long and twenty-five feet high, advertised "WADC 1350 On Your Dial," "Over 200,000 Friends" and "Home of CBS Programs."

When the atmospheric conditions were just right, the 5,000-watt station could be heard as far away as South Africa and Australia.

Over the decades, the station's on-air talent included Bob Wilson, Estelle Ruth, Johnny Martone, Jack Clifton, Harold "Red" Hageman, Gladys Ammon, Roger Carter, Joe Grant, James Dunlevy, Ernie Stadvec, and Nina Magno.

After spurning offers for decades, Simmons sold WADC in 1964 for $1.3 million to Welcome Radio Associates led by Cleveland attorney Harrison Fuerst. The call letters changed to WSLR, a country station.

WFJC

WFJC is a forgotten radio station in Akron. It's better known for what it became than what it actually was.

Akron automobile dealer William F. Jones bought the equipment of defunct WDRK in Cleveland and leased space in the *Beacon Journal's* new building at 140 East Market Street. The call letters stood for William F. Jones Company.

After weeks of testing, the 500-watt station premiered November 4, 1927. Mayor D. C. Rybolt introduced announcer Walter Haushalter, who welcomed listeners to a three-hour program. Performers included Walter Logan's Orchestra, trumpeter Alois Hruby, contralto Alice McCullough, tenor Albert Downing, and soprano Leona Brown Woodcock, the station's program director.

The station, which operated at 1320 kilocycles, operated three nights a week but had to share its time with WCSO in Springfield, Ohio. As an NBC Red affiliate, it offered national programs such as *The Voice of Firestone*, *The Seiberling Singers*, *The Rudee Valley Show*, and *The Goldbergs*.

The station lasted only three years. Detroit radio executive George A. Richards, a former Firestone tire salesman, bought WFJC in 1930, merged it with WCSO, and started a 24-hour Cleveland station, WGAR, whose call letters represented the new owner's initials.

WGAR became a Cleveland institution, launching the careers of such personalities as Norm N. Nite, John Lanigan, and Don Imus.

Akron orchestra leader Eddie Ballway signed off WFJC at midnight, December 14, 1930, with "Going Home" from Dvorak's New World Symphony.

WJW

Here's another local obscurity. Radio executive John Weimer moved 6-year-old WJW from Mansfield to Akron in 1932, leasing the fourth floor of the Arcade Garage at 41–49 South High Street for a studio.

The call letters were a reference to the owner's initials. The 100-watt station, which operated at 1210 kilocycles, signed on October 15, 1932, with Samuel W. Townsend as manager.

Radio personalities included Everett "Bud" Pritchard, DeForest Winter, Bill Griffith, and Akron taxidermist Ben Morgan. It was a revolving door of on-air talent with at least nine announcers leaving the station over a two-year span in the mid-1930s.

In 1940, Weimer sold the station to William O'Neil Jr., the son of General Tire & Rubber Co.'s president. Initially unaffiliated, WJW joined the Mutual network to carry programs by Guy Lombardo, Art Kassel, Fulton Lewis Jr., and Shep Fields. It also aired Akron Yankees games.

After a decade, the station left Akron. It signed off at 2:30 p.m. on November 14, 1943, and then moved to Cleveland, where it switched its wavelength to 850 and enjoyed a good run through the 1970s.

Although WJW-AM abandoned its call letters in 1986, its television sister, WJW-TV (Channel 8), has been a Northeast Ohio fixture since 1956.

Who knew that WJW used to be in Akron?

WAKR

The grande dame of Akron radio has such a rich history that it merits a book of its own. Until that time, we offer highlights.

Akron attorney S. Bernard Berk, owner of Sun Radio Company, founded WAKR in 1940 as president of the Summit Radio Corp. His wife, Viola, served as secretary-treasurer and attorney Donald Gottwald was vice president. They financed the venture through the sale of 250 shares valued at $300 apiece.

Berk borrowed the first three letters of "Akron" for the call letters.

WAKR built its studios in First-Central Tower (later known as First National Tower, FirstMerit Tower, and Huntington Tower). The station occupied 5,200 square feet and operated under the Main Street storerooms with entrances from Main, Mill, and Howard streets.

The station went on the air at 6:30 p.m. October 16, 1940.

NBC announcer Milton Cross, a star of the radio quiz *Information Please*, emceed the program and performed the sign-on. The Rev. Noble S. Elderkin, pastor of First Congregational Church, delivered the invocation. Mayor Lee D. Schroy and Goodyear co-founder C. W. Seiberling offered prepared remarks. The evening's network fare included orchestra music by Glenn Miller, Gene Krupa, and Jan Savitt.

"This is, in fact, an important moment in the history of Akron," Berk advertised. "For WAKR is dedicated to the interests of its listeners, and will serve the people of this area by bringing a superior quality of programs ... outstanding national radio entertainment and information ... plus alert, complete coverage of local events. And so, with sincere friendliness and in good faith WAKR salutes Akron, pledging loyalty and public service through the years to come."

The station initially operated at 1530 kilocycles but switched to 1590 within a year while boosting its power from 1,000 to 5,000 watts.

Affiliated with NBC's Blue Network, WAKR carried national shows like *Inner Sanctum*, *Easy Aces*, *Death Valley Days*, and *Gang Busters*, but it increasingly emphasized local programs, news, and public service.

WAKR attracted a bevy of top-notch talent over the years. Its first big star was disc jockey Alan Freed, who arrived in June 1945. As host of *Jukebox Serenade* in the afternoon and *Request Review* in the evening, Freed became an idol to bobby-soxers, receiving more than five hundred letters a day.

After leaving Akron in 1950, Freed joined Cleveland's WJW, where he played rhythm and blues and popularized the term "rock 'n' roll."

Other WAKR employees to find fame included announcer Art Fleming, the first host of "Jeopardy," receptionist Lola Albright, the star of "Peter Gunn," announcer Mark Stevens, a Hollywood actor in film and television, and disc jockeys Scott Muni and Charlie Greer, who became legends in New York.

WAKR added an FM station in 1947 and a TV station in 1953 and consolidated all three operations under one roof at 853 Copley Road.

The AM station was a behemoth in ratings, obliterating the Akron competition for decades. It served as the flagship station for Group One Broadcasting, a national chain run by the Berk family.

The 1980s brought a whirlwind of changes, however. In 1986, the Berks sold all eight of their stations for $60 million to DKM Broadcasting of Atlanta. In 1987, WAKR-AM and sister station WONE-FM moved to studios at 853 Copley Road. In 1989, US Radio of Philadelphia bought them for $13 million. In 1993, Gordon-Thomas Communications of Cleveland scooped them up for $10 million to form the Rubber City Radio Group with WQMX at 1795 West Market Street in Wallhaven.

It's impossible to sum up eighty years of talent, but some of WAKR's memorable voices included Jerry Healey, Jack Ryan, Bill Murphy, Jack Fitzgibbons,

Akron in Broadcasting

WAKR disc jockey Alan Freed is surrounded by young fans from the studio audience during a 1946 radio broadcast of *Request Review*. \ Photo courtesy of the *Akron Beacon Journal*

Wes Hopkins, Harriet Leaf, Frank Ward, Russ Knight, Larry Crawford, Bob Friend, Bob Wylie, Billy Soule, Adam Jones, Bob Allen, Kenny Halterman, Larry States, Ray Horner, Fred Anthony, Tim Daugherty, Chuck Collins, Jasen Sokol, Sandy Bennett, Nick Anthony, Bobbi Horvath, and Jeanne Destro.

In addition to music and news, WAKR served as the radio home of the Browns, Cavaliers, Guardians, and Buckeyes.

The station has offered local talk shows, syndicated programs, satellite packages, and streaming services.

So much has changed since 1940, but WAKR keeps rolling.

WHKK

Cleveland invaded Akron during World War II. In 1944, the FCC approved the relocation of WCLE to Akron under the call letters WHKK.

The United Broadcasting Co., a subsidiary of Forest City Publishing Co., owned WCLE along with its sister station WHK, the *Plain Dealer*, and the *Cleveland News*.

WHKK, which operated at 640 on the dial, built a studio at 51 West State Street at the back of the M. O'Neil Company parking deck in downtown Akron. Russell "Bud" Richmond served as general manager.

The 1,000-watt station signed on February 25, 1945, with a 6:40 p.m. concert at Goodyear Theater. Entertainers included soprano Jean Merrill, jazz pianist Harry "The Hipster" Gibson, violinist Joseph Knitzer, comedian Hank Lawson, and the WHK Orchestra.

"WHKK will contribute substantially to the information and entertainment of service people, war workers, and the general public in Akron," United Broadcasting Vice President H. K. Carpenter told the audience.

The station operated during daytime hours, roughly 6 a.m. to 8:30 p.m., and carried the Mutual network, which WJW had abandoned when it left for Cleveland in 1943.

Over the next fifteen years, the Akron station's most popular disc jockeys were Cliff Rodgers and Pete "Mad Daddy" Myers.

Rodgers was a guitar-strumming, cowboy-singing host who welcomed such acts as Johnny Cash, Red Foley, Kitty Wells, and Marty Robbins. In 1953, he was the emcee who broke the news to the Canton Memorial Auditorium crowd that Hank Williams had died on the way to the show.

When he sponsored WHKK Day at Summit Beach, more than ten thousand fans showed up.

Akron in Broadcasting

"With rock and roll music sweeping the country today, I'm proud to be a hillbilly man," he told the *Beacon Journal* in 1956. "I used to feel a little guilty when I'd tell anyone I was a country disc jockey. Not anymore."

Myers was the opposite. An early champion of rock 'n' roll, he hosted sock hops and developed a cult following among teens. He spoke in rhyme and popularized catchphrases such as "Hang loose, Mother Goose," "Wavy gravy," and "Mellow Jell-O."

He eventually moved to Cleveland, where he donned a cape and briefly hosted "Shock Theater" on WJW-TV paving the way for horror icon Ernie "Ghoulardi" Anderson.

WHKK's other memorable personalities included Joel Rose, Happy Hank Pawlak, Bill Pierson, Peg Rodgers, Hal Murray, Jack Morrissey, Bruce Blake, and Rick Reighard.

Clevelanders Philip R. Herbert and Jackson B. Maurer bought the station for $100,000 in 1952 and sold it to the Susquehanna Broadcasting Company of Pennsylvania for $600,000 in 1959.

Not a bad profit. The station became WHLO in 1960.

WHLO

Goodbye, WHKK. Hello, WHLO.

With a change of call letters, the "Hello Radio" era began January 18, 1960, on 640 AM. The Susquehanna Radio Corporation, a unit of the Pennsylvania kitchenware company Pfaltzgraff, owned the Akron station.

The FCC required the 5,000-watt station to sign off at California sundown and sign on at Akron sunrise because it interfered with clear-channel station KFI in Los Angeles. In the summer, WHLO operated from 6 a.m. to 11 p.m., but only 7:45 a.m. to 7:45 p.m. during the winter.

It touted its disc jockeys as "The WHLO Good Guys." The early voices were Steve Fullerton, Warren Duffy, Bill Ridenour, Johnny Andrews, and Joe Cunningham. WHLO touted a Top 40 format just in time for the British Invasion of The Beatles, The Rolling Stones, and The Dave Clark Five.

Other on-air talent included Bob Ancell, Todd Taylor, Carl Day, Bill Miller, and Ralph Lockwood.

WHLO began losing young listeners as FM gained popularity in the 1970s. General manager Allen Saunders increasingly focused on news content.

In 1974, with a dozen reporters in the newsroom, WHLO established a reputation for in-depth, award-winning journalism. The radio station at 2650 West

Market Street in Fairlawn considered itself a direct competitor of the *Akron Beacon Journal*.

WHLO billed itself as NewsTalk 64, offering a formidable lineup of shows with Steve Fullerton from 9 a.m. to noon, Steve "Boom Boom" Cannon from noon to 3 p.m., Nick Anthony from 3 to 6 p.m., and Lee Hamilton from 6 to 9 p.m.

Other on-air talent from the era included David Lieberth, Bill Jasso, Larry States, Rich Barnett, Jim Carney, Marilyn Miller Paulk, Dick Russ, Scott Thomas, Tom Krisher, Phil Ferguson, and Bill Younkin.

The wheels came off in the early 1980s. Following a series of shake-ups in management, WHLO lost about thirty employees in one year.

The FCC allowed the station to operate twenty-four hours a day in 1980. Affiliated with the CBS and Mutual networks, WHLO became the radio home of Major League Baseball, the World Series, Monday Night Football, and the Super Bowl.

640 AM switched to a "Memories" music format in 1981. Three years later, Susquehanna Radio sold the station to Xen and Lee Zapis of Cleveland.

WHLO changed its format again, switching to contemporary Christian radio on Christmas Day 1985 and finishing last in the Arbitron ratings among twenty-nine area stations. Religious broadcaster Mortenson Broadcasting of Lexington, Kentucky, bought the station in 1986. Salem Communications took the reins in 1997 and moved WHLO to Independence.

Clear Channel, later known as iHeartRadio, gobbled it up in 2001. After a few more attempts at local programming, most notably Matt Patrick in 2008, WHLO switched almost entirely to syndicated talk shows.

WCUE

Another Akron station? Sure, why not? WCUE, located at 1150 on the AM dial, was "Your Cue to Better Listening."

Businessmen Tim Elliott and George K. Stroupe, owners of the Akron Broadcasting Company, founded the 1,000-watt independent station. Its studio was in the Palace Arcade in downtown Akron and its transmitter was at Cuyahoga Street and Sackett Avenue.

"Coming your way will be programs for young and old—fun and excitement for all the family," the station promised. "It's a happy situation, and we feel happy about it. But we feel a deep responsibility too, and this, we promise: WCUE will always be operated in the public interest, WCUE will always be a vigorous station—working to keep the Akron area a better place in which to live and make a living."

Akron in Broadcasting

WKDD disc jockey Matt Patrick bids farewell to co-host Barbara Adams in 2002 as she prepares to leave the morning show. \ Photo by Phil Masturzo, courtesy of the *Akron Beacon Journal*

WCUE went on the air at 1:10 p.m. on February 12, 1950, with a program titled "Sunday Serenade." The original on-air roster included Jack Crocker, Kitty Brown, Jack Larson, Gene Davis, Paul Hill, Bud Del Vecchio, and Rick Reighard.

During its formative years, the station was at a competitive disadvantage, operating only during the day, roughly 5 a.m. to 5 p.m., until 1963.

Jack Clifton was the best-known deejay in the 1950s. He served as program manager, hosted the morning show, and emceed events across the city. Singer Pat Boone credited him with being one of the first disc jockeys to play his music. When Clifton died in 1956, Boone headlined a memorial concert at the Akron Armory.

Ted Estabrook of New York City and Jack Valdes of Princeton, New Jersey, bought WCUE for $600,000 in 1958. The new owners promised "the newest concepts of modern radio," and that meant lots of rock 'n' roll—up to one hundred songs daily.

"Sure, we're a glorified jukebox," Estabrook acknowledged in 1959. "But there are many people who like this kind of radio. And somebody has got to give it to them. If we don't, someone else will."

A year later, it abandoned rock for a "modified good music policy."

WCUE launched an FM station on January 21, 1961, at 96.5 megacycles. The FM carried the same programming as the AM during the day, but it provided classical music and old standards at night.

George W. Mamas, general sales manager, bought the station for more than $600,000 in 1962 and operated it for two decades. The studio moved to 1424 Sackett Avenue in Cuyahoga Falls.

WCUE switched to a contemporary, personality-oriented format in the 1970s and spent $200,000 on new studios at 1675 State Road.

Morning host Sweet Richard was one of the best-known personalities of the era. A shock jock with suggestive humor, he hosted wet T-shirt contests at local discos.

"Blatant obscenity is where I draw the line," he noted in 1977. "I can say obscene things in a more refined way and get my point across."

Over the decades, the station's memorable voices included Jack Chenoweth, Bob Forster, Dick Reynolds, Bob Ancell, Art Roberts, Jerry Healey, Charlie Cooper, Bob Alexander, Joel Rose, Keith London, Tim Phillips, Mike O'Brien, and Don Christi. Matt Patrick, soon to be a star at WKDD, got his start there in 1980.

On March 6, 1981, it changed formats to "Music of Your Life," a playlist featuring Frank Sinatra, Doris Day, Ella Fitzgerald, and other pre-rock vocalists. Three months later, Mamas sold WCUE for $1 million to Sackett Broadcasting, a group led by Akron attorney David L. Brennan.

The station suffered poor ratings for five years. In 1986, Sackett Broadcasting donated WCUE to nonprofit Family Radio, a Christian broadcasting network that beamed its religious programs by satellite.

The network boosted the station's power to 5,000 watts. No more rock, no more shock, no more local. WCUE became a noncommercial station spreading "the comfort and hope of the Gospel."

WSLR

It takes a legend to replace a legend.

When Cleveland attorney Harrison Fuerst's Welcome Radio Associates bought WADC for $1.3 million in 1964, the company had some pretty big shoes to fill. It chose cowboy boots.

Akron radio host Jack Clifton, whose real name was Louis K. Salzburg, dons a cowboy hat in 1950 as the emcee of WADC's "Jamboree" program. \ Photo courtesy of the *Akron Beacon Journal*

"A new era of Akron radio is beginning," the station advertised. "WADC pioneered radio broadcasting and served well, since 1925. There have been many achievements and there are many fine memories of this station's past. But now, WADC is being retired."

WSLR, "Whistler Radio," premiered February 1, 1965, on 1350 AM with "a new concept of public service, a new concept of entertainment, a new blend of music you will enjoy."

WSLR disc jockey Jaybird Drennan works the microphone during the morning show in 1986. \ Photo courtesy of the *Akron Beacon Journal*

Returning from the WADC staff were Bob Wilson, Gladys Ammon, and Roger Adams. New on-air personalities included Steve Stone, Norm Tester, Mike Metz, and Ken Speck.

"Please listen!" the station implored. The public happily obliged.

WSLR made the masterstroke of hiring Jay "Jaybird" Drennan, an amiable, 6-foot-3 Texan with a velvety voice, as morning host. Never before had a local station been so thoroughly identified with a single personality.

Drennan emceed country concerts, broadcast live from local businesses, lent his voice to commercials, recorded a gospel album, and played record after record after record. In Akron, he helped popularize such artists as Waylon Jennings, Glen Campbell, Willie Nelson, Johnny Cash, Loretta Lynn, Charlie Pride, and Tammy Wynette.

"I love this kind of work and I really enjoy Akron," Drennan admitted. "The people have been so great."

In 1974, the studio moved from Main and Mill streets to 369 South Portage Path behind the Click store at Five Points Shopping Center. Its transmitter was at Steels Corners Road and Route 8 between Akron and Cleveland.

For a time, it was the only 24-hour country station in Ohio.

Akron in Broadcasting

In addition to Drennan, WSLR's on-air talent included Bob Fuller, Craig Scott, Dude Walker, Bill Coffey, Jim Huitt, Bill Love, Buddy Ray, Nick Anthony, and Steve Fullerton.

WSLR finished in the Arbitron ratings as the No. 2 AM station in the Akron market behind powerhouse WAKR.

In 1983, WSLR and WKDD-FM moved to Fairway Center off West Market Street. A year later, Welcome Radio sold the sister stations for $8.9 million to OBC Broadcasting Company, a Boston company owned by Albert J. Kaneb.

Perhaps the best-known voice in Akron, Jaybird Drennan retired in 1992 after 27 years at WSLR. His shoes could not be filled.

In 1994, the station changed its call letters to WTOU.

And "Whistler Radio" rode off into the sunset.

WAKR-TV/WAKC-TV

The test pattern aired for a month as Akron's first television station prepared to go on the air. Technicians scurried about the studio and control room, making final adjustments to cameras, equipment, and monitors.

WAKR radio owner S. Bernard Berk had applied to the FCC in June 1952 for permission to bring a TV station to Akron. He had hoped for a powerful VHF station between channels 2 and 13, but he would settle for a lower-range UHF channel between 14 and 83.

Three months later, the FCC assigned Channel 49 to Akron and authorized Summit Radio Corp. to begin construction. WAKR built a temporary location at its radio quarters in the First National Tower.

Older television sets did not have UHF on their dials, so customers had to buy converter strips ranging from $14.95 to $39.95.

The TV station premiered July 19, 1953. Three men of different faiths— a priest, a minister, and a rabbi—gave blessings at the opening ceremonies.

Akron Mayor Russell M. Bird told the audience: "I'm sure I'm expressing the proud and happy feelings of every Akron man and woman today." Program manager Blue Wright called the first telecast "the beginning of a new entertainment and community service era."

WAKR drafted radio personalities for television duty. Bill Murphy, a bearded man with an eyepatch, anchored the news with Jack Fitzgibbons. Bob Wylie provided a sports update and swimsuit-wearing Jo Anne Ybarra delivered a weather forecast.

The station had acquired the rights to more than 275 movies. On its first evening, it aired a double feature: "The Cheaters" (1945) and "Magnificent Rogue" (1946). Akron viewers marveled at the clarity of the broadcast.

The ABC affiliate aired programs five to six hours a night and carried a test pattern from 10 a.m. to 6:15 p.m. daily. WAKR offered quiz shows, amateur hours, children's programs, church sermons, and panel discussions.

WAKR opened a $500,000 "ultramodern television center" on April 23, 1954, in the former Copley Theater at 853 Copley Road. Each TV camera cost $28,000. Station officials invited the public to watch live broadcasts in the 250-seat studio.

Local programs included *Hinky Dinks*, *The Record Hop*, *The Teen-Who Club*, *The Professor Jack Show*, *Akron Tonight*, *Civic Forum of the Air*, *Sports View*, *Talk Back*, and *Spectrum*.

In 1963, WAKR began transmitting in color. In 1967, it switched from Channel 49 to Channel 23 and increased its power from 220,000 watts to 1.2 million watts. Nearly one million homes were in the signal's 60-mile radius.

Ange Lombardi sits at the piano while Torey Southwick hosts the *Hinky Dinks* children's show in the WAKR-TV studio in 1954. \ Photo courtesy of the *Akron Beacon Journal*

Akron in Broadcasting

By the late 1970s, the station employed a 100-member staff who produced seven local shows and two nightly newscasts.

Channel 23 served as a pipeline of talent for Cleveland television. Among the personalities who traveled north were Ted Henry, Dick Russ, Carole Sullivan, Rose Gabriele, Eric Mansfield, Mark Nolan, Mark Johnson, and Jeff Phelps. Other memorable broadcasters included Mark Williamson, Jim Kambrich, Billy Soule, Opie Evans, and Phil Ferguson. Reporter Carol Costello went to work for CNN.

In 1986, WAKR-TV switched its call letters to WAKC, a reference to Akron and Canton. In 1993, ValueVision, a home shopping network, purchased the station for $6 million. In 1996, Paxson Communications bought it for $18 million, dropped local programs, changed the call letters to WVPX, and moved to Warrensville Heights.

Akron's first television station is a memory. WVPX broadcasts Ion Television, which airs old movies and TV programs.

WAPS

Akron Public Schools went on the air in 1955 with an FM station in the Board of Education building at 70 North Broadway in downtown Akron.

Philanthropist Grace Crawford, who lived at Hower House on Fir Hill, donated $8,000 to establish the commercial-free station.

WAPS operated at 89.1 megacycles with 1,300 watts of power. The call letters stood for Akron Public Schools. The station, which operated four days a week, had a normal operating range of 25 miles.

Cyril Jones, director of radio and television for the district, explained that the station's purpose was "to beam educational broadcasts into the schools." Every classroom was outfitted with an FM radio, although teachers were not compelled to use the service.

Hower Vocational High School students installed the equipment and served as engineers. Students from other schools were announcers. The station began operating on a test basis June 10, 1955, but officially opened in September when school was in session.

"The programs, mainly recorded by system specialists in music, speech, and social sciences, are repeated over and over, to allow fitting into varied classroom schedules," the *Beacon Journal* reported.

WAPS operated four days a week, six hours a day. Cyril Jones provided science lessons. Dorothy Kester taught speech correction. Mary Helen Bowers gave music lessons from 1956 to 1976.

In 1959, the district began airing French classes over WAPS to elementary students. Parents could learn the lessons at home with their children.

"These radio classes may be the answer to the demand for foreign language teaching in the lower grades," Superintendent Martin Essex explained.

The pledge of allegiance and national anthem were played three times between 8 and 9:30 a.m. to account for different starting times at schools.

The station aired the May Festival as well as educational lectures.

Most programs continued to be educational in the 1970s, but the district allowed students to play Top 40 songs in the late afternoon. In the 1980s, WAPS served as a training ground for disc jockeys. By the 1990s, the station had nine paid announcers, sixty volunteers, and two students.

The station carried an eclectic mix of alternative music, jazz, and ethnic programs: Arabic, Hungarian, Indian, Irish, Latin, Polish, and Slovenian.

"Our mission is to serve the unserved radio market," operations director Bill Gruber explained in 1994, the year it switched from 89.1 to 91.3.

WAPS rebranded as The Summit 91.3 FM in 1999. Its format became adult album alternative with indie, pop, rock, reggae, blues, and country.

Through high definition, it offered new channels: The 330, featuring Northeast Ohio music; KIDJAM! Radio, providing programs geared toward children; and Rock and Recovery, a resource for the recovery community.

Memorable on-air talent has included Jim Chenot, Bill Hall, Ryan Humbert, Marc Lee Shannon, Brad Savage, Garrett Hart, Chad Miller, and Tim Greathouse.

Although the Akron school district still holds the license, The Summit is self-sufficient, depending on financial support from listeners, philanthropic groups, and the Corporation for Public Broadcasting.

Tommy Bruno, executive director and general manager, supervised the 2,000-watt station's move in 2019 to a 5,000-square-foot studio at Ellet Community Learning Center following a $750,000 capital campaign.

As always, The Summit continues to educate.

WAUP/WZIP

Reading a textbook is one thing. Running a radio station is another.

University of Akron students learned real-life lessons in broadcasting when WAUP hit the airwaves in 1962. Trustees paid $12,000 to equip the noncommercial station, which operated in Kolbe Hall on a frequency of 88.1 megacycles with a signal radius of twenty miles.

Administrators had dreamed of having a campus radio station since the 1930s. The call letters stood for "Akron University Programs."

Akron in Broadcasting

Students handled programming, scheduling, announcing, and engineering with the assistance of faculty. Seventy students in the Radio Workshop, a speech department group that had produced programs for decades on WAKR and WADC, coordinated broadcasting efforts.

Speech instructor Phyllis Hardenstein served as faculty advisor, succeeded in 1968 by Dr. Ruth Lewis, who added the title Station Manager.

Students supplemented the WAUP schedule with recordings from the library of the National Association of Educational Broadcasters.

Broadcasts originally aired from 6 to 10 p.m. Monday through Friday. The 330-watt station premiered at 6 p.m. December 10, 1962, with a schedule of decidedly highbrow material.

The evening began with *UA News*, a recap of campus-related events of interest to the community. Next, Robert Monaci of Bath and Fairlawn schools provided an Italian lesson. Then students began a series on "The Federal Government and Higher Education."

Other programs included a discussion of novelist James Fenimore Cooper, art commentary by Professor Bernard Weiner, a folk music review by Professor Walter Lehrman, a student production of Archibald MacLeish's play "The Fall of the City," and a recorded recital by soprano Leontyne Price. Sign-off was at 10 p.m.

"In a few weeks of initial broadcasting, WAUP-FM has proved a stimulating source of learning, entertainment and educational news to a community which had no previous educational programming," *Akron Alumnus* magazine noted in January 1963. "The future will see an increase in original programming as The University of Akron expands its role as intellectual and cultural leader in the community."

Students produced shows about classical music, opera, drama, Broadway, literary figures, alumni news, and current affairs, with a special emphasis on educational lectures and commentary. In 1968, the station added an Associated Press service and expanded hours of broadcasting fifty-two weeks a year under student manager Dave Lieberth. Play-by-play coverage of Zips teams with Don Read was added as well. By the 1970s, the format had loosened to allow more topics of student interest: US politics, civil unrest, women's rights, and professional sports.

WAUP provided a training ground for disc jockeys playing a variety of music, including rock, folk, soul, jazz, punk, and new wave. It also provided more than twenty hours of ethnic programs, including Arabic, Croatian, German, Greek, Hungarian, Indian, Irish, Italian, Polish, and Slovenian.

The station moved to Guzzetta Hall, grew to 3,000 watts, widened its range to 40 miles, and offered 24-hour programming.

The call letters changed to WZIP at 12:01 a.m. June 5, 1989.

"WZIP-FM more clearly identifies us with the university and the Akron Zips," station manager Tom Beck told *The Buchtelite* student newspaper.

A month later, it dropped most of its ethnic programming to provide more airtime to students interested in pursuing careers in broadcasting.

In 1998, the university celebrated a $7.4 million renovation of Kolbe Hall, including new studios for WZIP. It boosted its power to 7,500 watts.

Known as Z88, the modern station played a format called "rhythmic contemporary hit radio" and boasted more than 125,000 listeners a week. It also offered news, sports, a polka program, and syndicated shows.

Students continued to work as DJs, reporters, anchors, sportscasters, and programmers. They had come a long way since James Fenimore Cooper.

WDBN

Ahhhhhhhh. WDBN was an island of tranquility when rock 'n' roll spread like wildfire around the world. Its music was soft, soothing, serene.

Licensed to Barberton in 1960, the station and 118,000-watt transmitter were built in Medina County's Guilford Township on County Road 55, soon to be renamed Tower Road. Operating at 94.9 megacycles, WDBN debuted on FM when few people listened to that broadcast band.

Ted Niarhos of Independent Music Broadcasters Inc. was owner and general manager. With its "good music" format, WDBN was unabashedly unhip, catering to older listeners who liked orchestral and choral artists.

The call letters were chosen because they sounded smooth and easy. According to Niarhos, they coincided with "Dog, Baker, Nan," a phrase that engineers used when testing equipment.

The station operated from 7 a.m. to midnight when it debuted October 14, 1960. It had only six minutes of commercials each hour and no newscasts. It could reach listeners within a 100-mile radius.

Montovani and Ferrante & Teicher were in heavy rotation along with Henry Mancini, Percy Faith, Sergio Mendes, and Burt Bacharach.

In 1961, WDBN installed $17,000 in Multiplex equipment, becoming one of the first stations in Northeast Ohio to broadcast in stereo.

"This is the thing that will eventually kill AM radio," Niarhos predicted.

The FCC granted a license change from Barberton to Medina in 1965.

In 1968, Robert M. Miller, former program director at WERE in Cleveland, bought WDBN for $1 million, a record amount for an FM station. His wife, Pam, served as program director.

Critics labeled the easygoing songs as elevator music, but the Millers doubled down with a memorable nickname: "The Quiet Island."

"Isn't the rattle of your neighbor's garbage can lids enough without having to listen to freaked-out music?" the station advertised. "Pull yourself out of your old radio routine and get onto something nice and sweet. WDBN. The Quiet Island in radio's sea of noise."

In 1974, WDBN moved into the Great Northern Building at 4986 Gateway Drive in Montville Township near Interstate 71 and Route 18. The station was heavily automated, not big on on-air personalities, but its well-known announcers included Bill Miller, Len Anderson, Ken Courtright, Tom Field, Walter Henrich, David Mark, and Tom Cullison.

By the mid-1980s, the station had built a loyal following of 250,000 listeners a week, although the older demographic was perhaps not the most desirable among advertisers.

Business partners Thom Mandel and Gordon Stenbeck bought the station for $4.6 million in 1988. They changed the call letters to WQMX and switched to adult contemporary radio on August 14, 1988.

The Quiet Island sank into an ocean of soft rock.

WAEZ

The top-selling artists of 1973 included Pink Floyd, Led Zeppelin, Lynyrd Skynyrd, and Aerosmith. None of them got any airplay on WAEZ-FM.

Since its debut in 1947, Akron's first FM station, WAKR-FM, had maintained a low profile, mostly replicating the programming of its popular AM sister. It didn't establish its own identity until it changed the call letters to WAEZ and began playing easy-listening music July 9, 1973.

Owned by Group One Broadcasting, the station was located in the WAKR complex at 853 Copley Road. The 50,000-watt station had an 80-mile range from its transmitter in West Akron.

Located at 97.5 on the FM dial, the format was as plain as the name.

"We chose it because it best represents what we're all about. EZ listening," the station advertised. "Music so relaxing you'll wish you had a second set of ears. WAEZ Stereo is a soothing sound. We play the kind of soft, EZ-to-listen-to music that un-jangles your nerves."

The original playlist included Roger Williams, Ray Conniff, Andy Williams, Doc Severinsen, Enoch Light, Nat King Cole, The Sandpipers, Mantovani, Henry Mancini, Percy Faith—a lot of the same artists heard at easy-listening rival WDBN.

Announcers were required to have soothing voices. WAEZ even refused to air noisy commercials, not wanting to destroy the mellow vibe.

"About 52 minutes of beautiful music each hour," it advertised.

Listeners and advertisers flocked to the station.

"Our only regret is that we didn't change the name sooner," station manager Allen G. Grosby told the *Beacon Journal* in 1974.

By the end of the decade, WAEZ had climbed to second in Arbitron's Akron survey with 6.7% of the market behind sister station WAKR's whopping 16.1%.

Using music prepackaged in Chicago, the station was mostly automated so it required only two local disc jockeys. David Bennett, Dave Bradley, and Jim Kambrich were among the on-air personalities.

But the beautiful music format began to lose steam in the 1980s, catering mostly to 35-or-older listeners.

WAEZ confirmed in December 1984 that it would change its format to "adult rock" to attract a younger audience. Summit County's last easy-listening station faded away January 1, 1985.

Taking its place was WONE-FM with a playlist that included—you guessed it— Pink Floyd, Led Zeppelin, Lynyrd Skynyrd, and Aerosmith.

WKDD

WCUE-FM had been around for fifteen years without making a name for itself. Operating since January 21, 1961, the nondescript station withered in the shadow of its AM sister, airing much of the same content.

That began to change in 1976 when WCUE moved into new studios at 1675 State Road in Cuyahoga Falls. The FM station began broadcasting in stereo on July 12 and switched its call letters to WKDD on July 16.

The letters didn't mean anything at 96.5 FM. Station owner George Mamas just liked the way they sounded.

The original lineup of personalities included Debbie Ullman, Bobby Knight, Kevin Coan, Brother Louie, Vince, and Greg Morrison.

A new 500-foot tower in Northampton Township allowed the 50,000-watt station to improve its signal to an 85-mile radius.

WKDD began as a progressive rock station, trying to compete with WMMS in Cleveland, but pulled the plug after only a year. In 1977, it changed its format to "mellow rock" and languished at the bottom of the ratings.

In 1981, Mamas sold WKDD for $3 million to Welcome Radio Associates, a group led by WSLR owner Harrison M. Fuerst. In 1984, Welcome Radio sold the two stations for $8.9 million to OBC Broadcasting of Massachusetts.

Operations manager Nick Anthony switched to Top 40, contemporary music, and advertised WKDD as "Akron's Next No. 1," a self-fulfilling prophecy that came true in less than a year.

Akron in Broadcasting

A big reason for the success was music director Matt Patrick, a funny, charismatic personality who hosted "The Waking Crew" morning show with Barbara Adams and Steve French. Patrick was Akron's top-rated (and best-paid) disc jockey, serving as morning host for thirty years.

WKDD was the most popular radio station in Summit and Portage counties during the 1980s and 1990s. Its studio was at 1867 West Market Street in Akron.

Over the years, the on-air talent included Nancy Alden, Angela Bellios, Keith Kennedy, Krissy Taylor, J. R. Richards, Doc Reno, Tom Sullivan, Lynn Kelly, Eric Cramer, Danny Wright, Sue O'Neil, Katrina Curtiss, Dave Sharp, Jenn Ryan, Dave Nicholas, and Kat Jackson.

WKDD's annual "Have a Heart, Do Your Part" marathon raised millions of dollars for Akron Children's Hospital.

In 2000, Clear Channel Communications bought the station. In 2001, WKDD changed its frequency to 98.1, the former WTOF in Canton, while 96.5 became WAKS (KISS-FM), a Cleveland station. The frequency swap involved seven stations in Ohio.

Matt Patrick left the station December 18, 2009.

"I have decided the time has come for me to step away from this microphone," Patrick announced on the air. "I have the greatest job in the world, but now the time has come to say goodbye."

He died in 2017 after a battle with cancer.

Owned by iHeartRadio, WKDD moved its studios to 7755 Freedom Avenue NW in Jackson Township.

Local talent Keith Kennedy and Tony McGinty hosted the morning show in recent years. The rest of the schedule was filled with iHeartRadio personalities like Delana Bennett, Toby Knapp, Chris Davis, and Maddox.

"Akron's Best Music" played the music of such artists as Harry Styles, Miley Cyrus, Ed Sheeran, Taylor Swift, and Lady Gaga.

WNIR

WNIR, which bills itself as "The Talk of Akron" but is headquartered near Kent, merits discussion because of its longtime focus on Summit County and its history of high ratings in the market.

It debuted February 19, 1962, as WKNT-FM, a 250-watt station "operating on a good music policy" at 100.1 megacycles. Licensed to the Kent-Ravenna Broadcasting Company, the Record-Courier newspaper was its original owner.

Alternating between music, news, sports, and weather, it initially operated from 6 a.m. to midnight with a primary focus on Portage County. The station

WNIR host Howie Chizek makes a face while talking with a caller in 1994. \ Photo courtesy of the *Akron Beacon Journal*

covered Kent City Council meetings, announced club bulletins, carried high school games, and aired local church services.

Family-owned MediaCom Inc., led by Richard M. Klaus, bought the station and its AM sister in 1971 for $275,000. Three years later, Klaus made the sage decision to hire 26-year-old Howie Chizek as an on-air personality, a move that would raise the station's visibility in the years to come.

With a booming voice, a gift for gab, expert comedic timing, and a sarcastic demeanor, Chizek hosted a midday talk show that became No. 1 in the afternoon ratings. Even people who didn't like his viewpoint tuned in to hear what he would say. He was a fixture for thirty-eight years until his death in 2012.

"If you listen to the show and take the whole five hours seriously, you're doing it an injustice," Chizek once told the *Beacon Journal*. "There's news at the top and bottom, and what's in between is over-the-back-fence talk."

WKNT-FM changed its call letters to WNIR on August 4, 1980, to "soften the association with Kent." The station promoted itself as "Winner 100," and gradually adopted an all-talk format.

Akron in Broadcasting

Longtime listeners would argue that WNIR's golden era was in the 1980s and 1990s. Chizek's conservative viewpoint was balanced by Joe Finan's liberal counterpoint in the afternoon. Morning host Stan Piatt's laughter was contagious as he dispensed bawdy humor while evening host Jim Albright's dial-a-date show was outrageously fun in the days before the internet.

A short list of the 4,200-watt station's other memorable voices would include Bob Golic, Janet DiGiacomo, Steve French, Phil Ferguson, Joey Harper, Bill Hall, Angela Bellios, John "Couch Burner" Denning, Jim Midock, Tom Erickson, Jim Midock, Mark Richards, Jim Isabella, Joyce Johnson, Chris Casale, Bryce Wilson, Pat Rose, Maggie Fuller, and Bob Earley.

"Our philosophy has always been to provide our listeners with the finest news and talk programming available," station manager Bill Klaus, son of the founder, explained in 1986.

He and his brother, Bob Klaus, continued to operate the family-owned business long after rival stations were gobbled up by national chains.

"The Talk of Akron" still has a local voice (even if it's located near Kent).

WBNX-TV

The Reverend Ernest Angley, a televangelist and faith healer, is the personality most associated with this television station in Cuyahoga Falls.

The FCC issued a permit in 1984 to the Akron-Rhema Television Corporation, a nonprofit group led by North Ridgeville minister Amer Shab, but when it ran out of funding, Ernest Angley Ministries provided financial backing for Channel 55.

A minister with a lilting voice, Angley had been a well-known figure in Akron since conducting tent revivals in the mid-1950s. The North Carolina native opened the $1 million Grace Cathedral on Canton Road in 1958. Long associated with Akron radio, he branched out into television in 1972.

"I didn't know the expense of television," Angley later recalled. "I didn't know what it would cost. The Lord just said, 'Do it.'"

"The Ernest Angley Hour," broadcasting from Grace Cathedral, aired in more than one hundred markets in the United States, Canada, Africa, and the Philippines.

In 1984, Ernest Angley Ministries paid $2 million for the Rex Humbard Foundation's television studio and office complex on State Road in Northampton Township (now Cuyahoga Falls).

WBNX went on the air December 1, 1985, with reruns of classic TV programs such as *Father Knows Best, The Donna Reed Show, Lassie, Gunsmoke, My Three*

Sons, and *Family Affair*. The call letters referred to the Winston Broadcasting Network. Angley's middle name was Winston.

The Channel 55 schedule also featured Angley's religious programs *The Ninety and Nine Club* and *The Ernest Angley Hour*.

Angley bought the domed 5,400-seat Cathedral of Tomorrow from Humbard for $2.47 million in 1994.

In 1997, WBNX affiliated with The WB, the Warner Brothers network, after Channel 43 in Lorain declined to renew its contract. Channel 55 carried such hit shows as *Dawson's Creek*, *Gilmore Girls*, and *Buffy the Vampire Slayer*.

After The WB merged with UPN to form The CW network in 2006, WBNX aired such hits as *Smallville*, *One Tree Hill*, and *Arrow*. It remained the local affiliate until 2018 when the network rejoined WUAB.

The Rev. Ernest Angley died in 2021 at age 99.

The independent TV station went back to basics, leaning heavily on reruns of programs such as *Friends*, *The Goldbergs*, and *Family Feud*.

WONE

A rollicking piano intro broke the silence before dawn on New Year's Day.

"Just take those old records off the shelf," Bob Seger sang. "I'll sit and listen to 'em by myself."

"Old Time Rock and Roll" was the first record that WONE-FM played after it signed on at 5:30 a.m. on January 1, 1985. It was a rude awakening for older listeners expecting to hear the familiar sounds of WAEZ on 97.5.

The easy-listening station had been successful, but its audience wasn't getting any younger, so station owner Summit Radio Corporation, a member of Group One Broadcasting, changed the call letters ("One," get it?) and shook up the format.

"It's classic album-oriented rock—music that has been stored away for years," Fred Anthony, vice president and general manager, explained at the time. "It's the music people 25 and older grew up with."

Program director Ward Holmes described it as "a breath of fresh air."

"The Home of Rock & Roll" offered a mix of classic rock and new songs. Its original on-air staff included Deeya McKay and Rich Barnett from 6 to 10 a.m.; Tim Daugherty, 10 a.m. to 3 p.m.; Mike Michelli, 3 to 7 p.m.; Jim Chenot, 7 p.m. to midnight; and Dan Slentz, midnight to 6 a.m.

WONE surged in the Arbitron ratings, jumping to fourth place out of twenty-nine stations in the market and becoming a local fixture in rock radio.

Over the years, it became a kaleidoscope of "Twofer Tuesdays," "Get the Led Out," "No Repeat Weekends," "Mini Concerts," "The Vinyl Word," "The 5 O'Clock Traffic Jam," and "Rock the Lock."

Following a series of ownership changes and physical moves in the 1980s, WAEZ joined WAKR and WQMX in Rubber City Radio Group and settled into an Akron headquarters at 1795 W. Market Street.

By 1991, it went to No. 1 in the Arbitron and Birch books.

The station's rocking personalities have included Brian Fowler, Joe Cronauer, T. K. O'Grady, Jim Chenot, Jeff Kinzbach, Steve Hammond, Sandra Miller, Tim Daugherty, Kathy Vogel, Wendy Miller, Matt Spatz, Amanda Casey, Erin Carmen, Bill Hall, Dana Durbin, Ryan Lang, Ben McKee, Carrie Danger, and others.

A check of the playlist finds a heavy emphasis on classic songs from the 1970s, 1980s, and 1990s.

Nearly forty years after its debut, WONE still likes that old-time rock 'n' roll.

WQMX

It billed itself as "Mix 95," promising "a better mix of favorites from yesterday and today."

After business partners Thom Mandel and Gordon Stenbeck bought WDBN for $4.6 million in 1988, the easy-listening station switched formats to adult contemporary at noon August 14.

"If you decide you don't like us, we'll understand," Mandel told regular listeners at 94.9 FM. "You can still find your soft-and-easy favorites on WHBC at 94.1 or WQAL at 104.3."

With that advice, "a new era in Akron radio" began with the 1977 hit "Smoke from a Distant Fire" by the Sanford-Townsend Band.

In 1989, the station moved from its headquarters in Medina to new studios at Jefferson Park, west of Summit Mall in Fairlawn.

Mix 95's on-air talent included Tom Sullivan, Bill Miller, Brian Chase, Steve Frazer, Catrina Severson, Chuck Abel, Jerry Heckler, Bill Shield, Danny Wright, Lucy Otto, Brian Chase, and Steve Cherry.

"A better mix" turned out to be the wrong mix for Akron, though. The adult contemporary station peaked at ninth place in the Arbitron ratings and eventually dropped to sixteenth.

WQMX switched to country music on April 5, 1993. Similar to Top 40, the station played only new songs and billed itself as "Akron's Hot Country."

"It's the happening format around the country," program director Steve Cherry told the *Beacon Journal*.

Gordon-Thomas Communications changed its name to Rubber City Radio Group in August 1993 after buying WAKR and WONE. The three stations consolidated at 1795 West Market Street in Akron.

The format switch paid off. By 1994, WQMX was No. 1 in the Arbitron ratings among listeners twelve or older.

Memorable on-air talent included Cherry, Kathy Cistone, Kris Taylor, Jim O'Brien, Ken Steel, Lynn Kelly, and Scott Wynn.

WQMX adjusted its slogan to "Akron's Own Country" before settling on "Your Country."

With a series of concerts at Tangier, the station introduced Akron to up-and-coming stars like Eric Paisley, Luke Bryan, Eric Church, Scott McCreery, Big & Rich, Kellie Picker, and Cassadee Pope.

The station's modern on-air personalities included Scott Wynn, Sarah Kay, Cherise, Ben McKee, Rachel Evans, and Eric Mathews.

With country music's popularity holding firm, WQMX seems to have found the right mix.

WTOU

Listeners must have suffered whiplash when they turned on the radio. Country music station WSLR changed its format to urban adult contemporary September 1, 1994.

Owner Barnstable Broadcasting of Waltham, Massachusetts, switched the call letters a few weeks later to WTOU 1350-AM, "The Touch." Using a syndicated package from ABC, the station played a mix of classic R&B with no rap, aiming for an audience of twenty-five to fifty-four years old.

Lunzy Armstrong Jr. served as program director. Other on-air personalities included Maurice Turk, Ike Thomas, and Connie Young. The station aired religious programs featuring Henry Dunn, Denver Wilborn, Ann Robinson, Ginger Johnson, and Paul and Susie Finney.

WTOU billed itself as "The Heart & Soul of Akron." It sponsored concerts, festivals, programs, parades, and fireworks to raise its profile.

Increasingly, however, the station offered sports. WTOU aired Ohio State football and basketball games, hired veteran sportscaster Rudy Piekarski to call plays for Akron high school games, and carried Cleveland Crunch soccer games.

In 1998, it signed a deal to become the flagship station of University of Akron sports with broadcasters Steve French and Joe Dunn. Then the Akron Aeros signed a contract with Jim Clark and Todd Bell calling the plays.

Akron in Broadcasting

Listeners again experienced whiplash November 13, 1999, when the station switched from adult urban contemporary to the ESPN radio network.

"The urban community—the African American community—has a lot of choices," program director Chuck Collins told the *Beacon Journal*.

"It seemed to be more of a natural fit to go to a 24-hour-a-day sports format when we're already serving Akron sports like no one else in town."

In 2000, Clear Channel bought WTOU and sister station WKDD. In 2001, WTOU affiliated with Fox Sports. In 2005, it transformed into WARF to offer a syndicated format of progressive hosts talking politics.

Talk about whiplash.

WARF

On Monday, the topic was Major League Baseball. On Tuesday, it switched to President George W. Bush.

WARF 1350-AM, which billed itself as "Radio Free Ohio," launched June 2, 2005, with a syndicated format of political talk. Intended as a liberal counterpoint to conservative hosts like Rush Limbaugh and Bill O'Reilly, it advertised as "Talk Radio for the Rest of Us."

The call letters were a reference to "Radio Free." Its national lineup included progressive hosts such as Al Franken, Rachel Maddow, Randi Rhodes, Ed Schultz, Stephanie Miller, and Bill Press.

Cleveland entrepreneur Tom Embrescia was one of the original investors in Air America, saying he thought it was good to offer "an alternate voice."

Broadcasting veteran Joe Finan, most recently of WNIR, came out of retirement in February 2006 to host a local midday show, but the program was canceled in October and he died on December 19, 2006, at age 79.

Air America filed for bankruptcy October 13, 2006.

WARF, which had continued to broadcast Akron Aeros and University of Akron games during "Radio Free Ohio," returned to an all-sports format March 30, 2007. Initially called "Sportsradio 1350," it affiliated with Fox Sports Radio and called itself "The Gambler."

The station that traced its roots to WADC in 1925 moved to Independence in 2022 to focus on the Cleveland market.

Postscript

Today, everyone in Akron is a broadcaster. Most folks have smartphones that can record video and audio to publish on the internet.

People have become their own personalities, announcers, disc jockeys, podcasters, videographers, and engineers. In the palm of their hand, they have the power to reach a global audience.

The future of broadcasting is unknown, but you can bet it will look a lot different than the previous 125 years.

Bibliography

Braden, James, ed. *A Centennial History of Akron: 1825–1925*. Summit County Historical Society, 1925.

Grismer, Karl H., *Akron and Summit County*. Summit County Historical Society, 1952.

Knepper, George W., *New Lamps for Old: One Hundred Years of Urban Higher Education at the University of Akron*. The University of Akron, 1970.

Tel-Buch, University of Akron yearbook. The University of Akron.

Van Tassel Warner, Deb, and Stuart Warner, eds., *Akron's Daily Miracle: Reporting the News in the Rubber City*. University of Akron Press, 2020.

Periodicals

The Akron Alumnus
The Akron Beacon Journal
The Akron Evening Times
Akron Life & Leisure
The Akron Press
The Akron Times-Press
Billboard Magazine
The Buchtelite
The Plain Dealer

Websites

The Akron Beacon Journal. beaconjournal.com
Ancestry.com
Case Western Reserve University. case.edu
Family Radio. familyradio.org
Find a Grave. findagrave.com
Newspapers.com
Nostalgia Central. nostalgiacentral.com
Ohio History Connection. ohiomemory.org
The Plain Dealer. cleveland.com

The Summit FM. thesummit.fm
The University of Akron. uakron.edu
WAKR radio. wakr.net
WBNX-TV. wbnx.com
WHLO radio. 640whlo.iheart.com
WKDD radio. wkdd.iheart.com
WNIR radio. wnir.com
WONE radio. wone.net
WQMX radio. wqmx.com

\ **18**

The Rise and Fall of Howard Street as a Black Business District

Rose Vance-Grom

One of Akron's earliest Black-owned businesses, Henry Pickett and Charles Alexander's Excelsior Whitewashing Company, was listed in the Akron City Directory at 190 North Howard Street.[1] Several of the first Black political clubs of Akron met on Howard Street: The Black Grant and Wilson Club in 1872, organized in support of President Ulysses S. Grant, the Grand United Order of Odd Fellows in 1891, and the Union League Club in 1894.[2] These early businesses and organizations were among the first of many Black-owned businesses and organizations that would eventually find themselves on Howard Street.

In the early twentieth century, people flocked to the Rubber Capital of the World in search of jobs, with the population growing from around 70,000 in 1910 to nearly 210,000 in 1920. Akron's Black population increased eightfold in that time, from 657 to 5,580, many of them settling in what had historically been a Jewish neighborhood between Downtown and West Akron.[3] This neighborhood—dubbed Little Harlem—became the lifeblood of a business and entertainment

295

district along Howard Street, with Black-owned hotels, restaurants, clubs, tailors, barbershops, and beauty salons that served the tight-knit community.

Because of Akron's central location between bigger cities like New York and Chicago, it became a hotbed for jazz. Renowned artists, including Ella Fitzgerald, Cab Calloway, and Count Basie among many others, performed in Akron while touring the country. Beyond these national acts, there was a thriving local jazz scene. According to the *Ohio Informer*, Akron's short-lived Black newspaper, there was no shortage of things to do on Howard Street, also known as Rhythm Row.

For live music, dancing, and drinking, the Hi-Hat Club, the Green Turtle, and the Cosmopolitan to name only a few, were popular spots. The Akronite Jazz Society met on Sunday nights, while the Akron Jazz Club met on Mondays. There was always something going on at Benny Rivers: Thursdays were Talent Night with jam sessions and battles of the bands, while Friday was Mambo Night, and Family Night on Saturday. The *Ohio Informer* claimed that Akronites, or "A-Towners," "like all good music whether it be progressive or just plain gutty jazz."[4]

The Cosmopolitan was hailed as "Akron's most sophisticated hot spot" after it opened in 1936.[5] The club, owned and operated by Charles Fitzhugh, was a popular place for touring musicians to stop through as well as for local musicians who played there regularly. Patrons could also rent rooms at the club; many galas, wedding receptions, and community events were hosted there. Before Fitzhugh opened the Cosmopolitan club, he was an entertainer in his own right, performing in vaudeville shows as a dancer and comedian. He was also co-owner of the J. C. Wade Dance Studio at 33 South Howard Street.

J. C. Wade was a talented local dancer discovered after he won a Charleston dance competition in 1925. He moved to New York City and joined a theatre troupe as a tap dancer for several years. Wade moved back to Akron in 1933 and opened his first dance studio at 324 Gold Street, making him the city's first Black dance teacher and studio owner.[6] He outgrew that studio and moved to the Howard Street location in 1935, where he taught tap and ballet to both white and Black students and hosted an annual recital at Goodyear Theatre.

Hundreds of people made their livelihoods on Howard Street over the years, but the life of George Washington Mathews mirrors the trajectory of this business and entertainment district better than any other. Born the eldest of ten sons on a cotton farm in rural Georgia, Mathews moved to Akron in 1920. He purchased an old eleven-room boarding house at 106 North Main Street and opened his first barbershop. Using every penny he had, he purchased a rooming house at 77 North Howard Street, where he opened the Mathews Hotel in 1925, which

The Rise and Fall of Howard Street as a Black Business District

"Hotel Matthews" at 77 N. Howard Street, c. 1930s. The hotel sign reads "Matthews" although the owners, George and Alberta, spelled their name with only one "t". They continued to advertise their business as "Mathews Hotel" in local newspapers and *The Negro Motorist Green Book*. \ The University of Akron Archives and Special Collections.

he eventually expanded to a sixty-room operation.[7] By 1930, he opened a barbershop and a beauty salon in the hotel, which at one point was "Akron's largest colored barbershop."[8]

The Mathews Hotel became Akron's premier Black hotel and was listed in *The Negro Motorist Green Book*, a guide that helped Black Americans safely travel the country, from 1938 to 1967. Its central location on Howard Street and on-site amenities made it a popular spot for traveling musicians who were often on the road for long periods of time. A haircut, a clean suit, a nice dinner, and good music were all within walking distance from the hotel. Mathews, with his wife Alberta, ran the establishment and was considered "one of Akron's most successful business men."[9] They were also active members of their church and local

NAACP. The hotel itself served as a community meeting place for various organizations including the Carver Club, which was formed to "attempt to elevate the status of the Negro locally."[10]

In June of 1945, Duke Ellington and his famous orchestra played a four-night stand at the Palace Theatre on Main Street. This was not their first time playing in Akron, but these shows were part of a tour sponsored by the US Treasury Department to promote war bond sales. The orchestra traveled all over the country from 1943–1946, and *Your Saturday Night with the Duke* was broadcast on ABC. The series was released in 1974 as an eight-album set called *A Date with the Duke*, with the Akron show featured on Volume 6. Ellington and his orchestra all stayed at the Mathews Hotel because the Mayflower and Portage Hotels turned away Black patrons, no matter how famous they were.[11]

Howard Street was subjected to regular police raids by "vice squads" targeting liquor and narcotics violations, gambling, and disorderly conduct. The raids became so frequent that *The Ohio Informer* referred to these constant drills as "Operation North Howard" and said cops "in Gestapo-like fashion pour down on Howard Street" every chance they get. It further states that Akron police officers were indoctrinated to believe that this area was a "friction spot," but that "the only friction that has occurred on the street recently has been that created by some trigger-happy cop or several cops themselves."[12]

By the mid-1960s, Howard Street was in decline, and urban renewal efforts across the city sealed its fate. The Innerbelt highway, first proposed in 1962 as a key component of several projects to revitalize Downtown, was meant to connect the larger interstate network.[13] When construction began in 1970, the planned route was criticized by the Akron Chapter of the American Institute of Architects, claiming it would "wipe out a Black business district" and "foster segregation."[14] Two alternate routes were proposed, but neither of them was adopted. The Mathews Hotel was forced to close in 1978 and was razed in 1982. George Mathews died the same year at age 95.[15]

Throughout the rise and fall of Howard Street, the Stewart Photography Studio was there to document it. The studio, located at 11 ½ North Howard Street, opened in 1934 and was owned and operated by Horace and Evelyn Stewart. This husband-and-wife team photographed special events and the everyday lives of Black families in Akron, from wedding and graduation portraits to baby announcements and funerals. The Stewarts were also active in their community beyond photography. Horace spent as much time on community affairs as he did photography, with the education of Akron's citizens his main concern. He presented lectures on Black history, led discussions in the Akron Public Library's Great Books Program, and was recognized as a scholarly educator.[16] In addition

The Rise and Fall of Howard Street as a Black Business District

The Elks Parade down Howard Street, c. 1940s. The Improved Benevolent and Protective Order of the Elks of the World is the largest Black fraternal organization in the world. The Akron chapter of the Elks was located on Howard Street, as seen here. \ The Horace and Evelyn Stewart Photograph Collection, Archives and Special Collections, University Libraries, The University of Akron

to her work at the Stewart Studio, Evelyn was also a photographer for the *Cleveland Call and Post*. Horace died in 1968, and the Akron Board of Education renamed an elementary school on Wooster Avenue the Horace St. John Stewart Primary School, making him the first Black Akronite to have a school named after him. Evelyn ran the studio on her own for another ten years before closing it in 1978.

The Innerbelt, or "the road to nowhere," was never completed to its original plan, and today stands partially abandoned. A memorial sits on the site of the former Mathews Hotel, at the corners of Howard Street and Martin Luther King, Jr. Boulevard. Miller Horns spent fourteen years advocating for a memorial before it was finally realized in 2011. He designed the monument to pay homage to Mathews, the great entertainers who once stayed at the hotel, and the historic

Black business district.[17] This remains the only visual reminder of Howard Street and its rich history.

While the loss of this neighborhood was undoubtedly devastating, it was not the end of the jazz scene. It lived on in small clubs and church basements, and through the people who continued to play anywhere they could. The University of Akron Jazz Studies program, started in 1974, has also fostered an environment for young musicians to get together and play. Today, the Rubber City Jazz and Blues Festival, started in 2016, celebrates Akron's musical legacy. The echoes of jazz can be heard throughout the city, and many musicians will tell you that Akron still has a unique sound.

Notes

1. Shirla Robinson McClain, *The Contributions of Blacks in Akron: 1825–1975* (1975; University of Akron, 1996), 103.

2. McClain, 99.

3. A. Kingsberry, *The Akron Negro Directory* (1940), 15.

4. The Night Owl, "The Rambler," *The Ohio Informer*, January 22, 1955, 7, Summit Memory.

5. "Cosmopolitan Club Has Anniversary," *Cleveland Call and Post*, November 11, 1937, 12.

6. McClain, 227.

7. Lloyd Stoyer, "His Formula: You Work a Little Harder," *Akron Beacon Journal*, February 2, 1955, 83.

8. "Matthews Called Akron's 'Modern Period Moses,'" *Cleveland Call and Post*, July 15, 1937, 12.

9. "Akron Hotel Owner Buys Kraus Estate," *Cleveland Call and Post*, May 20, 1944, 1B.

10. "Group Formed to Uplift Negro in Akron to Meet," *Cleveland Call and Post*, January 27, 1938.

11. Mark Price, "Orchestra Leader Duke Ellington took 'A' Train to Akron for Concerts," *Akron Beacon Journal*, June 21, 2015.

12. "A Sad Note on Brotherhood Month," *The Ohio Informer*, February 19, 1955, 2. Summit Memory.

13. *Akron Innerbelt: The Reconnecting Our Community, Phase 1 Report* (Studio O, December 2023), 15.

14. Jerry Eyster, "How Akron's Roadbuilding Program Stacks Up," *Akron Beacon Journal*, June 21, 1970, 10.

15. Albert E. Fitzpatrick, "George Mathews Battled Hard for All of His 95 Years," *Akron Beacon Journal*, October 4, 1982, 4.

16. McClain, 351.

17. Jim Carney, "Memorial Recalls Akron's Jazz Era," *Akron Beacon Journal*, January 9, 2012, B01.

\ **19**

Julia Perry's Musical Legacy Shines a Light on Akron

Karla Tipton

In 1972, *Akron Beacon Journal* music critic John Von Rheim lamented that "Julia Perry ... has been steadfastly ignored by her city's musical establishment."[1] At that writing, Perry was forty-eight years old and struggling to regain her health after a series of strokes that paralyzed the right side of her body.[2] Cared for by her mother in a house that still stands on Euclid Avenue, Perry taught herself to write with her left hand and continued composing.[3] In 1979, she died at age fifty-five at Akron General Medical Center.[4]

Not long after the family moved to Akron in 1934, Julia Amanda Perry's accomplishments graced the society pages of the *Akron Beacon Journal*. She performed on violin at age fourteen at programs sponsored by Akron Story League and the First Presbyterian Church, among others.[5]

The seeds for Perry's musical career were planted in Lexington, Kentucky. Born the fourth of five daughters to Dr. Abe Murphy and America Lois (Heath) Perry on March 25, 1924, Perry spent her first ten years in an affluent neighborhood made up of predominantly upper middle-class African American families and located a few blocks from the Kentucky Race Association. Julia's grandfather Abraham Perry was connected with the racing establishment through his skill as a thoroughbred horse trainer. His horse Joe Cotton won the 1885 Kentucky Derby.[6]

Abraham Perry died in 1908, but not before using his wealth to build a big house on two lots in the East End for his wife Clara and their children. His son Abe, a physician and amateur pianist, raised his family in the same Vertner Street home (now 216 East Avenue).[7] The Perrys participated fully in the high society of the East End, a community segregated by color, where Julia was influenced by the adults around her. As members of First Baptist Church, they placed an importance on faith and participated regularly in the church's religious programs rooted in African American spirituals, as well as in charity fundraising, social events, and the arts. The family encouraged the children's musical education, and the Perry sisters rehearsed, got dressed up for, and performed as vocalists and instrumentalists at recitals in schools, churches, and auditoriums.[8]

After relocating to Akron in 1934, the family settled on Berg Street in an integrated neighborhood near The University of Akron.[9] Her father opened a medical practice and her mother continued to work in local charities and religious organizations. In 1943, her father founded the A. Lois Perry medical clinic at 911 Bell Street, where he practiced until his death in 1961.[10]

Before high school, Perry attended Spicer Observation School for exceptional children. She was a tomboy who played baseball with the neighborhood kids, said Kermit Moore, the late acclaimed cellist and conductor, who grew up a block from her. Together they performed in a junior choir formed by his mother and sang for church teas and occasionally on WTAM-AM radio. He described Perry's vocal style as dramatic and uninhibited.[11]

At Central High School, she sang in the a cappella choir and played violin in the orchestra, studying under Mabel E. Todd, who "discovered" her. Todd had connections to East Coast music circles. In a 1950 interview with *Beacon Journal* music critic Oscar Smith, Julia said, "Miss Todd was a great inspiration to me in my work. She induced me to go to Westminster Choir College."[12]

But Julia was not the first of the Perry sisters to pursue a career in music. She followed in the footsteps of her older sister, America Lois, a gifted vocalist and instrumentalist named after her mother. In 1935, Lois had been chosen to perform on cello as one of twenty Akron-area students in an all-high-school 144-piece orchestra for a concert in Cleveland.[13] In her late teens, she attended the Oberlin Conservatory of Music and the Cleveland Institute of Music. On July 31, 1940, on a return trip from New York City where she had been a featured

Julia Perry's Musical Legacy Shines a Light on Akron

Julia Perry. \ Permission to use this photograph is granted by Talbott Music Library Special Collections and Westminster Choir College Archives (Julia Perry Collection), Rider University. Digital image, copyright 2021.

vocalist on a radio show, Lois was killed in the Doodlebug commuter train crash in Cuyahoga Falls. Only twenty years old, she was one of forty-three fatalities. Four months before her death, she performed a benefit recital broadcast on WHK-AM radio, supported by her sisters Julia and Lucie.[14]

Perry spoke rarely of the tragedy, even to friends, but it may have inspired her best-known composition, "Stabat Mater," which she dedicated to her mother. The piece is a minimalist work about shared suffering, written for a soprano soloist against a string orchestra backdrop. In early performances, Perry sang the solo part herself.[15]

After graduating high school in 1942, Perry spent a year at The University of Akron. She then studied at Westminster Choir College in Princeton, New Jersey, as the recipient of the Knight Memorial Education Fund, established by John S. Knight in memory of his late father. She earned her bachelor's degree in music in 1947 and a master's in 1948. She continued her formal training at the Julliard School in New York, with the nephew of Gustav Mahler; and the Berkshire Music Center in Tanglewood, Massachusetts.[16]

Beacon music critic Smith posited that her approach to music differed from many young people. "She composes music, conducts, plays the violin, and writes the words to many of her songs," he wrote. "She believes a composer should know as much about music as possible, for she knows that composing is not all inspiration. She has learned there is a great deal of hard work in it."[17]

Her earliest compositions drew from her roots, and were primarily arrangements of African American spirituals, such as "Free at Last" and "I'm a Poor Little Orphan Girl."[18] Perry sang her own compositions for mostly white audiences and was an effective vocalist. "Julia's singing of 'The Lord's Prayer' and a Negro spiritual practically 'brought down' the house with applause," reported the *Beacon Journal* on its society page in 1941.[19] "One way to ensure your pieces were being heard, if you were a Black composer, was to write things that white audiences associated with Black composers, but she's also writing these pieces because she's genuinely inspired by the history of Blacks in the United States," said musicologist Kendra Preston Leonard, who is writing about Perry for a book.[20]

She broadened her composition skills under the tutelage of Italian Luigi Dallapiccola, who influenced her use of *serialism*—a twelve-toned technique that avoids setting the music in a specific key—which she incorporated into "Stabat Mater."[21] Performed throughout Europe and America, it received critical acclaim and remains one of Perry's most performed pieces.

In 1951, after a benefit performance of the piece at Central High School to finance her trip, she traveled by sea to Florence, Italy. Julia's mother went to New York to see off her daughter on the ship *Independence*.[22] Once in Florence, Julia continued studying with Dallapiccola, attended the American Conservatory in France, and then studied composition in Paris with Nadia Boulanger, a French music teacher who tutored many twentieth-century composers such as Aaron Copland.[23] She also studied composition in Florence with composer and conductor Roberto Lupi. During the mid-1950s, Julia was awarded two Guggenheim Fellowships.

Julia's most prolific period of composition was spent during this decade in Europe. Fluent in Italian, she wrote three operas, including "Cask of Amontillado," a dozen symphonies, and other commissioned pieces for individual instruments or ensembles. She lectured and conducted orchestras, sometimes of her own works, throughout Europe for the US Information Service, including at the BBC in London. She announced she would no longer perform as a vocalist in 1953. On her passport renewal in 1957, she identified her occupation as "composer." But after her death, it was her rich mezzo-soprano voice that people remembered.[24]

When Julia returned to Akron in 1960, she moved into the apartment over her father's practice on Bell Street, where she wrote a groundbreaking piece for percussion and harp, *Homunculus C. F.*, released by CPI Records in 1969. In the liner notes for the recording, she describes its inception "in my apartment situated on the top floor of my father's (physician and surgeon) office, equipped with all the necessary facilities except a piano. These clinical surroundings evoked memories of the medieval laboratory where Wagner, youthful apprentice to Faust, made a successful alchemy experiment, fashioning and bringing to life a creature he called homunculus."[25] The piece was unusual in that it was chamber music written specifically for percussionists. As a result, "Homunculus" continues to be performed regularly. The minimalist style in her compositions "predates what we hear from male composers ten and fifteen years later," said musicologist Leonard. "Those male composers—Philip Glass is one of them—get the credit for having developed these particular methods of composition, and Perry was doing it way before them."[26]

By the time she returned, the United States had changed, altered by unrest and the struggle for civil rights. Inspired by social justice movements, she composed pieces that incorporated more accessible influences, such as "Symphony No. 5," titled "Integration"; "Module for Orchestra," incorporating Black folk songs; and "Symphony No. 10," called "Soul Symphony," including movements based on rock and roll and rhythm and blues styles.[27]

Much had changed for Perry, too, and she entered into a period of difficulties that continued to the end of her life. She developed chronic health issues and struggled to find employment to pay her way in the world. "She is described as having become very difficult, quick to take offense," said Leonard. "She cuts off many of her friends and she stops performing."[28]

She commuted between Akron and New York City and did find occasional success. In 1964, a short orchestral composition titled "Study" was performed by the New York Philharmonic Orchestra at Lincoln Center. The same year, the Akron Symphony Orchestra presented "Contretemps," a short piece for orchestra commissioned by the Great Akron Musical Association. "Miss Perry is not afraid of dissonance, but wisely uses it as pepper and salt rather than as an end in itself," wrote the *Beacon Journal*. "It is 'modern' music that need scare no one."[29]

Perry placed classified ads in the *Akron Beacon Journal*, offering music lessons. Read one 1963 ad: "Distinguished composer Julia Perry will teach private and group lessons in orchestration, composition and conducting." She earned money from teaching for one semester at Florida A&M University and for substitute teaching French and German for Akron Public Schools.[30]

Her experience at Florida A&M resulted in a charge by the university for writing a bad $90 check, reported the *Beacon Journal* in 1970. The institution later dropped the charges, but Perry was arrested for it in Akron. She sued the university for malicious prosecution, but the case was blocked by the Summit County Common Pleas Court. She took it to the 9th District Court of Appeals, which allowed her to move forward with the suit.[31] Nothing further was reported.

A few months later, she suffered her first stroke. Over the next several years, more strokes followed. Perry never stopped composing, and corresponded with numerous institutions, proposing pieces for publication and performance, but could not regain the attention she had enjoyed earlier in her career.[32]

"She was probably not the easiest person to work with. She didn't get as many commissions as she would have liked and she didn't get the care for her health," said Leonard.[33]

When her father died in 1961, Perry moved in with her mother, who had purchased property on Euclid Avenue after the City of Akron bought the Berg Street house to make way for urban renewal. Around 1966, her childhood home and the neighborhood she grew up in was razed.[34]

As Perry's health declined, she spent the rest of her life in Akron with her mother as caregiver, sharing the residence with her sister Lucie Bigby and her children.[35] Friends suggested that Perry donate her music catalogue to Fisk University, or another historically Black college or university, where it would be preserved, but she never did.[36] On her tombstone at Glendale Cemetery, the birth year of 1927 is incorrect.

Of the approximately one hundred compositions she wrote during her lifetime, about half are lost.[37] Perry's works continue to be performed across the world by distinguished musicians and orchestras. Many can be heard on YouTube.

Notes

1. John Von Rheim, "Music Fans Who Bothered Could Find Gold in '72," *Akron Beacon Journal*, December 24, 1972.

2. Helen Walker-Hill, *From Spirituals to Symphonies: African-American Women Composers and Their Music* (Greenwood Press, 2002), 104–105.

3. Ohio, Summit County, Grantee Deed Books, 1961–1965, Volume 4303, Page 653, Summit County Recorder's Office, Digital Images, Index Book Archive Viewer (https://ibav.summitoh.net).

4. "Services are Saturday for Composer Julia Perry," *Akron Beacon Journal*, April 27, 1979.

5. "Members of Story League Will Attend Christmas Meeting Monday," *Akron Beacon Journal*, December 9, 1938, 20; and "Socially Speaking," *Akron Beacon Journal*, December 5, 1939, 14. Unless otherwise noted, newspapers are cited from digital versions through Newspapers.com.

6. Dr. Abe Murphy Perry and America Louis (Heath) Perry marriage record, "Ohio, County Marriages, 1789–2016," 1915, FamilySearch, http://familysearch.org; Julia Perry birth record, Kentucky Birth, Marriage, and Death Databases: Births 1911–1999, Kentucky Department for Libraries and Archives; Abraham Perry (1842–1908) memorial plaque digital photograph, African Cemetery No. 2 (Lexington,

Julia Perry's Musical Legacy Shines a Light on Akron

Kentucky), Chronicle of African Americans in the Horse Industry (https://africanamericanhorsestories .org/research/people/abraham-perry).

7. Death notice for Abraham Perry, *Lexington Herald-Leader*, February 9, 1908, 19; "Sheriff's Sale: District No. 4, Colored, City," *Lexington Herald-Leader*, March 18, 1905, 8; "Perry Abe (America)," *Lexington City Directory 1923* (Baldwin-Franklin Directory Company, 1923), 634, Lexington Public Library, https://rescarta.lexpublib.org; Colored Notes, "Abe Perry, solo instrumentalist," *Lexington Leader*, March 22, 1930.

8. "Russell School Notes," *Lexington Herald*, January 31, 1932, 9.

9. Obituary for Julia A. Perry, *Akron Beacon Journal*, April 27, 1979, 34; "Perry Dr Abe," Akron, Barberton and Cuyahoga Falls City Directory (Burch Directory Company, 1936), 143, Akron-Summit County Public Libraries, http://akronlibrary.org; Abraham Perry, Berg Street, United States of America, Bureau of the Census; Washington, D.C.; Seventeenth Census of the United States, 1950; Record Group: Records of the Bureau of the Census, 1790–2007; Record Group Number: 29; Residence Date: 1950; Home in 1950: Akron, Summit, Ohio; Roll: 727; Enumeration District: 89–76

10. 911 Bell Street, Ohio, Summit County, Grantee Deed Books, 1935–1944, Volume 1996, Page 618, Summit County Recorder's Office, Digital Images, Index Book Archive Viewer (https://ibav.summitoh.net).

11. Helen Walker-Hill, *From Spirituals to Symphonies: African-American Women Composers and Their Music* (Greenwood, 2002), 98; Kermit Moore, interview with Helen Walker-Hill in New York, December 11, 1995.

12. Oscar Smith, "The Town Crier," *Akron Beacon Journal*, September 19, 1950, 27; Bea Jay, "It Was a Tuesday Tradition," *Akron Beacon Journal*, September 23, 1953, 12.

13. "20 Akronites Enter All-High Orchestra," *Akron Beacon Journal*, October 21, 1935, 3.

14. "Akron Clubs Sponsor Lois Perry Recital," *Akron Beacon Journal*, September 4, 1936, 34; "Deaths in Akron District," *Akron Beacon Journal*, August 3, 1940, 12; Walker-Hill, *From Spirituals to Symphonies*, 98.

15. Walker-Hill, *From Spirituals to Symphonies*, 98; Oscar Smith, "Julia Perry acclaimed in Europe for Music," *Akron Beacon Journal*, July 6, 1952, 16.

16. Smith, "Town Crier," 27; Walker-Hill, *From Spirituals to Symphonies*, 93–94.

17. Smith, "Town Crier," 27.

18. Walker-Hill, *From Spirituals to Symphonies*, 129.

19. "Here and There," *Akron Beacon Journal*, April 24, 1941, 16.

20. Kendra Preston Leonard, interview with Karla Tipton, July 22, 2022.

21. Leonard, interview.

22. Julia A. Perry, departure date November 22, 1951, from New York, New York, ship Independence, The National Archives at Washington, DC; Washington, D.C.; Series Title: Passenger and Crew Lists of Vessels and Airplanes Departing from New York, New York, 07/01/1948-12/31/1956; NAI Number: 3335533; Record Group Title: Records of the Immigration and Naturalization Service, 1787–2004; Record Group Number: 85; Series Number: A4169; NARA Roll Number: 144.

23. Leonard, interview.

24. Walker-Hill, *From Spirituals to Symphonies*, 101, 97.

25. Julia Perry, liner notes for *Homunculus C. F.* Composers Recordings, CRI-SD 252, 1969.

26. Leonard, interview.

27. Walker-Hill, *From Spirituals to Symphonies*, 108.

28. Leonard, interview.

29. "Will Play Composition," *Akron Beacon Journal*, June 10, 1964, 21; Oscar Smith, "Symphony Bows Out," *Akron Beacon Journal*, April 19, 1964, 126; Robert Finn, "'Sure Hand' Shown in Music Premiere," *Akron Beacon Journal*, April 29, 1964, 59.

30. Walker-Hill, *From Spirituals to Symphonies*, 103; Classified ad, *Akron Beacon Journal*, January 16, 1963, 59.

31. "Wins Right to Sue Florida A&M Here," *Akron Beacon Journal*, January 8, 1970, 84.

32. Walker-Hill, *From Spirituals to Symphonies*, 104–106.

33. Leonard, interview.

34. "Perry, Dr. Abe," obituary, *Akron Beacon Journal*, November 1, 1961; Berg Street, Ohio, Summit County, Grantor Deed Books, 1961–1965, Volume 4301, Page 30, Summit County Recorder's Office, Digital Images, Index Book Archive Viewer (https://ibav.summitoh.net); "OK Study of University Concourse," *Akron Beacon Journal*, January 18, 1966, 21.

35. *Akron, Barberton, and Cuyahoga Falls Official City Directory, 1966–67* (Burch Directory, 1966), Historic City Directories, Akron-Summit County Public Library, akronlibrary.org.

36. Leonard.

37. Leonard.

\ **20**

The Failure of the Akron Innerbelt

Seyma Bayram

In 1956, Flanvis J. Johnson set his eyes on a white-paneled, three-bedroom house with a sunroom on Akron's Douglas Street, just west of downtown.

The Camilla, Georgia, native and decorated World War II veteran had been working two jobs to save up for this moment. To realize his dream of homeownership, Johnson, thirty-seven, alternated between shifts at Leeds Jewelry store downtown, where he cleaned and maintained the shop, and Babcock & Wilcox, a power plant where he worked as a millwright—the first African American to hold that role in the company.

Johnson purchased the home at 533 Douglas Street for $11,000—the equivalent of $112,750 today—and settled into the vibrant neighborhood with his wife, Evelyn, and their children.

His sons, Joey and Willie, quickly bonded with the other kids who lived on the block. After walking home from Grace School, the children played football and foursquare in the street, frequently drawing the ire of an elderly neighbor, Mr. Holloway, who didn't want the boys running through his immaculate yard. They bought penny candies from Harry's corner store and rode their bikes the short trip to the custard stand at Edgewood and Euclid avenues, where they

309

feasted on hot dogs, hamburgers, and frozen custard, and where teenagers gathered after basketball games to catch glimpses of their crushes.

There were painful memories, too.

One year, a baby died when the house across the street caught fire. The father of another household struggled with alcoholism. But the community on Douglas Street was tight knit. Neighbors supported and looked out for each other through the ups and downs of life.

Then, one by one, people began to leave the neighborhood in the late 1960s. Rumors circulated that a highway was coming through, and the city was taking people's homes to make way for it.

City leaders had big plans for the Akron Innerbelt, a highway connecting downtown Akron to the suburbs. Instead, it became a highway to nowhere—a never-completed road that tore apart a neighborhood and pushed hundreds of Black families out of their homes and off the path to generational wealth.

Black families that had worked hard to buy houses—long the standard for accruing and passing on generational wealth—lost them overnight. Many became renters and entered public housing developments. Some were able to purchase homes in other parts of the city, though white flight followed them. Those who kept their homes also lost, as declining property values prevented them from being able to build equity.

Incomplete records mean that we do not know the exact number of houses razed or individuals displaced by the Akron Innerbelt. A 1975 document compiled by the Akron Department of Planning and Urban Renewal notes that at least 737 households were displaced during the highway's first two phases of construction. But that figure does not account for two later phases lasting until 1987, and former city employees, displaced residents, advocates, and local historians believe the number is higher.

In 2017, the Ohio Department of Transportation began to decommission a portion of the highway, which the city acquired in September 2021. Now, the mistakes of the past are guiding discussions about the future of a thirty-acre decommissioned stretch of the highway in the heart of Akron.

Akron officials seized property to make way for Innerbelt

To make way for the Innerbelt in the late 1960s, city officials seized property through eminent domain and offered small amounts of cash to homeowners for relocation. The payouts, which frequently were contested by homeowners, were often not enough to purchase new homes.

The Failure of the Akron Innerbelt

In the late 1960s and early 1970s, the city was offering about $5,000 to each homeowner, though on rare occasions payments were as high as $15,000.

When the city did not approach Johnson to buy his house, he was devastated. Johnson knew that if he stayed in the neighborhood, his house would end up being worth next to nothing.

All of the homes to the south of his were razed to make way for the highway. The Innerbelt cut through the middle of Douglas, Bell, Berry, and other nearby residential streets, turning them into dead ends.

A comparison of Akron street directories from 1968 and 1988 offers a glimpse into the extent of the destruction on Douglas Street, which lost about 150 buildings. Bell Street lost 160 buildings and Berry Avenue lost about thirty.

Property values on Douglas Street and the surrounding areas impacted by the highway construction began to plummet. With so many families leaving the neighborhood, school enrollment also declined, which led to school closures, further depreciating home values.

By 1996, forty years after Flanvis Johnson purchased it, the Johnson home was worth only $11,940. Meanwhile, average property values in Akron stood at $45,931.

Still, the Johnsons tried to maintain their home.

After Flanvis died in 2002, an aging Evelyn lived alone at 533 Douglas Street.

Joey, who is now the senior pastor at The House of the Lord, paid off the rest of the mortgage, but the home had fallen into disrepair, and insurance companies refused to insure it unless costly renovations were made.

Joey faced a dilemma.

He could continue pouring money into the property—money that the family would never recover—to make it safe and habitable for his mother, or he could move her into a senior living facility.

"That was a very difficult proposition. . . . She wanted to stay," Joey said.

When the day came to move Evelyn into the assisted living facility, she was in tears.

"I don't want to move. This is my house," she cried to her son.

After Evelyn left, her son Willie, who had been renting another property at the time, moved into the home on Douglas Street. But he inherited unpaid bills and fell behind on taxes, and eventually lost the house in 2008. The home went into foreclosure and was sold to a private company in 2017 for $2,500.

Occupied by another owner today, 533 Douglas Street is appraised at $18,500. The home lies in a census tract where, in 2020, average property values hovered at $18,948, a fraction of the citywide average of $66,184.

Flanvis Johnson was never able to pass on the fruits of his labor to future generations of his family.

"In the African American community, rarely does anybody leave anybody anything. You end up paying to have them buried.... I was left nothing. I was left with bills," Joey Johnson said.

"Every time I got ready to buy a house, buy a car, go to school, there is no wealth accumulated, so you have to do all of that on your own," he said, reflecting on how the loss of property value on his family's home after the Innerbelt's construction decimated his family's wealth.[1]

After marrying, Joey and his wife moved into the Spring Hill subsidized housing development. He was not able to purchase a home until later in life and, even then, he was limited in the kind of home he could buy.

At age sixty-nine, Joey continues to work because he is unable to afford retirement.

Today, the median US Black household possesses less than 15 percent of the net wealth of median white households.[2] Homeownership and home equity account for two-thirds of a family's net wealth, according to LaDale Winling, a professor of urban history at Virginia Tech.[3]

In 1960, 53 percent of nonwhite families in Akron owned their homes, according to the US Census Bureau. Though homeownership rates in Akron have since fallen for both white and Black families, in 2019, only 34 percent of Black families in the city lived in owner-occupied homes compared to 59 percent of white families.

"Equity is the key to social mobility and generational wealth accumulation and for African Americans and other racial groups, the odds have been stacked against homeownership because of racial discrimination, racial segregation," said Eric Avila, an urban planning professor at UCLA. "When folks were able to buy a home in segregated neighborhoods, that was an achievement, but it was undermined.

"Highway construction devalued property among homeowners who lived in the vicinity of highway building projects. That story is repeated on the national level, and I think partly helps to explain the racial wealth gap.... The racial biases inherent within the federal highway building program disproportionately affected African American homeowners and prevented an entire generation of Black homeowners from realizing generational wealth," he said.[4]

Why the Innerbelt was built

First proposed in 1960, the Akron Innerbelt was conceived as part of a fifteen-mile-long expressway that would run from US Route 224 in Barberton through downtown Akron to state Route 8 and then through to Kent.

The Failure of the Akron Innerbelt

The rationale behind the Akron Innerbelt, which began to be built under Mayor John Ballard in 1970, was linked to a larger trend in urban planning and highway projects throughout the country.

With the rise of the automobile and the proliferation of suburban housing developments after World War II, many Americans flocked to the suburbs. Retail businesses and newly constructed malls followed them there, while downtowns began to decline. In Akron, good-paying rubber factory jobs began disappearing in the 1960s.

With support from the Federal Aid Highway Act of 1956, planners looked to the interstate highway system as a way of reversing urban decline by making it easier for suburbanites to drive to and from downtowns, where they would shop or work.

The Akron Innerbelt would "provide the much-needed stimulation for further economic growth in the Akron Metropolitan Area," concluded a 1963 report from the Akron Department of Planning and Urban Renewal.[5]

But the proposed location of the Innerbelt points to the structurally racist underpinnings of urban renewal and housing policies of the era nationwide, experts say. It also ran counter to a federally funded effort to invest in that neighborhood through the Model Cities Program.

A 1939 map of Akron shows that the areas slated for demolition to make way for the Innerbelt had been redlined.[6]

The term was used to denote neighborhoods—usually predominantly Black—that the federal government had labeled undesirable or "hazardous" and therefore risky for lenders. Consequently, banks often refused to lend to Black homeowners living in redlined areas, whether to buy homes or repair the ones they owned.

The area designated for the Innerbelt construction contained "enough blighted housing and substandard conditions to warrant either total clearance or almost total clearance," according to the 1963 Akron report.[7]

To enact their vision for urban renewal, planners and developers across the country followed paths of least financial and political resistance, Winling said. After decades of discriminatory lending, the new highways would run through neighborhoods where communities of color lived, which were deemed less valuable and therefore cheapest to bulldoze. These same communities also often lacked political representatives who would have stood up to the interests of the planners and builders.

Before the construction of the Innerbelt, Akron completed three major urban renewal projects around downtown—Grant/Washington, Lane/Wooster, and Opportunity Park—which displaced significant portions of the city's Black population. By 1975, urban renewal projects, including the Innerbelt, had relocated 3,197 households, according to municipal records. Meanwhile, in the mid-1960s, residents in the nearby affluent and white suburb of Fairlawn successfully protested and prevented the state from running Interstate 77 through their community.[8]

"White affluent or white middle-class communities had the wherewithal to block highway construction," Avila said. "They had the political clout. They had connections in city hall. They had resources and access to forms of mobilization that African Americans and other minority communities did not have. So the existing pattern of highway construction today—what was built and what wasn't built—conforms to a racially and economically skewed pattern of political resistance that was successful largely in white affluent communities and not successful in poor and/or minority communities."[9]

As historian Richard Rothstein notes in his book, *The Color of Law: A Forgotten History of How Our Government Segregated America*, by the 1950s and 1960s, terms like *slums* and *blight* were tossed around euphemistically to refer to Black neighborhoods. City officials tried to control the movement of Black people away from downtowns so that white suburban commuters would not have to interact with them, Rothstein wrote, and they did so through "slum clearance."

"One slum clearance tool was the construction of the federal interstate highway system," Rothstein explains.[10]

"Road to nowhere"

Backers of the Innerbelt project could have changed course.

In 1970, the American Institute of Architects met with Akron urban planners and proposed alternative routes to the east or west of the eventual path. They criticized the proposed route on the grounds that it would "wipe out a Black business district, slash through the heart of the Model Cities area and foster segregation."[11]

But Akron planners maintained that the route, which would also cut through the center of Black commerce on Wooster Avenue and shutter more than one hundred businesses, would be most efficient, best accommodate traffic, and greatly reduce costs. City officials said that adopting one of the alternative routes would have increased costs by $300,000 and delayed construction for up to two years.

Akron's current urban planner Jason Segedy explained that because wealth in Akron and its suburbs—like Fairlawn, parts of Copley and Bath—lie to the northwest, planners prioritized ramps to the west onto Interstate 76.[12]

The Reverend Greg Harrison, whose family was displaced from their home at 636 Douglas Street in the 1960s, said the lack of ramps enabled white people from the suburbs to travel to downtown Akron without having to enter any Black neighborhoods. At the same time, it severed access for the people living in the neighborhoods.

"It was a bypass of the Black neighborhoods.... at the cost of Black neighborhoods," Harrison said.[13]

Segedy, too, views the Innerbelt more as a "blight removal" tool and urban renewal project than a well-thought-out transportation project.

"It was literally a road to nowhere," he said.

Construction on the highway lasted until 1987. Despite its $300 million price tag—a combination of state and federal funds—the Akron Innerbelt ultimately never connected to Route 8 because the money had dried up.

The highway did not bring more traffic or wealth from the suburbs to downtown. On the contrary, Segedy believes the road made it easier for people, and wealth, to continue moving outward and away from the city.[14]

Designed to accommodate 120,000 cars daily, by the early 2000s the Innerbelt saw only about 18,000 cars per day.

A 1977 paper by Frank J. Kendrick, a political science professor at The University of Akron, details how the Innerbelt further segregated the city and carried with it a host of other negative socioeconomic and environmental consequences—in exchange for saving suburban drivers 1.25 minutes of driving time.[15]

"A tremendous loss"

Segedy said most people who were displaced by the Innerbelt ended up in worse housing situations.

Willie Johnson watched many neighbors, including homeowners, move into public housing, which municipal records show the city pushed aggressively during relocation efforts.

"I believe that a lot of people ended up in Section 8 because it was probably the quickest fix—not a real fix, but to solve an immediate problem of 'where do we go from here?' And I think many of them got trapped into Section 8 [housing]," he said.[16]

Tom Fuller, former executive director of Alpha Phi Alpha Homes Inc., a nonprofit that provides housing for low-income seniors in Akron, many of whom are Black, was a social worker in the city's relocation office in the 1970s when the Innerbelt was being constructed. He went door to door helping to implement the city's policy of relocation and supporting families that were being displaced to find new housing.

At the time, Fuller was unaware of how the Innerbelt project fit into larger systems of economic segregation and harm toward Black communities.

"I was interested in helping people get a leg up and that's what we were trying to do," he said. Though he was able to help some renters transition to first-time homeownership or otherwise improved conditions, he estimates that only about 25 percent of people ended up in better situations.

Today, Fuller sees the ongoing reverberations of the injuries inflicted by the Innerbelt and urban renewal more generally.[17]

The Innerbelt relocation program offered displaced renters the opportunity to purchase homes, with up to $4,000 in state funds toward a down payment. Renters had to match anything over $2,000.

Akron Beacon Journal reports from 1972 show the Ohio Department of Transportation dragged its feet on advancing down payment assistance to people experiencing hardship, in violation of state law. Without money for a down payment, many renters remained in limbo and unable to move. As a result, nearly a year after the city began to purchase homes in the path of the highway's second phase of construction, only 30 of the 487 affected families—many of whom were renters—were relocated.

In a 1972 *Beacon Journal* article, Roland A. Nesslinger, who was then deputy director of the State Highway Department's right-of-way division, justified the state's deferral of payments by claiming renters might spend relocation funds on color television sets or cars instead of the "more important responsibility of using the money for adequate housing."[18]

Fuller recalls how entire neighborhoods were declared "dilapidated" despite the quality of some of the homes in them. In order to secure federal funding for urban renewal and highway projects, cities had to deem entire neighborhoods as being "unfit for living."

"It would appear based upon my other reading that it was intentionally targeting African American communities," he said.

Once the damage was done, any good housing stock that remained in those neighborhoods became impossible to maintain. Homeowners would never see a return on their investment.

Lovie Moore's father purchased her family's home on Rhodes Avenue near the future site of the Innerbelt in 1957 for $14,450, or $143,370 today. Sixty-five years later, the 2,269-square-foot home is appraised at a mere $35,740.

Moore, who is seventy-three and inherited the home with her siblings, has lived on the street since she was a little girl.

"If it was white people that lived there, the value wouldn't be that low and they would have had more access to loans to renovate than we do," Moore said.

Moore has worked hard to maintain her home—her front lawn is perfectly manicured and the home was recently painted a bright white and green—but the

The Failure of the Akron Innerbelt

neighborhood looks different now. There are few homeowners left, and many people rent. Pockets of vacant land dot the landscape.

"It's just nothing like it used to be, you know, with the tearing down, with the Innerbelt and all of that. Everything is missing," she said.

"A lot of those homes were good homes," she added.

Neighborhoods destroyed by urban renewal projects like the Innerbelt were socioeconomically diverse and thriving, Avila said. He pointed to examples in other parts of the country where thriving middle-class neighborhoods—and even wealthy Black neighborhoods, like Sugar Hill in Los Angeles, which was cleared for the Santa Monica Freeway—were destroyed for highway construction.

Segregated housing policies of the early twentieth century forced Black families to live together regardless of income. Then urban renewal and highway projects destroyed this model of urban Black community and "fueled a kind of class segregation of African Americans," Avila said.[19]

Malcolm Costa, whose father used to own a barbershop on Wooster Avenue (now Vernon Odom Boulevard), remembers Black professionals, skilled workers, and low-income families living together in his neighborhood.

"Doctors and attorneys—because of the housing policies—they lived in the same type of community as other Blacks and, I mean, I know personally because our doctor lived two streets from where we lived.... You had the professionals as well as the skilled laborer ... plumbers, electricians, those types of households that were doing really well," he said.

"It was by no means dilapidated," he said of the neighborhood.

Costa now serves as CEO of Community Action Akron Summit, a nonprofit group that provides support to Akron's low-income communities. The organization was established in 1964 as the Community Action Council as a response to the growing problem of urban poverty and housing insecurity that intensified during and after urban renewal.

Many of the families displaced by the Grant/Washington urban renewal project of the early 1960s moved to West Akron, Costa said, unaware that they would be displaced again by Opportunity Park several years later. Eventually, the Innerbelt also came through West Akron, causing another round of displacement.

"In many cases, people moved two or three times," Costa said.[20]

From a child's perspective, relocation happened suddenly, seemingly without warning.

When Gordon Keaton and his family were displaced from their Damon Place rental when he was a teenager in the late 1960s, he didn't understand all the changes happening around him. Adults focused on surviving and often didn't talk about these things.

Where would his friends go, Keaton wondered, and where would his family end up when they were forced to vacate their apartment?

His family did not own a car. Keaton worried whether he would be able to walk to his friends' new homes and maintain the relationships that were so crucial to him.

"Losing my friends, my relationships that I had developed there, how do I grieve that? Nobody—we didn't know anything about the grieving process or grieving itself, the loss.... We're all being displaced," the seventy-two-year-old recalled.

"That was a tremendous loss for me," he said.

Equitable redevelopment

For Joey Johnson, the ill-fated Innerbelt destroyed Akron's Black cultural heritage, erasing hope and identity.

"If you don't have land, I'm not sure you can have an identity," he said. "It's very difficult to develop an identity with no stable land, foundation, community, those kinds of things. And areas where [Black people] develop those things.... White folks went in and burned them down because they recognized the power of what was going on," he said, drawing a connection between the ways officials used the law to destroy Black neighborhoods through highway projects and other stains in America's history, like the violent erasure of Black business districts in Tulsa and elsewhere.

Johnson, who chairs the mayor-appointed Racial Equity and Social Justice Task Force, urged city officials to keep an eye toward equity as they engage in conversations about how to redevelop the stretch of former highway north of Exchange Street.

As co-chair of the task force's housing subcommittee, one of Johnson's chief concerns is the lack of safe and affordable housing in a city where 85 percent of the housing stock is over one hundred years old. In addition to increasing homeownership rates among the city's Black residents, the subcommittee recommends new affordable housing or rehabilitation near the Innerbelt and in other socioeconomically disadvantaged neighborhoods.

"The people who are left down there, they are at a dead end, and we have to think about giving them opportunities, help them build wealth," he said.

Current residents and people whose families were displaced by the Innerbelt told the *Akron Beacon Journal* they want to see more investment in their neighborhoods, from affordable housing and increased opportunities for homeownership to workforce development, recreational and enrichment programs for children,

The Failure of the Akron Innerbelt

and support for small businesses. They also pointed out that the area is a food desert, with dollar stores and gas stations but few full-service grocery stores.

Including impacted communities in the redevelopment process is a priority for Liz Ogbu, a Bay Area-based urban designer who is committed to "engaging and transforming unjust urban environments."[21] The city hired her last spring to lead the informal advisory committee tasked with discussing the future redevelopment of the Innerbelt.

Launched by former Deputy Mayor James Hardy, the Innerbelt Advisory Committee consists of thirteen diverse community members, including former displaced residents, elected officials, downtown business people, artists, and community advocates.

The project comes at an opportune time.

President Joe Biden's $1.2 trillion infrastructure plan, signed in Fall 2021, includes a $1 billion initiative aimed at reconnecting communities that have been divided by local highway projects. Akron can apply for a share of that money.

At the core of Ogbu's mission is to use urban design as a vehicle to positively transform and heal communities.

"The way in which I work is often about 'What does a reparative [design] process look like?'" Ogbu told the *Akron Beacon Journal*.

"It's really easy to do an envisioning process that is like, 'What are all the cool things we can bring here? What are the beautiful spaces that we can create?' . . . [But] a lot of times we're actually building on a foundation of broken promises and crushed dreams. And when we build without a regard to also having an ability to hold space for that and acknowledge it and reckon with that, then oftentimes you don't engage people in the way that they need to be engaged and you create something that actually usually has a limited potential for success and also doesn't meet the needs of a lot of people," she said.

Exploring the possibilities

What could equitable redevelopment of the Innerbelt and its surrounding neighborhoods look like?

In January, Santa Monica launched the "Right to Return" program, which seeks to offer affordable housing to descendants of more than 100 Black and Latino families who were displaced by the Santa Monica Freeway in the 1960s.[22]

In St. Paul, Minnesota—home to the historically Black community of Rondo, which was demolished in the 1950s and 1960s for Interstate 94—residents and advocates teamed up with the state legislature and state department of transportation to devise a plan to reconnect the community while keeping the road intact. The proposal is to build a community land bridge to "cap" the freeway and allow for the construction of affordable housing and businesses on top of it.[23]

Ogbu said she is interested in implementing a community support program in Akron similar to the 11th Street Bridge Park in Washington, DC.

Initiated in 2016, the 11th Street Bridge Park will be an elevated park over the Anacostia River. To the east of the river are the predominantly Black communities of Wards 7 and 8, which have long experienced disinvestment.[24]

Vaughn Perry, director of equity at Building Bridges Across the River at THEARC, the nonprofit that spearheaded the park project, explained that when redevelopment projects come in, residents often rightfully fear their neighborhoods will be gentrified and that they will be displaced. To counteract this, the 11th Street Bridge Park, with the input of the community and extensive collaborations with other nonprofits and the local government, launched a series of programs to aid residents in workforce development, job training, homeownership, and cultural preservation.

Perry said his organization raised $75 million—almost as much as the construction cost of the park itself—to reinvest in Wards 7 and 8.

The nonprofit collaborated with other area organizations to host tenant rights workshops and launched the Ward 8 Homebuyers Program. Now in its fifth year, the homebuyers program has seen almost 1,400 participants and enabled about one hundred people to purchase homes in the neighborhood.

The nonprofit also established a community land trust as another avenue for affordable housing and wealth creation.

"These are people who have come from generations of renters who are now being able to shift the potential for wealth in their family by being able to purchase a home," Perry said.

Technical assistance, loans, and workshops also are available to small-business owners, and the nonprofit sees the construction of the bridge itself as an employment opportunity for Ward 7 and 8 residents.

Though Perry's organization is nonprofit, he said that this model of equitable redevelopment can be replicated by any organization, including local governments, because it requires deep collaboration among residents, elected officials, and community organizations.

"At the crux of this is relationship-building," Perry said. "All of the strategies came from our community.... We're not going in and trying to give solutions, but we believe that the solutions are always in the community. We believe the community can identify their own problems, and they also can identify their own solutions. And so for us, it's how do we bring additional resources to these solutions that the community says ... will help [them] become more resilient?"[25]

The Failure of the Akron Innerbelt

Whatever plan Akron adopts, it must take into account the unique challenges posed by the site itself, including accessibility, Segedy said.

The highway is sunken and filling it would be cost-prohibitive, he said, though he and other city officials did not offer a figure for how much filling the land would cost.

"Because the city owns the land, the city has a lot of power to steer how the land is developed, if they so choose," said Ben Crowther, program manager for the Congress for the New Urbanism's Highways to Boulevards and Freeways Without Futures initiatives.

"You can easily leverage that land's value to create reparative programs, one that restitches and heals community wounds," he added.[26]

Crowther encouraged meaningful public engagement efforts, including transparency in the request-for-proposals stage of the process.

In Akron, Ogbu emphasized the need for the city to build trust with residents.

"Those wounds are so deep that anytime you say you're going to do a big project, people go back to that story.... The onus is on us to build that relationship of trust and to show that we are completely clear on what has happened before," Ogbu said.[27]

Those who were adults when the city took the homes and dreams they had worked hard to build are no longer alive. But their surviving children, who are seniors now, continue to feel the economic and emotional shocks of dispossession.

One of them, Greg Harrison, is cautiously optimistic about the redevelopment of the Akron Innerbelt. He believes the city has a moral obligation to build trust with and engage the families whose communities, land, and wealth were stolen by the highway's construction.

"You can't repair all of the damage, but you can repair some of it," he said.

"If you really want to do what's right, talk to the children of the Innerbelt, and let's find a way to rebuild what you destroyed: African American community."[28]

This story was first published in the February 3, 2022, edition of The Akron Beacon Journal, *with the support of a fellowship from Columbia University's Ira A. Lipman Center for Journalism and Civil and Human Rights. Doug Livingston contributed. This story has been updated for this book.*

Editor's note

In 2021, the City of Akron launched an initiative called "Reconnecting Our Community," engaging former residents of the area—those most impacted by the building of the Innerbelt (Route 59) in the 1960s.

In 2024, Akron selected the nationally recognized planning and design firm Sasaki as the primary consultant to create an Innerbelt master plan.

In January 2025, the city announced that it had won a $10 million grant from the U.S. Department of Transportation to support future transformations of the site, which will be matched by an additional $10 million from local and state sources. Planners met with members of the public at a community workshop to gather feedback from residents to help guide the master plan that is expected to deliver actionable recommendations for developing the site by the fall of 2025.

Notes

1. Joey Johnson, interview with the author.
2. Neil Bhutta et al., "Disparities in Wealth by Race and Ethnicity in the 2019 Survey of Consumer Finances," *FEDS Notes*, Board of Governors of the Federal Reserve System, September 28, 2020, https://www.federalreserve.gov/econres/notes/feds-notes/disparities-in-wealth-by-race-and-ethnicity-in-the-2019-survey-of-consumer-finances-20200928.html.
3. LaDale Winling, interview the author.
4. Eric Avila, interview with the author, January 6, 2022.
5. "A Perspective of the Akron Innerbelt," City of Akron Department of Planning and Urban Renewal, August 1963, https://amatsplanning.org/wp-content/uploads/AMATS-A-Perspective-of-the-Akron-Innerbelt.pdf
6. "Map of the Akron Area," Mountcastle Map Company, 1939, https://library.osu.edu/documents/redlining-maps-ohio/maps/Akron_map.JPG.
7. "A Perspective of the Akron Innerbelt."
8. Coverage of these efforts include "Fairlawn Highway Battle to Resume," *Akron Beacon Journal*, January 7, 1964, 5; Don Kirkman, "State Redraws Freeway Line in Fairlawn," *Akron Beacon Journal*, May 11, 1964, 1; John Larabee, "I-77 Through Fairlawn Faces 5-Year Delay," *Akron Beacon Journal*, August 9, 1965, 1; John Larabee, "Fairlawn Highway Battle Going to Court," *Akron Beacon Journal*, October 28, 1965, 13; Kenneth J. Rabben, "I-77 About to Bridge Fairlawn Gap?," *Akron Beacon Journal*, July 11, 1966, B1.
9. Avila.
10. Richard Rothstein, *The Color of Law: A Forgotten History of How Our Government Segregated America* (Liveright, 2018), 127)
11. Jerry Eyster, "How Area's Roadbuilding Program Stacks Up," *Akron Beacon Journal* (June 21, 1970), 10.
12. Jason Segedy, interview with the author.
13. Rev. Greg Harrison, interview with the author.
14. Segedy.
15. Frank J. Kendrick, "Effects of Transportation Planning on Urban Areas," *The Ohio Journal of Science* 77, no 6 (November, 1977), 267–75.
16. Segedy.
17. Tom Fuller, interview with the author.
18. Ronald D. Clark, "Innerbelt Puzzle: Hardship," *Akron Beacon Journal*, March 15, 1972, A18.
19. Avila.
20. Charles Buffum, "She Packs Again—3rd Home To Fall For 'Progress,'" *Akron Beacon Journal* (July 16, 1970), 1.
21. Liz Ogbu, interview with the author.

The Failure of the Akron Innerbelt

22. Alisa Chang, Jonaki Mehta, Christopher Intagliata, "Santa Monica, Calif., Aims to Welcome Back Historically Displaced Black Families," *All Things Considered*, NPR, January 21, 2022, https://www.npr.org/2022/01/21/1074872905/santa-monica-calif-aims-to-welcome-back-historically-displaced-black-families

23. "A Progressive Purpose Needs a Progressive Path," *Reconnect Rondo: Build a Bridge to Better*, https://reconnectrondo.com/landbridge/project-2/.

24. "Bridging DC," *11st Street Bridge Park*, https://bbardc.org/project/11th-street-bridge-park/

25. Vaughn Perry, interview with the author.

26. Ben Crowther, interview with the author.

27. Liz Ogbu, interview with the author.

28. Greg Harrison, interview with the author.

\ **21**

1968

A Year of Drama. A Year of Change

David Lieberth

As Akron looks back at two hundred years of history, there are moments in time that are identifiable inflection points, years when momentous events changed Akron forever.

The year 1968 was a turbulent time for Akron, for the United States, and for the world. Akron was still heavily reliant on the tire and rubber industry, although the decline of its manufacturing industry was clearly evident.

In 2018 *Smithsonian* magazine remembered 1968 as "The Year That Shattered America." A year that began with the Tet Offensive in the Vietnam War went on to see a record number of military deaths for this conflict—more than sixteen thousand—more than in any other year. In March, President Lyndon Johnson announced that he would not run for re-election. On April 4, The Rev. Martin Luther King Jr. was assassinated in Memphis by a white gunman, igniting riots in Washington DC, Chicago, at least five other major cities, and hundreds of smaller cities. In June, Senator Robert F. Kennedy was assassinated.

In 1968, the Civil Rights movement was losing momentum nationwide, a few years after a possible peak with the 1965 Voting Rights Act. Akron was grappling with issues of racial inequality and social unrest. Like many American cities, Akron was undergoing urban renewal projects that impacted race relations, which have been difficult since Akron's beginning.

Akron was settled mainly by men and women from New England. Many brought with them a dedication to social movements of the time—education for all children, temperance, women's rights, and the abolition of slavery. And before the Civil War, the Akron area was a place where freedom-seeking people who had been enslaved south of the Mason-Dixon line found support and assistance. But Black people also faced discrimination in Akron, and the State of Ohio had "Black laws" designed to discourage their settlement in the state by depriving them of rights and privileges afforded to the rest of Ohio's people.

Between 1844 and 1854, Akron was home to the single most consequential person ever to live in Summit County, John Brown, who came to believe that violence was not only acceptable, but necessary to achieve the eradication of slavery in America. On the day of his execution, December 2, 1859, Akron stores and businesses closed, and church bells tolled for an hour.

His failed raid on the federal arsenal at Harpers Ferry, Virginia (now West Virginia), would ignite a national debate that rallied the abolitionist cause, struck fear in slaveholders, and would lead to the first shots fired in the American Civil War eighteen months later.

Akron's history of race relations has always been complicated.

In August 1900, a violent mob burned city hall to the ground after attempting to lynch a Black man named Louis Peck. The sheriff had anticipated their attack by moving Peck to Cleveland, and the mob violence was quelled after the governor called out the militia.

In the 1920s, Akron hosted one of the largest klaverns of the Ku Klux Klan in the country. The mass migration of Appalachian men to Akron during the explosive growth of the rubber industry would reflect the nativist sentiments of the men from the hills and hollers of Appalachia.

For most of the twentieth century, Akron was a city where Black and white people lived separately. A study of racial conditions in the 1950s, the Akron Community Audit documented patterns of racial segregation and discrimination illustrated by the following examples:

A white couple could check-in at a hotel. Researchers would send a Black couple to the front desk where they were told no rooms were available.

The Akron Metropolitan Housing Authority placed only white families at their 274 units on Edgewood Avenue and only Black families at the 276 units in Elizabeth Park under the North Main viaduct.

Of seven cemeteries in Akron, only five would accept a burial of an African American person, and even then burials were limited to a segregated area of the cemetery.

Four thousand Black men and women were employed at the rubber companies during the tire industries' heyday, mostly in positions as janitors or laborers. The cafeterias at Goodyear and Firestone were segregated.

The "royalty" of the shops were tire builders. Of two thousand such elite positions, twelve were held by Black men.

African American families reported that going to an Akron restaurant could be challenging. Either they'd be told to wait in line until they got tired and left, or if they were seated, no server would appear to take their order.

Skating rinks and swimming pools posted "Admissions for Negroes" on special days only. The only bowling lanes available to Black residents were at the YMCA.

In 1960, classified ads in the *Beacon Journal* still listed housing as being available to "Colored or White." When F. A. Seiberling and Harvey Firestone created their industrial residential neighborhoods, Goodyear Heights and Firestone Park, the land sales were specifically limited by covenants contained in the deeds to the properties. No transfer could take place to a person of "African or Ethiopian descent."

In 1968 Akron had a population of almost three hundred thousand, including sixty thousand residents of African American heritage.

When Akron's urban renewal programs were implemented earlier in the decade, the impact of the federal grant program disproportionately affected Black neighborhoods. Between 1960 and 1970, the City of Akron transplanted three thousand households. More than 80 percent—about twenty-four hundred homes—were owned by African Americans, effectively destroying a dozen intact Black neighborhoods. Almost no new housing was constructed under Urban Renewal, and this failure to provide accommodations for thousands of people dispossessed of their homes became one of the root causes of civil disturbances in 1968.

In July 1968, I was a twenty-one-year-old student at The University of Akron studying communications. On a Sunday in July, I launched my career in broadcast news with my first job at a commercial radio station as a news editor at WHLO Radio. The week of July 15, 1968, would be one of the most tumultuous weeks in Akron history.

It was to be a week of great celebration in northeast Ohio since the Cleveland Orchestra was due to christen its new summer home, the Blossom Music Center.

Riots in other cities were in the news. In Akron, young Black men on the west side were in a territorial dispute with groups from the east side. Police were called to break up crowds throwing rocks and bottles at each other.

Wednesday, July 17

It was a hot night—more than eighty degrees, with high, suffocating humidity.

At 1:00 a.m. (the early morning hours of July 18), a group of young men broke a window at the Olson Electronics store at the corner of State and Water Street in downtown Akron. Windows were broken at fifteen stores on South Main Street, including LeRoy's jewelers.

Police chased a crowd of Black teenagers down Bowery Street into the Wooster Avenue neighborhood. There, police were met by a group of youths breaking store windows, throwing Molotov cocktails and attempting to keep officers at bay by throwing rocks and bottles. Sholiton's drug store was being looted of cigarettes and watches.

Police estimated that perhaps four hundred young people had gathered in the four blocks of Wooster Avenue between Rhodes Avenue and Raymond Street.

At 1:45 a.m., flames broke out at Murphy Lumber on Moon Street, after a firebomb was pitched through a window.

A sixteen-year-old named Leo Stegall ran from Solomon's grocery store on Edgewood Avenue, which was also being looted. Police said they told him to stop running, and when he failed to heed the police officers' command, two Akron officers fired three shots, wounding him in the shoulder.

By 2:00 a.m., three hundred Akron police officers and Summit County sheriff's deputies had been called in for duty. Some teenagers gathered inside Calhoun's record store on Wooster Avenue until they were flushed out by tear gas.

At 3:00 a.m., Mayor John Ballard asked the governor to activate the National Guard.

By 8:00 a.m., thirty members of the National Guard with twenty police officers wearing riot gear formed a wedge to clear Wooster Avenue of people.

Twenty-three juveniles and nineteen adults were arrested that first night.

On Thursday night, Mayor Ballard imposed a curfew in Akron from 9:00 pm to 6:00 am. Neighboring cities followed suit. Downtown department stores announced they would close at 8:00 p.m. Akron buses halted all runs after 8:00 pm.

At a morning press conference at the Akron police station, National Guard General Sylvester Del Corso said. "I have 450 men. Their weapons are loaded. Their bayonets are fixed. We will use force if necessary to stop looting, arson, and disorder. When we order someone to stop, if they do not, they will be shot."

The Thursday edition of the *Beacon Journal* contained an insightful column by writer Kenny Nichols, the city's veteran Town Crier. "Wooster Avenue is where the Great Depression of the 1930s never ended," he wrote.

Mayor John Ballard said he was concerned about a deep and serious hostility toward Akron police. Attorney Edwin Parms, president of the NAACP, said he was concerned about a deep and serious hostility by some Akron police officers toward Black citizens.

The preeminent leader in Akron's Black community, Vernon Odom, Executive Director of the Akron Urban League, criticized the lack of training that Akron police had displayed in attempting to manage riot conditions, citing indiscriminate beatings of Black men by police, who even beat some of the adult leaders trying to quell the youth. Odom also expressed concern about the overuse of tear gas.

Thursday, July 18

It rained. All of the businesses on Wooster Avenue had closed. Twelve storefronts were attacked that night, often by groups of youth doing smash-and-grabs. Meat from one grocery store was thrown into the street.

Many young people gathered at the barbershop on Wooster Avenue. Next door to it was the office of the New Afro-American Liberation Front. It was surrounded by police, who smashed the windows so they could throw tear gas into the building.

On Thursday, 106 individuals were arrested, including eighty-three for curfew violations. Twenty-eight people were injured and treated at Akron hospitals. There were three firebombs thrown that night.

One of the targets for the two nights of violence was the Sparkle Market, the grocery store where most of the neighborhood residents shopped. The owner Carl Saferstein grew up in the neighborhood and described the two days as a "bad dream—I saw twenty-five years of my life go down the drain." Saferstein said he had enough and announced that he would shut down the store and dismiss his eleven employees—most of them African American residents of the Wooster Avenue neighborhood.

Stan Zalob of Stan's Family store said he'd been in business for twenty-two years. "We're closed for good," he announced.

Sixty-seven-year-old Max Minty ran the Lake Erie Fish Market, where the windows were smashed. "I've never felt so bad," he said.

A confederation of civil rights groups, the United Black Front, alleged that the store owners provided inferior merchandise at excessive prices.

1968 329

Friday, July 19

The city's elite population of professionals and business leaders were concerned about how they would get to the opening of Blossom Music Center with a 9:00 p.m. curfew in effect for the entire city. Mayor Ballard said anyone with tickets or headed to Blossom for lawn seats would be given a pass.

The Blossom pavilion, all 4,600 seats, was sold out. Fifteen thousand people were expected to sit on the lawn. Half that number showed up to hear Beethoven's Symphony No. 9, best known for its "Ode to Joy."

The National Guard set up headquarters at the fire station on Wooster Avenue. Major General DelCorso approached a young Black boy at the ball field next door to the fire station. The kid had a ball and a glove, and the general asked, "Why aren't you playing?" To which the boy replied, "Not until you guys get the hell out of here."

That night twenty fires were set along Wooster Avenue and in the west side neighborhood, including the Rosetani Club. Red's supermarket on Edgewood was gutted by flames. Fifty-three more arrests were made.

Saturday, July 20

African American leaders met with Mayor John Ballard and reminded him that they'd been telling him for three months that city was sitting on a tinderbox. They complained about the report from one neighborhood leader who saw five Black men beaten by police "for no reason." They asked him to remove the National Guard and pull back the police from the street.

The mayor agreed to move the guard to South High School and to delay the curfew Saturday night to give them a chance to establish peace.

That night, crowds assembled on Wooster Avenue and on Akron's east side main thoroughfare, Arlington Street. The gatherings were dispersed by tear gas. Two hundred people gathered in front of Allen Cleaners on Wooster Avenue. Rocks and bottles were thrown, and there were additional reports of looting.

Sunday, July 21

The National Guard encampment moved to Akron's Rubber Bowl and was now a force of nearly a thousand soldiers. They brought in armored personnel carriers to transport soldiers up and down Wooster Avenue. A machine gun emplacement was established on Wooster Avenue.

The Curfew that had been lifted Saturday night was now re-imposed. On Sunday, there were nine firebombings and eighty-one arrests.

Ed Davis, the distinguished councilman for the third ward, was in despair. "These kids are leaderless and running wild," he said.

Monday, July 22

Black leaders announced a boycott against all white-owned businesses.

The curfew began at 10:00 p.m. There were three firebombings, including a house on Copley Road that was some distance from the center of the Wooster Avenue neighborhood. Sixty-one more arrests were made.

A community meeting was held at the Urban League. White reporters were banned from attending. The *Akron Beacon Journal* had no Black reporters to send to the meeting. Mayor Ballard met with the Civic Unity Council headed by community activist, television host, and photographer, Opie Evans.

The *Beacon Journal* editorial page opined that white Akronites were not seeing the problems of Black residents—their experience of mistreatment by police, housing discrimination, and segregated schools.

Young African Americans were saying to their elders, "For all of your patience and forbearance—where did it get you?"

The curfew emptied streets as far north as Hudson, where John Ong resided. The chairman and CEO of the B. F. Goodrich Company, Ong, along with other Hudsonites, worried that the "gangs" of Black youth might migrate their protests as far north as Hudson.

Karl Hay, a distinguished attorney at Brouse McDowell and community leader, told an interviewer that as much as he hated guns, he started carrying a pistol to his office downtown.

Tuesday, July 23

The publisher of the *Akron Beacon Journal*, Ben Maidenberg, arranged what he called a "peace conference." An eleven-man peace committee of Black leaders asked the mayor for a chance to bring the disturbances to an end.

They said the curfew had clearly become a "Black man's curfew" and asked that it be lifted.

The talks continued off and on for much of the day. By 8:00 p.m. no resolution had been reached when Ballard received news from Cleveland that Fred Ahmed Evans, head of a Black nationalist group, had led an ambush in Cleveland's Glenville neighborhood that led to the death of three Cleveland police officers and seven Black men.

1968

Ballard was reluctant to pull back any of his forces or lose any of the tools that he thought would assist in controlling the violence.

That night in the mayor's office, Ben Maidenberg asked Black leaders to stand up if they would make a commitment to do everything in their power to end the violence. Eleven men stood. Ballard gave them till 9:00 p.m. to act.

At 8:40 p.m., the city's curfew was lifted. Akron police moved out to the perimeter of the neighborhood. The National Guard stood by at the Rubber Bowl.

Homell Calhoun brought a sound truck from his Wooster Avenue record store and played music. The young people of Wooster Avenue had a street dance. And then it rained.

After six nights, fifty-seven firebombings, some four hundred arrests, and the call up of a thousand soldiers, Wooster Avenue would never be the same again.

On July 27, Mayor Ballard wrote to Dr. Edwin Lively, head of the Sociology Department at The University of Akron, asking him to convene a ten-member commission to study the direct and indirect causes of the disorder and to make recommendations aimed at preventing similar occurrences in the future.

The commission held hearings that fall and winter, and in April 1969 issued its final report.

The commission found that the disorders were not deliberately started, although there were some persons and groups who were "receptive to trouble and willing to encourage and accentuate it."

The primary cause of the disturbances, said the commission, was the "resentment of discrimination toward Black [residents] in all areas of community life." This included the aggravated compression of Black families into what had become "ghettos," which were primarily a consequence of Urban Renewal relocation in the Grant-Washington area, the University area, Cascade and Route 59. Contributing factors, according to the commission, included "anti-Semitism, personal animosities, opportunism and hoodlumism, a lot of youthful excitement."

The commission documented complaints about the failure of law enforcement officers to distinguish those Black citizens who, at considerable personal risk, were attempting to ease the tensions and disperse those who were creating them, from those who were active contributors to the disorders. Black leaders were certain that there was an excessive and indiscriminate use of tear gas, although police were convinced that the use of chemicals minimized the need for physical force.

In his summation, Dr. Lively wrote, "No human, no matter what the color of his skin or the extent of his patience, can live without the hope of accomplishments. . . . The failure to show concern about the conditions of poverty, deprivation, degradation, inequality, and discrimination is the food on which tension and hostility feed," he wrote. "Collective violence is a measure of the extent of desperation of people who see no other way to be heard."

A year after the Lively Commission report was issued, the *Beacon Journal* reviewed the minimal progress on the commission's recommendations. In April 1969, Dr. Lively said, "There has been no systematic approach to the recommendations." Mayor Ballard said, "As Rome wasn't built in a day, the issuance of a report doesn't bring about change overnight."

Mayor Ballard listed improvements in the neighborhood, such as removing debris and addressing the problem with vermin. He noted that Wooster Avenue was the only neighborhood receiving twice-weekly garbage pick-ups.

Addressing the main issue in the report—the absence of recreational opportunities for youngsters, Ballard noted that the city hired ten new recreation supervisors, invested $800,000 in a new Lane-Wooster athletic field, installed a portable swimming pool on Wooster Avenue, commenced sensitivity training for police officers, and initiated a recruitment effort for African American candidates for the police and fire departments.

Dr. Lively felt some issues had been addressed, but too many issues raised had simply been ignored. "The public at-large," he said, "has remained apathetic. No one is pushing the City Council or the Police Department." With regard to the issue of recreational opportunities, Lively bemoaned the absence of a master plan for parks that would have taken funding for parks "out of the realm of political bargaining."

Councilman Davis questioned why the mayor had failed to appoint a Human Relations Commission that would replace the Council of Civic Unity, which was founded in 1948. Ballard would not appoint a fifteen-member commission with paid staff until December 1969.

Many problems in the Wooster Avenue area remained unresolved during the 1970s as the Ohio Department of Transportation obliterated whole neighborhoods to make way for an extension of Route 59 that would be called the "Akron Innerbelt." Under Governor John Gilligan, construction extended the limited-access highway only to the foot of Mill Street. His 1974 opponent, James Rhodes described the road as "Gilligan's Island." In the process, some eight hundred homes were removed, with insufficient compensation being paid to homeowners who were forced to relocate.

In 1987, funeral director Marco Sommerville, a Buchtel High School graduate and a past president of Akron's NAACP, ran for political office and was elected as the Council Representative for Ward 3, which included the entire Wooster Avenue neighborhood. He became Akron City Council President in 1999 and enjoyed fourteen years as its leader until 2013, when he was appointed Akron's Planning Director.

During his twenty-six years representing the ward, Sommerville aggressively advocated for city funds to be appropriated for development in the Wooster Avenue neighborhood. He led the initiative to re-name Wooster Avenue, "Vernon Odom Boulevard," for the fondly remembered president of the Akron Urban League. He developed housing projects like City View and Roulhac Circle and led revitalization efforts in the Summit Lake neighborhood. Sommerville was also an early proponent of police oversight calling for the appointment of a police auditor.

Investments in the neighborhood produced multiple "anchor" organizations. The Akron Zoo invested more than $100 million in infrastructure improvements over a twenty-year period. The City invested $5 million into a re-visioned Lane Field. The Akron Metropolitan Housing Authority was the agent for a federally funded "Hope VI" program Edgewood Homes, which built three hundred housing units, apartments and single-family homes at a cost of $50 million.

In 2003, the Helen Arnold Community Learning Center became the city and school district's first newly built school and community center at a cost of $8 million, joining with the Akron Urban League to share the property with its new headquarters that led to Akron's award as an "All-America City" in 2008. In all, over $200 million were invested in the Wooster Avenue area between 2000 and 2024.

Akron has always had the capacity to heal itself—whether the issues were related to public education, commerce, or social justice. In 1994, a successful dialogue on issues of race brought the *Akron Beacon Journal* a Pulitzer Prize for its series, "A Question of Color." This was followed by the Coming Together project, a community initiative launched to engage African Americans and white residents alike in conversations in churches, in schools, and in the community at large.

Akron earned a national reputation that caught the attention of the president of the United States. In 1997, Akron was chosen to host President Clinton's first Town Meeting on Race at E. J. Thomas Hall, which was televised nationally.

Today, the discussion of inequality—of race, gender identity, or national origin has changed. One question is, can our local economy succeed if we do NOT include all residents? In 2018, the Greater Akron Chamber launched a vision for the community's future, "Elevate Greater Akron," following a year-long study by the city, the county, the Chamber, and its foundation partners. Notable among the goals of this initiative is "economic inclusion and opportunity."

More than ever in our history, employers are challenged to view the entire community when making decisions about hiring and overcoming a past that has been a rocky road in accepting people of all sexes, races, and gender identities as equals in employment. It is a conversation that Akron has been having over three different centuries.

Bibliography

Books

Giffels, David, and Steve Love. *Wheels of Fortune: The Story of Rubber in Akron*. The University of Akron Press, 1999.

Grismer, Karl H. *Akron and Summit County*. Akron: Summit County Historical Society, 1952.

Knepper, George W. *Summit's Glory. Sketches of Buchtel College and The University of Akron*, The University of Akron Press, 1990.

Unpublished Manuscripts

Akron Committee for a Community Audit, *The Akron Community Audit: A Study of Discrimination in Akron, Ohio*. 1952. https://archive.org/details/the-akron-community-audit.

City of Akron Department of Planning & Urban Development, "Akron Redevelopment Program Project Data Completed as of Oct. 1979, prepared for Mayor John Ballard: Area of Project, Project Costs, Relocation Grants, Families and Individuals Relocated, Parcels Acquired and Other Data." Unpublished manuscript in the library of the City of Akron Department of Planning.

Lively, Edwin. "The Report of the Akron Commission on Civil Disorders." April 1969. https://www.akronlibrary.org/images/SpecCol/Akron_Commission_on_Civil_Disorders.pdf.

McClain, Shirla Robinson. "The Contributions of Blacks in Akron, 1825–1975." PhD diss., The University of Akron, 1975. https://www.akronlibrary.org/images/SpecCol/Contribution_-Blacks_Akron.pdf.

Periodicals

Akron Beacon Journal, July 18, 1968–July 24, 1968. Over seven days, a team of more than twelve reporters and writers covered the civil disturbances on Wooster Avenue and South Arlington Street. This account draws on more than seventy stories published during this seven-day period.

Twombly, Matthew. "1968: The Year That Shattered America." *Smithsonian*, January/February 2018.

Brett, Regina, and Jim Dettling. "Beacon Journal wins the Pulitzer Prize for Service." *Akron Beacon Journal*, April 13, 1994, A1.

Dyer, Bob. "Akron Speaks Up." *Akron Beacon Journal*, December 4, 1997, A1.

Gaynor, Donn. "Lively Report: What's Happened in Year?" *Akron Beacon Journal*, April 22, 1970, D1.

Websites

Elevate Greater Akron, https://elevategreaterakron.org/our-plan/#findings

Other

Hay, Karl. Interview with author. July 2001. https://www.summitmemory.org/digital/collection/p17124coll16/id/16/rec/1.

Ong, John. Interview with author. July 2001. https://www.summitmemory.org/digital/collection/p17124coll16/id/10.

Investments in the neighborhood since the year 2000 were calculated by the author from public sources including the *Akron Beacon Journal.*

\ **22**

Black Intracity Migration to Maple Valley and the Copley Corridor in the 1960s

Shaneen A. Harris

The arts replicate life and have illustrated the Black migration experience on its quest for upward mobility in literary works such as Lorraine Hansberry's *A Raisin in the Sun* (1959) and television shows such the *Jeffersons* (1975–1985) and other sitcoms. Each has depicted what is commonly called "The Great Middle American Dream Machine," the desire for financial prosperity and an ability to gain a higher social status.[1] This dream has been a nagging in the guts of many Black people throughout American history. In Akron, this transition from lower class to middle or high class was symbolized by living in Maple Valley, a.k.a. "Sugar Hill." It was so named because the perception was Black people could not afford to live there. They could only afford sugar.

Demographics of Maple Valley

During the 1960s and 1970s Black people in Akron were achieving financial gains as white- and blue-collar workers. However, finances were not the only obstacles to upward mobility. The lack of available housing created by the 1960s urban renewal projects, redlining practices, the desire for ethnic communities, and the growing migration of Black people to the city were also impediments. According to US Census records Akron's Black population increased by 28 percent from 37,636 in 1960 to 48,205 in 1970. In that same decade, the overall population of the city fell more than five percent, from 290,351 to 275,425.

Ironically, some of these obstacles along with the civil events of the 1960s would facilitate bulk, not incremental, Black migration into Maple Valley. According to the Census, the Black population in Maple Valley's Copley Road Corridor increased from one person in 1960 to 646 people in 1970.

Urban renewal could account for some of the growth in the Black population in this area. However, a fuller explanation is much more varied and best stated by those who experienced it.

Why They Migrated

"We made a lot of moves. We lived in a lot of apartments, from Perkins Street, to Raymond, to Cedar Court." When asked what drove the moves, Veeda Edwards replied, "My mom and dad were poor. We probably moved every two to three years." But being in poverty did not prevent them from having dreams when it came to home ownership. "We wanted a house; all the other places were apartments." Both her parents worked to provide a better life. Her dad, Rudolph Sewell worked as a meat cutter at Case Egg & Poultry and a mail driver for Ohio Bell Telephone Company. Her mom, Ruby worked as a housekeeper at Brown Derby Inn and Restaurant, for a doctor, and at Ohio Bell Telephone Company. Her parents' efforts paid off, and their dream materialized in the 1960s when her family moved on to "The Hill" to 556 Wildwood Avenue. This would be the first and only house Rudolph and Ruby owned.

Urban renewal rapidly displaced many families, white and blue collar, forcing them to leave their homes and take whatever they could find. Often multiple temporary dwellings were needed before families again found homes they could call their own. Such was the case with Carla Moore, whose family originally lived on Douglas Street. Her father, Robert, was military, in the Pacific Theater, and an educator who would later teach at Firestone High School and serve as

Assistant Principal of her alma mater, Buchtel High School. Her mother, Doris, was an X-Ray Technician at Edwin Shaw. Due to urban renewal, she says "We had to move fast." Fast meant moving from her birth home to the Akron's public project, Ardella Homes and Lodge, created to house Black World War II veterans.[2] Moore recalls that her parents' plight mirrored that of many other Black families displaced by urban renewal, regardless of their profession or education level. "We were surrounded by what turned out to be all these Black professionals. Looking back, retrospectively sort of a who's who of Black professionals in Akron." From Ardella her family would reside with an aunt in Edgewood. They, like many, had to cohabitate with another family in order save money, due to the high price of homes driven by availability shortages. They would and were able to purchase a home in West Akron on Packard.

"We just wanted to move from the neighborhood." Like many African Americans, her family originally migrated from the South and came to Akron looking for opportunities in 1932. Her father, James, found work at B. F. Goodrich, and her mother, Eula, in a doctor's office. They would initially reside at 701 Bowery Street. Sallie (Rowland) Christian has fond memories of playing holes; shooting marbles into holes; kids being dared to swing across the canal; racing bicycles; watching Tap, a neighborhood boxer, train; and fishing with her dad on family vacations. But the neighborhood was changing. The neighbors were still mostly homeowners, but a different class of worker mentality was developing, and the neighborhood was declining, according to Christian. A lot of the nicer homes and neighborhoods were in West Akron.

Racism might have been an external ill, but colorism was an internal one that was faced by many, including Christian. "My parents wanted a different experience for me. There were nicer homes, and the neighborhood had a little more of a mix." Her family left Bowery Street in 1958 and purchased a home at 736 Diagonal Road, less than a mile away from the mansion of Simon Perkins, the city founder, and the home of John Brown, the abolitionist.

Job opportunities brought Elton L. Henderson and Ora Dee Moore-Henderson to Kipling Street on the south side of Akron from Selma, Alabama, in 1945. They initially stayed with family members; however, their growing family necessitated moving from the twin plex, says Elder Josephine Henderson-Wilson, the eldest of the eight children. Her father already had family living in Maple Valley. Her mom wanted a home near family. She found it in 1960 on Dover Avenue.

The area was considered more expensive, and Henderson-Wilson could not understand how the family of ten would live "on the hill." But she says her mom "knew how to stretch," and her father would drive back to familiar areas to shop. Or they would get things on discount, like day-old bread from the Wonder

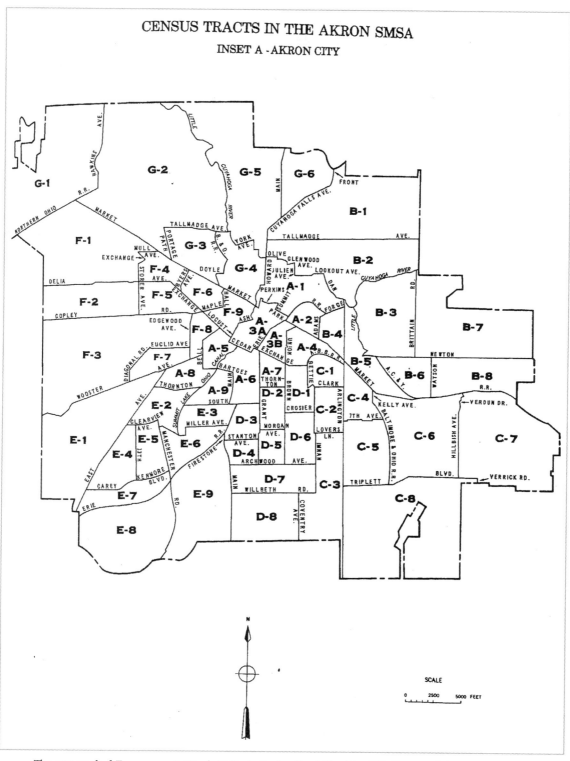

The area marked F-2 represents Maple Valley's Copley Road Corridor. U.S. Bureau of the Census, "Akron, Ohio: Standard Metropolitan Statistical Area," U.S. Censuses of Population and Housing: 1960. Census Tracts. Final Report PHC(1)-2. \ U.S. Government Printing Office, census.gov.

Bread thrift store. Her father would provide, despite layoffs, to ensure they kept their home.

Once Black families made it to "Sugar Hill" many stayed there. The parents of each of the above-mentioned interviewees would reside in their homes in West Akron for the duration of their lives, having achieved their piece of the American Dream.

Black Businesses

Tammy Monroe's family called Madison Avenue home in 1965. She too recalls the community being very connected. She affectionately remembers getting treats from Mrs. Snyder's plum tree. She indicated that, "they knew each other as family." She says, "If we were poor, we didn't know it." Her dad, Clyde Gray, worked for the Akron Meat packing company and her mom, Willie Maude, worked at St. Thomas. Both were heavily in the union and had migrated from the South, originally residing on Mays Street, near the Innerbelt.

By the 1970s Monroe, like Edwards, recalls not only her immediate but extended family living in Maple Valley. It provided a chance for families to live closer again and create their ethnic community. That community included the possibility for entrepreneurship.

Urban renewal, relocation of rubber company productions, and riots had destroyed or crippled Black business communities in other parts of Akron, but "Copley Road was thriving. The resources were there. Maybe that's why people came," says Monroe.

Dr. Ernest Ivan Stewart established his dental practice, originally located on Wooster Avenue in 1961, at 734 Copley Road in 1962. Stewart was not only a pioneer in Black business on Copley Road, but he and his family would also be pioneers for Black families in housing in the corridor.[3] A growing legacy of Black-owned businesses would develop in the area.

In 1963, Maple Valley was the home to Mapp's Service Station at 1261 Copley Road.

By 1964, Inetha Hodges would open A Touch of Paris Coiffures at 539 East Avenue, which still exists today.[4] Vel's Discount opened its doors at what was once 964 Copley Road and LeAnn Davis established Open Pantry convenience store (now Mr. Pantry). Today, the Copley Corridor continues to be a hub for Black business opportunities with Black hair salons, restaurants, and galleries.

Black Intracity Migration

Charles W. Mapp operated two west side service stations, one at 1210 Diagonal Road and this one at 1261 Copley Road. His stations were featured in the August 31, 1963 edition of the *Akronite*, an African American newspaper published in Akron. \ Opie Evans Papers, Archives and Special Collections, University Libraries, The University of Akron.

Black Churches

The Black church has been at the very heart of the Black community. Not only was it a place for spiritual connections, but it was also a space for social interaction and civil organization. Black churches established and migrated with their constituents. For instance, Reverend J. Milton Burrell and his wife Doris had a home on Peerless Avenue in 1958 and established Prince of Peace Baptist Church not far away at 844 Garth Avenue.[5]

In 1963, on the south side of Akron, Rev. Howard B. Washington led the congregation of Mount Olive Baptist Church at 637 Coburn Street.[6] Reverend Washington and Rabbi Morton M. Applebaum of Temple Israel came together to reflect the communal relationship that had existed between white people

Prince of Peace Baptist Church in 1979. \ Photo by Ron Kuner. *Akron Beacon Journal* Collection, Summit Memory, Akron-Summit County Public Library.

and Black people. They prayed for the communities and participated in the civil rights march to downtown Akron on March 15, 1965.[7] Not just a pastor, Washington was innovative, launching a weekly radio broadcast as well. Mount Olive Baptist Church would move from Coburn Street to its current location at 1180 Slosson Street on April 16, 1967.

Buchtel High School

America was newly off the heels of 1954's *Brown v. Board of Education*, 1957's Little Rock Nine, and 1960's Greensboro Four and Ruby Bridges. For Henderson-Wilson, the shift from a Black to a white school was alienating. She does not remember being welcomed to the community by white people nor engaging with them much in school. Her grandparents' stories of drinking from colored fountains and learning to be "cooperative" around white people, left her unsure of how to act or interact outside of the Black community. Initially, she kept to herself; however, she found community with other Black students at Buchtel.

Small percentages of Black students at Buchtel had not prevented their participation in choirs, sports, or student government. Nor did it impede great achievements. Black students were represented in various areas of leadership. Henderson-Wilson shared pride when her classmate Lynnette Miller became the first Black cheerleader. In 1963, Buchtel had a Black King B, Homecoming King. Edwards still speaks with pride at how her cousin Gwendolyn (Gwen) Corley in 1966 became Buchtel's first Black Homecoming Queen.

Black Intracity Migration

Moore remembers it being communal. "It was sort of like the neighborhood and the school became one and the same." Her class "was one of the most cohesive classes, just connected, white, Black even to this day." White students and Black students were "defying racial stereotypes, and pushing the envelope forming friendships and interracial dating."

If the school and the community were the same, the varied experiences seen at the school would also be reflected in the community. In its simplest state, it is a comradery forged from the empathy of what is perceived as similar plights. Redlining documents show how between 1935 and 1940 Jewish people experienced discrimination similar to that experienced by Black people. The D4 district (Raymond, Bowery, Summit Lake) in Figure 8 was 25 percent Jewish and 35 percent "Negro." It was described as a "declining district, heavily populated with low-class Jews." Compare this to the descriptions of A7 and A8 current Maple Valley and Fairlawn as "most desirable," "Clean," and full of "Pride of Ownership," which recorded 0 percent for Negros and Foreign Families Nationalities.[8]

Black and Jewish people have bonded for civil liberties and equities throughout history, as they would again in the 1960s Civil Rights era. In its most complex form, their differences would be highlighted. The desire of Jewish people to maintain their ethnic community and education would hasten the separation. Though the 1960s forged bonds, it also heightened tensions and fostered the lack of trust and fear.

Why They Left

New School

Families of Maple Valley were able to stay in what has been described as a communal state throughout the early to mid-1960s. However, the neighborhood's utopian existence would be tested. They could neither exist in a vacuum nor in a place devoid of change. By 1965, Buchtel High School had more than 40 percent Black students. There are many contributors to this shift.

The first is the construction of Firestone High School in 1963, which was located in northwest Akron. The immediate impact of Firestone High School was not felt on the Maple Valley community. The mix of Black and white students did not much change at Buchtel. The relationship between Black students and many of their white classmates was palatable and supportive. Moore recalls white classmates standing in solidarity with her regarding civil rights issues.

Ethnic Community

In the 1960s, more Black people began moving to the areas in and around the Maple Valley, which also had a healthy Jewish community. Initially, the slow influx did not produce a readily noticeable antagonist response, lending to the communal feel so many experienced. The community had accepted Black people as guests and members to the Jewish Center Pool when other organizations such as the YMCA and YWCA had refused.[9] Not only were Black people received at the center, but West Akron communities would also host Akron's first Black golf club, Tire Town Golf Club, at J. E. Good Park Golf Course, as early as 1952.[10] In addition, when the concerns of Black people over hiring practices for a grocery store were voiced, it was their white neighbors who worked with owners to come to a resolution.

However, in *A Century of Adjustment: A History of the Akron Jewish Community, 1865–1975*, Helga Eugenie Kaplan notes that the inverse growth rate of Black people to white people during the 1950s and 1960s was felt in the schools and amplified existing concerns for the ability to maintain a Jewish education and ethnic community. Further, the race relations crack that had been weaving its way through the nation found its way to the Maple Valley communities. The 1968 Wooster riots not only destroyed many Black businesses. It also strained relationships between Black and white neighbors.

Civil Unrest / Fear

The 1960s brought hope for Black people through the Civil Rights, Voting Rights, and Fair Housing Acts. However, it also brought a lot of despair. Kennedy's assassination agitated relations between Black people and white people, and King's assassination tipped Black Akronites over the edge, said Henderson-Wilson. Christian recalls, "Whites didn't know what to expect of Blacks; some whites appeared threatened, felt Blacks were trying to take over." Kaplan documents the shifting relationship between the Eastern European Jewish communities and the Black communities and the heightened tension this caused in the mid- to late 1960s. She cites a Jewish leader who stated they once had a "seat at the table" during the early to mid-1960s. But by the 1970s they had been completely isolated.

White Flight

Added tension and a new school in a desirable area in northwest Akron would lead to white flight from the Maple Valley neighborhood. But this also

Black Intracity Migration

created more available housing. The 1960 US Census shows area F2 in Figure 1 contained 5,619 white residents. By 1970 that number would drop to 5,099.

Likewise, by the mid-1960s Buchtel High School's senior class size would reduce by approximately 50 percent to just over 250 students. However, the number of Black students would increase more than 300 percent, from just over 30 to over 100 by the mid-1960s. Firestone would boast a class size of approximately 410 students. Less than 0.3 percent of Firestone students were Black.

Many homes like Moore's were being sold by Jewish owners who wanted to reclaim their ethnic communities. In a neighborhood where most Black people felt they could only afford sugar, some would acquire "Sugar Hill" at half the value as the existing homeowners marked down prices to facilitate a more rapid exodus.

Conclusion

Akron's 1960s urban renewal project can be credited with displacing and causing the migration of Black Akronites between 1960 and 1970. However, it alone does not account for the influx of Black people into the Maple Valley area. This migration can also be credited to the natural desire for better homes and neighborhoods and the increased availability of homes caused by the departure of the white community. No matter how it started, the Maple Valley community afforded the opportunity for success so many Black people had desired, whether they migrated from the southern United States or the south side of Akron. It did so with a communal grace that allowed it to be reflective of how relationships across ethnic boundaries could exist. However, like so many communities, it was plagued by civil unrest, fear, and a desire to maintain ethnic communities and education systems reflective of those communities. Maple Valley is constantly reinventing itself, showing its pride, its collective strength, and its desire to endure. It is still a vibrant community for Black business, church, education, and most of all, family.

Notes

1. For more about this, see Lynn Berk, "The Great Middle American Dream Machine," *Journal of Communication* 27, no 3 (September 1977), 27–31.

2. Warren Louis Woolford, "A Geographical Appraisal of Major Distributional Changes in the Akron, Ohio Black Population, 1930–1970." Master's thesis, University of Akron, 1974.

3. Seyma Bayram, "Beloved Papa: Akron Dentist, Veteran Contributed to Polio Vaccine Research," *Akron Beacon Journal* (December 30, 2020), A1.

4. "Inertha Hodges and Petty Duhart." University Libraries Archives and Special Collections Digital Collections, The University of Akron, https://cdm15960.contentdm.oclc.org/digital/collection/p15960coll3/id/93/rec/214

5. "Prince of Peace Baptist Church." University Libraries Archives and Special Collections Digital Collections, The University of Akron, https://cdm15960.contentdm.oclc.org/digital/collection/p15960coll3/id/28436/rec/36

6. "Rev. Howard B. Washington." University Libraries Archives and Special Collections Digital Collections, The University of Akron, https://cdm15960.contentdm.oclc.org/digital/collection/p15960coll3/id/215/rec/113

7. "History." Mt. Olive Baptist Church, http://www.teammtobc.org/History.html

8. To view and interact with this map, see Robert K. Nelson, LaDale Winling, et al., "Mapping Inequality: Redlining in New Deal America," ed. Robert K. Nelson, *American Panorama: An Atlas of United States History*, 2023, https://dsl.richmond.edu/panorama/redlining

9. Helga Eugenie Kaplan, "A Century of Adjustment: A History of the Akron Jewish Community, 1865–1875." Ph.D. dissertation, Kent State University, 1978, 464.

10. Jim Mackinnon, "Tiretown Golf Club Celebrates New Home," *Akron Beacon Journal* (May 29, 2022), 1B.

\ **23**

The Great Transition

Remembering the Akron Renaissance

Stephen H. Paschen

Approaching downtown Akron in my car on a gray day in early January 1975, I was nervous and enthusiastic about my first day as a landscape architect for the city. As I exited Route 8 and continued onto Buchtel Avenue, the smell of burnt rubber hit me but was mingled with another more pleasant aroma. Was it baking bread? Yes, as I drove through The University of Akron campus, the scent of freshly baked bread nearly masked the pungent, acrid stink of rubber. That distinctive combination, a by-product of B. F. Goodrich making tires and the Wonder Bread Bakery turning out fresh baked goods, became a familiar daily experience. My new colleagues in the City of Akron Planning Department explained that in this city, the stench of tires being manufactured was "the smell of money." I was not surprised by the rubber smell. After all, this was the Rubber City. Akron's rubber companies—including giants Goodyear, Firestone, Goodrich, and General—employed more than 34,000 Akron workers in 1975.[1]

However, Akron's reputation as the Rubber City was faltering in the 1970s. Foreign competition, aging factory buildings, and rising energy prices were taking a toll on the rubber companies, and rampant inflation in this era neutralized recent wage gains by rubber workers. An *Akron Beacon Journal* article concluded

347

that "Akron's Rubber Heyday is Gone Forever."[2] City leaders, urban planners, and a growing number of private stakeholders slowly realized that for Akron to thrive in the future, it would have to become a different kind of city.

Living in Akron

Akron was daunting to a small-town arrival like me, but I was excited that the city provided so many new activities and experiences that could only be found in a larger urban area. Soon I learned that there were beautiful city parks, a metro parks system, and the newly created Cuyahoga Valley National Recreation Area. Akron had pleasant leafy neighborhoods like Goodyear Heights, Firestone Park, Ellet, Kenmore, North Hill, and the two I would call home: Middlebury and Wallhaven. I had never lived in a city this big. The streets seemed busy, teeming with traffic, but I soon learned that it did not take long to drive anywhere in Akron.

For the first time in my life, professional sports teams were nearby, and as a lifelong baseball fan, it was easy to adopt the Cleveland Indians as my favorite

The author wearing a headband and approaching the batter's box in a 1981 softball game played at Summit Lake ballfields. Weekday recreational league ballgames were going on every evening in parks all over Akron. \ Photo courtesy of the author.

The Great Transition

American League team. The team was mediocre, which was no change for me, having followed the National League's Chicago Cubs while growing up in rural Illinois. Even more importantly, organized recreational softball and baseball leagues were popular and playing fields abundant in the city's many parks. One year I played on six different softball teams spanning the summer and fall seasons. In the winter, I played racquetball, volleyball, and bowled. I took up cross-country skiing, made easy by affordable equipment and abundant places to ski, such as scenic Metroparks trails and accommodating local golf courses.

I inherited a love of history and museums from my mother, who was a teacher. There were three historic house museums in Akron—Perkins Stone Mansion (1837), Hower House (1871), and Stan Hywet Hall and Gardens (1915), as well as nearby Hale Farm and Village (a living history museum)—more choices available to me than in any previous place I had lived. Akron's history was rich and fascinating, and I was keen to explore it.

Leadership in the community was a vestige of Akron's prosperous past. Rubber company executives, bankers, and businessmen, along with influential local journalists like John S. Knight had led for most of the twentieth century and several of these people were still around when I arrived. These leaders built a city that became home for thousands of immigrants and migrants, rubber workers toiling around-the-clock shifts, attractive neighborhoods and parks, a major university, and a rich cultural landscape.

Despite my first impression of bustling traffic and big buildings, I learned that Akron's downtown was declining and had already been the main focus of redevelopment for a generation. The streets were dotted with restaurants (some were only open for lunch) and retail, but a closer look revealed some establishments were on their last legs. There was a new hotel recently built on Cascade Plaza, but no other hotel remained downtown after the Portage (1969) and Mayflower (1971) closed. A few fading low-rent housing hotels hung on, not contributing much to livening up the streets. No grocery stores remained; the closest were just outside the downtown by this time. Two or three older theaters recently transformed into adult movie venues, a handful of small bars, and even a couple of old-style burlesque houses were scattered down the streets among the retail shops. Vacant buildings stood in nearly every block, with more appearing all the time. After dark, most workers left the downtown for homes in the surrounding neighborhoods and suburbs.

Two big downtown department stores, O'Neil's and Polsky's, stood on South Main Street directly across from each other just a block away from the Municipal Building where I worked. Conveniently, during the next few years I could do all my Christmas shopping on lunch hours. A few dime stores, on which

I depended for a quick lunch or small everyday necessities, lingered on Main Street. I enjoyed the aging but gorgeous Civic Theatre and the iconic Peanut Shoppe on Main Street, which reminded me of the caramel corn shop in my Illinois hometown.

There was ample evidence of how and why the downtown was declining. Rolling Acres Mall was just opening the year I arrived, joining Summit Mall and Chapel Hill Mall, existing fully enclosed shopping malls. Popular malls with their massive parking lots were drawing retail, restaurants, and entertainment from downtown as well as from older neighborhood business districts and strip malls built in the 1960s and 1970s.

Gradually I realized all of this was a trend in progress, getting a little worse all the time. It would be a decade or more before the decline in some blocks would begin to reverse. When I joined the Planning Department design staff, our work focused heavily on revitalizing the downtown, but we also prepared plans for restoring and revitalizing neighborhoods and neighborhood business districts, parks, and other public spaces. Oddly, all of my five design studio mates— landscape architects, architects, and urban planners—were recent arrivals from other states. None of us were born or raised in Akron, and at first, we knew little about its history. It would take time to get to know the city better, but we believed we could play a part in its future.

Each workday morning, I parked my car in a lot on Summit Street next to a long narrow building featuring a sign that said, "Garlando's Produce," adjacent to the former Quaker Oats complex at Mill Street and Broadway. When I started my job downtown, the Quaker buildings were being adapted for use as a shopping and restaurant complex. Landscape design for the project was provided by my design staff colleagues. When Quaker Square opened later that year— with its many specialty shops, restaurants, and offices—it was an immediate hit. The success of this adaptive reuse project increased interest in the restoration of handsome older buildings and caught the attention of the design staff.

Soon, other deteriorating or vacant downtown buildings were considered for restoration or adaptive reuse, including the Portage Hotel, YMCA, YWCA, Gothic Building, Ohio Building, United Building, Polsky's, O'Neil's, Akron Armory, the Mayflower Hotel, and a slew of other smaller storefront structures. We designers produced numerous drawings proposing restoration of these downtown buildings. Some of these ideas came to fruition, but others did not capture the interest of developers or financial backers. But it was the beginning of a nationwide trend in preservation of architectural heritage.

Vestiges of Urban Renewal

The imprint of urban renewal, the city's first effort to stem the tide of deterioration, was visible in downtown Akron. A recently reconfigured block anchored by the iconic First National Tower (built in the 1930s) felt like the center of the city. New buildings surrounded a landscaped, paved, open public space called Cascade Plaza, but I had no clue as to why *cascade* was used in its name. I learned the reference was to the Ohio & Erie Canal, once the primary transportation and shipping lifeline of the city, now buried underneath the plaza and reduced to functioning as a drainageway and overflow storm sewer.

Further south, just beyond the still-active B. F. Goodrich complex, tracts of land cleared during urban renewal were now being redeveloped as Opportunity Park, a multi-use area blending light industry with new multifamily residences and parkland. My earliest work for the Planning Department was streetscape design (landscaping and decorative pavements) in Opportunity Park and landscape plans for the contemporary-styled park alongside the canal surrounding the newly built Channelwood apartments.

North of Cascade Plaza were empty blocks cleared of all their older streets and buildings. This urban renewal area, dubbed "Superblock" by city leaders, was also under development in 1975. Just beyond Market Street, the canal emerged from the ground and flowed north through its ruined and abandoned locks.

Running along the west edge of the downtown was a short piece of freeway called the Innerbelt. Curiously, it was incomplete and did not provide quick access to highways in either direction. There was so little traffic on this road when I arrived in 1975 that when Akron celebrated its Sesquicentennial that summer, the roadway was closed and used as a pedestrian walkway lined with booths, food vendors, and other activities. The Innerbelt was part of a transportation plan designed and built in the previous few decades and eventually created a significant challenge to the downtown's vitality. Highways veered around the city's center, and one-way streets speeded traffic quickly through it. Annexation of large undeveloped tracts of land further away from the downtown increased city revenues, but coupled with residential migration to the suburbs, it pushed industry, business, and retail outward.

Traffic was altered once again in 1977 when the crumbling North Hill Viaduct connecting the downtown to North Hill had to be shut down due to large chunks of the bridge falling on homes and businesses in the valley below.[3] The bridge was demolished and a new Y-shaped bridge designed to funnel traffic from twin one-way downtown streets—Broadway (running north) and High Street (running south)—to and from North Hill. The design staff drew plans for streetscaping Perkins Street (later renamed Martin Luther King Boulevard) which connected the new bridge (opened in 1982, it was named the All-America Bridge) to the Innerbelt and Route 8 on the east edge of the downtown.

In the city's neighborhoods during the late 1970s, we designers created plans rehabilitating neighborhood business districts in Kenmore, Copley Road, Temple Square (North Hill), Highland Square, Aster Avenue, and Goodyear Heights. Special grants and capital improvement projects refreshed many small businesses in these areas, and the design staff provided design consultation to scores of business owners. Also, many of the city's parks and neighborhood facilities were redesigned or restored by our staff, including Prentiss, Mason, Perkins, Lisa Ann, Chestnut Ridge, Hereford, Lane Field, Hardesty, Summit Lake, Margaret, Forest Lodge, Elizabeth, Talbot, Patterson, Reservoir, and Hyre. I worked on these plans during the day and played softball and baseball in many of these same parks on summer evenings.

The Beginnings of Change

American City Corporation of Columbia, Maryland, was hired by the city in 1979 to prepare a phased master plan to redevelop the downtown. The city's planners and design staff worked with American City to prepare the plan. Two years later I was one of twenty-two Akron representatives who flew to Houston, Texas, where we competed with 140 other cities for a prestigious award given by the National Municipal League. Akron was chosen as one of only ten cities to receive the title *All-America City*. The League's citation listed three accomplishments: the recent passage by Summit County voters of a measure creating the first county charter government in Ohio; completion of the magnificent community-funded Civic Theatre renovation; and implementation of the new downtown redevelopment plan we created.[4]

Many Akronites were baffled in the early 1980s when a new park was built on Lock Two of the Ohio and Erie Canal in a neglected area of the downtown. Lock Two Park was the first city park purposely designed to educate visitors about canal history. The design staff prepared landscape plans for the park, which was situated behind deteriorating structures on South Main Street. This park, with its full-scale replica of a canal boat, was among the last projects I worked on for the Planning Department.

City leaders and downtown civic groups began to consider vacant office buildings and factories as potentially useful for other purposes. In 1982, the city's first business *incubator* was established in a building previously occupied by a steel company behind E. J. Thomas Performing Arts Hall on the campus of the

The Great Transition   **353**

University of Akron. Initially, sixteen fledgling businesses were established there at favorable leasing rates. In the coming years, the incubator grew and migrated to a few other downtown buildings, giving new life to old structures and districts while helping many small companies take hold in the community.[5]

There was more visible downtown development activity during the 1980s. The Ocasek state office building replaced the old Akron Armory in the government sector and was connected by a skyway to the Municipal Building across the street. The YWCA building at the intersection of Bowery and High Streets was renovated for offices, a health club, and a new adjoining parking deck built. The Delaware Building on South Main Street was renovated and became the Huntington Bank Building. Across the street from Quaker Square, the former Nobil Shoe Warehouse at Mill and Summit Streets was adaptively reused as an office building. Akron's beautiful YMCA Building was extensively remodeled into the Canal Square apartments. City leaders, downtown business groups, and newspaper editorials discussed the potential of building a downtown convention center. Sadly, both of Akron's downtown department stores, Polsky's (1978) and O'Neil's (1989) closed forever by the end of the decade.

The pace of downtown transformation began to quicken. Communication and coordination between city and county government and collaboration with the private sector greatly improved. Other entities like the Akron Regional Development Board, The University of Akron, Goals for the Greater Akron Area, Akron Urban League, Downtown Akron Association, the League of Women Voters, Keep Akron Beautiful, Akron's NAACP, and United Rubber Workers Local 9 worked together effectively to keep important projects on track.

Civic leadership in Akron began to change in the 1980s, becoming more diversified and inclusive due to Leadership Akron, a new community-based program that brought together men and women selected for their potential as community leaders. The year-long program informed selected participants about Akron's economy, history, culture, and plans for the future. Its alumni became key players in the city's revitalization. Later, in the early 1990s, I would be selected for a Leadership Akron class and eventually became the Akron history presenter in the program.

The Return of Community Pride

My working life changed in the early 1980s. I left the Planning Department and turned to part-time freelance landscape architecture while entering graduate studies in history at The University of Akron. I spent much of my time over the next few years commuting to classes. At that time, the university was still a commuter campus with streets cutting through it, large surface parking lots, and parking decks. Soon, the university took its first steps toward becoming a more attractive pedestrian campus by closing Buchtel Avenue and creating a park-like mall. While finishing my degree, I was hired as curator of the Summit County Historical Society. My workplace shifted to the Perkins Stone Mansion at Copley Road and Portage Path.

It seemed to me that community pride was on the rise. Public events like the July 4th International Festival were increasingly drawing people back downtown. During the 1980s, concerts, films, farmer's markets, summer arts festivals, holiday celebrations, and other public activities took place on Main Street and Cascade Plaza, the Akron Art Museum, Civic Theater, The University of Akron, and other venues. We also enjoyed neighborhood events like the African American Festival at Lane Field, the Highland Square Festival, the Summer Festival at the Perkins Stone Mansion on Copley Road, Victorian Faire at Hower House, and the car show at Stan Hywet Hall and Gardens. The popular Akron Arts Festival at Hardesty Park was near my home, and Ohio Ballet staged performances at Cascade Plaza and several neighborhood parks, including Forest Lodge Park in my neighborhood.

In 1986, I was among many Akron residents who got a peek inside the famous Goodyear Zeppelin Airdock when it was opened to the public for the first time in decades.[6] And while we worked on a lighter-than-air (blimps and Zeppelins) history exhibit, a colleague and I were invited to take a blimp ride. On a bright sunny afternoon, we got a rare "blimp's-eye" view of the city—a uniquely Akron experience. We observed many signs of Akron's progress along with some unhealed scars where development had not yet taken place. Goodyear blimps were a familiar sight to everyone in the community. One of my daughter's earliest memories was sitting on my shoulders one dark night looking up through our open skylight, hearing the distinctive buzz of the blimp's engines, and seeing a dazzling lightshow on the outside of a blimp that drifted directly over our house.

The End of Big Rubber

Akron's rubber industry declined relentlessly in the 1980s. General Tire ceased producing tires in 1982. By 1985, there were only 15,000 rubber workers in Akron, less than half as many as ten years earlier.[7] Then, corporate raider James Goldsmith attempted to take over Goodyear in 1986. The city rallied around the beleaguered company, which found a way to outmaneuver Goldsmith, but at great cost to the company and community. Goodrich announced in 1987 that it would no longer produce tires in Akron. Firestone announced it was moving its

The Great Transition

World Headquarters to Chicago and was acquired by Japanese company Bridgestone in 1988.

What kept me and others in Akron after the demise of Big Rubber? One reason was the feeling that the city was successfully moving beyond its halcyon rubber days. The community's public and private leadership had faced the fact that the city's once glorious rubber years could not be sustained any longer, and they worked together to forge a new path. A spirit of teamwork generated pride and momentum. As a public historian, I collaborated with a growing number of people who regarded Akron's past as an asset in building a more diverse economy and vibrant city. Another astounding development was on the horizon: baseball, my favorite sport, would contribute to Akron's renaissance.

The Renaissance Begins

The Cleveland Indians professional baseball team, which had suffered decades of losing seasons, was acquired in 1986 by Akron brothers David and Richard Jacobs. The two were tremendously successful businessmen, and under their leadership, and to my great delight, the Cleveland Indians began to build a contending team. Also, I became a fan of the Canton-Akron Indians, a minor league affiliate of the Cleveland team, which began playing their games in a modest Canton ballpark during the 1989 season. Astonishingly, the minor league team would become a catalyst for revitalizing a whole sector of downtown Akron.

Another surprising scheme in the 1980s was the idea of attracting the Philadelphia-based National Inventors Hall of Fame to relocate to Akron. In 1987, local attorney Ned Oldham approached city leaders, touting potential economic and cultural benefits to Akron should the city become the Hall of Fame's new home. Oldham convinced the city to apply and a group of like-minded leaders quickly secured commitments for a bid of $9 million. The Hall of Fame board voted to move to Akron.[8]

Much of the massive vacant Goodrich complex on South Main Street was converted into Canal Place in 1988, a fresh new location for warehousing, businesses, restaurants, artist studios, and art galleries. The University of Akron launched its "span the tracks" strategy, leasing an office building across the railroad tracks on South Broadway and acquiring in 1987 the vacant Polsky's department store and its skyway-connected parking deck. The building would be renovated to accommodate university classrooms and offices. The university also completed the Akron Polymer Science Center in 1989, a crystalline glass building that dramatically enhanced the city's skyline. Polymer research was linked to rubber's past.

Two new grassroots groups, the Ohio and Erie Canal Coalition and the Cascade Locks Park Association were formed in 1989 and began working to promote the recreational and economic benefits of restoring historic canal locks, towpaths, and buildings. Soon after I became executive director of the Summit County Historical Society in 1990, my organization began supporting these groups and hosting their meetings. An ambitious plan emerged, proposing restoration of the historic Ohio and Erie Canal towpath, creating miles of parkland, providing a greenway through existing neighborhoods, and stimulating businesses all along it. By 1994, canal groups and other community groups along the 87-mile path of the canal from Cleveland to the Ohio River assisted in the passage of state legislation creating the Ohio and Erie Canal Heritage Corridor. The historic canal corridor and the Cuyahoga Valley Recreation Area became major elements of the region's future.

The effort to draw people back downtown and other places of community pride accelerated in the late 1980s and early 1990s. Events were sprinkled all through the calendar year. In the summer there was the annual AA Founders Day (commemorating the founders of Alcoholics Anonymous), July 4 fireworks, the Akron Symphony concert on the Innerbelt, the Professional Golfers' Association (PGA) World Series of Golf at Firestone Country Club, Highland Square Festival, Portage Lakes Boat Parade, African American Festival, and the traditional late summer event: the Soap Box Derby. The Fall schedule was full as well, including events at the Akron Zoo, Stan Hwyet, Hower House, Cuyahoga Valley National Recreation Area, Hale Farm and Village, Akron Art Museum, athletic events at the Rubber Bowl, and even a Three Stooges Film Festival (featuring a world record pie fight on Main Street in front of the Civic Theater). The annual Civil War Homecoming Days at the Perkins Mansion where I was director was held on an autumn weekend, drawing our biggest crowds of the year. In winter we could attend the Professional Bowling Association's PBA Tournament of Champions, the Holiday Tree Festival (at Quaker Square), the downtown Holiday Parade, the Tuba Christmas concert at the Civic Theatre, and a multitude of cultural events on The University of Akron campus. Along with major community events there were scores of indoor and outdoor art shows, concerts, historical tours, lecture series, and other smaller events.

Charging into the Millennium

In the 1990s, The University of Akron dedicated the Paul E. Martin University Center on Fir Hill and the campus continued spreading into the downtown with the opening of a newly constructed College of Business building on South

The Great Transition

Broadway. The pedestrian skyway across the railroad tracks was restored, providing a sheltered pedestrian crossing into the downtown and running to the Polsky Building, which was crowded each day with university students, faculty, and staff. Inspired by skyways connecting buildings over streets in cities like Minneapolis, Portland, and Cincinnati, the city was planning other new covered walkways over the alleys that ran mostly north and south behind the Main Street buildings. It would eventually be possible to walk inside new skyways and through a tunnel under Main Street from the Polsky Building all the way to Cascade Plaza.

A thriving new arts community was establishing itself on South Main Street between Cedar and Exchange Streets. New art galleries, along with efforts further down Main Street (at Canal Place) were evidence that this part of the downtown was becoming a trendy area of galleries, eateries, and nightclubs. Just a few years before, this block was lined on both sides with vacant buildings. A notable survivor, the venerable Diamond Deli, a restaurant that adaptively re-used a long-closed jewelry store, had now thrived in this location for over two decades. Given the university's Polsky Building and stronger connection to the downtown there was even talk about developing student housing in and around these blocks. Already some nightclubs were opening up nearby. Just a few blocks away, Inventure Place, the spectacular new science museum and home of the National Inventors Hall of Fame, opened in July 1995 featuring interactive exhibits, fireworks, and great fanfare.[9]

Like most Akronites, I was stunned when the city began campaigning to bring the Canton-Akron Indians to Akron. Akron Mayor Don Plusquellic saw the economic potential of having a minor league team play baseball downtown. City council authorized an agreement with the team's owner in November 1994.[10] The new ballpark was beautifully designed with Lock Two Park just behind the outfield wall. Aptly named Canal Park, the striking red brick architecture was handsome and its scale was perfectly compatible with existing buildings fronting on Main Street.

My son and I stood in line with hundreds of others outside the newly completed Canal Park one snowy February morning in 1997 waiting to buy tickets for the first Aeros (the team's new name) game. Opening Day, April 10, 1997, attracted more than 9,000 fans. Spurred by the ballpark, development interest in the south downtown exploded, and soon new restaurants and nightclubs popped up in the area. Nightlife in the downtown became much more exciting than it had been in decades.

I became a downtown worker once again in 1997 when I became an archivist at The University of Akron Archives, in the university's redesigned Polsky Building. By this time the change in the downtown was extraordinary. I could work all day, walk to any of several nearby bright new restaurants for dinner, and join thousands of fans for a baseball game in the beautiful ballpark a few steps down the street.

The city was changing in exciting ways. Its economy was much stronger and more diversified than it was when I arrived in 1975. Population decline had slowed down from 14 percent in the 1970s to 6 percent in the 1980s and 3 percent in the 1990s.[11] Goodyear was still the leading employer with 4,700 workers, but now Summa Health System was close behind with 3,850 and Summit County government with 3,470.[12] The University of Akron, another large employer, had become much more visible and connected with the downtown, with a student population of 23,000 (of which rapidly increasing numbers were living on campus).[13]

In the late 1990s, community workshops were held all along the canal corridor to collect public feedback that would help identify the elements to complete the Ohio & Erie Canal Heritage Corridor management plan. The Mustill Store and house at Lock 15 and related facilities (restroom building and parking lot) were completed along with Towpath Trail extensions downtown from Locks 11 through 15 on the old waterway. The Ohio and Erie Canal not only survived, it became the backbone for new development linking the city's recreation, culture, and economy. The quality and popularity of the completed portions of the towpath provided momentum for completing the heritage corridor in the new millennium.

Beginning in 1996, downtown Akron was the focus of a big family-oriented annual event that was designed to show off the city's renaissance in the form of a community New Year's Eve Party. The celebration, called "First Night," was coordinated by the Downtown Akron Partnership (founded in 1996), which brought together private business owners, government officials, university officials, and citizens with a common goal of promoting the downtown. Many rehabilitated buildings and spaces, new businesses, and restaurants were featured as venues for performances of music, dance, magic shows, and many other attractions at this "ring in the New Year event." The star of the show was the nearly completed Canal Park, from which there was a public countdown of the last seconds of 1996 and a heralding in of the new year with a grand show of fireworks.

Akron celebrated its 175th birthday in 2000. My wife and I attended an autumn ceremony at the historic Perkins Stone Mansion in which a community time capsule buried in the porch stones fifty years earlier was unearthed and opened. It was a memorable occasion for me, a moment of reflection on having taken part in the city's renaissance as a designer, student, historian, and archivist. More than half my life I had lived, studied, and worked in Akron. Both of my

The Great Transition

children were born in Akron and attended local schools and universities. I was both a student and an employee of The University of Akron, which underwent its own renaissance.

One year in the late 1990s, I traveled to London, Ontario, to play in a vintage (Civil War-era rules) baseball tournament along with my Stan Hywet Black Stockings teammates. While there I visited the Canadian Baseball Hall of Fame and happened to meet the museum's curator. After we chatted for a few minutes, he asked, "Are you by chance from Akron, Ohio?" I said, "Yes, how did you know?" He replied, "I can tell by your accent."

Notes

1. Abe Zaidan, *Akron: Rising Toward the Twenty-First Century* (Windsor Publications, 1990), 30.

2. Pat Englehart and Peter Geiger, "Akron's Rubber Heyday is Gone Forever," *Akron Beacon Journal*, March 16, 1975. Unless otherwise noted, newspapers are cited from digital versions through Newspapers .com.

3. Mark Faris, "2-foot Hole Halts All Viaduct Traffic," *Akron Beacon Journal*, February 15, 1977.

4. "Welcome to the All-America City: It's Official: Akron Shares National honor," *Akron Beacon Journal*, April 13, 1975.

5. Marilyn Geewax, "Akron Launches Plan to 'Hatch' New Businesses," *Akron Beacon Journal*, July 28, 1982.

6. Larry Pantages, "We Expect to Be the Winner," *Akron Beacon Journal*, September 13, 1986.

7. Steve Love and David Giffels. *Wheels of Fortune: The Story of Rubber in Akron* (University of Akron Press, 1999), 185.

8. Zaidan, 43.

9. "Inventure '95: Celebrate the Place," *Akron Beacon Journal*, July 9, 1995.

10. Jim Quinn, "AA Tribe Agrees to 20 Years in Akron," *Akron Beacon Journal*, November 11, 1994.

11. Frances McGovern, *Written on the Hills: The Making of the Akron Landscape* (University of Akron Press, 1996), 210.

12. Love and Giffels, 332.

13. "Total UA Enrollment, Fall Semesters 1997–2018," The University of Akron website, accessed March 25, 2023, https://www.uakron.edu/ir/docs/HistoricalEnrollment_TotalSince1997.pdf.

\ **24**

The Akron Sound

David Giffels

It began in the radio, when the radio was a piece of furniture in virtually every Ohio household, a portal to worlds unknown. It began in the voice of Alan Freed, an eager young announcer playing music that had never been heard on the airwaves and giving it a name:

Rock 'n' roll.

That phrase introduced one of the most vibrant cultural movements of the twentieth century, influencing and defining everything from sexuality to race relations to linguistics to technology to the amount of denim one might include in one's wardrobe.

And its voice owed everything to Akron.

Alan Freed began his radio career in the Youngstown area and he popularized the phrase "rock 'n' roll" in Cleveland, but it was his stint in between, working at Akron's WAKR in the late 1940s, that proved pivotal. While here, he discovered the newly emergent rhythm and blues style and began to push the boundaries he would bust wide open a short time later.

From Freed's 1945 arrival on Main Street through Devo's 2021 nomination for the Rock and Roll Hall of Fame, Akron has held a significant presence in the landscape of pop music and its larger culture. The city's homegrown artists and their music represent an important part of our civic identity. As a medium-sized, relatively unglamorous locale in what much of the larger world thinks of as

360

The Akron Sound

"flyover country," Akron has always carefully fostered and valued its ambassadors to the world at large. Freed's Akron story is as important to the story of American popular music as it is to the story we tell about ourselves.

He was born Aldon James Freed in Western Pennsylvania in 1921. The family moved several times over the next dozen years before settling in Salem, Ohio. "Al J," as he was known before eventually settling on "Alan," developed an early interest in music, listening to swing and big band on the radio and teaching himself to play trombone on an instrument handed down from an uncle. After enrolling at Ohio State University, Freed discovered the campus radio station and, as he later told a biographer, "That was it. I was gone!" Following a stint in the army, from which he received a medical discharge shortly before the outbreak of World War II, Freed attended broadcasting school in Youngstown then landed a newscasting job at the tiny WKST Radio in New Castle, Pennsylvania.

An ambitious self-promoter, he soon talked his way into a full-time job at the much larger WKBN in Youngstown, where he began announcing news and sports in 1943. He lasted less than two years at the station, and while accounts vary about where he went next, it was in that spell that he chanced to meet S. Bernard Berk, who had founded WAKR in Akron in 1940. Berk recognized Freed's talent, offered him a job, and in June 1945, Freed walked into the studio in the First National Tower on South Main Street. Radio would never be the same.

Freed began his WAKR career as the play-by-play announcer for University of Akron sports, but two months into his tenure, the night disc jockey failed to show, and Freed was enlisted to take the microphone and spin records. Berk knew a good thing when he heard it and, as Freed later said, "He fired the other guy and gave me the job."

At age twenty-four, Freed became the host of "Request Revue," a call-in show that played jazz and popular music. His popularity skyrocketed, and by 1947 "Request Revue" was the station's top-rated show. Freed was a local star. His ambition continued to surge, both for career advancement and musical discovery. He was growing tired of the big bands whose performances he often emceed live in the ballroom of downtown's Mayflower Hotel, gravitating toward the more adventurous edges of jazz. The hotshot deejay soon discovered the allure of rhythm and blues music, a style previously associated with Black culture but gaining in popularity with white teenagers.

Freed's popularity and ego led to growing tension with station owner Berk. As the deejay demanded more money, Berk rebuffed him and tried to put him in his place. Freed brashly cut a deal with a local promoter to launch a new program on station WADC, directly across the street from WAKR, and in the same time slot as "Request Revue."

But Freed's contract included a no-compete clause, prohibiting him from broadcasting from any radio station within seventy-five miles for one year if he left WAKR. A court battle ensued, and Freed sidestepped the radio competition restriction by taking a job with a television station—Cleveland's WXEL—until his banishment ended. In February 1951, Alan Freed went on air at Cleveland's WJW, dubbed himself "The King of the Moondoggers," and began spinning the music he proclaimed "rock 'n' roll."

• • •

Alan Freed was a pioneer in a grassroots American revolution, as R&B and rock 'n' roll traveled through the airwaves and into the bedrooms and basements of young people who sang into hairbrushes, shook their hips in the mirror, plucked new sounds on department-store guitars, and looked around their neighborhoods for like-minded souls.

Born in Akron in 1934, Ruby Nash was a teenager attending Central High School when Freed's influence took over the region. The new sound he promoted led to one of the most significant events in American cultural history, the Moondog Coronation Ball, held March 21, 1952, at the Cleveland Arena, considered the first-ever rock concert. A crowd composed mostly of young Black music fans overwhelmed the venue's 10,000-person capacity, causing police and fire officials to eventually pull the plug, but there would be no closing the floodgates.

Teenagers across the region were energized, and while Nash's influences may have been tamer—the shy, soft-spoken girl was drawn to the likes of Nat King Cole, Ella Fitzgerald, and Cab Calloway—her love of singing coincided with the sudden rise of new stars who looked like her and suggested the glimmer of possibilities for an African American teen from Akron.

After graduating from Central and taking a job at O'Neil's department store, Nash began performing at talent shows at the Akron Community Center on East Market Street. She put together various groups, entering contests, but never won until one night in 1961 when she sang in a group with her sister and two friends. In the audience that night were members of a singing group called the Feilos. The all-male quartet had been trying to get a career off the ground, without success. Nash's performance sparked an inspiration—what if they brought a female voice into the mix? They asked, and she said yes.

After more than a year of rehearsal and preparation in their hometown, the group was invited to New York City by a talent scout from Kapp Records. Following an hours-long audition, the record executive determined that Nash should be the lead singer, with the others singing backup, and he came up with a new name to fit: Ruby and the Romantics.

The Akron Sound

1963 photo of Ruby Nash, of Ruby and the Romantics. \ Photo courtesy of the *Akron Beacon Journal*.

"But the guys didn't like it at first," Nash told the *Akron Beacon Journal* in 2021. "I said 'Hey, that's cool. I'll be calling you guys 'Romantics,' and then the guys said, 'Well, OK, we'll go with it.'"

The group immediately went into a recording studio and only a month after that initial meeting released their first single—"Our Day Will Come." And indeed it would. In February 1963, Ruby & the Romantics had a No. 1 hit on both the *Billboard* Top 100 and R&B charts, eventually reaching sales of more than one million copies.

The upward spiral was dizzying for the quiet, humble girl from Akron. Two more Top 40 hits followed: "My Summer Love" and "Hey There Lonely Boy." The group, with its lush, complex vocal arrangements and sophisticated ballroom attire, set off on a tour with James Brown and rode its wave of success for a decade, touring America and Europe. They shared stages with many of the biggest R&B stars of the era, including the Temptations, Smokey Robinson, Gladys Knight and the Pips, and many, many others.

Along the way, Nash married an Akron schoolteacher, Robert Garnett, keeping one foot in her hometown and one on the tour bus. As the Romantics' celebrity waned, Ruby made the decision to return home. The group broke up in 1971, and the artist now known as Ruby Nash Garnett started her family. She and her husband had three children, and Ruby took on less glamorous work, with jobs at Ohio Bell in Akron and the Salvation Army store in Barberton.

In her late eighties in 2021, the singer was still living in Akron, where "Our Day Will Come" was a cornerstone of both her personal legacy and the narrative of her hometown.

"You know, I still hear it today," she told the *Beacon Journal*. "They still play it around here in Akron. I can go over to Walmart and hear it or Walgreens and hear it."

• • •

Throughout the second half of the twentieth century, Akron had a nuanced relationship with Cleveland, drawing much of its pre-digital-age media influence from the major market forty miles to the north, yet carefully maintaining its own distinct cultural identity.

The era of Alan Freed was followed by the ascendence of FM station WMMS. In the early 1970s, the so-called "Home of the Buzzard" was one of the few stations in the country taking chances with artists outside the classic rock and Top 40 mainstream, playing adventurous new music by the Velvet Underground, New York Dolls, the MC5, Soft Machine, and others.

This music fueled the interest of a core of like-minded outsiders, young burgeoning musicians who had grown up fixated on another key Cleveland influence: Ghoulardi, the television alter-ego of Ernie Anderson, host of a late-night B-movie showcase. In a lab coat, fake Van Dyke beard, and sunglasses with a missing lens, and speaking in a campy hipster spiel, Ghoulardi exuded an aura of anti-establishment absurdity against a soundtrack of primitive instrumental rock 'n' roll.

These signals reached a city whose young people were seeking new venues beyond the rubber factories that had defined the lifestyle of their parents and grandparents, whose political awareness had been gut-punched by the May 4, 1970, National Guard shooting deaths of four students at nearby Kent State University, and whose musical sensibilities were piqued by rumors of a punk rock revolution taking place in New York City.

Bands formed and soon a scene began to emerge among misfits who shared this ground in common.

There were the Rubber City Rebels, a straightforward punk band with power-pop sensibilities who wore their hometown pride on their leather-jacketed sleeves. Their signature song, "Rubber City Rebel," included the lyrics, "Daddy

The Akron Sound

works for Goodyear / Mama works for the 'Stone." Like their peers who played original music, they had a hard time getting gigs in Akron. One day, lead singer Ward Welch (stage name Rod Firestone) and guitarist Buzz Clic happened into an Akron bar called the Crypt, a block from the Goodyear Tire & Rubber campus and owned by a rubber worker. This was 1976, at the end of a historic 141-day strike that marked the beginning of the end of tire production in Akron. The prevailing culture was in a tenuous state.

The two musicians, noticing the place had a stage, asked if their band could play there. The owner, beaten down by the long, contentious strike, offered them one better. If they were willing to run the place and make his lease payment, he said, they could have it all to themselves. With that, the Crypt became what is generally believed to be the American first punk rock club outside New York City. In Akron, of all places.

Their first shows, in late 1976, featured three bands that would put Northeast Ohio in the international spotlight, and eventually the history books, as a key outpost of the punk and New Wave movement: Devo, from Akron, and Pere Ubu and the Dead Boys, both from Cleveland.

The Akron scene was thriving, with what seemed an inordinately high number of serious, innovative bands. These included an adventurous quintet, Tin Huey, influenced by Roxy Music and Captain Beefheart; the Bizarros, a riff-driven group with a Velvet Underground vibe; and Chi-Pig, a smart, funk-pop, female-fronted trio.

While the music was interesting and fresh, it was the blue-collar work ethic and ambition of the players that led to Akron becoming a musical hotbed. The Crypt represented not only a place to perform, but also a forum where ideas were exchanged, an audience gravitated, and alliances were formed.

Nick Nicholas, singer for the Bizarros, was a rubber worker's son with an entrepreneurial spirit. He formed a label called Clone Records and began releasing music by his peers, including two compilations of Akron bands—*Bowling Balls from Hell* and *Bowling Balls II*.

Devo soon emerged as the breakout band from this scene. The group had first come together as a wide-ranging conceptual art project, with a rock band as just one component of a philosophy of "devolution," the notion that humans were regressing, rather than progressing. Initially launched by Kent State University students Gerald V. "Jerry" Casale and Bob Lewis in the wake of the campus shootings, the group would eventually include art student Mark Mothersbaugh and play its first concert at a KSU arts festival in 1972.

In 1976, Devo finally settled on the lineup that would carry it into the mainstream consciousness, with Mark's brother Bob and Jerry's brother, also named

Bob (hence their nicknames Bob 1 and Bob 2) and drummer Alan Myers, fresh out of Firestone High School.

This lineup cut their teeth at the Crypt and other area clubs, released a single, and soon began generating buzz in the New York scene. Their hype reached its boiling point on the evening of November 15, 1977, when David Bowie stepped onto stage at Max's Kansas City, a New York rock club, and introduced the boys from Akron.

"This is the band of the future," he declared. "And I'm going to produce them in Tokyo this winter."

The band did enter the studio, although it was in Germany, with famed producer Brian Eno rather than Bowie at the helm, and would soon complete the recording of their debut album, *Are We Not Men? We Are Devo!* and sign with Warner Bros. During their stay in Europe, they were invited to play some concerts, including one in Liverpool, where a music journalist, interviewing Mark Mothersbaugh, asked what Akron was like.

"Actually, it's a lot like Liverpool," Mothersbaugh responded. He was referring to the dingy, monochrome industrial landscape. But the reporter went away with the impression that Akron might be a Liverpool-esque hotbed like that which had spawned the Beatles and the Mersey Beat movement of the early 1960s. Very soon, thanks in great part to Devo's ascendance and the world's curiosity about this "Akron" place that had spawned them, journalists, music fans, and record company executives began making a pilgrimage. At the same time, a term began appearing in the music press and on the tongues of record company executives: "The Akron Sound."

What was it? It's hard to say, considering the eclectic range of sounds, from hard rock to cold electronics to saxophones. Noted rock journalist Robert Christgau of the *Village Voice* was one of those who made the trek to the Rubber City, looking to answer that question. He didn't arrive by accident. As he noted in an insightful 1978 feature story, "A Real New Wave Rolls Out of Ohio," he'd been enticed by "a smart, rambling letter" from Chris Butler, a member of Tin Huey who also had a new band of his own called the Waitresses. The local musicians, much like Dr. Seuss's "Whos" on Horton's clover, were clamoring, "We are here!"

As Christgau noted in his story, "There's ... a possibility that bands in other cities are making rock and roll every bit as good and not recording it—but I doubt it."

Soon, Stiff Records—the influential London-based label that had released the first recordings by punk and New Wave acts including Elvis Costello, Nick Lowe, and the Damned—jumped on the bandwagon, releasing *The Akron Compilation*, featuring an array of local artists and a scratch-and-sniff tire on the cover. It smelled like burning rubber.

The Akron Sound

Tin Huey in the early 2000s. Clockwise from upper left: Harvey Gold, Chris Butler, Bob Ethington, Ralph Carney, Mark Price, Michael Aylward, Stuart Austin. (Chris Butler was also the founder of the Waitresses.) \ Photo courtesy of the photographer, Dolli Quattrocchi Gold

By late 1978, almost all the "Akron Sound" artists of note–Devo, Tin Huey, the Bizarros, the Rubber City Rebels, the Waitresses, and singer Rachel Sweet–had been signed by major labels. It's a hard road, however, and only Devo, the Waitresses, and Rachel Sweet managed to gain some level of national recognition.

Devo would make it the farthest, reaching No. 14 on the *Billboard* Hot 100 chart with its song "Whip It" in 1980 and helping define the look and sound of rock's New Wave era, as well as pioneering the art of the music video in the early years of MTV. The red, ziggurat-shaped "energy dome" hats they wore in the "Whip It" video—often mistaken for upside-down flowerpots—remain in iconic image of 1980s pop culture.

Especially in their early years, Devo drew heavily from its working-class, industrial surroundings, filming videos in Goodyear's "World of Rubber" exhibit and on the streets of Akron, for instance, and buying its trademark yellow Tyvek jumpsuits from the local Portage Broom & Brush catalogue.

The Akron cityscape "worked as an art-directed backdrop for this kind of music we were making," Jerry Casale said in an interview. "It had this hellish, depressing patina, this kind of dirty latex layer that fills the air, and the people in Akron seemed–their spirits were depressed; they were desperate; their kids were kind of like the characters in *Island of Lost Souls* that rebelled in the pit. In other words, they were just ready to go over the edge at any moment. They were so beaten down that they were gonna freak out. And it fit in with the early-twentieth century art movements—Expressionism, Dada, and others that were influenced by those kinds of environments in Germany and England. We had our very own backyard version of it. A rubber version."

Devo released eight studio albums between 1978 and 1990 and remained a highly respected and influential band. Front man Mark Mothersbaugh went on to a career scoring music for television and film and the band continued to tour and occasionally release new music.

In 2021, the band was nominated for the Rock and Roll Hall of Fame. To celebrate, the City of Akron issued a proclamation declaring April 1 "Devo Day" and installed fifty energy dome-inspired sculptures around town, created from discarded tires, painted red and stacked in upwardly descending sizes to replicate the ziggurat shape.

• • •

The most notable local musician of that same era, and one of the most notable ever to be closely associated with Akron, is Chrissie Hynde. As the kid sister of Terry Hynde, saxophone player for legendary Kent group the Numbers Band (with whom both Chris Butler and Jerry Casale had played bass), Chrissie had an early exposure to the thriving local music scene. While still a student at Firestone High School, she played briefly in a band called Sat Sun Mat with Mark Mothersbaugh and she was on campus the day of the Kent State shootings.

But her inherent ambition and wanderlust soon jettisoned her from her hometown. She moved to London in 1973 at age twenty-two and began writing for the rock magazine *New Musical Express* while looking to start a band of her own. It wasn't long before she found herself, mostly by chance, at the center of London's seminal punk scene, first working at Malcolm McLaren and Vivienne Westwood's clothing shop SEX, which became headquarters for the Sex Pistols, then crossing paths with most of the musicians who would become synonymous with the British punk explosion.

She finally formed her own group in 1978: the Pretenders, whose self-titled first album is often noted by critics as one of the greatest debuts in rock history.

The Akron Sound

Chrissie Hynde performing with the Pretenders, 1984. \ Photo by Paul Tople, courtesy of the *Akron Beacon Journal*

Hynde's smart lyrics were delivered in a soulful, vibrato-tinged voice that ranged from a tender croon to a streetwise growl against the tough backbeat of bassist Pete Farndon and drummer Martin Chambers and the sprawling guitar leads of James Honeyman-Scott. The single "Brass in Pocket" hit No. 1 on the British charts and the Pretenders were on their way to worldwide success.

The Pretenders became a mainstay on the international pop charts and in concert halls, with a string of gold records in the US and UK stretching into the mid-1990s. Their *Billboard* Top 20 hits include "Back on the Chain Gang," "Middle of the Road," "Don't Get Me Wrong," and "I'll Stand By You."

Despite her residence in London and a band composed of British musicians, Hynde maintained a strong association with her hometown, frequently referencing Akron in her lyrics and interviews. Her song "My City Was Gone" serves as a mournful paean to the Akron of her youth, detailing the disappearance of the downtown train station and South Howard Street and lamenting the shopping malls that replaced "the farms of Ohio." Another song, "Downtown (Akron)," references the Portage Hotel, the Cuyahoga Valley, and the "burning sulfur skies." And she took the name of a Northeast Ohio landmark for her song "Dragway 42."

Hynde has remained an ambassador, with Akron-themed T-shirts (often from the local Rubber City Clothing) as part of her standard stage attire and frequent comments about her strong affinity for Akron. In 2007, she opened a vegan restaurant called VegiTerranean in Akron's Northside district. It closed four years later after suffering financially but represented the pop star's stake in her hometown.

In 2005, the Pretenders were inducted into the Rock and Roll Hall of Fame in Cleveland, just a short drive up the highway from the city where it had all started.

• • •

A number of Akron-born performers have left their mark on the history of American pop and rock music, even though they are less directly associated with the city of their birth.

James Ingram, an East High School graduate who attended The University of Akron on a track scholarship, moved to Los Angeles and gained fame as a singer on the R&B charts, often in collaboration with other artists. Throughout the 1980s he sang on such hits as "Baby, Come to Me" with Patti Austin, "What About Me?" with Kenny Rogers and Kim Carnes, and "Somewhere Out There" with Linda Ronstadt. He was nominated for thirteen Grammy Awards through the 1980s and '90s, winning two.

Howard Hewett followed a similar path, leaving his hometown for Los Angeles at age twenty-one to begin his music career. He rose to prominence as the lead singer for the soul/R&B group Shalamar, which helped define the look and sound of the disco era. Shalamar's hits included "The Second Time Around," "Uptown Festival (Part 1)," and "Dead Giveaway." Hewett left the group in 1985 to begin a solo career, producing Top 10 R&B hits "I'm For Real," "Stay," and "Show Me."

David Allan Coe was born in Akron in 1939 and spent much of his youth in Ohio, although perhaps not all by choice, as he did time in various prisons and reform facilities, including a stint in the Ohio State Penitentiary. He'd always loved music, and so he developed his singing and songwriting in tandem with his outlaw image. A prison spell alongside legendary Cleveland R&B singer Screamin' Jay Hawkins turned into a mentorship of sorts, as Hawkins encouraged the

The Akron Sound

younger inmate's musical ambitions. In his late twenties, Coe made his way to Nashville and became part of the burgeoning "outlaw country" movement. In 1975, he scored a Top 10 hit with "You Never Even Called Me By My Name." His other country hits included "Mona Lisa Lost Her Smile," "The Ride," and the outlaw country anthem, "Willie, Waylon and Me."

Glen Buxton and Neal Smith were both born in Akron in 1947, and both migrated with their families to Phoenix, where they began playing in rock bands. While in high school, Buxton, a guitarist, met a fellow rock fan named Vince Furnier, formed a group to perform at a talent show, and soon became a full-fledged band. In 1967, the group brought Smith on board as its drummer and the following year Furnier changed his stage name to Alice Cooper, adapted a campy shock-rock persona, and the rest is rock history. Buxton and Smith were a core part of the group until Cooper went solo in 1974, contributing to all seven of the band's studio albums, including the breakout *Billion Dollar Babies*. Both Akron musicians are credited as songwriters on the classic songs "I'm Eighteen" and "School's Out," with Cooper crediting Buxton for coming up with the latter song's main riff. In 2011, Buxton and Smith were inducted into the Rock and Roll Hall of Fame as members of the original Alice Cooper band.

• • •

Patrick Carney and Dan Auerbach grew up on the same block in West Akron, just off Palisades Drive, and were classmates at Firestone High School, but hardly knew each other. Dan was a jock, captain of the soccer team, with a cool, laid-back demeanor and fascination for blues music, and Pat was a tall, lanky indie-rock geek in horn-rimmed glasses with a quick ironic wit.

Despite their seeming differences, each shared a distinct link to Akron's rock 'n' roll legacy. Patrick was the nephew of Ralph Carney, Tin Huey's saxophonist who had gone on to a robust career playing with many artists—the B52's, Elvis Costello, and St. Vincent among them—but most notably serving as longtime sideman to Tom Waits. Dan was the cousin of Akron-born guitarist Robert Quine, a member of the seminal New York punk band Richard Hell and the Voidoids who went on to play with Lou Reed, Brian Eno, Matthew Sweet, and others. And their high school had its own de facto rock 'n' roll hall of fame, with an alumni list that included Chrissie Hynde, Devo drummer Alan Myers, Ralph Carney, Rachel Sweet, and noted singer-songwriter Joseph Arthur.

When their musical paths finally crossed, it was not so much by fate as by convenience and necessity. As a guitarist in various loosely organized indie rock bands, Patrick had cobbled together a rudimentary recording studio in his parents' basement. Dan was trying to make a go of it as a blues guitarist and needed a demo. So they got together one day to jam. Pat wasn't really a drummer, but no

The Black Keys performing at Quicken Loans Arena in Cleveland. \ Photo by Mike Cardew, courtesy of the *Akron Beacon Journal*

one else was available, and he had a cheap drum kit to beat on. They found a connection, recorded a handful of songs, and decided to make it official, taking the name the Black Keys in 2001. The name was inspired by a man Patrick's father, Jim Carney, had encountered as a reporter for the *Akron Beacon Journal*. Alfred McMoore was a local character, an outsider artist diagnosed with schizophrenia who, when frustrated by having to leave an answering machine message, would declare, "Your black key's taking too long!"

The duo began sending out demo tapes and before they'd even played a live show, they were offered a contract by small independent label Alive Records. They played their first show at Cleveland's Beachland Tavern, soon followed by another at Akron club the Lime Spider, where their frenzied mashup of stomping blues and garage rock quickly became a big draw. The Black Keys became the focal point of a vibrant early 2000s local rock scene.

With stubborn ambition and a classic Akron work ethic, the band toured the country in a 1994 Chrysler van, often playing to small crowds and sleeping on floors. They kept recording and releasing their music, slowly but surely building a grassroots following despite little radio airplay. Piece by small piece, their reputation and success gained momentum. An appearance on *Late Night with Conan O'Brien*. A song in a Nissan commercial. Invitations to major music festivals.

The Akron Sound

373

Nearly a decade into their career, the band reached a height they couldn't have imagined in those early days in the basement. Their 2010 album *Brothers* produced a hit, "Tighten Up," which spent 10 weeks at No. 1 on the *Billboard* Alternative Songs chart. *Brothers* went platinum in the United States, topped many critics' year-end Top 10 lists, and was nominated for five Grammy awards, winning three.

By this time, the Black Keys had relocated to Nashville, but their postindustrial Midwestern hometown, as it always had been, was central to their identity. Much like LeBron James, whose career trajectory ran parallel to theirs, they regularly cited Akron's influence on their worldview in interviews and public appearances. They named their third album *Rubber Factory*, having recorded in a temporary studio in a former General Tire plant. Their stage props included a giant inflatable tire as a backdrop (with "Black Keys" mimicking the Goodyear logo) and a replica of the iconic Indian chief sculpture, "Chief Rotaynah," which had stood for years in front of the Judith A. Resnik Community Learning Center. In 2008, the group co-headlined a benefit concert at the Akron Civic Theater with Devo and Chrissie Hynde, representing a sort of three-headed "Monsters of Akron Rock."

"The Akron aesthetic is honest and unpretentious," Dan said in a 2012 interview. "I'd like to think you don't have to dress in fancy clothes, drive fancy cars, or live in a big house to be able to say or do something profound. A lot of people look at some of the Akron imagery as being dismal but I always felt the opposite about it all—it always made me feel energized. It was like I'd grown up in a magic city that had been frozen in amber. Oftentimes, directors and writers try to make their movies resemble what Akron looks and feels like naturally. It's easy to overlook that if you never get to see the outside world but we toured so much that when we would come home it would just smack you in the face."

With the release of their 2011 album, *El Camino* (whose cover art featured photos of minivans shot around Akron), the little band from Akron emerged as one of the biggest rock groups in the world, headlining arena concerts and reaching critical and commercial peaks. The album debuted at No. 2 on the *Billboard* chart and went double platinum, producing the hit singles "Lonely Boy," "Gold on the Ceiling," and "Little Black Submarines." Mirroring *Brothers*, it was nominated for five Grammys and won three.

Their artistic output and success continued into the third decade of the twenty-first century, with 2022's *Dropout Boogie* reaching No. 8 on the *Billboard* album chart. In an interview following the record's release, Patrick Carney reflected on the continued importance of his hometown to his life and work.

"I love Ohio," he told *Under the Radar* magazine. "I lived there for almost thirty years and it definitely informs every single bit of my personality...

I highly recommend, if you want to start a band, to move to a place like Ohio, to Akron because there's so many cool people there and it's affordable, you know. That's why I stayed there for so long."

• • •

The local music scene continues to thrive as the city enters its third century, with Kenmore Boulevard emerging as "Akron's Music Row," featuring a pair of live music venues, the Rialto Theater and Buzzbin; a pair of independently-owned guitar stores, the Guitar Department and the world-renowned Lay's Guitar Shop; a music boutique, JuJu Bonz Records; and an old building renovated into a studio space by Chris Butler, still holding forth as a prime mover and advocate of the ever-evolving "Akron Sound."

Bibliography

Adams, Deanna R. *Rock 'n' Roll and the Cleveland Connection.* Kent State University Press, 2002.

Christgau, Robert. "A Real New Wave Rolls Out of Ohio," *Village Voice,* April 17, 1978.

Dellinger, Jade and David Giffels. *The Beginning Was the End: Devo in Ohio.* University of Akron Press, 2023.

George-Warren, Holly, ed. *The Rolling Stone Encyclopedia of Rock & Roll.* Third edition. Fireside, 2001.

Giffels, David. "Interview with Black Keys Singer Dan Auerbach." *Rubbertop Review,* 2012.

Heylin, Clinton. *From the Velvets to the Voidoids: A Pre-Punk History for a Post-Punk World.* Penguin Books, 1993.

Hynde, Chrissie. *Reckless: My Life as a Pretender.* Doubleday, 2015.

Jackson, John A. *Big Beat Heat: Alan Freed and the Early Years of Rock & Roll.* Schirmer Books, 1991.

Love, Steve and David Giffels. *Wheels of Fortune: The Story of Rubber in Akron.* University of Akron Press, 1998.

Price, Mark. J. "Akron Singer Ruby Nash Garnett Recalls 1960s Success with Romantics." *Akron Beacon Journal,* March 26, 2021.

Price, Mark. J. "'School's Out' Forever: Alice Cooper Original Drummer Neal Smith Recalls Akron and Anthem." *Akron Beacon Journal,* April 24, 2022.

Russell, Nicholas. "The Black Keys on 'Dropout Boogie.'" *Under the Radar,* June 2, 2022.

\ **25**

Akron's Queer History

Fran Wilson

Below the Belt, 1950–1970s

At the corner of Howard and Perkins currently stands a theater turned scrappy, gay nightclub: The Interbelt. It's one of the last remaining structures on what was once an active social and economic block for the local Black and queer communities, a district torn apart by an urban renewal infrastructure project in the late 1960s that's now an unused highway with knee-high weeds poking between the cracks in the concrete. The kids who sneak into the bar for drag nights with their fake IDs are probably oblivious to the history of LGBTQIA+ suppression on that very block.[1]

Queer Akronites have long lived and loved in the shadows. Interlocking systems of oppression cracked down on queer living, perpetuated discrimination and isolation, and denied queer Akronites basic rights and liberties. In some ways, discrimination against LGBTQIA+ folks is still legal, and for most of our collective history being out and proud was illegal and punishable in brutal ways.

Many queer folks led two different lives: one public, one private. Queer Akron renters feared eviction, and employees feared being fired if outed.[2] In the 1950s, the United States experienced a wave of homophobic persecution known as the Lavender Scare. It began as an effort to purge homosexuals from the federal government, leading to similar efforts by state and local governments and

375

the private sector. Countless government workers, suspected or known to be LGBTQIA+, were dismissed. The fear and prejudice from this era impacted employment practices for decades, with LGBTQIA+ people facing intrusive psychological evaluations and job limitations.[3] In Akron, John Grafton, as a former Director of Housing at The University of Akron in the 1960s, faced issues when colleagues and students found out he was gay: "I would get mysterious phone calls in the middle of the night. And it got so bad I had to disconnect my phone. And then there were things written on the walls in the residence halls. And so I resigned in 1969."[4]

Discrimination and ostracism from society created a need for safe spaces for queer Akronites. Thus, churches, hidden-away or invite-only bars and speakeasies, bathhouses, and parks became extensions of home. While nightlife scenes were not the only gathering spots for the community, they were some of the most lively. The freedom to find community and opportunities to explore pleasure were rare and often only possible in private or hidden places after dark.

Akron's first gay bar of note, the Lincoln Bar, opened at 28 South Howard Street in 1948,[5] From the 1950s through the 1960s, Howard Street, known as a cultural and economic hub for the local Black community, was also a staple of queer social life—though, it should be noted that gay and lesbian communities often socialized separately.[6] Drag nights at The Lincoln Bar were said to be full of "gayety and a festival atmosphere." All within a short distance were other establishments: Cadillac Cafe, a lesbian bar; Eli's, a "dumpy" gay and lesbian bar; and Hi-Hat, a "mixed gay/straight Black bar."[7] Discos, drag, and drugs fueled Akron's largest-ever collection of gay bars, a nightlife district that would have rivaled today's Highland Square.

Max Turner Monegan, a Kent graduate researcher, describes these bars in his 2019 thesis. Hung in the front window of some of Akron's late-night gay establishments were "members only" signs, meant to discourage or, at the very least, warn hetero patrons that this was not some average straight bar. At some places, like Club Akron's Bathhouse, new folks had to have guest passes or even be vouched for by a current member with a signature. Other establishments had patrons sneak in through the back or through alleyways with boarded up windows and doors. An Akronite once described these measures as protections: "the imagined boundary between the bar's interior and the straight world beyond all contributed to the sense of community that began to emerge in the 1970s."[8]

Outside of the discos, bars, and bath scenes, some Akronites, primarily gay men, would also cruise parks and gyms. *Cruising* can be described as discreetly searching for a sexual encounter in a public space. As homosexual behavior was illegal for so long, it was difficult for folks to find an outlet for sex and other physical pleasures. Akron's Grace Park, off Perkins Street downtown, from the

50s to the 80s, was a hot spot for cruising, particularly after the bars closed for the night.[9] And while some patronized parks, bars, and the baths, some gay men lived at the local YMCA, which provided opportunities to meeting and encounter each other.[10]

While some of these spaces were claimed by the queer crowd, the threat of hate and violence loomed over these places. Queer gathering spaces were targets for police, with an understood fear that these sorts of places could get busted, raided, or even burned down.[11] Those who took an oath to protect and serve have a demonstrated history of beating, arresting, jailing, and even killing queer people.[12] For example, "cross-dressing" was grounds for arrest, and same-sex activity could land you in jail.[13]

Here at home, queer Akronites were afraid of being found out, afraid of police brutality and random violence. And while one 1969 police raid-turned-rebellion at New York's Stonewall Inn sparked national dialogue on police violence toward LGBTQIA+ civilians, particularly people of color, Akronites feared the same thing happening here. And their fear was real. Akron police frequently raided local queer bars and bathhouses. Officers, sometimes in plain clothes, would shake down customers and bar owners. Some spaces even adopted safety protocols to protect patrons. One bar that had a large, private dark room had someone assigned to flick the lights to "make sure your zipper's up ... and you're just standing around having casual conversation ... and what you're smoking is just an ordinary cigarette."[14] Beyond cops, patrons knew to be cautious of college boys and strangers when walking home, for there were incidents of queer patrons getting beaten up leaving the bars.[15] The Deucers Wild, a 1950s teen "gang" from South High, were known to put on their matching light-blue corduroy jackets (with a wolf wearing a hat with two playing cards) and harass patrons. And in 1956, the school club was disbanded after a rash of fights, beatings, and disturbances that included breaking into the Lincoln Bar and trashing it "just for kicks."[16]

The gayety of Howard Street, however, did not survive past the 60s. At the end of the decade, the City of Akron's urban renewal project to build the State Route 59 Innerbelt decimated important spaces to the LGBTQIA+ and Black communities. As Max Monegan explains, both Black and queer community institutions "were targeted by the Howard Street demolition" because "they did not fit" with "the city planner's idea of what the central business district should look like."[17]

The Innerbelt project, in the guise of progress, development, and urban renewal in Akron, further marginalized the local Black and queer communities, demolishing important gathering spaces and disrupting community networks. Apart from the electropop pulsing from inside the Interbelt Nite Club today, the block stands an empty shell of its former self, on a highway to nowhere.

Rubbers City, 1980s

On April 17, 1986, Franklin D. Vitatoe Jr., a twenty-eight-year-old man from Wooster, was walking around Grace Park when he ran into another man and struck up a conversation. Quite suddenly, Vitatoe found himself under arrest. The man turned out to be an Akron police officer on the department's vice squad, tasked with dealing with issues like prostitution and gambling. Vitatoe was charged with soliciting for sex. Vitatoe, who was gay and had AIDS, told police he had only a year to live.[18]

Within two hours of his arrest, Vitatoe landed in a courtroom, and swore to a judge that he wasn't soliciting and that the encounter was entrapment. City prosecutors argued that he was a danger, that he was spreading AIDS. Akron Municipal Judge Monte Mack decided to dismiss his charges, partly because staff at the Akron Corrections Facility where he was taken feared the disease would spread there. Vitatoe was ordered to leave the city immediately.[19]

Ten days later, Akron police received a tip that Vitatoe was "loitering" at Grace Park. They arrested him again. On the way to his hearing, inmates were said to have yelled, "AIDS! AIDS!" at Vitatoe. In a phone interview with the *Beacon Journal*, Vitatoe explained that he had returned to Akron to raise money to help his mother move. Back home in Wayne County, his relatives were harassed after a Wayne County newspaper published the family's address with the story of his arrest. In court, the judge set a bond of $1,500, which Vitatoe had no way of paying. So, he spent twenty-one days in jail. Instead of holding him at the workhouse, where folks facing misdemeanor charges were typically placed, Vitatoe was held at the Summit County Jail and confined in isolation because he had AIDS. Health officials advised that there should be no fear of contracting the disease from him, yet he was led to the showers and recreation apart from the others, and a corrections employee at the time noted that officers were encouraged to wear rubber gloves around him.[20]

Vitatoe pleaded guilty to the original soliciting charge, and the judge allowed his release on probation, with the stipulation that Vitatoe went nowhere near common cruising spots around Akron and that he take part in a treatment program to keep him in good behavior. His public defender, Karen Schneiderman, had trouble finding a good program for him. Schneiderman told the *Akron Beacon Journal* that "agencies she had regarded as open and nonjudgmental had been unwilling to consider helping Vitatoe." "It's clear that his life on Earth will be limited," she also said. "The trick is to make his time on Earth better than it has been."[21]

Akron reported its first locally originated AIDS cases in 1986: two suburban cases and one in the city. At the time, officials declared that these cases were "probably the beginnings of a local AIDS epidemic."[22] Human immunodeficiency

Akron's Queer History

virus (HIV) and acquired immunodeficiency syndrome (AIDS) hit the Akron queer community hard. One Akronite living at the time reflected on the tragedy around her: "There were many Saturday nights that I left the bar and went to the hospital because somebody I knew was dying."[23]

When the Akron City Council began to take action on AIDS in 1987, there was a hiccup: a forgotten, twenty-year-old restrictive ban on the sale and distribution of prophylactics. In 1960, the City of Akron—just a few decades after leading the nation in condom production—instituted measures to restrict condom sales beyond doctors, drugstores, and supermarkets with pharmacies.[24] According to then-City Councilor Ed Davis, the restriction was to prevent kids from accessing condoms through vending machines without someone asking why they needed them. The 1960 law made violations a third-degree misdemeanor, punishable by up to sixty days in jail and a $500 fine. No one was ever charged under the law, and by 1987 most had forgotten about it.

On March 30, 1987, the condom ban was repealed without discussion to promote condom use to fight the spread of AIDS.[25] However, at the same meeting, Councilor John Frank advocated for another change in city code: allowing judges to order AIDS testing and dropping the obligation for the city to pay for court-ordered sexually transmitted disease treatment if someone charged with prostitution was found positive. He stated that "Some of these diseases are incurable. The times we live in, it is better to have this out."[26]

Shortly after, city council approved the use of $5,000 of state funds to purchase 70,000 condoms for the Health Department. This aided the work of contracted educators hired by the city to go out into the community and share information about the disease.[27] But even before local officials finally took action, community groups and neighbors were already advocating and fulfilling needs. Drag queens hosted fundraisers for AIDS support groups, and bars offered HIV testing by the Health Department. And a neighbor named Vince stood at the corner of Grace Park saying, "There is a disease out there, you've got to take care of yourself," while handing out condoms to anyone who could spare a quarter.[28]

Fear of the deadly spread of HIV/AIDS fueled misinformation and hate. Speaking for the Moral Majority, one of the most influential political organizations of the 1980s, televangelist Jerry Falwell called AIDS "the gay plague."[29] And while the pastor faced instant national backlash, the damage was done. News outlets, magazines, and leaders in churches and elected office shared this idea widely, stoking misconceptions of and apprehension toward LGBTQIA+ individuals.[30]

One Akron factory employee in the 1980s shared their story with the local news: they were being harassed and threatened in their workplace for being homosexual. People feared getting infected from simply working alongside queer folks.[31] A former Akron police officer of twenty-five years, Cindy Christman, noted that she witnessed anti-gay stigma while serving on the force: from officers not wanting to ride with gay partners in their cruisers to one incident where officers were told to be careful on a crime scene in case the queer victim had a disease. Officers had yelled out, "Be careful. They're gay, and there's blood."[32]

The HIV/AIDS crisis was only another phase in the long struggle for queer health support and bodily autonomy. Before the AIDS crisis, in addition to direct forms of state persecution, lobotomies, which are invasive and irreversible procedures, were utilized as a tool to control and "treat" for queer folks. Forced castration and sterilization were once terms for parole or prison release. And Ohio lawmakers once sought to pass sterilization policies to further dehumanize queer individuals. While none were adopted into law, informal sterilization procedures took place in prisons and mental institutions.[33]

In 1973, the American Psychiatric Association decided that "homosexuality per se" should no longer be considered a "psychiatric disorder," redefining it instead as a "sexual orientation disturbance." This change was a step toward changing the notion that same-sex attractions and gender nonconformity were diseases that could be cured.[34] For so long, these misconceptions had allowed for discrimination and medical abuse. Up until that time, and still after, LGBTQIA+ people were sent to asylums, faced conversion therapies, and were lab rats for inhumane medical and mental health procedures and practices.[35] In the 1980s, the idea that queerness was somehow a "disease" exacerbated already-existing critical health and equity concerns and tormented the queer community during a pivotal health catastrophe.

The HIV/AIDS crisis led to the death of a generation of queer folks.[36] Nationally, a lack of leadership and governmental response, doubled with the weaponization of existing anti-queer criminal codes, oppressed communities in the midst of a crisis. The HIV/AIDS epidemic killed over 100,000 people in the United States between 1981 and 1990.[37] By 1989, an estimated 1,500 Summit County residents had been infected with HIV, and over one hundred cases of AIDS were recorded to have been treated by Akron healthcare facilities.[38]

In the wake of the HIV/AIDS health crisis locally, community organizers, nonprofits, and philanthropists began to build lasting resources to support the Akron queer community. Today's organizations like The Bayard Rustin Center, Akron AIDS Collaborative, CANAPI, and the Akron Community Foundation's Gay Endowment Fund make up just a handful of the initiatives that have blossomed from decades of organizing and advocacy.

Out in Akron, 1990s

Amid devastating grief and loss, queer Akronites found solace, community, and defiant joy by gathering together. In some ways it was an escape; in others, it was an unapologetic reclamation of identity and celebration of survival.

From strip shows and poppers to drag queens performing in stilettos and fishnets, the 1990s boasted spectacles of local queer late-night fantasies.[39]

One 1992 ad for Westgate, an Akron bar on West Market, boasted a Wednesday night like no other. The poster featured four costumed hunks: a construction worker, a shirtless man with a US flag draped over his shoulder, one man posing in just a jockstrap, and a buff, shirtless man whose name just read "Josh." Another Westgate ad encouraged folks to "put on your boots and kick up your heels" to get down to some country tunes and line dancing.[40] One bar patron's scrapbook from the 1990s—now tucked away in our local library's special collection archives—shows pictures of folks out at the bars: one of someone dancing with a tank top and thong made of glittery material, another of someone wearing a sash displaying the words "cash only $," and yet another, a blown up image of someone's rear-end in a thong. Below the image read: "'Look what's cooking' after hours at 1223 Niteclub."[41]

Drag queens held a spotlight at many of these establishments along with the lesser known and documented drag kings. From the 1940s to the 1980s, several drag queens stood out as prominent figures in the community: Contessa, Hestia, Rosita Estefan, and Valerie Hill.[42] And up through the 1990s and beyond, many other queens took the stage: Trixie Morgan, Carla Visconte, Samantha Styles, Mackenzie Spencer, Tyranny Fox, Danyel Vasquez, and many others. The "Lavender Ladies" were also a hit: Destiny Dawn—pictured in a scrapbook wearing a red dress and matching gloves with a foot-wide brimmed hat—Little Trixie, Miss Barberton, and others. While a majority of drag bars at the time catered primarily to gay men, The Roseto Club was an exclusive women's club that opened in 1982 on Arlington Street.[43] They held Drag King shows on Thursdays and Hip Hop nights on Fridays.[44]

One of the most known drag performers of the time was Valerie Hill.

Valerie Hill was born in Canton, Ohio, and lived in Akron for twenty-eight years. She lived on Mildred Avenue in North Akron and had a partner and lover of eighteen years, Edward Blazeff.[45] Hill was a drag queen or "impressionist artist" for over twenty years. She lived for decades of her life as a woman, and one front-page newspaper profile describes her as "an Akron man who lived as a woman." Even her neighbors knew her as a woman and referred to her with female pronouns.[46] She was an AIDS activist and a fundraiser for AIDS benefits.

From the 1960s to her passing, every stage graced with Hill's presence lit up bright. One friend recalled a night out with her: "on a small stage, [Valerie] would pantomime to the latest Supremes hit. I can see her, even now as only she could, her hand criss-crossed her body while snapping her fingers and saying 'Innn Deeed!' She will leave a lasting memory and be missed, indeed."

While some might have called her a star, Akron police labeled her a prostitute.[47] In one *Akron Beacon Journal* article, the caption beside a photo of Hill reads "Akron Police say these two prostitutes are among the best-known in town." Hill, whose picture is captured on the left of the page, is seen posing in a one-strap red dress, full makeup, and matching red earrings, crossing her arms in a fluffy white boa and standing in front of a dead-end street sign.[48] In 1995, Hill's life was cut short at forty-eight years old. She was shot in the abdomen by her partner in their home, reportedly a homicide turned suicide. The community mourned her loss, leaving flowers and notes at their door.[49]

The death of Hill and its related news coverage was difficult for Akron's queer community. The 1990s also saw many national stories on LGBTQIA+ issues, from the implementation of President Bill Clinton's "Don't Ask, Don't Tell" policy (1993) and his 1996 signing of the Defense of Marriage Act (DOMA), which legally defined marriage as between men and women, to the brutal murder of a young, gay man named Matthew Shepard in Wyoming in 1998.

In Akron, collective advocacy work and community programming combated stigma and anti-queer bills from the Ohio legislature, giving Akronites a glimpse into a more hopeful future. In 1995 in the little town of Peninsula just outside of Akron, the Among Friends Gallery hosted an event called All Out Art, showing and selling the works of LGBTQIA+ artists and craftspeople. This benefit to support the Stonewall Akron advocacy group and the work of Summit AIDS Housing was a hit. Some six hundred visitors came to a little town of five hundred people, located between Cleveland and Akron. Over forty works were sold at the opening, and hundreds of dollars were raised. Chris Hixson, who led the event, said that the goal of the show was to "promote an understand[ing] and education within the non-gay community that being gay is about a lot more than sex."[50] The success of this event showed that more people in Northeast Ohio were beginning to back the queer community.

In 1997, Stonewall Akron, an LGBTQIA+ civil rights group, held a rally downtown to protest Ohio House Bill 160, which sought to outlaw same-sex unions. Hixson, then president of Stonewall Akron, also noted that the rally culminated in a kiss-in, where protestors voluntarily kissed the stranger beside them as an act of defiance and solidarity.[51] Two years later, just a year after the killing of Matthew Shepard, a rally bringing together thirty locals advocated

Akron's Queer History

for hate-crime protections. Some held signs that read "stop hate crime now" and "stop anti-gay violence." The group gathered to advocate for strengthening Ohio's hate crime laws to include crimes against homosexuals. Organizer and President of Stonewall Akron, Judy Byrd, told a journalist at the protest that "homosexuals have been the target of hate crimes" and that she recently spoke with a homosexual man about being beaten outside an Akron gay bar. Byrd noted that "the man did not go to the police because he does not want people to know he is gay."[52] One event in October of 1999 advertised a vigil at the courthouse, stating, "A year has passed since Matthew's death, and we still do not have state or federal hate crime legislation."[53]

While Columbus and Cleveland had already hosted vibrant festivals for Pride month and Coming Out Day, it wasn't until 1997 when Stonewall Akron and other community organizers created Akron's first official Pride. A group of locals met at Angel Falls Coffee Company in the Highland Square neighborhood, bringing together different organizations to discuss an event that would include films, theater, visual arts, and public forums. The weekend-long event was called "Out in Akron: GLBT Pride Weekend."

The schedule of events included a Pride rally, a "comedienne" show, a meet and greet with Mark Sadlek and Steve Habgood—who had a feature in *Life* magazine about same-sex marriage—and a live one-man play at the Highland Square Theatre. Also on display was a touring photo-text exhibit, "Love Makes a Family: Living in Lesbian and Gay Families," which portrayed stories of queer families to "combat homophobia by breaking silence and making the invisible visible." Dozens of sponsors supported the event, including Angel Falls Coffee Company, Gay People's Chronicle, Stonewall Akron, Akron Sewing Machine Center, The Highland Square Theatre, Roseto Club, Mother Wit (a group for lesbian and bisexual mothers), What's Up Publication, Temple Israel, PFLAG, and so many more.[54]

The event opened with a National Coming Out Day rally on High Street, where folks gathered with signs and spoke about the importance of equality and love. But the moment was also partly tarnished by passersby who were vocally against Pride. The *Akron Beacon Journal* noted that the crowd of thirty to fifty people gathered for an hour to hear speeches that were occasionally interrupted by mean slurs yelled out of passing cars. "When they hurt one of us," Eric Resnick, a speaker, said, "They hurt all of us." "If anything," reporter Bill O'Connor wrote, "the rally showed that gay people, as many minorities before them, are making their way into the tent of acceptability."[55]

Today, Akron Pride stands as a regional celebration of our city's LGBTQIA+ community, from Akron AIDS Collaborative's vogue ball and Family Black

An Out in Akron rally outside Akron's Highland Theater, 1998. \ Photo by Jocelyn Williams, courtesy of the *Akron Beacon Journal*.

Pride picnics and scholarship banquets to recent Pride events that have brought out over thirty thousand people to march, dance, and uplift all of Akron's beautiful colors.[56]

Equal-ish, 2000–2010s

"Should gay couples marry?" Akronite Chris Hixson answered this question in a letter printed in the *Akron Beacon Journal* on January 22, 2000. The topic of equal rights in marriage weighed on him, as before he came out and married his now-partner, he was married to a woman.[57] "I am a taxpayer, a voter, a business owner, and a law-abiding citizen of Ohio. I happen to be gay. Am I not worthy of the same treatment under the law as my heterosexual neighbors, family, and friends?"[58]

The turn of the century brought with it some advances in equality under the law nationwide. In 2003, the Supreme Court struck down sodomy laws in *Lawrence v. Texas*, declaring criminal punishment for consensual, adult same-sex

Akron's Queer History

A page from the 1997 Out in Akron program. \ Christopher Hixson collection.

activity unconstitutional. In 2004, Massachusetts became the first state to legalize same-sex marriage. In 2009, President Obama added sexual orientation and gender identity to federal hate crime laws. The 2010s saw a number of significant victories for the LGBTQIA+ community as well. "Don't Ask, Don't Tell" was repealed, the Supreme Court ruled in favor of same-sex marriage nationwide in *Obergefell v. Hodges* (whose plaintiffs were from Ohio), and the fight against anti-transgender bathroom restrictions gained national attention and helped combat hateful legislation. Akronites were also grappling with these issues at home, debating the topic of marriage, as well as housing and employment protections. It was not until the 2000s that queer Akronites began to gain the same rights and privileges of loving, working, and living as freely as their hetero neighbors.

For many LGBTQIA+ Akronites before the new millennium, the idea of having the legal right to marry their same-sex lovers or partners was just a dream.[59] And because of this, some closeted Akronites decided to marry people of the opposite sex, and even had kids.[60]

When John Grafton, a gay Akronite, went to work at Goodyear in the late 1990s, he was asked how he'd like to set up his retirement benefits. His employer didn't know about his partner of thirty years. Grafton decided to take a smaller amount, a lump sum, to ensure he would legally be able to pass on his earnings to his partner. These types of benefits, a few years later, would be the center of a nurses' strike at Akron's largest healthcare provider. In 2004, nurses walked out of Akron General after collective bargaining negotiations broke over the topic of salary, pensions, and benefits that included same-sex partners and dependents. The strike over issues were eventually settled after eleven days of picketing. While negotiations failed to deliver full same-sex domestic partner benefits, the strike was successful in achieving paid bereavement leave for same-sex partners.[61] Up until recently, many companies were not welcoming to LGBTQIA+ employees and had restrictions for workers who were not straight and not married to the opposite sex. Federal protections for queer workers were strengthened and clarified in the 2020s.[62]

Little stopped landlords from evicting Ohioans and Akronites who identified as LGBTQIA+, who were outed, or even simply suspected to be queer. A 2002 case from the Ohio Civil Rights Commission upheld that a landlord's religious rights can trump discrimination based on marital status. An article about the case in the *Gay People's Chronicle*, a popular queer Ohio publication at the time, stated that "the landlord David Grey has the right to refuse to rent to an unmarried couple because their living arrangement violates his religious beliefs.... The commission's decision allows landlords in cities such as Akron that do not specifically include designations for marital status and sexual orientation to legally refuse to rent to or to sell to unmarried couples, same-sex and different sex."[63]

In Akron, in 2001, at a city council and school board debate led by Stonewall Akron, candidates were asked if they support a proposal to add sexual orientation and gender to the city's equal rights ordinance. The night was said to have gotten heated.[64] After almost a decade of debate, Akron City Council reconsidered and passed the historic equal opportunity and anti-discrimination ordinance that protected individuals from discrimination based on their sexual orientation and gender identity and expression in 2009.[65] The next year, in 2010,

Akron's Queer History

Akron's first openly LGBTQIA+ elected official, Sandra Kurt, took her oath of office for city council. Seven years later, through a joint legislative act of Akron City Council and the mayor of Akron, the Akron Civil Rights Commission was established to investigate complaints of discrimination in employment, housing, and places of public accommodation, and act as an avenue to file complaints and seek justice and remediation.[66]

While the 2000s and 2010s brought more debate on basic civil rights and protections for LGBTQIA+ Akronites, the power of pride and acceptance was underscored when Akron won the international bidding to host The Gay Games in 2014.[67] With Cleveland as a co-host, the 9th Gay Games brought twenty thousand local and international visitors to the region. Welcoming thousands of athletes, the two cities split between them different sporting events—from soccer and golf to baseball and even the international competition's first ever (and maybe last) gay rodeo. According to an economic impact study, the games injected over $52 million into the local economy.[68]

Rain and Rainbows, 2020s

Light rain fell on a body lying face-up on the sidewalk on East Buchtel Avenue. Brian "Egypt" Powers, a forty-three-year-old Black transgender Akronite from the south side, was found dead by a groundskeeper in the early hours of June 13, 2020. Powers was shot through the legs and left for dead.[69]

Powers was kind and social, a graduate of Garfield High School, a fighter who battled addiction and housing insecurity, and often wore long, pink and blue and green braids—lovingly called Powers' "unicorn braids." An obituary tells of Powers' infectious laugh, and about a love of cooking and old movies.[70]

A question was inked boldly above the fold on the front page of the *Akron Beacon Journal* on July 24, 2020: "Who Killed Brian Powers?" For up to a month after the murder, the Powers family reported hearing next to nothing from local law enforcement, worrying that sexual orientation or gender identity played a role in how much effort investigators put in. The Akron Police Department's spokesperson told a reporter, "until we identify and/or have a suspect in custody, it's really hard to infer that his lifestyle was a contributing factor.... I hate to even suggest that that even played a role." And if Powers' identity did play a role, Ohio hate crime laws excluded protections for gender identity and sexual orientation.[71]

Long after that June morning, there was still no surveillance footage, no witnesses, no leads. It was not until March of 2023 that the man responsible was arrested and charged. A month after arrest, a grand jury found him guilty of murder.[72]

Vivian Powers-Smith shows photos of her brother Brian "Egypt" Power after his slaying in 2020. \ Photo by Phil Masturzo, courtesy of the *Akron Beacon Journal*.

"We need to be talking about how stigmatized the Black community and white community is about transgender life and death," Steve Arrington, a local LGBTQIA+ advocate, shared with the news following the murder. "We don't talk enough about it, [we] sweep it under the carpet."[73]

Northeast Ohio in recent years has seen a sharp rise in homicides and violence against transgender people.[74] One 2022 study by a Kent State graduate student, Andrew Snyder, surveying hundreds of queer folks in Akron and surrounding counties, recorded 172 Akron respondents who had faced discrimination at home and in public. When asked about the primary issues affecting LGBTQIA+ locals, 82 percent of Akron respondents identified hate crimes as their foremost concern, while 62 percent highlighted the significant problem of physical assaults targeting queer community members.[75] And while 50 percent of those surveyed said they didn't feel safe interacting with police, sixty-nine Akronites who have encountered the criminal justice system shared bad experiences related to the lack of proper accommodations and respect for their LGBTQIA+ identities.

Steve Arrington, leader of Akron AIDS Collaborative and the Bayard Rustin LGBTQ+ Resource Center, cuts through with clear words: "The current climate is what we're used to anyway.... We're not privileged people here."[76]

Portraits of the gay and Black civil rights activists hang on the walls of the Rustin Center. Laughter fills the room as chairs tuck in at the table, plates bursting with food made with loving hands. Arrington leans forward in his chair to ask

Akron's Queer History

Community dinner at the Bayard Rustin Center. Seated in the front left is Steve Arrington. \ Photo by Karen Schiely, courtesy of the *Akron Beacon Journal*.

how everyone is doing. A group of once-strangers start to talk about joy, about race and identity, gender and sexual health, about family. This is what Wednesday nights are like at the center's weekly community dinners.

For decades, good-troublemaker Steve Arrington has been a vocal and active advocate for more robust support and funding for Akron's Black gay community. In 1995, when he came back to Ohio, Arrington coordinated the Ohio Department of Health's HIV/AIDS programs supporting Black men—speaking before Congress about the real need for more funding to serve people of color with HIV.[77] Today, Arrington heads a center that serves not only as an HIV testing hub and weekly dinner meetup, but also as a walk-in service provider. Any day of the week, just about anyone can—and does—walk through their doors looking for housing, health support, a place to escape the bad weather, or something warm to put in their stomachs. Social workers welcome neighbors from all walks of life, helping folks navigate tough moments.[78]

Next door to the new Rustin Center location on Exchange Street is the newly minted Equitas Health facilities. Equitas is one of the nation's largest LGBTQIA+ and HIV/AIDS-serving organizations.[79] Across town, the ever-growing Summa Pride Clinic provides not just primary physician care, but gender-affirming care and other specialized services.[80] The care they give is life-altering because hundreds of surveyed LGBTQIA+ Akronites have reported never visiting a doctor's office specifically tailored to their needs. And 249 surveyed locals mentioned receiving inadequate sexual health education. Needless to say, this emerging network of healthcare providers is offering crucial support to a historically neglected community at a time when it is most needed.[81]

Today, almost half a million LGBTQIA+ folks call Ohio home.[82] And yet, queer Ohioans are still fighting for basic protections, amid escalating violence. On the national level, some progress has been made within the last decade: from the expansion of awareness, resources, healthcare access for LGBTQIA+ individuals to federal anti-discrimination protections for queer employees, not to mention gender-inclusive passports, and the end of the Food and Drug Administration's tissue and blood ban for gay and bisexual men. But deep-rooted issues and violence against queer folks permeate life in the Buckeye state. Here, alongside a rise of far-right protests at drag brunches, a renewed wave of anti-queer bigotry has washed through the state legislature: political attacks on transgender rights, gender sports bans, "Don't Say Gay" bills, educational censorship, and book bans.[83] In Akron, there has been progress: we have witnessed the passage of healthcare for transgender city employees, faith communities using their platforms to discuss gender identity and sexual orientation, and the slow but steady expansion of funding for queer organizations on the frontlines of health and social services. But overall, as civil rights and funding expand in some areas, liberties are encroached in others.

Akron's rich and sometimes difficult queer histories—those hidden in plain sight, carried to a closeted grave, or told out and proud—tell of a people and place that has seen the rain yet has also seen some rainbows. Indeed, Akron, Ohio, is a queer place.

Notes

1. I use the terms "queer" and "LGBTQIA+" as these are used mostly interchangeably in our time, especially among younger Akronites. Where I am writing about specific sub-communities under these umbrellas, I will identify them as such. These terms are used not to rename or redefine, but to refer to the collective experience of the non-heterosexual and gender-different.

2. Cindy Christman, conversation with the author, 2022; John Grafton, conversation with the author, 2022.

3. For more on the Lavender Scare and its impact on people in the Midwest, see Heather Hines, "The LGBT Community Responds: The Lavender Scare and the Creation of Midwestern Gay and Lesbian Publications" (master's thesis, Bowling Green State University, 2017).

4. John Grafton, conversation with the author, 2022.

5. Max Turner Mohegan, "A Different Kind of Community: Queerness and Urban Ambiguity in Northeast Ohio, 1945–1980," (master's thesis, Kent State University, 2019), 44.

6. James Zwisler, email to Fran Wilson, 2023; Mohegan, 96.

7. Gary Felsinger, "A History of Akron Gay Life, 1948–2009: 61 Years Out in The City," unbound manuscript history of the Akron gay community, 2009, Akron-Summit County Main Library Special Collections.

8. Monegan, 50.

9. Monegan, 61.

10. James Zwisler, email to Fran Wilson, 2023.

11. Mohegan, 51–52.

12. MJ Eckhouse and Saxen MJ, "Police Brutality and Why It Is an LGBTQ+ Issue," *FUSION*, Spring 2017, 30–35, https://www-s3-live.kent.edu/s3fs-root/s3fs-public/file/Police_Brutality.pdf.

13. Kate Redburn, "Before Equal Protection: The Fall of Cross-Dressing Bans and the Transgender Legal Movement, 1963–86," *Law and History Review* 40, no. 4 (2022): 679–723, https://doi.org/10.1017/S0738248022000384.

14. Monegan, 52, 47.

15. Stephanie Warsmith, "Vigil honors Shepard," *Akron Beacon Journal*, October 13, 1999, B3; Monegan, 52. Unless otherwise noted, newspapers are cited from digital versions through Newspapers.com.

16. Don McClure, "South High Gang Breaks Up After Police 'Get Tough,'" *Akron Beacon Journal*, May 10, 1956, A1.

17. Felsinger, "A History of Akron Gay Life"; Monegan, 39–40.

18. William Canterbury, "AIDS Victim Pleads Guilty to Akron Soliciting Charge," *Akron Beacon Journal*, May 7, 1986, D4.

19. William Canterbury, "AIDS victim told to leave Akron." *Akron Beacon Journal*, April 25, 1986, A1.

20. William Canterbury, "Man's Rearrest for Soliciting Came After AIDS Counseling," *Akron Beacon Journal*, April 29, 1986, A1.

21. William Canterbury, "Agencies Reluctant to Accept AIDS Patient," *Akron Beacon Journal*, May 17, 1986, 21.

22. Randolph Smith, "Life and Death in Akron: Bad News, Good News," *Akron Beacon Journal*, August 13, 1986, B1.

23. Cindy Christman, conversation with the author, 2022.

24. Killian Manufacturing, L. E. Shunk Latex Products, and Youngs Rubber were three of the four largest condom manufacturers in the 1930s. Killian's plant was located near Bartges and South High Street, L. E. Shunk Latex Products was on Morgan Street, and Youngs Rubber was based in Barberton. For more on Akron as a center of condom production see Sarah Ruth Payne, "Cleaning Up After Sex: An Environmental History of Contraceptives in the United States, 1873—2010" (PhD diss., University of New Mexico, 2010).

25. "Legal Notice," *Akron Beacon Journal*, April 8, 1987, D9; Randolph Smith, "Akron Health Commission Seeks Repeal of Condom Law," *Akron Beacon Journal*, February 25, 1987, A1.

26. Charlene Nevada, "Akron Council Set to Ease Sale of Condoms," *Akron Beacon Journal*, March 24, 1987, D1.

27. "Contract for Sexual Health Educational Programming," Akron City Council Ordinance 110–1987.

28. Felsinger; Monegan, 96.

29. Mary McGrory, "The Spread of Fear," *The Washington Post*, September 17, 1985, https://www.washingtonpost.com/archive/politics/1985/09/17/the-spread-of-fear/ee19427b-3894-4eaf-9082-cb3823920e96

30. Thrity Umrigar and Robin Witek, "Loving, Dying," *Beacon* (Sunday supplement to the *Akron Beacon Journal*), August 30, 1992, 2; Erin Ruel and Richard T. Campbell, "Homophobia and HIV/AIDS: Attitude Change in the Face of an Epidemic," *Social Forces* 84, no. 4 (June 2006), https://www.jstor.org/stable/3844494.

31. Randolph Smith, "Couple's Infant Daughter at Risk; Student Lives Life of Uncertainty," *Akron Beacon Journal*, March 8, 1987, 12.

32. Cindy Christman, conversation with the author, 2022.

33. Felsinger.

34. Today, "gender nonconforming" is defined by Merriam-Webster Dictionary as "exhibiting behavioral, cultural, or psychological traits that do not correspond with the traits typically associated with one's sex" and "having a gender expression that does not conform to gender norms." "The APA Ruling on Homosexuality: The Issue Is Subtle, The Debate Still On," *The New York Times*, December 23, 1973, 109, https://www.nytimes.com/1973/12/23/archives/the-issue-is-subtle-the-debate-still-on-the-apa-ruling-on.html.

35. *Tommy Dickinson, Curing Queers: Mental Nurses and Their Patients, 1935–74* (Manchester: Manchester University Press, 2014), 23, 46.

36. Peter Piot, Sarah Russell, and Heidi Larson, "Good Politics, Bad Politics: The Experience of AIDS," *American Journal of Public Health*, 97, no. 11 (November 2007), 1934–36, https://ajph.apha publications.org/doi/full/10.2105/AJPH.2007.121418.

37. "Current Trends Mortality Attributable to HIV Infection/AIDS—United States, 1981–1990," *MMWR* 40, no. 3 (January 25, 1991), 41–44, https://www.cdc.gov/mmwr/preview/mmwrhtml/00001880.htm.

38. Akron City Council Ordinance 239–1989.

39. Felsinger.

40. Local Makeup Publication, March 27, 1992, in Gary Felsinger, "A Gay History Supplement: Reflecting Our Lives, Gay-Lesbian, Bi-Sexual, Two Spirit, Queer and Questioning." Akron-Summit County Public Library Special Collections.

41. Felsinger.

42. Felsinger; Monegan.

43. Felsinger, 5.

44. "Roseto Club (Akron, Ohio)," *Our Community Roots*, 2019, https://ourcommunityroots.com/?p=95121.

45. Felsinger.

46. Thrity Umrigar, "Gay Community Says Goodbye," *Akron Beacon Journal*, July 14, 1995, 1.

47. Felsinger.

48. Stuart Warner, "On the Streets of Akron, What You See Isn't Always What You Get," *Beacon* (Sunday supplement of the *Akron Beacon Journal*), February 3, 1985, 6.

49. Umrigar, "Gay Community."

50. Daniel R. Mullen, "First Lesbian-Gay Art Show Brings 600 To Tiny Town," *Gay People's Chronicles*, October 1, 1995, 6, https://www.pridemuseum.plus.

51. Chris Hixson, conversation with the author, 2022.

52. Stephanie Warsmith, "Vigil honors Shepard," *Akron Beacon Journal*, October 13, 1999, 17.

53. "Out in Akron" (pamphlet), October 1999.

54. "Out in Akron" (pamphlet), October 1997.

55. Bill O'Connor, "Coming Out in Akron," *Akron Beacon Journal*, October 11, 1997, B1.

56. Grace Springer, "2023 Akron Pride Festival Celebrates History, Diversity, Acceptance," Ideastream Public Media, August 25, 2023, https://www.ideastream.org/community/2023-08-25/2023-akron-pride -festival-celebrates-history-diversity-acceptance; Steve Arrington, conversation with the author, 2023.

57. Chris Hixson, conversation with Fran Wilson, 2022.

58. Chris Hixson, "Marriage Is a Legal, Not a Religious, Contract," *Akron Beacon Journal*, January 22, 2000, 9.

59. Cindy Christman, conversation with the author, 2022.

60. Steve Schmidt, conversation with the author, 2022.

61. Eric Resnick, "Akron General Nurses Settle Strike Without Benefits," *Gay People's Chronicle*, July 2, 2004, 3, https://www.pridemuseum.plus

62. John Grafton, conversation with the author, 2022; Joseph R. Biden Jr., "Executive Order on Preventing and Combating Discrimination on the Basis of Gender Identity or Sexual Orientation," The White House, https://www.whitehouse.gov/briefing-room/presidential-actions/2021/01/20/executive -order-preventing-and-combating-discrimination-on-basis-of-gender-identity-or-sexual-orientation/.

63. Eric Resnick, "Religious Rights Trump Fair Housing Rights in Akron Case," *Gay People's Chronicle*, September 13, 2002, https://www.pridemuseum.plus.

64. Eric Resnick. "Akron Council Candidates Say They Support Equal Rights Law." *Gay People's Chronicle*, October 12, 2001, https://www.pridemuseum.plus.

65. Anthony Glassman, "Akron Considers Adding Gays, TGs to Rights Law," *Gay People's Chronicle*, September 22, 2000, https://www.pridemuseum.plus. Akron City Council. Ordinance 514-2009:

Akron's Queer History

"Amending and/or Supplementing the Code of Ordinances of The City of Akron to Provide Equal Opportunity and Prohibit Discrimination on the Basis of Sexual Orientation and Gender Identity; and Declaring An Emergency."

66. City of Akron, Akron Civil Rights Commission Presentation, 2021.

67. Dirk Breiding, conversation with the author, 2022.

68. Riley Simko and Grace Howard, "Gay Games 9," *Encyclopedia of Cleveland History*, last updated July 29, 2022, https://case.edu/ech/articles/g/gay-games-9.

69. Family and news refer to "Brian" Powers (legal name) as "Egypt," using he/him/his pronouns. While news outlets conducted interviews with those who knew this individual, both names have been included in this story because names are sacred to many in the LGBTQIA+ community. The author attempted to reach out to the family to confirm details, but could not get a response.

70. Brian Joseph Powers obituary, Newcomer Cremations, Funerals & Receptions, https://www.newcomerakron.com/Obituary/185884/Brian-Powers/Akron-OH.

71. Seyma Bayram, "Who Killed Brian Powers?," *Akron Beacon Journal*, July 24,2020, A1.

72. Akron Municipal Court Case Docket. Case # 23-CR-01727 Count 1, https://courts.akronohio.gov/AkronCaseInformation/cases/criminal/23-CR-01727-001; Summit County Court of Common Pleas. #CR-2023-03-1053.

73. Seyma Bayram, "Who Killed Brian Powers?".

74. Kelley Kennedy, "Violence Against Transgender Community Grossly Underreported in Cleveland," *19 News*, March 3, 2022, https://www.cleveland19.com/2022/03/04/ive-been-sexually-assaulted-pistol-whipped-19-investigates-violence-against-transgender-community-grossly-underreported/.

75. A. M. Snyder et al. "Greater Akron LGBTQ+ Community Needs Assessment." Kent State University College of Public Health. https://www.lgbtqohio.org/greater-akron.

76. Derek Kreider, "Despite Rough Seas for LGBTQ Rights, Akron-Area Organizations Stay the Course," *Akron Beacon Journal*, June 23, 2023, https://www.beaconjournal.com/story/news/local/2023/06/25/akron-lgbtq-orgs-facing-legislative-headwinds-stay-the-course/70329649007.

77. John Russell, "Steve Arrington Has Spent His Life Making Sure the Black LGBTQ+ Community Gets Their Due," *LGBTQ Nation*, September 22, 2023, https://www.lgbtqnation.com/2023/09/steve-arrington-has-spent-his-life-making-sure-the-black-lgbtq-community-gets-their-due/.

78. Noor Hindi, "Akron's Steve Arrington on 30 Years of Advocacy for Men With HIV," *Cleveland Scene*, December 4, 2019, https://www.clevescene.com/news/akrons-steve-arrington-on-30-years-of-advocacy-for-men-with-hiv-31866429.

79. "About Us," Equitas Health Website, accessed August 8, 2024, https://equitashealth.com/about-us/; Steve Arrington, conversation with the author, 2022.

80. "Pride Clinic," Summa Health, accessed August 8, 2024, https://www.summahealth.org/specializedservices/pride-clinic.

81. A. M Snyder et al.

82. "Ohio's Equality Profile," Movement Advancement Project, accessed August 8, 2024, https://www.lgbtmap.org/equality_maps/profile_state/OH.

83. "Mapping Attacks on LGBTQ Rights in U.S. State Legislatures: 2024 Anti-LGBTQ Bills," ACLU, accessed August 8, 2024, https://www.aclu.org/legislative-attacks-on-lgbtq-rights?state=OH.

\ **26**

"You'll Be Hearing from Us, Too"

Citizen Volunteers and Environmentalism in Akron

Megan Shaeffer

When the Cuyahoga River caught fire in 1969, national attention turned to the pollution the river had suffered for decades. Cleveland became the focus of much of the media surrounding the state of the river, as well as an environmental movement centering on the improvement of water quality. Upstream of the burning river incident, however, Akronites were also concerned about the health and quality of not only the Cuyahoga River and her tributaries, but the air they breathed and the land they lived on. In Akron, movement toward environmental policies and regulations was driven in no small part by the actions of dedicated citizens, the results of which can be felt in the city, the state, and the country even today.

The story of environmentalism and volunteer action in Akron has two sides, both of which are rooted in larger historical contexts in the United States. The first is the American cultural ideal of volunteerism as a means to enact social and

"You'll Be Hearing from Us, Too" **395**

community change outside of a government framework. The second is the increased understanding of the effects that environmental degradation has on the health and welfare of individuals both within and outside of one's community. The citizens who laid the foundation of Akron's environmental successes drew together both of these threads in their campaigns to improve their community.

Here I present two instances in Akron's history where her citizens took matters into their own hands to enact environmental change. The first is the story of the women of Akron and their campaign for air quality in the late 1900s through the 1940s. The second is the tale of enthusiastic environmentalists in the 1970s and 1980s and their quest to turn a largely misused and forgotten tract of land into a park along the Cuyahoga River. They are separated by decades and took place in different sociocultural circumstances, but these stories exemplify the spirit that drove and still drives an environmental ethos in Akron's citizenry.

The Smoke Nuisance and the Women of Akron

Volunteerism has a long history in the United States, where collective action organized through clubs and associations helped lay the foundation of American cultural life from its earliest days.[1] Mid-nineteenth-century Akron had no shortage of groups, clubs, or organizations that citizens could join. Both men's and women's groups existed, but women in particular found clubs and associations to be a mechanism for realizing social or political change in their city. The Woman's Christian Temperance Union (WCTU) influenced the adoption of Prohibition, while the Woman's Suffrage Association (WSA) lobbied for women's voting rights, for example, and both groups had enthusiastic memberships in Akron.[2]

Leaders from the Akron WTCU and WSA brought their organizations and many others together by forming the Women's Council. The Women's Council was a confederation that sought to familiarize members of Akron's women's organizations with one another's initiatives and to foster collaboration between the groups. Representatives from thirty local organizations attended the first organizational session of the Women's Council[3] in 1893.[4] The Council thereafter played a part in directing the goals of its member organizations.

Women's societies of the late 1800s and early 1900s often set goals in line with their social roles in a society where gender and class dictated opportunity and prestige. Health, safety in the home, and welfare and happiness of the family was the domain of women, and this included both domestic and municipal cleanliness.[5] The Women's Council took up causes related to the sanitary conditions in Akron, advocating for better sewerage, less factory smoke, and cleaner streets.[6]

The environmental issue that got the most interest and support from the Women's Council was smoke abatement. Industrial smoke was viewed as unsightly, unsanitary, and contrary to the City Beautiful Movement at the turn of the twentieth century, which emphasized urban beautification.[7] Controlling smoke through the use of smoke abatement technology or "smoke consumers" was one strategy.

In 1891, Akron's Board of Health announced its intention to adopt smoke consumers in the city, but no ordinance requiring their use was put into place.[8] In 1893, Akron's city commissioners recommended, but pointedly noted they could not require, the use of smoke consumers and hoped manufacturers would adopt them because they could save costs by decreasing fuel waste.[9] The issue of an official ordinance requiring smoke consumers (or any type of smoke abatement) was discussed and debated by city officials throughout 1892 and 1893 with no resolution.[10] Despite these good intentions, the smoke consumer ordinance issue was tabled indefinitely by the city council in 1893, having received little support for its passage.[11] In 1906 an ordinance was finally passed that fined businesses for "smoke nuisance," but this ordinance did not in any way regulate emissions.[12]

Just as local governmental support seemed to be waning, the Women's Council stepped in to take up the cause. It became a frequent topic of discussion at conferences and meetings, where participants set out to understand the technical and practical aspects of the smoke nuisance. At an 1894 conference of the Council, a Mrs. Bennett gave a presentation on smoke abatement where various methods of smoke prevention or reduction were discussed; the topic was noted to be "of such universal interest."[13] A similar presentation made in 1900 by a Mrs. Julius Lane went into technical details on the mechanics of smoke abatement,[14] and in 1909, the president and corresponding secretary of the Women's Council were given a demonstration of a smoke consumer in use at a local pottery.[15]

In 1909, the Women's Council attempted to take the smoke nuisance problem head-on, once and for all. It was adopted as the reform initiative that the Council would work towards to make Akron a "city beautiful."[16] In July of 1909, the Women's Council drafted a resolution to ask the city to enforce its smoke nuisance ordinance as a way of pushing violators to lessen their smoke output or employ smoke abatement measures. They provided a list of fifty-five manufacturers or institutions in what was called "the opening gun" fired by the Women's Council. The City agreed to notify the offenders and make sure they would take steps to take care of the nuisance, but it would not fine or shut down any businesses on account of their smoke emissions.[17] It would be several decades before further strides against smoke emissions were made, and it would again be heavily influenced by the women of Akron.

With the passage of the Nineteenth Amendment, 1920 was a turning point for women's participation in politics. The League of Women Voters (LWV) was founded in 1920 and was the successor of the National American Women's Suffrage Association (NAWSA).[18] The LWV combined the goals of the women's suffrage movement with those of many women's associations such as the Women's Council. The LWV encouraged women to use their newfound voice in government to focus policy agendas that enacted their civic agendas concerning the health and well-being of the family and the community.[19] In Akron, this meant that the smoke abatement issue would be taken up by the LWV, and their efforts proved more successful than those of their forebears. At a meeting of the Akron chapter of the LWV in 1921, a regional director of the National League of Women Voters told attendees, "[i]t was thought that women would use the franchise merely in the interests of prohibition and municipal cleaning up ... but their influence is going to extend much further than that."[20] She was right.

Later, in January 1946, the City of Akron embarked on an anti-smoke campaign. Goals included studying and reporting on Akron's coal usage, recommending an ordinance to control smoke output and potentially developing a department to enforce such an ordinance.[21] Members of city administration, the Akron Coal Exchange, the Coal Producers Committee for Smoke Abatement, and a number of city and industrial engineers comprised the group tasked with addressing the problem.[22] Akron's LWV had already made smoke abatement their focus for 1946[23] and were invited to take part in the campaign to convey the merits of the plan to other organizations in the city and engage support for the program.[24]

By the end of 1946, it became apparent that the anti-smoke campaign had slowed,[25] but the LWV refused to let the issue stall. The LWV had created a smoke control committee headed by Adelaide McDonnell Briscoe.[26] A 1946 biography of Briscoe printed in the *Akron Beacon Journal* notes the surprise she was met with when she started attending city council meetings, but her knowledge and motivation regarding the subject were reflective of the LWV's drive to find a solution for the smoke nuisance once and for all.[27] The LWV mustered not only the political will of its own members, but also the influence of the media. *Akron Beacon Journal* reporter Paul Campbell wrote pieces on the anti-smoke campaign starting in September of 1946, noting that no action on the problem had been taken despite the planned study having been conducted and the results reported.[28] Opinion pieces were also published in the *Beacon*, including one from Briscoe herself, criticizing the lack of progress on the smoke abatement program.[29] The LWV took to the radio on local station WAKR to discuss the proposed ordinance.[30] By this time, Briscoe and the LWV were viewed as

Smoky Akron, circa 1914. \ Archives and Special Collections, University Libraries, The University of Akron.

active leaders on the issue, representing public interest in crafting an ordinance on smoke control.[31] Their role became that of "citizen experts," a well-informed base who could act as the liaison between city officials and concerned residents and who could take the lead in informing local pollution policy.[32]

A breakthrough on the issue finally came at the end of 1946. The LWV announced that it would begin a renewed campaign on smoke abatement in November of 1946, kicking it off with a radio forum featuring their own members, as well as the mayor of Akron, Charles E. Slusser.[33] Over fifty area organizations joined in support of the LWV's efforts.[34] The city council immediately announced that it was preparing to pass a smoke regulation and enforcement ordinance.[35] After another six months of discussion and debate (in which the LWV was enthusiastically involved), a smoke control ordinance finally passed in Akron on July 1, 1947.[36] An editorial in the *Akron Beacon Journal* recognized the work of the LWV in getting the ordinance crafted and passed, noting that it was the persistence of the women of the LWV that kept the issue alive and pushed the city council to act.[37] The LWV likewise thanked the *Beacon* for their role in keeping the issue alive in the public eye.[38]

Even after the ordinance took effect, the LWV made it clear they would remain involved in smoke abatement. When the city created the job posting for Akron's new smoke regulation engineer, the LWV argued that the proposed salary was too low to attract a competent applicant. After a back-and-forth on the matter at a city council meeting, a council member dismissed the LWV representatives, telling them, "[y]ou'll be hearing from us." "You'll be hearing from us, too," responded one of the women as they left.[39] This proved to be true, as later in 1947 Briscoe was named by Mayor Slusser to a three-year appointment as a member of the advisory board to assist the new smoke regulation engineer.[40] Like the earlier Women's Council, the LWV had taken up an issue that affected the environment of their community, but unlike the earlier organization, the LWV was able to firmly establish a prominent role beyond advocacy into policymaking.

Cascade Valley: A Masterful Plan

I cannot here do justice to the monumental strides of the multi-faceted environmental movement that took shape in the 1960s and 1970s in the United States. Rachel Carson's *Silent Spring*, published in 1962, became a touchstone for citizens concerned with pollution and the policies that governed it. In 1969, the burning of the Cuyahoga River brought national attention to the highly contaminated waterway, which helped spur passage of the Clean Water Act in 1972. Also in 1972, the United States and Canada reached the Great Lakes Water Quality Agreement, which defined Areas of Concern (AOC). An AOC is an area suffering environmental degradation, which impairs its use by aquatic life.[41] The Cuyahoga River met the criteria to be designated as an AOC, and work to clean her began in earnest.

Public interest in environmental issues grew in the 1960s and 1970s. New conservation-oriented clubs formed and memberships to many existing ones increased. Between 1960 and 1980, the World Wildlife Fund, Environmental Defense Fund, Friends of the Earth, Natural Resources Defense Fund, the League of Conservation Voters, Earthjustice Legal Defense Fund, Clean Water Action, Greenpeace U.SA, Trust for Public Land, the Ocean Conservancy, American Rivers, and the Sea Shepherd Conservation Society all formed—and this is not an exhaustive list![42] The Sierra Club (founded in 1892) saw its membership jump from about 31,000 to 246,000 between 1965 and 1981. In the same time period, the National Audubon Society's (founded in 1905) membership grew from 40,500 to 400,000, and the National Wildlife Federation's (founded in 1936) membership increased from 256,000 to 818,000.[43]

Such is the background to one of the most dramatic examples of the impact that citizen volunteers have had on Akron's greenscape, in the story of turning a neglected tract of land between the Cuyahoga River Gorge and the Little Cuyahoga River into a park. The Cuyahoga River forms a U across northeastern Ohio, flowing south from Geauga County down to Summit County before making a sharp turn north again as it heads out into Lake Erie. The geography of the eighty-five-mile river is a remnant of northern Ohio's ancient glacial past, though its legacy of pollution was the result of Ohio's much more recent industrial history.

Approximately two miles of the Cuyahoga River that cut through northern Akron and Cuyahoga Falls had been converted to parklands in the 1930s. The Akron Metropolitan Park District[44] (AMPD) was created in 1921 and in December of 1929, the Northern Ohio Traction & Light Company (NOT&L) donated the land at the Cuyahoga River's turning point to the young park district.[45] This became Gorge Metro Park. To the west, just beyond the confluence of the Cuyahoga and the Little Cuyahoga Rivers, another AMPD park, Sand Run, was formed. The land in between had remained largely undeveloped along the Cuyahoga, though some of it had been used as a municipal dump in the 1950s. This was Cascade Valley.

In 1973, the City of Akron's Department of Planning and Urban Development completed a comprehensive study of the city's park and recreation needs over the next twenty years.[46] One of the areas highlighted for park development was

Cascade Valley, or "the site of the old landfill and parcels around it."[47] 1973 was also the year the Portage Trail group of the Sierra Club (PTSC) was founded in Akron by Dr. Walter Sheppe, a professor of biology at The University of Akron.[48] One of the group's primary aims was the restoration and conservation of the Cascade Valley area. Sheppe suggested that through scenic easements, government ownership, and rezoning efforts, this section of the Cuyahoga River Valley could be protected from development and used by Akron citizens for recreation.[49] The PTSC intended to be part of the transformation process.

The natural partner for the park project was the AMPD, not only because it was a park district, but because of the proximity of its other parks and because of its longstanding dedication to conservation in Summit County. In 1974, the PTSC submitted the Cascade Valley Park project to the Board of Trustees of the Summit-Portage Comprehensive Health Planning Agency. The Board asked the AMPD to coordinate the project with the PTSC and with the landowners in Cascade Valley.[50] The AMPD agreed to maintain and operate the park (contingent upon the passage of a park levy in 1976), and the City of Akron would provide the money for its planning and construction.[51] The PTSC took on the role of representing public interests in the project, as well as educating citizens of Akron on the benefits of the new park.[52]

The PTSC wasted no time making their plans for the area known. In 1976, the group issued a 48-page booklet to the city and the AMPD outlining their proposal for Cascade Valley Park.[53] The proposal advocated the development of a master plan for the park and called for public involvement in removing trash, planting trees, and building new trails throughout the area. The proposal suggested that youth groups might provide labor and older volunteers could help pay for materials. Sections of the trail could also be "adopted" by volunteer groups who would be responsible for constructing and maintaining their own stretches. Public involvement in the form of letter-writing and city council attendance was also encouraged.[54] This park was to be a deeply engaging project for Akron citizens.

After the passage of a park levy in 1976, the AMPD and the City of Akron hired Wallace, McHarg, Roberts & Todd (WMRT), an architectural planning firm, to create a master plan for Cascade Valley Park. Walter Sheppe acted as the ecological consultant for the document. The ambitious plan was for a 1,500-acre park encompassing the Cuyahoga River and its confluence with the Little Cuyahoga River. Along with athletic fields, picnic areas, and hiking trails, the project would include two amphitheaters, tennis courts, canoe and bike rentals, an observation tower, a swimming area, and a nature center.[55] The plan predicted that the park would mostly serve neighborhood users from the Akron area, creating much-needed recreational opportunities for the public.[56]

The project group hosted public meetings on the master plan throughout the first half of 1978.[57] The project was presented to Akron's Parks and Recreation Committee, who had very strong feelings about public use of the new park: they wanted ballfields. "Don't even bring it (the plan) in (to council) unless you have six or seven fields (in the first phase)," Councilman (and later mayor of Akron) Don Plusquellic told the WMRT.[58] The committee felt that Akron's lack of lighted ballfields was a major recreational deficiency that the new park should alleviate. Accordingly, the revised master plan called for four lighted ballfields in the first phase of development and a total of fourteen overall. No money was appropriated for hiking trails.[59] Work on the first phase of park development soon began, and the Oxbow area of Cascade Valley Park opened for baseball and softball starting in 1981.[60]

Undeterred, members of the PTSC took matters into their own hands. The group formed a Cascade Valley Trail Committee, which aimed to develop trails through overgrown and forested areas of the park for its next development phase. In 1982 PTSC volunteers began the difficult work of flagging and clearing trails for hikers to enjoy.[61] The trails would focus on the river as well as cultural features, like two sets of stairs that had been built by the Works Progress Administration in the 1930s for a small early park called High Bridge Park.[62]

The physical labor was arduous as the volunteers picked up trash and cut through weeds and brush, but a path was also being cut through new bureaucratic ground. The park was being developed by the City of Akron and maintained by the AMPD; thus, the PTSC needed approval from both for any work they did. Both the city and the AMPD seemed amenable to working with the PTSC volunteers, though not without some ground rules. AMPD's Chief Landscape Architect Ken Avery laid out a number of guidelines the volunteers would have to follow while cutting in trails, including the preferred width of the trails (no more than four feet) and directions for removing brush and rubbish from around the trail. If these rules could be followed, Avery wrote to Bill Hahn of the city's Planning Department, "We (the AMPD) can turn the Sierra Club 'loose' on this project."[63] The City followed up with the PTSC in the spring of 1983, granting them permission to continue to construct trails.[64] Through the summer of 1983, PTSC volunteers spent their weekends toiling through the vegetation at Cascade Valley.[65]

The group's efforts met with success. By the fall of 1983, the Chuckery Trail had been completed, and the PTSC was able to enjoy it for their tenth-anniversary celebration.[66] It was also included in the AMPD's popular annual Fall Hiking Spree in 1983.[67] Locals were hiking the Chuckery even before the City of Akron and the AMPD developed the Chuckery Area in 1985 and 1986; the PTSC had opened it up for the enjoyment of Akron's hikers.

The Volunteer Environment and Akron

In 1979, members of the PTSC attended a conference in Detroit, Michigan, sponsored by the National Urban League called the City Care conference. In summing up the involvement of the PTSC in the creation of Cascade Valley Park, member Peg Schneider Bobel stated, "The story stresses the role that a volunteer organization such as the Sierra Club can take in the democratic political process, and illustrates the ways that city people can become directly involved in influencing the future of their urban environment."[68]

This is the story not just of Cascade Valley Park, but of Akron. Through voluntary efforts, the Women's Council, the LWV, and the PTSC shaped their local landscape and directed conservation in Akron. The impact of volunteers from the late 1800s through the 1980s is still felt today in the ownership and engagement that Akron's citizens feel in the conservation of their environment.

Notes

1. Kathleen L. Endres, *Akron's "Better Half": Women's Clubs and the Humanization of the City, 1825–1925* (The University of Akron Press, 2006), 3–4.

2. Endres, 85.

3. Also known as the Akron and Summit County Federation of Women's Clubs.

4. "A Woman's Council: Preliminary Steps Take for Its Organization," *Akron Beacon and Republican*, March 4, 1893. Unless otherwise noted, newspapers are cited from digital versions through Newspapers.com.

5. Terrianne K. Schulte, "Citizen Experts: The League of Women Voters and Environmental Conservation," Frontiers: A Journal of Women Studies 30, no. 3 (2009). http://www.jstor.org/stable/40388745.

6. Endres, 89.

7. David Stradling and Peter Thorsheim, "The Smoke of Great Cities: British and American Efforts to Control Air Pollution, 1860–1914," Environmental History 4, no. 1 (1999): 9. https://doi.org/10.2307/3985326; "Smoke Consumers Are a Necessity: Dr. Frederich Tells of Need of Cleanliness in Cities," *Akron Beacon Journal*, May 20, 1905; "Smoke Reducing is Tackled by Women," *Akron Beacon Journal*, July 9, 1909.

8. "Smoke Consumers: Plan for their General Adoption," *Akron Beacon and Republican*, December 5, 1891.

9. "Smoke Consumers: City Commissioners Will Recommend Their Use," *Akron Beacon and Republican*, July 25, 1893.

10. "That Smoke Nuisance," *Akron Beacon and Republican*, February 5, 1892; "Let's Have Smoke Consumers," *Akron Daily Democrat*, October 10, 1892; "Auburn Hued Was the Temper of President Chandler Last Night: He Will Have Meetings Promptly on Time Hereafter or Not at All," *Akron Daily Democrat*, November 1, 1892; "Smoke Consumers: The Ordinance that the Board of Health Wants Adopted," *Akron Beacon and Republican*, December 19, 1892.

11. "Council Sits on Two City Ordinances," *Akron Beacon and Republican*, September 19, 1893.

12. "The Smoke Nuisance in Akron Must Stop," *Akron Beacon Journal*, May 8, 1906.

13. "In a New Light: Advantages of the Free Kindergarten Presented at the Woman's Council," *Akron Beacon and Republican*, May 23, 1894.

"You'll Be Hearing from Us, Too"

14. "Women's Council: An Interesting Program for the Annual Meeting," *Akron Beacon Journal*, November 12, 1900; "What Can She Do? An Expression of Akron Women Upon the City's Needs," *Akron Beacon Journal*, November 16, 1900.

15. "Practical Test Made of Smoke Consumer," *Akron Beacon Journal*, May 31, 1909.

16. "Smoke Consumption Considered by Women," *Akron Beacon Journal*, July 8, 1909; "Smoke Reducing is Tackled by Women," *Akron Beacon Journal*, July 9, 1909.

17. "Crusade Against Smoke Started: Women's Council Submits List of Firms and Corporations Alleged to be Violating Law–Sanitary Officer Will Notify Them, but Will Not Be Radical," *Akron Beacon Journal*, July 29, 1909.

18. Schulte, 1.

19. Schulte, 1.

20. "Urges Creation of Public Sentiment Upon Women Voters," *Akron Beacon Journal*, April 1, 1921.

21. "Fight to Check Smoke Nuisance Starts This Week: Engineers' Survey to Bring Controls, Rigid Enforcement," *Akron Beacon Journal*, January 27, 1946.

22. "Fight to Check Smoke Nuisance Starts This Week: Engineers' Survey to Bring Controls, Rigid Enforcement," *Akron Beacon Journal*, January 27, 1946.

23. "League Will War on Smoke," *Akron Beacon Journal*, January 20, 1946.

24. "Fight to Check Smoke Nuisance Starts This Week: Engineers' Survey to Bring Controls, Rigid Enforcement," *Akron Beacon Journal*, January 27, 1946.

25. Campbell, Paul, "Smoke–The Black Nuisance," *Akron Beacon Journal*, September 29, 1946.

26. Briscoe, M. L., "Housewives Back Campaign Against Akron Smoke, Grime," *Akron Beacon Journal*, October 6, 1946.

27. Smith, Oscar, "Biography in Brief: Mrs. Adelaide Briscoe, *Akron Beacon Journal*, November 24, 1946, B3.

28. Paul Campbell, "Smoke–The Black Nuisance," *Akron Beacon Journal*, September 29, 1946; Paul Campbell, "War Against City Smoke is Launched," *Akron Beacon Journal*, November 11, 1946; Paul Campbell, "Council Orders New Law in Smoke Fight," *Akron Beacon Journal*, November 12, 1946; Paul Campbell, "Strict Anti-Smoke Ordinance Faces 'Worst' Violators Here: Program Offered by Women," *Akron Beacon Journal*, November 24, 1946.

29. M. L. Briscoe, "Housewives Back Campaign Against Akron Smoke, Grime," *Akron Beacon Journal*, October 6, 1946.

30. Paul Campbell, "War Against City Smoke is Launched," *Akron Beacon Journal*, November 11, 1946.

31. Paul Campbell, "Waste Burning at Two Sites Stopped," *Akron Beacon Journal*, December 5, 1946.

32. Schulte, 2.

33. Paul Campbell, "Council Orders New Law in Smoke Fight," *Akron Beacon Journal*, November 12, 1946.

34. "League of Women to Demand 'Teeth' in Smoke Curb Law," *Akron Beacon Journal*, January 30, 1947.

35. Paul Campbell, "Anti-Smoke Law Here predicted Within 10 Days: Council Planners Vow Speedy Action on Curb Measure," *Akron Beacon Journal*, February 3, 1947; Campbell, Paul, "Industry Vows Ban on Smoke," *Akron Beacon Journal*, February 13, 1947.

36. "New Smoke Ordinance Takes Effect on July 15" Five-Year Program Adopted," *Akron Beacon Journal*, July 1, 1947.

37. "Smoke Control," *Akron Beacon Journal*, July 2, 1947.

38. M. L. Briscoe, "Smoke Control Victory," *Akron Beacon Journal*, July 5, 1947.

39. "Council Moves Against Smoke," *Akron Beacon Journal*, July 8, 1947.

40. "Slusser Names 8 to Assist Smoke Regulation Chief," *Akron Beacon Journal*, November 26, 1947.

41. United States Environmental Protection Agency, "Great Lakes Areas of Concern," last updated March 21, 2023, https://www.epa.gov/great-lakes-aocs.

42. Christopher J. Bosso, Environment, Inc.: From Grassroots to Beltway (University Press of Kansas, 2005), 19–20, Table 1.1.

43. Bosso, 54–55, Table 3.1.

44. The AMPD was founded in 1921 and retained this name until 1987, when the name changed to Metro Parks, Serving Summit County. In 2014 the name changed to Summit Metro Parks, which it remains as of the publication of this work.

45. Summit Metro Parks Board Meeting Minutes, December 21, 1929, Series 1, Vol. 2, Summit Metro Parks Collection, Akron-Summit County Public Library Special Collections, Akron, OH.

46. Sierra Club, Portage Trail Group. Akron's Cascade Valley Park: A Proposal for the Development and Use of a Park in the Valleys of the Cuyahoga and Little Cuyahoga Rivers in Akron, Ohio (The Sierra Club, 1976), 7.

47. "Here's Planning Concept Behind Parks in Akron," *Akron Beacon Journal*, May 21, 1973, C1.

48. Gene Winski, "Akron Area Sierra Club to Be Formed," *Akron Beacon Journal*, February 17, 1973; "Sierra Club Formed in Five-County Area," *Akron Beacon Journal*, March 1, 1973, C19.

49. Bruce Larrick, "New Cuyahoga Park Urged by Sierra Club," *Akron Beacon Journal*, August 26, 1974, B1.

50. "Falls-Akron Park Plan Is Endorsed," *Akron Beacon Journal*, November 27, 1974, B8.

51. Summit Metro Parks Board Meeting Minutes, September 4, 1975, Series 1, Vol. 13, Summit Metro Parks Collection, Akron-Summit County Public Library Special Collections, Akron, OH.

"Cascade: 1,400-Acre Akron Park Hinges on Levy," *Akron Beacon Journal*, October 22, 1976, B6.

52. "Ecology Programs for this Month," *Akron Beacon Journal*, May 2, 1976, C2; "Cascade Park Still Not a Reality," *Akron Beacon Journal*, May 21, 1977, B3.

53. Sierra Club, Portage Trail Group, Akron's Cascade Valley Park: A Proposal for the Development and Use of a Park in the Valleys of the Cuyahoga and Little Cuyahoga Rivers in Akron, Ohio (The Sierra Club, 1976).

54. Sierra Club, Portage Trail Group, 42.

55. Wallace, McHarg, Roberts, and Todd, Cascade Valley Park Master Plan, (Philadelphia, PA, 1977).

56. Wallace, McHarg, Roberts, and Todd, 12.

57. "Speak Out: Wednesday," *Akron Beacon Journal*, February 20, 1978, A2; "A Park in the Valley," *Akron Beacon Journal*, July 22, 1978, D5.

58. William Canterbury and William Hershey, "Akron Councilmen Want More Ballfields in New Park," *Akron Beacon Journal*, July 25, 1978, B4.

59. Bruce Larrick, "Akron Park Plan to Be Made Public," *Akron Beacon Journal*, April 12, 1979, C1.

60. Summit Metro Parks Board Meeting Minutes, Series 1, Vol. 15, Summit Metro Parks Collection, Akron-Summit County Public Library Special Collections, Akron, OH.

61. Peg Bobel and Elaine Marsh, interview with the author, April 6, 2021.

62. Bobel and Marsh.

63. Kenneth U. Avery to Bill Hahn, April 15, 1983.

64. William C. Sigel to Elaine Marsh, May 9, 1983.

65. "Hikes," *Akron Beacon Journal*, July 14, 1983, B3; Barbranda Lumpkins, "New Trail Cleared in Cascade Valley," *Akron Beacon Journal*, July 17, 1983, B1.

66. "Help Chop a Path Through Valley's Underbrush," *Akron Beacon Journal*, September 15, 1983, B3.

67. Webb Shaw, "Fall Spree 20-Year Hiking Habit for 16," *Akron Beacon Journal*, November 10, 1983, D1. Note that the article incorrectly states that the PTSC helped create the Oxbow Trail, a trail that extends through the adjacent section of Cascade Valley. The trail constructed by the PTSC was the Chuckery Trail; Bobel and Marsh.

68. Peg Bobel, "Prepared Notes for City Care Conference Workshop #13," April, 1979.

\ **27**

Neighborhood Development in the Twenty-First Century

Melanie Mohler

Introduction

Neighborhood development is by no means a new phenomenon. Like many American cities, Akron utilized an Urban Renewal template in the late twentieth and early twenty-first century to distribute development funds to neighborhoods, primarily acting as a conduit of federal funds. One major source of federal funding was the Community Development Block Grant (CDBG), a federal grant administered by the US Department of Housing and Urban Development (HUD) since 1974.[1] Akron still receives CDBG funding, but the city receives about three to four times less today than in the past.[2] In the 1990s and 2000s, the city created Urban Renewal Plans focused on moderate and low-income areas to eliminate blight using various methods, including rezoning and acquiring land.[3]

In more recent years, federal funding has dwindled, and the city has shifted focus to financially support neighborhood organizations to carry out neighborhood development work. Beginning with the 2019 Capital Investment and

Community Development Program, $300,000 was specifically allocated to supporting community development corporations (CDCs).[4] Other current efforts led by the city for neighborhood development include a partnership with the Akron Community Foundation to offer Neighborhood Partnership Program (NPP) grants and the Great Streets program which launched in 2019 to assist thirteen designated Neighborhood Business Districts through business façade grants and other resources.[5]

However, with significant initial funding from the Knight Foundation and the hosting of four Better Block events around the city, four prominent CDCs have emerged in the past ten or so years: North Hill CDC (NHCDC, formerly known as North Akron CDC), The Well CDC in Middlebury, Better Kenmore CDC (formerly known as Kenmore Neighborhood Alliance), and Progressive Alliance CDC (PACDC) in West Akron.

Community development corporations are nonprofits and organizations that support the revitalization of a particular community, typically one that has historically experienced disinvestment, by focusing on solutions such as safe and affordable housing, economic development, and neighborhood revitalization. CDCs first formed as a response to urban renewal projects led by the federal government in the 1950s and 1960s; however, CDCs were not seriously recognized as their own "field" of organizations until the late 2000s.[6] According to the Sixth National Community Development Census Survey published by the Urban Institute in September 2023, there were just over 6,200 CDCs operating in the U.S. between 2019 and 2021.[7]

North Hill, Middlebury, Kenmore, and West Akron have all hosted Better Block events. Better Block is a nonprofit based in Dallas, Texas, that organizes Better Block events in neighborhoods across the country. An underutilized block within the neighborhood is reimagined for a weekend with pop-up vendors, blocked-off roads, bike lanes, and other amenities all led with community input and support in mind. The events are meant to give residents an idea of what the block could look like and inspire change.[8]

In September 2017, the Knight Foundation awarded NHCDC, The Well, and Better Kenmore $240,000 to each organization. The Knight Foundation "follow[ed] years of experimentation and observation in communities that the city consider[ed] on the tipping point between success and ruin." The Knight Foundation first awarded $50,000 to these neighborhoods to host Better Block events in North Hill in 2015, Middlebury in 2016, and Kenmore in 2017,[9] and later awarded $73,600 to Copley Road in 2019.[10]

Neighborhood Development in the Twenty-First Century

The Exchange House, located at 760 Elma Street. The Exchange House was purchased by Jason Roberts, founder of Better Block. Ownership transferred to NHCDC in 2019. \ Photo courtesy of NHCDC.

North Hill

In May 2015, North Hill was the first Akron neighborhood to host a Better Block event. It was held in the Temple Square business district at North Main Street and East Cuyahoga Falls Avenue. With $50,000 of funding from the Knight Foundation, the event was organized by residents, the Akron Metropolitan Area Transportation Study (AMATS), the International Institute, and led by Tina and John Ughrin. The goal of the event was to celebrate the neighborhood's history, celebrate its newer immigrant population, bring about changes to the event area to make it more pedestrian- and biker-friendly, and add more trees. There was an open-air market with different activities and events throughout the three-day event.[11] Overall the Better Block event was a success, drawing in thousands of people to an area that typically sees little foot traffic. Data collected from the Better Block event showed that participants wanted the bike lanes to remain and the road to be reduced to two lanes to slow traffic.[12]

By 2017, NHCDC had formed and was led by John Ughrin.[13] The Exchange House also opened that year at 760 Elma Street and was managed by Katie Beck, who worked as an AmeriCorps VISTA volunteer for Better Block.[14] Better Block founder Jason Roberts had purchased the vacant home in 2015. The Exchange House's first floor served as a community event space while the second floor offered rooms to rent via Airbnb.[15] Ownership of The Exchange House was later transferred to NHCDC in 2019. Beck credits The Exchange House as the real catalyst for getting NHCDC going. In early 2020, Beck was appointed Executive Director. The Exchange House temporarily closed due to COVID-19, but later reopened as a community space and upstairs rooms for rent.[16]

Entrepreneurship has been one of NHCDC's main areas of focus to bolster one of Akron's only growing neighborhoods in terms of population, according to the 2020 US Census. Opportunities NHCDC has offered have included The Maker House, NoHi Pop-Up, and NoTique.[17]

The Maker House opened in March 2021 next door to The Exchange House with the intent to promote entrepreneurship of women. As the name suggests, it offers a maker space with studio space and equipment such as sewing machines available for community use. NoHi Pop-Up opened at 778 North Main Street in 2020 during the COVID-19 pandemic and thrived despite offering takeout only.[18] The space was a commercial kitchen for minority and women food entrepreneurs to host weekly kitchen takeovers and offer their own menus. NoHi was a great success and generated $600,000 in sales for the food entrepreneurs over its nearly three years of operation. Unfortunately, due to program costs and inflation, NHCDC was unable to provide an affordable opportunity for participants and closed NoHi in December 2022.[19] NoTique, a store for local entrepreneurs and makers to sell their goods, opened around the holiday season of 2020 but closed a year later.[20] A newer program to assist entrepreneurs has been an Aspiring Entrepreneurs program in partnership with Bounce Innovation Hub. It is a ten-week program for North Hill residents interested in starting a business.

Justin Chenault, NHCDC's former Operating Director, became the Executive Director in 2022. There is now a focus on revitalizing certain areas in the North Hill neighborhood, namely Temple Square and Howard Street, as well as outdoor recreational areas such as Waters Park and fostering further growth in People's Park.[21] The backyards of The Exchange House and The Maker House were imagined as People's Park, an outdoor community event space beginning in 2018.[22] A NoHi Food Truck Park opened in May 2023 adjacent to People's Park to support food truck businesses and further promote the use of a community gathering space.[23] As of May 2024, the Howard Street Heritage Courtyard project, a creative placemaking initiative installed at the intersection of North Howard Street and West Cuyahoga Falls Avenue to celebrate North Hill's diverse heritage and the history of African Americans on Howard Street, was nearly complete. Murals created by local artists will be part of the project and rotated out twice a year.[24]

Middlebury

In July 2016, Middlebury was the next Akron neighborhood to host a Better Block event. The event activated the intersection of North Arlington Street and East Market Street with food trucks, outdoor seating, a community garden, live entertainment, and improved bicycle and pedestrian infrastructure. The crosswalks created for the event later became permanent. A drive-thru bank was also renovated to act as a coffee shop.[25]

After the Better Block event ended, there were concerns from Middlebury residents that nothing would change. Many members of the planning team continued to work on the newly formed What's Next Committee. The following year, the What's Next Committee developed the Middlebury Neighborhood Survey. 211 survey responses were collected from April to November 2017 by canvassing the neighborhood. The survey data then informed the Middlebury Neighborhood Plan, which was published in March 2019.[26] The Committee also determined five contradictions of Middlebury based on current conditions: a central neighborhood without a center; a walked neighborhood that isn't walkable; a working-class neighborhood without enough work; a neighborhood surrounded by anchors that don't anchor wealth here; and a neighborhood of

Volunteers from the Middlebury Better Block event in 2016. \ Photo courtesy of Better Block

homes without enough homeowners. Residents, business owners, leaders from nonprofit and community-based organizations, and the city of Akron all contributed to the creation of the plan.[27]

Around the same time as the Middlebury Better Block event, The Well CDC was founded by Zac Kohl. Kohl grew up attending First Presbyterian Church located at 647 East Market Street and later moved to Middlebury with his family in 2012. While renovating his home on Jewett Street, he noticed that many homes near him were vacant. Kohl worked with neighbors and friends to renovate some of the houses and worked with the city to demolish others. Eventually Kohl had reached his financial capacity to renovate houses and looked to create a CDC to continue this work in Middlebury.[28]

The Well has three initiatives: restoring housing, creating economy, and supporting place. The Well purchased their first home in 2018 and began the "60 homes for 60 months" program. As of February 2023, they have renovated eighty-four homes in the Middlebury neighborhood. The focus has been on renovating existing housing, not building new homes; however, The Well did build new housing in 2022. Along with home renovations, The Well offers other programs to help Middlebury residents with their homes. In the summer of 2020, the Community Tool Library was launched, making more than five hundred tools available for an annual membership fee.[29] Home maintenance classes were also launched. Together, these two initiatives give residents an opportunity to develop skills for home maintenance and easily obtain the tools needed for a project or repair.[30]

At the end of 2019, The Well launched Akron Food Works, a shared space inside The Well's headquarters (in the former First Presbyterian Church on East Market Street). It is a shared kitchen space that can be rented out hourly by small-scale food entrepreneurs. The program is meant for small food businesses that want to work past cottage laws and operate in a fully licensed kitchen. By the summer of 2021, the Workforce Development program had ramped up. The program is a five-week development course that partners with local employers such as Summa Hospital and Children's Hospital to help people find jobs in the area.

The Well's final prong is supporting place. Since 2018, The Well has partnered with Mason Community Learning Center through the Akron Hope program to provide support and resources to students, teachers, and families to make them feel part of something that's bigger than themselves.[31] 647 Coffee is another initiative that opened inside The Well's headquarters in 2017 to help fund The Well's mission and provide a sense of community in Middlebury.[32]

The Well continues to make an impact in Middlebury. Their 2023 Community Impact Report documented the organization's achievements in 2023, which

Neighborhood Development in the Twenty-First Century

included the renovation of eight single-family homes and an investment of $2.1 million into affordable housing in Middlebury. The Well also received The Ohio CDC of the Year Award from the Ohio CDC Association in 2023.[33] Highlights from 2024 included The Well purchasing their one hundredth home and hosting events such as the Meet the Maker Mixer for Akron Food Works entrepreneurs.[34]

Better Kenmore CDC

In September 2017, Kenmore held a Better Block event on Kenmore Boulevard focusing on the blocks between 13th Street and 16th Street. The event used community input to focus on imagining businesses that acted as third spaces and would encourage residents to linger on the Boulevard and make the area more pedestrian-friendly.[35]

Better Kenmore CDC,[36] initially founded in 2016 by Angela Miller and Dave and Kathy Hoppe, focused on bettering Kenmore through revitalizing business and culture.[37] Shortly after the Better Block event that Better Kenmore helped organize, the neighborhood group received $240,000 from the Knight Foundation. Tina Boyes was hired as Executive Director and the organization transitioned from a neighborhood volunteer group to a CDC.[38]

Better Kenmore CDC has a strong focus on physical space and placemaking, particularly for Kenmore Boulevard between 13th Street and 16th Street. [39] After the Better Block event, it became clear that Kenmore's niche is music, with several local music venues and businesses on the Boulevard and musicians living in the neighborhood. A Better Block event survey also found that many residents felt that Kenmore Boulevard was unsafe.[40] The CDC has worked to support businesses and bring more people to the Boulevard so that more is happening, and to create a safer environment. First Fridays, sponsored in part by Better Kenmore and Akron Civic Commons, are held on the first Friday of warmer months to activate the area with live music and promote local businesses.[41]

A 2019 Neighborhood Vision Plan outlined five goals for Kenmore: create a culture of collaborative planning among the city, residents, community groups, businesses, and property owners; initiate a shared vision of development for Kenmore; make Kenmore a more walkable, bikeable, and livable neighborhood; provide opportunity for economic development and attract businesses and jobs to Kenmore; and create a blueprint for short-term and long-term improvements.[42] A market study was also completed in 2019, which offered insight into the businesses that could be sustained in Kenmore. It found that the neighborhood could support four restaurants, two of which, SRINA Tea House and the Nite Owl, have opened as of the summer of 2022.[43] Since 2020, sixteen businesses and organizations have opened on the Boulevard. The CDC has worked to support these businesses and their growth to encourage Kenmore residents to stay in the neighborhood for amenities and entertainment.[44] Better Kenmore also partnered with the JOBS (Jump on Board for Success) program and CareSource Insurance to offer culinary classes to moms and young women. After completion of the course, participants can look for opportunities in Kenmore.[45]

In 2023, the CDC rebranded to Better Kenmore CDC and Josh Gippin became Executive Director.[46] The CDC's focus has been on Kenmore Boulevard, but there have been more recent efforts to advocate for Kenmore's schools. After successful lobbying, Akron Public Schools will rebuild Miller South and Pfeiffer Elementary on the former site of Kenmore High School. Better Kenmore's 2023 Annual Impact Report, published in 2024, highlighted their achievements from 2023 based on the organization's strategic priorities: amplify Akron's Music Row, ignite neighborhood-friendly investment, create spaces that sing, and engage the community.[47]

The last two years have brought more changes for Better Kenmore. In July 2024, Better Kenmore opened a new headquarters and small business resource center in the neighborhood's business district at 1028 Kenmore Boulevard. The building had been vacant for over twenty years and was donated to Better Kenmore by the owners of Kenmore Comics. Better Kenmore was then able to renovate the building through funding from the city, GAR Foundation,

A performance during a First Friday Kenmore event. \ Photo courtesy of Emmy Strong

Neighborhood Development in the Twenty-First Century

Summit County Land Bank, and Akron Community Foundation.[48] In February 2025, the Development Director Eleni Manousogiannakis was named the Executive Director.[49]

Copley Road/West Akron

Akron's most recent Better Block event was hosted on Copley Road between Hawkins and Nome Avenues in the Maple Valley district of West Akron. Progressive Alliance CDC partnered with the Knight Foundation, Summit County Think Tank Coalition, and community members to facilitate the event in May 2019.[50] Community input leading up to the event voiced concerns regarding safety and aesthetics of the area. As part of the event, a pop-up police department was provided to connect police with the community. They created three parklets to use for seating and music performances. Microgrants were offered to businesses in the area to improve their façades. Similar to previous Better Block events, foot traffic increased in an area that had not seen a lot of activity in years and provided a safe space for community members to gather.[51]

PACDC was formed in 2018 by Reverend Dr. David Nelson. As Senior Pastor of New Hope Baptist Church in the Sherbondy Hill neighborhood, he saw first-hand a need for a neighborhood organization to address the issues his congregants were experiencing. The Better Block event helped PACDC gain legitimacy as a neighborhood organization.[52]

PACDC has focused on economic development in West Akron, primarily in the main corridors of Copley East, Sherbondy Hill, and the Maple Valley business district. The areas of economic development include small business microenterprise, digital inclusion, and workforce development. PACDC supports small minority-owned businesses with microgrants and support for those looking to start a business, such as workshops, scholarships, and a business development cohort. Digital inclusion efforts in 2021 and 2022 were led in part by funding from Summit County.[53] PACDC distributed devices and offered technical support to qualifying Temporary Assistance for Needy Families-eligible residents in West Akron.[54] PACDC also fosters workforce development with their Work Forward program. The first cohort has had seven participants placed in jobs.[55] Additionally, during the height of the COVID-19 pandemic, PACDC distributed COVID-19 safety kits and partnered with local restaurants to give out over six hundred free meals to residents.[56]

PACDC led the creation of a West Akron Neighborhood Plan beginning in 2022. The plan was published in the spring of 2024 and covers the West Akron and Sherbondy Hill neighborhoods, from Mull Avenue to the north, Exchange

Street to the northeast, Route 59 to the east, I-76 to the south, and Collier Road to the west. The project team consisted of MKSK, an urban planning firm based in Cleveland that has worked with other Akron CDCs to produce neighborhood plans, Project Ujima, and KM Date Community Planning. Based on community input gathering during the planning process, ten big ideas were identified: foster vibrant neighborhood districts; announce West Akron; grow local businesses and jobs; support housing opportunity for all; cultivate neighborhood third places; activate park and public spaces; create safe streets; expand food access; heal the Route 59 divide; and build capacity to realize plan ideas. These big ideas will serve as a roadmap for future planning in West Akron and Sherbondy Hill.[57]

Other Neighborhood Development Efforts

The four previous CDCs mentioned are not the only neighborhood organizations in Akron. Other organizations have developed, with some having been formed as far back as the 1980s. East Akron Neighborhood Development Corporation (EANDC) was formed in 1982 with a mission to provide affordable housing.[58] Other notable neighborhood organizations include the Downtown Akron Partnership, created in 1996 to enhance Downtown Akron[59]; West Hill Neighborhood Organization (WHNO) in West Hill, Highland Square, which first formed in 1997[60]; and Neighborhood Network of Habitat for Humanity of Summit County in Middlebury and University Park, which held its first community meeting in 2012.[61] While many of Akron's neighborhood organizations have been successful, not all of them have been. University Park Alliance (UPA) was formed in 2001 to revitalize a fifty-block radius around The University of Akron. They had received over $13 million in funding from the Knight Foundation since 2002, but it was later discovered in late 2012 that funding was mismanaged.[62]

Conclusion

This chapter is only a glimpse into the more recent efforts of neighborhood development in the city of Akron. NHCDC, The Well, Better Kenmore, and PACDC in particular have emerged relatively recently, and have experienced great success to date; we are now beginning to see the fruits of their labor. Other neighborhood organizations are also growing and providing resources to their respective communities. Each organization is finding what niche they need to fill in terms of services and resources within their own neighborhood and build trust among residents. Partnerships between neighborhood organizations, the city, businesses, foundations, and other sources of funding are flourishing in Akron, and it seems that this will be the case for years to come.

Neighborhood Development in the Twenty-First Century

Musicians perform in front of businesses at the corner of Copley Road and South Hawkins Avenue during the Copley Road Better Block event in 2019. \ Photo courtesy of Better Block

Notes

1. "Community Development Block Grant," US Department of Housing and Urban Development. Last updated December 22, 2022. https://www.hud.gov/program_offices/comm_planning/cdbg.

2. Jason Segedy, City of Akron's Director of Planning and Urban Development, interview with the author, February 21, 2023.

3. Segedy.

4. "2019 Capital Investment and Community Development Program," City of Akron. https://www.akronohio.gov/cms/2019CIPprogram/2019_capital_investment_community_development_program.pdf.

5. Segedy.

6. Erekaini, Rachid. "What is a Community Development Corporation?" National Alliance of Community Economic Development Associations. September 17, 2014. https://www.naceda.org/index.php?option=com_dailyplanetblog&view=entry&category=bright-ideas&id=25%3Awhat-is-a-community-development-corporation-&Itemid=171

7. Corianne Payton Scally, Will Curran-Groome, Alexa Kort, and Shubhangi Kumari, "The State of US Community-Based Development Organizations, 2019–2021," Urban Institute, September 2023, 1.

8. "About Us." Better Block. Accessed March 31, 2023. https://www.betterblock.org/about.

9. Doug Livingston, "Grants Aim to Stabilize Districts," *Akron Beacon Journal*, September 27, 2017.

10. Doug Livingston, "Copley Road Next Up for Better Block Makeover," *Akron Beacon Journal*, February 1, 2019.

11. Stephanie Warsmith, "Weekend Activities Offer Hope for Future," *Akron Beacon Journal*, May 14, 2015.

12. Rick Armon, "Lively Time in North Hill," *Akron Beacon Journal*, May 18, 2015.

13. Initially known as North Akron CDC (NACDC), which encompassed the North Hill, Chapel Hill, and Cascade Valley neighborhoods. NACDC was later changed to North Hill CDC (NHCDC) in 2022 to focus on the North Hill neighborhood.

14. Katie Beck, former Executive Director of NHCDC, interview with the author, January 24, 2023.

15. Theresa Cottom, "Exchange House Opens," *Akron Beacon Journal*, March 4, 2017.

16. Beck.

17. Justin Chenault, Executive Director of NHCDC, interview with the author, February 20, 2023.

18. Beck.

19. Kerry Clawson and Tawney Beans, "NoHi Closing Pop-Up Saturday in Akron's North Hill," *Akron Beacon Journal*, December 2017, 2022.

20. Beck.

21. Justin Chenault, Executive Director of NHCDC, interview with the author, February 20, 2023.

22. Beck.

23. "NoHi Food Truck Park," North Hill CDC, https://northhillcdc.org/nohi-food-truck-park/, accessed March 31, 2023

24. "Howard St. Heritage Courtyard," North Hill Community Development Corporation, accessed July 21, 2024, https://northhillcdc.org/howard-street-heritage-courtyard/

25. "Middlebury Better Block," Better Block, Accessed March 11, 2023. https://www.betterblock .org/2016/middlebury-better-block.

26. Marissa Little, Vice President of Programming, Habitat for Humanity of Summit County, Ron Shultz, Neighborhood Network Founding Member and Core Member, and Rochelle Sibbio, President & CEO, Habitat for Humanity of Summit County, interview with the author, March 17, 2023.

27. "Middlebury Neighborhood Plan," March 8, 2019. https://thewellakron.com/wp-content/ uploads/2018/08/Middlebury-Book-REVISED-LR.pdf

28. Zac Kohl, Founder and Executive Director of The Well CDC, interview with the author, February 14, 2023.

29. Zac Kohl, Founder and Executive Director of The Well CDC, interview with the author, February 14, 2023.

30. "Community Tool Library," The Well CDC, https://thewellakron.com/community-tool/.

31. Kohl.

32. 647 Coffee was initially known as Compass Coffee until May 2024.; Theresa Cottom, "Compass Coffee Fills Up for Mixer," *Akron Beacon Journal* (Akron, OH), March 5, 2018.

33. "2023 Community Impact Report," The Well Community Development Corporation, 2024, 1, 5.

34. The Well Community Dev. Corp. (@thewellakron), "2024 was full of milestones and new opportunities...", Instagram, December 31, 2024.

35. "Kenmore Better Block," Better Block. https://www.betterblock.org/2017/kenmore-better-block accessed March 31, 2023.

36. Initially known as Kenmore Neighborhood Alliance (KNA), KNA was later rebranded as Better Kenmore CDC in April 2023 (https://www.betterkenmore.org/post/kenmore-neighborhood-alliance -rebrands-as-better-kenmore-community-development-corporation)

37. Theresa Bennett, "Angela Miller Builds Connections in Kenmore," *Akron Beacon Journal*, December 29, 2019.

38. Doug Livingston, "Grants Aim to Stabilize Districts," *Akron Beacon Journal*, September 27, 2017.

39. Tina Boyes, Consultant, former Executive Director of Better Kenmore CDC), interview with the author, March 14, 2023.

40. Malcolm X. Abram, "Let's Hear it for Kenmore," *Akron Beacon Journal*, January 11, 2018.

41. Tina Boyes, Consultant, former Executive Director of Better Kenmore CDC, in discussion with author, March 14, 2023.

42. "Kenmore Neighborhood Plan," January 2019.

43. Kerry Clawson, "Joy of Tea: Akron Native Brings SRINA Tea House to Kenmore," *Akron Beacon Journal*, August 12, 2022.

Neighborhood Development in the Twenty-First Century

44. Boyes.

45. "JOBS Culinary Classes," JOBS, accessed April 2, 2023. https://jumponboardforsuccess.org/jobs-culinary-classes.

46. "Kenmore Neighborhood Alliance Announces New Executive Director," Better Kenmore, accessed April 1, 2023, https://www.betterkenmore.org/post/kenmore-neighborhood-alliance-announces-new-executive-director

47. "2023 Annual Impact Report," Better Kenmore Community Development Corporation, 2024, 3–4.

48. Thompson, Anthony. "Better Kenmore CDC to Unveil New Headquarters, Resource Center Friday," *Akron Beacon Journal*, July 31, 2024.

49. Better Kenmore CDC, "New Executive Director!," Facebook, February 8, 2025, 3:14PM.

50. Livingston, Doug. "Copley Road Next Up for Better Block Makeover," *Akron Beacon Journal*, February 1, 2019.

51. Nightingale, Krista. "Re-Imagining Copley Road," Better Block. June 11, 2019. https://www.betterblock.org/post/re-imagining-copley-road.

52. David Nelson, Executive Director of Progressive Alliance CDC, interview with the author, March 7, 2023.

53. "Community Impact Report," Progressive Alliance Community Development Corporation. 2022.

54. Emily Mills, "'People Need Help Now More Than Ever," *Akron Beacon Journal*, July 5, 2021.

55. David Nelson, Executive Director of Progressive Alliance CDC, interview with the author, March 7, 2023.

56. "Community Impact Report," Progressive Alliance Community Development Corporation. 2022.

57. "West Akron Neighborhood Plan," Progressive Alliance Community Development Corporation, City of Akron, MKSK, 2024, 39.

58. "East Akron Neighborhood Development Corporation," Candid GuideStar, accessed April 2, 2023. https://www.guidestar.org/profile/34-1365690

59. "About DAP," Downtown Akron Partnership, accessed April 2, 2023. https://www.downtownakron.com/about

60. "West Hill Neighborhood Organization," West Hill Neighborhood Organization, accessed April 2, 2023. http://www.whno.org/

61. Little, Shultz, Sibbio.

62. Betty Lin-Fisher, "Akron Officials Piece Together Grand Collapse," *Akron Beacon Journal*, May 11, 2014.

Index

AA Founders Day, 356

abolitionism, 28, 29, 30, 39–40, 42–51, 54–56, 59

AIDS epidemic, 378–80

Akron Aeros, 292, 293, 357

Akron AIDS Collaborative, 380, 383, 388

Akron Anti-Slavery Society, 87

Akron Area Interfaith Council, 104, 211

Akron Armory, 71, 96, 139, 157, 275, 350, 353

Akron Art Museum, 27, 354, 356

Akron Baptist Temple, 98, 205, 206–12, 214, 218, 221, 223

Akron Bible Church, 97–98

Akron Bicentennial Commission, 2

Akron Candy Company, 133–34

Akron Chamber of Commerce, 128

Akron Children's Hospital, 22, 190–91, 287, 412

Akron City Council, 25, 210, 357, 379, 386–87, 396, 400

Akron City Hospital, 128

Akron Council of Churches, 100, 104

Akron Department of Planning, 310–22, 332–33, 401

Akron *Germania* (newspaper), 130, 131

Akron Gospel Tabernacle, 182, 204, 212

Akron Innerbelt, 298–99, 309–22, 332, 351, 377

Akron Interfaith Council, 104, 211

Akron Law School, 157

Akron Ministerial Association, 91, 96, 100, 104

Akron Plan, the, 90, 126–27

Akron Police Department, 180, 185, 187, 189, 19, 193, 198, 327–33, 377, 387, 415

Akron Pride, 383–84

Akron Symphony Orchestra, 305

Akron YWCA, 72, 114

Akron Zoo, 333, 356

Akron-Canton Regional Foodbank, 103

Alcoholics Anonymous, 34, 356

All-America City, 333, 352

American Marble and Toy Manufacturing Company, 129–30

American Professional Football Association (later the National Football League), 257

American Revolution, 9

Anderson Rubber Company, 139–40, 144

Angley, Ernest, Rev., 104, 205, 217, 218–30, 289–90

Annunciation Catholic Church, 99–100

Annunciation Greek Orthodox Church, 93–95, 96

Anti-Slavery Bugle (newspaper), 56–59, 61

Appalachian peoples, 96–97, 100, 201–202, 254–55, 325

Applebaum, Morton M., Rabbi, 341

Arlington Church of God, 102, 216

Armstrong, Tim, Rev., 216, 217

Arrington, Steve, 388–89

Asia Services in Action (ASIA Inc.), 75

Aster Avenue (neighborhood), 352

Auerbach, Dan, 371–74

421

B.F. Goodrich Company, 143, 237

Ballard, John, 313, 327–32

Barber, Ohio Columbus, 128–29

Bartges House, 27

Bartges, Catharine Ann Crump, 27

Bartges, Dr. Samuel F., 27

baseball and softball, 165–75, 348–49, 355, 357, 403

Battered Women's Shelter, 187

Bayard Rustin LGBTQ+ Center, 388

Better Akron Foundation, 99

Better Block, 408

Better Kenmore CDC, 408

Bierce, Lucius V., 48

Billington, Charles, Rev., 210–12

Billington, Dallas, Rev., 98, 205–12, 218

Black Keys, The (band), 371–74

Black laws, 40, 325

Black peoples, 295–300, 309–22, 336–45

blimps, 354

Bliss, George, 35

Blossom Music Center, 329

Bob Denton Safety Forces Support Center, 195–99

Brown Street Baptist Church, 98

Brown, John, 39–51, 236–37, 325, 338

Brown, Owen, 39–40, 42

Buchtel College, 90

Buchtel High School, 214, 338, 342–43, 345

Buchtel, John R., 90, 126

Buckeye Mower and Reaper Works, 126

Burnham, Carl, Rev., 104, 182, 203, 205, 212–14, 217, 230

Burnham, David, Rev., 104, 211, 212–15

Burrell, J. Milton, Rev., 341

Buxton, Glen, 371

Calvary Temple, 221

canal boat captains, 32–35

Canal Park, 355, 357

Carney, Patrick, 371–74

Carney, Ralph, 371

Casale, Gerald "Jerry" V., 365–68

Cascade (North Akron), 22

Cascade Locks Park Association, 356

Cascade Mill Race, 16, 18–21, 29, 124

Cascade Plaza, 351

Cascade Valley Park, 400–404

Cathedral Buffet, 222, 229–30

Cathedral of Tomorrow, 205–6, 211, 217–26

Cathedral Tower, 222

Catholic peoples, 71, 86, 87, 91, 95

Cayuga peoples, 7, 8, 9

Central High School, 302

cereal manufacturing industry, 124

Chapel Hill Mall, 350

Chapel, The, 205–6, 211–17

Chief Logan, 9, 12n16

children, 16–17, 111

Chinese, 74

City Church A/C, 212

City of Akron Planning Department, 347–59

Civic Theatre, 350, 356

Civic Unity Council, 330

Civil Rights movement of the 1960s, 324, 344

clay products industry, 122–23

Cleveland, 33

Clinton, Bill, 216, 333

Coe, David Allan, 370

Coming Together project, 216, 333

Community Action Akron Summit, 317

Community Chest, 72, 210

community development corporations (CDCs), 407–16

Conageresa (Broken Kettle), 8

Conageresa's town, 10

Copley Road (neighborhood), 352

Cosmopolitan club, the, 296

Croatians, 66

Crosby, Dr. Eliakim, 16

Crosby, Marcia Calista, 16, 29

Crypt, the (music venue), 365

Cuyahoga Town (exact location unknown, but possibly near Peninsula, Ohio), 8

Cuyahoga Valley National Park, 24, 240, 348, 356

Index

Delaware, *see* Lenape
Denton House, 184, 189
Denton, Bill, Rev., 178–99, 202–5, 206, 208, 212–14, 230
Denton, Bob, Rev., 178–99, 205
Devo (band), 360, 365–68, 373
Diamond Deli, 357
Diamond Match, 128
divorce, 29, 195
domestic workers, 109–18
Doodlebug commuter train crash (1940), 303
Douglas, Lloyd C., Rev., 96, 98–99
Douglass, Frederick, 42, 45, 49, 56
Downtown Akron Partnership, 358, 416
Du Bois, W.E.B., 61
Dum-Dum lollipops, 134
Dyke, Samuel C., 129

East Akron Neighborhood Development Corporation, 416
East High School, 370
Edison, Thomas and Mina, 127
Elevate Greater Akron, 333
Ellet Brethren Church, 103
Enterprise Manufacturing Company, 133
Equitas Health, 389
ethnic clubs, 66–69, 75, 91
Evans, Opie, 330

Fairlawn, 314
Fairlawn Heights Golf Club, 238
Fenn, Jonathan, 23
Firestone, 354
Firestone Country Club, 236–40, 356
Firestone High School, 343, 371
Firestone, Harvey, 158, 326
First Church of Christ, Scientist, 92
First Congregational Church, 87, 104
First Methodist Episcopal Church, 87, 90, 93, 126
First Night (New Year's Eve party), 358
First Presbyterian Church, 87, 301
First United Methodist Church, 90

Fitzhugh, Charles, 296
football, 252–63
Ford, Mark, 216
Fort Island (Fairlawn, Ohio), 7
Fowler, Ron, 216
Franklin Mills (Kent), Ohio, 39, 43
Freed, Alan, 270–71, 360–62
Fry, Shirley, 242–44
Furnace Street Mission, 177–199, 203–5, 212, 213

GAR Foundation, 414
Garfield High School, 387
General Tire, 64, 143, 165, 167, 171, 174–76, 269, 354, 373
George, Edward A., 78–79
George's Tangier, 78–79
Germans and German Americans, 64, 66, 86, 91, 124, 130
Ghoulardi (alter ego of Ernie Anderson), 273, 364
Glendale Cemetery, 18, 23, 126, 127, 131, 157, 306
Glory Barn, 97–98
golf, 236–41
Goodrich, Charles C., 236
Goodyear Heights (neighborhood), 42, 167, 170, 326, 348, 352
Goodyear Tire & Rubber Company, 72, 143, 145, 167, 237, 354, 358, 367
Goosetown (neighborhood), 64, 66, 75
Gore, the, 22, 87
Gothic Building, 350
Grace Cathedral, 205, 206, 217–30, 289
Grace Park, 376–79
Great Depression, The, 99, 100, 114, 119, 131, 175, 204, 212, 238, 328
Grismer, Karl, 2, 14, 87, 266
Guyasuta, 9

Halas, George, 258–61
Hale Farm and Village, 53, 347, 356
Hall, Philander, 24
Hall's Corner, 24–25

Harbel Manor, 115
Harrison, Greg, Rev., 314–15, 321
Haven of Rest, 103
Heart to Heart, 103
Hewett, Howard, 370
Highland Square (neighborhood), 34, 66,
    352, 356, 376, 383, 416
Hill, Valerie, 381–82
Holland, Ed, Rev., 212
Horns, Miller, 299–300
House of the Lord, The, 210, 311
Howard Street, 23–24
Howard, Charles Wesley (C.W.), 13–38
Hower family, 117
Hower House and Hower House Museum,
    116, 349, 354, 356
Hudson, Ohio, 39, 42, 43
Humbard, Rex, Rev., 104, 205, 217–26, 230
Hungarians, 66, 67, 83, 92
Hynde, Chrissie, 368–70

Ingram, James, 370
Innerbelt, 298–99, 309–22, 332, 340, 351–52,
    356, 377
International Institute of Akron, 72–74
Iredell, Seth, 23, 25, 32
Irish (people) and Irish Americans, 15, 63,
    86, 87
Italians and Italian Americans, 66, 95, 180

James, LeBron, 79, 244, 246, 247, 253, 373
jazz, 296
Jenkins, Carol Heiss, 250–51
Jenkins, David, 249–51
Jenkins, Hayes Alan, 249–51
Jenkins, Hayes R., 251
Jews, 65–66, 67, 71, 91, 295, 343, 344
Johnson, Gus, 246–47
Johnson, Joey, Rev., 311–23
Jones, Bob, 202

Kenmore (neighborhood), 352, 408, 413–15
Kent State University, 364

Ketchum, Charlie, 175
King, Judge Leicester, 29
King, Martin Luther, Jr., 61
Knepper, George, 2
Knight Foundation, 408, 413
Knight, John S., 161, 303, 349
Knight, Katharine, 117
Kohl, Zac, 412
Ku Klux Klan, 70–72, 98, 159–60, 202,
    253, 325
Kuhlman, Katharine, 210, 218

Lane, Samuel, 26, 28
Larson, Knute, Rev., 215
Leadership Akron, 353
Lee, Robert E., 49
Lenape (Delaware), 8, 9
Little Harlem, 295
Little Tikes, 148
Lively Commission, 332
Lively, Edwin, 331
Lock Two Park, 352
Lord Dunmore's War, 9
Love Akron, 103, 216

Mahican peoples, 8
Malik, Shammas, 79
Maple Valley (neighborhood), 336–46
marble manufacturing industry, 129–30
matchmaking industry, 128
Mathews Hotel, 296–300
Mathews, George Washington, 296–300
Mayflower Hotel, 350
McMoore, Alfred, 372
Merriman Valley, 240
Miami peoples, 8
Middlebury (village and neighborhood),
    14, 123, 348, 408, 411–13
Miller, Lewis, 90, 126
Mohawk peoples, 7
Mothersbaugh, Mark, 365–68
Mount Olive Baptist Church, 341
Mustill Store, 358

Index

Nash, Ruby, 362–64
National Inventors Hall of Fame, 355, 357
National Organization for Victim
   Assistance, 190
Negro Business Directory, 102
Negro League Baseball, 174
Nied, Frank, 254, 257
North Hill (neighborhood), 66, 75, 95, 96,
   352, 408, 409–10
North Hill CDC, 408
North Hill Methodist Church, 103
North Hill Viaduct, 351
Northern Ohio Traction and Light
   Company, 158–59

O'Neil, Michael, 64, 95
O'Neil's department store, 64, 66, 349,
   353, 362
Oak Place, 127
Ohio and Erie Canal, 10, 15, 25, 63, 87, 351,
   352, 356, 358
Ohio and Erie Canal Coalition, 356
Ohio and Erie Canal Heritage Corridor,
   356, 358
Ohio and Erie Towpath Trail, 356, 358
Ohio Ballet, 354
Ohio Building, 350
Ohio Informer, 296, 298
Ojibwe peoples, 8, 10
Olin, Oscar, 2
Oneida peoples, 7
Onondaga peoples, 7
Opportunity Park, 351
Ottawa peoples, 8

Panic of 1837, The, 27, 43
Parseghian, Ara, 247–48
Peanut Shoppe, The, 22, 350
pedestrian skyway, 357
Pennsylvania and Ohio Canal, 18, 63
Perkins Mansion, 44, 349, 354
Perkins, George T., 117, 236
Perkins, Simon, Jr. ("Colonel"), 42–52, 338

Perry, Julia, 301–6
Pflueger, Ernest, 132
Plusquellic, Don, 357, 403
Pollard, Fritz, 252–63
Polsky, Abraham, 66
Polsky's department store, 66, 67, 349, 350,
   353, 355, 357
Pontiac's Rebellion, 9
Portage Country Club, 237–40
Portage Hotel, 350
Portage Path, the, 10
Pretenders, The (band), 368–70
Prince of Peace Baptist Church, 341
Pro Football Hall of Fame, 261–63
Progressive Alliance CDC (West Akron),
   408
Prohibition, 91
Proyecto RAICES, 78

Quaker Oats Company, 124
Quaker peoples, 32

Rempel Manufacturing, 145–46
Rempel, Dietrich and Ruth, 145–46
Reynolds, Butch, 248–49
Richfield, Ohio, 44
Robinson, Marius R., 59
Rockefeller, John D., Jr., 261
Rolling Acres Mall, 350
Roosevelt, Franklin, 161, 205
Rubber City Jazz and Blues Festival, 300
Rubbermaid, 148
Ruby and the Romantics, 362–63

Saalfield Publishing, 137
Sartarelli, Paul, Rev., 216
Schaller, Lyle, Rev., 102
Schumacher, Ferdinand, 64, 124–26
Scullen, John J., Rev., 87
Second Adventism (Millerites), 87
Second Congregational Church, 87
Seiberling Field, 170
Seiberling Latex, 144

Seiberling, F. A., 115, 167, 239, 326
Seneca peoples, 7, 8, 9
Serbian Orthodox Church, 93
Serbians, 92
Seven Years' War (French and Indian War), 9
sewer pipe industry, 123
Shawnee peoples, 8
Sisler, George, 165
Six Nations, 8
Slovaks, 66, 92, 99
Slovenians, 66
Smith, Gerrit, 45, 47–48
Smith, Neal, 371
Soap Box Derby, 356
Sommerville, Marco, 332–33
South Akron (neighborhood), 22, 66
South Park Village (near Independence, Ohio), 6, 7, 10
Spiritualism, 89
St. Bernard Catholic Church, 78, 89, 92, 94
St. Hedwig Church, 92, 95
St. John's Christian Methodist Episcopal Church, 103
St. Martha's Catholic Church, 95
St. Mary Catholic Church, 91, 99
St. Paul's Episcopal Church, 126
St. Thomas Hospital, 95
St. Vincent Church, 89
Stan Hywet Hall and Gardens, 110, 115, 349, 354, 356
Step2, 149
Stewart Photography Studio, 298–99
Stewart, Horace and Evelyn, 298–99
Stone Mill, 18
Suddeth, George W., 100
Summa Health System, 358
Summit County Historical Society, 354
Summit Lake, 15
Summit Mall, 350
Sun Rubber, 140–43
Sweet, Rachel, 367
Syrians, 78

Tabernacle Movement, 180–82, 202
Tallmadge, Ohio, 42
Tappan, Arthur, 28–29
Temperance Movement, 31–35
Temple Israel, 341
Temple of Healing Stripes, 220–21
Temple, Shirley, 131, 138–39
The Chapel, 104
The Well CDC in Middlebury, 408
Thorpe, Jim, 257
Thurmond, Nate, 244–46
Tin Huey, 365–68, 371
Tire Town Tabernacle, 97
Todd, Mabel E., 302
Treaty of Nanfan (1701), 7, 8
Truth, Sojourner, 45, 54–62
Turner, Captain Reuben, 33–35
Tuscarora peoples, 8

Underground Railroad, 40, 42, 45, 59
unions, 114
United Building, 350
Universalist Church, 85, 88, 90
University of Akron, The, 61, 66, 90–91, 186, 190, 228, 251, 282–84, 292–93, 300, 303, 315, 326, 331, 333, 347, 353–59, 376
University Park (neighborhood), 211, 215
University Park Alliance, 416

Vernon, R.A., Rev., 212
Victim Assistance Movement, 177–99

WADC (radio station), 182, 267–68
Wade, J.C., 296
WAEZ (radio station), 285–86
Waitresses, The (band), 367
WAKR (radio station), 269–72, 360–61
WAKR-TV / WAKC-TV (television station), 279–81
WAPS / 91.3 The Summit (radio station), 281–82
WARF (radio station), 293
Washington, Booker T., 61